BLIND TRUST

/ also by vamık volkan

Bloodlines: From Ethnic Pride to Ethnic Terrorism
Richard Nixon: A Psychobiography (with Norman Itzkowitz and
   Andrew Dod)
Turks and Greeks: Neighbours in Conflict (with Norman Itzkowitz)
*The Need to Have Enemies and Allies: From Clinical Practice to
   International Relationships*
The Immortal Ataturk: A Psychobiography (with Norman Itzkowitz)
*Cyprus—War and Adaptation: A Psychoanalytic History of Two Ethnic
   Groups in Conflict*

BLIND TRUST

Large Groups and Their Leaders in Times of Crisis and Terror

Vamık Volkan

PITCHSTONE PUBLISHING
Charlottesville, Virginia 22901

PITCHSTONE PUBLISHING
Charlottesville, Virginia 22901

Library of Congress Cataloging-in-Publication Data

Volkan, Vamik D., 1932-
  Blind trust : large groups and their leaders in times of crisis and
terror / Vamik Volkan.-- 1st ed.
      p. cm.
Includes bibliographical references and index.
  ISBN 0-9728875-2-0 (hardcover : alt. paper) -- ISBN 0-9728875-3-9
(pbk. : alk. paper)
  1. Group identity. 2. Social psychology. 3. Crises--Psychological
aspects. 4. Regression (Psychology) 5. Trust. 6. Civic leaders. I.
Title.

  HM753.V65 2004
  302.4--dc22
                                2003026253

/ for norman itzkowitz

/ contents

/ BLIND TRUST

/ introduction

When Einstein wrote to ask him what he thought
Science might do for world peace, Freud wrote back:
Not much. And took the occasion to point out
That science too begins and ends in myth.

—Howard Nemerov,
  "Einstein & Freud & Jack"

The terrorist acts of September 11, 2001, were brutally inhumane, but the people who planned and carried out those acts were not inhuman. Their personal motivations—about which we know very little—for bringing about such monumental devastation were entwined with the more well-known and articulated motivations of the large group to which they belonged—al Qaeda. The events and consequences of September 11, including the tendency in the United States to divide the world into those who are "with us" and those who are "against us," have sharpened the need to further understand human nature, especially the relationships between individuals and their large groups and those between large groups themselves.

This book is not about September 11 or terrorism or more recent events in Afghanistan and Iraq *per se*. Rather, it examines how certain *universal* elements of human nature converge to create an atmosphere that both gives rise to violent aggressive acts, such as the September 11 attacks or war, and allows the smothering of individual rights and freedoms, such as by a repressive totalitarian regime—or even, more subtly, by a democratic state preoccupied with "national security" concerns. This book focuses on large-group identity, how societies under threat are subject to large-group regression, and how political leaders may manipulate this regression. The concept of *large-group identity* describes how thousands or millions of individuals, most of whom will never meet in their life-times, are bound by an intense sense of sameness by belonging to the same ethnic, religious, national, or ideological group. Interestingly, large-group identity is not something on which we consciously focus in our routine, everyday lives. We do not wake up in the morning feeling intensely Egyptian, Vietnamese, or American. Belonging to a large group does not necessarily come to our minds while walking or driving to work, even though we may see symbols of that group identity, such as a flag, during the journey. Our relationship with our large-group identity, in ordinary times, is like breathing. We breathe constantly, and we are unaware of it unless someone reminds us of the fact that we need air to survive. Consider having pneumonia or being in a smoke-filled building: in those circumstances, we do not need to have our need for breath brought to our attention; we are instantly aware of every breath we take. If our large-group identity is under attack, we behave like an individual with pneumonia or in a burning building; we are acutely aware of our large-group affil-iation, its perceived characteristics, our emotional investment in it, and how we are "similar" to thousands or millions of others who also belong to the large group. At the same time, we separate ourselves from those we consider to be different from us. Under such circumstances, we see how our individual sense of self, our personal identity, becomes entwined with our large-group identity. We may even experience that being Egyptian, Vietnamese, or American may be more important than being Abdullah, Phuong, or Stephanie.

Threats to the abstract psychological creation that is large-group identity produce shared anxiety, and this may lead to a societal regression among the members of the large group. In general terms, regression in an individual involves a return to some of the psychological expectations, wishes, fears, and associated mental defense mechanisms of an earlier stage of human development. For example, for many weeks after the September 11 attacks, Beth, an American woman living in Virginia, found herself eating only macaroni and cheese. Her eating behavior rep-resented a personal regression; when Beth was a child, her mother used to feed her macaroni and cheese whenever Beth felt anxious. Beth's mother, who lived in New York City, was not directly hurt on September 11. Beth knew intellectually that her mother had survived the World Trade Center attack, but she unconsciously feared that her mother had died or had come close to death. By regressing and eating only macaroni and cheese, she utilized a mental mechanism that kept her mother "alive." Some weeks later, her mother came to visit, and after actually seeing her,

Beth gave up obsessively eating macaroni and cheese. She now "knew" that her mother was alive.

Large groups also regress. Activities such as rallying around the leader, exhibiting flags, attempting to "purify" the group from those whose names or skin colors suggest that they may be affiliated with the enemy, and dividing the world into clashing civilizations may be related to concepts such as patriotism and national security. But they are also aspects of large-group regression, as I will illustrate. Thus, a group's realistic efforts to feel secure merge with expressions of human nature under stress, and, in certain areas, reality and fantasy become blurred. Regression itself is not good or bad; it is a human condition that appears in individuals and large groups. But regression in large groups is subject to manipulation by political leaders.

The relationship between a political leader and his or her followers is rather like a busy street. In normal times, the traffic—information and political decision-making as well as other means of influence—flows smoothly in both directions between the leader's influence and the public's awareness. Naturally, the flow is sometimes greater in one direction and sometimes in the other, as at rush hour on a busy highway. At other times, however, for one reason or another, the street is officially declared "one-way" from leader to public: this is seen in the political propaganda of totalitarian regimes. Even in democratic countries, during times of crisis and terror, there is more focus on the "traffic" traveling from the leader/government to the public, since the public seeks a "savior" to protect them and their personal and large-group identities.

Leaders and governments can exaggerate people's "need to have enemies and allies."[1] Some leaders may help people differentiate where the reality of threat ends and where the fantasy of threat begins. This lessens anxiety. Other leaders, due not only to what is called "national interests," but also to their own personality characteristics, may magnify the dangers, increase anxiety, and help the group to remain in regression, which itself will have further societal and political consequences. In times of crisis and terror, leaders can heal or poison their followers.

Large-group regression disturbs what the late psychoanalyst Erik Erikson called basic trust, a concept that describes how a child learns to feel comfortable putting his or her own safety in a caretaker's hands; by developing basic trust, a child discovers, in turn, how to trust him or herself. In normal circumstances, adults also depend on trusting themselves and others to remain functioning citizens. Without basic trust, for example, I would not be able to board an airplane without extreme anxiety because I could not feel comfortable putting my life in the hands of the designers, builders, and pilots of the plane. Basic trust is so fundamental that those who have functional basic trust are not even aware of using it.[2] Once the basic trust of members of a group is shaken, it gets perverted and is replaced by a *blind trust*. In such a societal regression, we tend to follow leaders' views and directions, whether they are reparative or destructive.

Before proceeding, I must add that large groups as I describe them here do not speak with one voice; they include subgroups and each subgroup is composed of individuals with varying patterns of thinking and feeling. However, when I write of large-group processes, I am referring to general observable patterns of thinking and feeling that to a great extent are shared by the group. For example, when I refer to a large group that is composed of followers of a particular ideology, I do not focus on dissenters, however interesting their psychology may be. Also, as I will demonstrate, the more a large group is under stress, the more individual differences in thinking and feeling disappear in response to the trauma.

The aim of this book is to illustrate how manipulation of large-group regression and its accompanying large-group rituals in the service of maintaining, protecting, and repairing identity may create an atmosphere ripe for unspeakable, seemingly inhumane acts of violence. The examination of large-group psychology and leader-follower relations gives us a broader view of what goes on in international relations above and beyond the usual economic, legal, military, and other real-world issues that are commonly considered to be explanations for such violence.

After September 11, the leadership and the media in the United States primarily focused on local interests and referred to others in terms of identified enemies or allies, dividing the world into "us" and "them." A look at human nature, whether we like it or not, connects all humans. Without lowering our guard against realistic security threats, this kind of global approach, I believe, may serve civilization better than fueling the idea of a clash of civilizations, which in fact helps to bring it to reality.

Newly graduated from the University of Ankara medical school in Turkey, I immigrated to the United States in the mid-1950s and trained as a psychiatrist at the University of North Carolina.[3] But I never wanted to open an office and plunge into private practice. So I followed in the footsteps of my parents and two older sisters (and their husbands), all of whom were teachers: I became a professor. Since the early 1960s, I have held a post at the University of Virginia School of Medicine (as an emeritus professor since the fall of 2002), working beneath the shadow of Thomas Jefferson, the author of the Declaration of Independence and the university's founder.

I graduated from the Washington Psychoanalytic Institute in 1970 and had been involved in clinical work and teaching for ten years when an event that would be decisive in my professional life occurred half a world away from me—though at first I was not aware of its significance. In 1977, then-president of Egypt Anwar Sadat made a historic visit to Israel; addressing the Knesset (Israeli Parliament), he declared that 70 percent of the problems between Arabs and Israelis are psychological. Subsequently, the American Psychiatric Association's (APA) Committee on Foreign Affairs developed plans to explore Sadat's suggestion: to investigate the psychological aspects of Arab-Israeli relationships and to examine how certain ethnic sentiments create resistance to peaceful resolution of conflict between opposing parties. Between 1980 and 1986, I was involved in a series of unofficial Egyptian-Israeli dialogues (during the last three years of these dialogues, Palestinians were also present) as a member of the APA committee.[4] During this period, the focus of my research slowly began to shift away from understanding the individual's internal world; though I continued to see individual patients up until 1998, large-group psychology and manipulation of mass movements have been my main object of investigation over the last two decades.

I quickly realized that my own training as a physician and psychoanalyst would be insufficient for the task of fully understanding the psychology of large-groups and the relationship between leaders and followers. I needed help from diplomats, political scientists, historians, and others, and I needed to develop sufficient knowledge of their disciplines' traditions and methodologies. In 1987, under the auspices of the University of Virginia School of Medicine, I organized the Center for the Study of Mind and Human Interaction (CSMHI) to advance this confluence of disciplines: an institution unique, as far as I know, in medical school circles, CSMHI counts psychoanalysts, psychiatrists, and psychologists as well as political scientists, historians, and former diplomats among its faculty. Collectively and separately, the faculty of CSMHI have worked in many areas of the world where ethnic, racial, religious, or other large-group tensions and violence have existed or currently exist: from South Ossetia, a region within the legal boundaries of the Republic of Georgia that fought a bloody war with the Georgian government after declaring its independence in the early 1990s, to the predominantly African American community of Blackwell in Richmond, Virginia, where illegal drugs, murder, and dysfunctional family conditions are common.

Thus Anwar Sadat, whom I never met, changed the course of my career. Gradually I left the traditional psychoanalyst's post (behind a couch) and began to participate—unofficially, of course—in negotiating-table activities between opposing or enemy groups such as Arabs and Israelis, Russians and Estonians, Turks and Greeks, and Georgians and South Ossetians. As might be expected, my journey from the safety of my clinical office to the uncertainty of traumatized societies and the heat of intense negotiation was full of resistance. Taking a "trip" with a patient into his or her internal world from the psychoanalyst's usual seat behind the therapeutic couch is one thing; sitting down between opposing or enemy representatives hurling acutely aggressive sentiments at one another, or standing among massively traumatized persons in situations of real and imminent danger, is quite another.

A psychoanalyst in his or her office is something of a lonely figure: he or she alone (though with the analysand's input, of course) assesses the patient's internal conflicts and adaptations and decides what to interpret and how to react. But being the "boss" of a situation, as a psychoanalyst is, can also be a narcissistically gratifying experience. Good training in a reputable institution vaccinates against potential misuse of that position of "control" by solidifying the analyst's personal and professional integrity and knowledge of him or herself; it is for this reason that, in accepted schools of psychoanalysis, the future psychoanalysts must themselves undergo analysis with a senior colleague as part of their training. But as soon as I began my involvement in international, interethnic, and other large-group processes, I was no longer in control of the situations before me. In a sea of complicated conflicts, it was often difficult simply to sort out unfolding events, let alone to figure out what hidden shared psychological processes were attached to them. Furthermore, I was, at times, rubbing elbows with world leaders and other major public figures— among them Mikhail Gorbachev, Jimmy Carter, Yassir Arafat, and Desmond Tutu. It was essential for me to work through the emotions and perceptions that associating, even if briefly, with such "celebrities" induced in me. How could I stay "neutral"? How could I tame my own prejudices? I had a great deal of internal work to do to adjust to my new career.

When it comes to ethnic, national, religious, or ideological sentiments, psychoanalysts, like diplomats and anyone else, may exhibit prejudices and respond to manipulations by political leaders. One's training analysis—unless the psychoanalyst-to-be suffers from malignant prejudices and/or paranoia, in which case these issues are brought up on the couch—usually does not deal with large-group sentiments effectively. Sigmund Freud himself, perhaps without even being aware of it, had assimilated a degree of European ethnocentrism and a tendency to stereotype and denigrate other cultures. In his correspondence with Albert Einstein,[5] Freud made certain "racist" remarks about "Turks and Mongols." He also jokingly referred to his patients as "Negroes."[6] These were not necessarily vicious or hateful attacks, and racism in general was prevalent—and to a degree accepted—in late nineteenth- and early twentieth-century Europe. Freud may have identified with the aggressor in an attempt to defend against mounting anti-Semitism, but his remarks nevertheless should serve to remind psychoanalysts that our own personal analyses, self-analyses, and extensive study of and training in human nature do not easily free us from investment in certain cultural norms, the attitudes of our own large group, or even racism. A psychoanalyst working in ethnic, national, or other large-group problems must gain first-hand experience with many cultures, and must work through, as much as possible, his or her own prejudices. I long ago concluded that, just as I would not take into analysis a friend or family member, I would not become the key figure involved in an unofficial diplomatic project to which my own original large group was a party in conflict.

As a psychiatrist and psychoanalyst, I had done my share of work with small "therapy groups" and had long been familiar with the psychodynamics typical of such groups.[7] As my focus shifted away from traditional clinical work, I observed that most psychoanalysts and other mental health professionals often erroneously apply their knowledge of small therapy groups or organizations of a few hundred members[8] to the psychodynamics of large ethnonational, religious, or ideological groups comprising hundreds of thousands or even millions of members. I became convinced that the psychology of large groups needed to be understood as a distinct dynamic in its own right. Since large groups are made up of individuals, individual psychology would obviously be reflected as a shared phenomenon in large-group psychology. Nevertheless, I came to note that large-group psychology, once initiated, assumes a life of its own. For example, we know how an individual mourns after the death of a loved one, how his or her psychological wound will heal, and what kinds of conditions may infect this psychological wound. After massive disasters, large groups also mourn losses. A large group's mourning process, however, takes a course that is not necessarily analogous to that of individual mourning and may affect societal and political movements that, on the surface, seem to have no connection with the individual members' shared emotional state, past or present.

The course of my career was influenced by several significant obstacles to collaboration between psychoanalysis and official diplomacy. Some of these obstacles come from within the psychoanalytic discipline itself, whereas others come from the realm of political science and diplomacy, and still others emerge when these two distant cousins actually try to collaborate.[9] Even when psychoanalysts have turned their attention to large-group processes and leader-follower relationships, ideas theoretically valid and meaningful to psychoanalysts have had only a very limited impact on political theory, and diplomats have found them substantially inapplicable to their practical analysis of international events, decision-making, and propaganda. The primary reason for this limited impact is that most psychoanalytic theories of large-group dynamics focus on the individual's perception and experiences of his or her own large group and its leaders: for example, a large group represents an idealized mother, or the leader represents a father figure for the individual group member. In general, the psychology of particular large groups themselves and the nature of relationships between large groups have not been systematically studied in their own right. The result has been a rather generic sort of theoretical understanding of what a large group and its leaders mean to individual members of that group.[10] By contrast, my work has sought to explain the behavior of specific groups and the psychological components of particular historical situations.[11]

This book relies heavily on my general observations in the international field since 1979. I had two principal "laboratories." First, when we brought together influential representatives of enemy groups for a series of dialogues—often lasting several years—these participants evolved as spokespersons of their respective large groups. Again and again, they verbalized the sentiments, feelings, and thoughts shared within their respective groups. Thus, I could collect repeated themes that illustrated how large groups relate to one another. Second, as a member of CSMHI, I have visited many locations, from Kuwait to South Ossetia, where post-war conditions had made inhabitants keenly interested in their own shared traumatized conditions and their shared perceptions of their enemies. In such locations, we often carried out hundreds of in-depth interviews with men and women, adults and children, from all levels of society. Thus, through these interviews, I once more examined repeated themes in order to understand human nature and the psychological workings of specific large groups. Furthermore, as I stated earlier, I came to know many political leaders and observed their way of behaving toward their followers.

I have divided this book into four parts. In Part One, I begin with a description of large-group identity. The chapters that follow this first one deal with large-group regression and large-group rituals. Part Two examines the nature of extreme fundamentalist religious groups that preoccupy us so much at the present time. Part Three focuses on political leader-follower relations and how leaders can be destructive or reparative and how they tame or inflame large-group processes. In Part Four, I examine in detail the consequences of entrenched societal regression years after the leader and the conditions he or she created no longer exist. I hope that the reader will find new ways of conceptualizing large-group psychology and leader-follower interactions. These general findings, I believe, can be used as a foundation for further study, from a different angle, of terror and terrorism, including the most recent events.

/ part one: large-group psychology

1 / the seven threads of large-group identity

The mind has no freedom
Its thoughts
Are nurtured
By old ideas

—Fazil Husnu Daglarca, "Our First Bondage"
translated from Turkish by Talat S. Halman

Soon after the 1991–1992 war between Serbs and Croats that followed the post-Soviet collapse of the Yugoslav federation, Maja Bajs-Bjegovic, a young Croatian psychiatrist from Zagreb (Croatia's capital) accompanied a team of German mental health workers assigned to the ruined border city of Vukovar. During the war, Serbian troops had forced the city's Croatian residents into central Croatia and had burned their houses, so Vukovar's population after the war was almost entirely Serbian, though the city itself remained within Croatia's boundaries. At the time that Bajs-Bjegovic went to help assess Vukovar's postwar needs, even a civilian Croat strolling through its streets was at risk; the Serbs exhibited hostility toward anyone or anything Croatian. Acutely aware of the danger, the German team asked Bajs-Bjegovic to pretend to be German during their visit and, above all, not to speak Croatian. At one point, the group entered a restaurant where no one spoke German or English, and the team members found themselves unable to order. It was then that Bajs-Bjegovic, spontaneously emphasizing her Zagreb accent, began to tell the waiter what they wanted to eat. As she addressed him, she later said, she felt increasingly agitated and found herself speaking very loudly, as if she wanted everyone in the restaurant to hear her. As she told me later, she felt almost obliged to show every Serb nearby her true large-group identity. After a few tense minutes, the group was able to eat, and they returned to Zagreb without incident.

In that moment, protecting her psychological existence as a member of her large group was more important to Bajs-Bjegovic than the risk of bodily injury or even death. Large-group affiliation can be so powerful because an individual's sense of ethnic, religious, or national identity is so closely tied to his or her "core" identity—his or her deep, personal sense of sameness, of stable gender and body image, and of continuity between past, present, and future.[12] Most of the time, we are not even aware of this link until our large-group identity is threatened or until an event occurs in which group-belonging gives us pleasure. The fortunes that bless and the misfortunes that befall our large groups make us happy or sad, and they reinforce our sense of belonging: This is especially clear in groups that are otherwise relatively homogeneous—in countries such as North and South Korea, for example. Even in nations with a nonhomogeneous population, such as the United States, the umbrella of large-group identity covers everyone, whatever their ethnic background: Americans go about their daily lives without thinking much about it, but, when American identity is threatened, most Americans tend to personalize that threat immediately and to experience it as an attack upon themselves, as we saw so dramatically after the September 2001 terrorist attacks on New York and Washington, D.C.—and with subsequent events in Afghanistan and Iraq.

But here already we encounter the challenge of large-group categorization. In everyday speech as well as in formal scientific and policy discourses, we use terms such as race and nationality to classify large groups. On the other hand, much scholarly work has debunked the scientific reality of "racial" difference and has demonstrated the "invention" of modern national communities.[13] For the very reason that these are conventional categories, however, they are also the categories by which the vast majority of people understand the structure of their own (and others') large-group identities; for our purposes, the experience of oneself as a member of an ethnic, racial, national, or religious group is in fact the relevant criterion for using such classifications. My focus here is not on these classifications *per se* but rather on the psychological processes, common to all large-group entities, which bring these classifications "to life." Therefore, only a brief sketch of the most important large-group identity categories is necessary here.

The word "ethnicity" is derived etymologically from the Greek word *ethnos*, meaning company, people, or tribe. Roger Scruton defines an ethnic group as one fixed "by virtue of long-standing association across generations, complex relations of kinship, common culture, and usually religious uniformity and common territorial attachments."[14] Anthropologist George De Vos cites a set of elements—including folk religious beliefs and practices, language, a sense of historical continuity, a belief in a common ancestry and place of origin, and a collective history—shared by members of an ethnic group and absent in others with whom the group associates.[15] As we can already see, categories of large-group identity, in practice, do not swing free of one another; ethnicity incorporates religious identity, and perhaps national identity as well. But I begin with ethnicity because I believe it is the privileged category of large-group identity. Anthropologist Howard Stein has observed that ethnicity is not a category of nature, but a mode of thought;[16] we can go further and say that what lies at the foundation of one's sense of ethnicity is a mode of affect. Ethnicity reflects the feelings and thoughts that connect people with those who unconsciously and symbolically "feel" like their mothers or like other important caretakers of childhood. Thus ethnicity not only refers to a human sense of belonging at a basic emotional level, but also defines "we-ness" by defining the "other" who is not "like us."

Religion—from the Latin *religare*, meaning "to bind together again"—is also connected with individuals' basic modes of feeling and thinking from their early childhood. It has historically provided not only a bond between human beings and a sense of the divine, but also a feeling of collectivity among followers. But religion is usually less specific than ethnicity in defining the uniqueness of a group of people and the specificity of their shared identity. Different groups may share the same religion while each of them hold on to their specific characteristics as ethnic groups, which may at times supercede the religious bond. For instance, though extremist religious fundamentalism initially bonded followers of the Taliban together, the followers' own ethnic affiliations resurfaced as the Taliban was being toppled by the pressure of U.S. attacks during the fall of 2001: Afghans placed a renewed emphasis on the "foreignness" of some Taliban followers and of Osama bin Laden's Arab supporters. Sometimes groups who are from the same ethnic "root," such as South Slavs, absorb different religions and emerge as distinct groups—in this case, as Catholic Croats, Orthodox Serbs, and Muslim Bosniaks. But I consider Croats, Serbs, and Bosniaks to constitute different ethnic groups because, over centuries of historical experience, their religious affiliations have come to define these groups as distinct cultural-ancestral units.

Though it is fair to say that in Europe, newer concepts of nationality have tried to fill a vacuum that was previously filled fully by religion—after the 1789 revolution and the tragedies of the Napoleonic wars, for instance, the French people continued to share religious beliefs with others outside their nation-state, but the nation now provided a more restricted frame of reference for their shared identity—religious belief nevertheless has remained powerful. Human ideologies have not fully replaced divine directions,[17] then, but rather have combined with them in sometimes strange and unpredictable ways. Scruton observes:

> Religion and politics can never be separated in the minds either of believers or of those who seek to govern them, and religious conceptions have influenced almost all of the concepts and institutions of modern Western government: the law, through canon law and natural law; sovereignty, through the doctrine of international jurisdiction; property, through the doctrines of the just prize and usury; social welfare and education, through the command of charity; political obligation, through the commands of piety and obedience; and political stability, through the belief that perfection belongs not to this world but to another.[18]

Today, ethnic terrorism in the Middle East and Northern Ireland as well as the terrorist attacks perpetrated by al Qaeda are openly associated with religion. In the United States, militia associations and their sympathizers are influenced not only by the literature of the radical political right, but also by apocalyptic evangelical Protestantism, as political scientist Michael Barkun comments:

> [T]he militias' superficially secular ideology—the belief that constitutional government is threatened by clandestine political and economic forces—masks close and direct religious associations. These associations link the conspiracy with Satan's struggle against God, the rise of the Anti-Christ, and the imminence of the end-times.[19]

Religion as a demarcation of large-group identity continues to play a role—often a key one—in ethnic and national politics and in international relationships.

Ethnicity, then, incorporates religion as well as *language*; connected with shared images of the group's history, it establishes an especially sharp sense of "us" and "them." Perhaps when nationalism swept through Europe after the French Revolution, it created modes of feeling and thought among national groups resembling the ones we find in ethnic groups. The nation-state as it is now commonly understood is indeed a relatively recent Western invention, and creating the Western nations did require struggles, often bloody ones. In other places, nations have been "born" by different means. Kuwait, for example, was founded by the Al-Sabah dynasty and two other families who migrated from the Arabian Peninsula. Over the centuries, they were joined by others of both Arab and Persian origin from surrounding areas. Slowly, a national identity developed that can best be described neither as inevitable nor as accidental, but rather as the product of both conscious and unconscious decisions, shared dedication, and a common history.[20] In this, Kuwait is what historian Peter Loewenberg would call a "synthetic nation."[21] Synthetic nations—such as the United States, Brazil, and Indonesia—are "invented" when people otherwise diverse in ethnicity, race, and/or religion transcend their differences within a particular geographic space. Loewenberg cites Otto Bauer's notion of "continuity of fate" (*schicksalsgemeinschaft*) as the common element linking such disparate individuals into a cohesive large group—a community constituted and shaped by shared experiences.[22] Since nations are "born" differently, the degrees of inclusion and exclusion, of grievance and entitlement, differ from one particular nation to the next. After the collapse of the former Yugoslavia, for example, when the state of Macedonia was "born," issues of inclusion and exclusion and of grievance and entitlement surfaced because one-third of the people in Macedonia are ethnic Albanians.

During my spring 2000 fellowship at The Yitzhak Rabin Center for Israel Studies, I had the opportunity to observe firsthand an especially difficult process of "synthetic" nation-building in progress. Israel, though nominally a "monoreligious" state, in fact seeks to synthesize a population of immense ethnic and cultural diversity into a nation. To pre-Holocaust Zionist settlers, Holocaust survivors, and their descendants (all mostly European in origin), more recent immigration has added a million Jews from the former Soviet Union and more than 80,000 Ethiopian Jews to Israel's population. Consider Israel's one million (mostly Muslim) Arabs and its small but significant Christian and Ba'hai minority communities as well as the substantial number of sects and variations within Judaism in Israel, and it is not difficult to see the task that faces the Israeli government's Ministry of Immigrant Absorption, which offers services that include career guidance, counseling, and financial aid to the nation's prospective and new residents.

It is obvious that Israelis themselves are very much aware of the synthetic nature of their nation-building. On the evening of May 10, 2000, during the fifty-second anniversary of the founding of the state of Israel, a ceremony took place in Jerusalem in the area surrounding Theodor Herzl's tomb. I had the opportunity to attend the ceremony, which was presided over by Avraham Burg, then Speaker of the Knesset. I had met Burg at the Knesset just a few days earlier, when both of us participated in a meeting that dealt with the themes of cultural diversity and coexistence. I remember thinking that he was an exciting speaker and I could see that most of the two thousand or so Israelis in attendance were stirred by his remarks. My Israeli friends who accompanied me to Mount Herzl translated Burg's remarks. He was urging his audience to live up to the vision of an idealized Israel where deep and troublesome societal divisions no longer exist, when the synthetic nation becomes cohesive.

The assassination of Yitzhak Rabin on November 4, 1995, by Yigal Amir, a Bar Ilan University law student, shocked Israeli society and left them asking how it was possible for one Israeli to kill another. Rena Moses-Hrushovski, an Israeli psychoanalyst, describes an Israeli "soul-searching" that took place after the assassination.[23] Israeli intellectuals wondered how they could facilitate the coexistence of different political and religious groups and overcome the destructive splits among Israelis' multiple religious factions and ethnicities. In the long run, however, according to Moses-Hrushovski, this did not occur. At the time of the ceremony, the country still had deep divisions. Burg's address referred to this condition and cried out for a solution.

When Burg's address was finished, twelve Israelis, representing different groups within the country, spoke briefly in front of lit torches and symbolically presented themselves as a unified Israel. A young woman, Oz (Sveta) Tokaev was a member of a group of one million recent "immigrants" from Russia. Zehava Baruch was the spokeswoman for Ethiopians. Boaz Kitain, whose son was killed in a helicopter crash, reminded everyone of grieving parents in a country where young people face real dangers. Two teenagers, one Jewish and one Druze, Ziv Scachar and Daniella Nadim Issa, spoke together, suggesting that Jews and non-Jews can coexist in the state of Israel. Others among the dozen speakers reminded the audience that there were citizens who were directly affected by the Holocaust and citizens who were representatives of women's rights groups; however, Muslim Israeli Arabs and ultra-Orthodox movements were not represented. In the excitement of the evening, however, one could visualize an idealized and unified Israel.

Though I differentiate between "synthetic" nations and those in which one ethnically homogeneous group of people are dominant, making these distinctions is not always as easy in practice as it might seem. Over time, "synthetic" nations evolve a kind of homogeneity defined by common historical experience that can be spoken and expressed in a common language. Nevertheless, the synthetic/nonsynthetic distinction remains useful for our purposes for several reasons. For example, a synthetic nation under stress may develop "cracks" in the society's "mosaic" of various ethnic, racial, and religious groups. During World War II, for example, more than 100,000 Japanese Americans were isolated in concentration camps, despite the fact that they were not disloyal.[24] After September 11, cracks appeared within the United States between those who are considered "us" and those who may be directly or symbolically connected with Islam.

In practice, certain definitions of nationalism are very similar to definitions of ethnicity. For example, Rita Rogers, a psychiatrist at the University of California, Los Angeles who has been studying international relations for decades, suggests that "[n]ationalism is a state of mind,"[25] echoing Stein's definition of ethnicity; William Petersen describes a nation as "a people linked by common descent from putative ancestors and by its common territory, history, language, religion, and/or way of life."[26] We find parallels with definitions of ethnicity in Hans Kohn's remarks, too:

Nationalism—our identification with the life and aspirations of uncounted millions whom we shall never know, within a territory which we shall never visit in its entirety—is qualitatively different from the love of family or of home surroundings. It is qualitatively akin to the love of humanity or of the whole earth.[27]

Kohn's definition only takes us so far, for there are varieties of nationalism, including varieties of postcolonial nationalism. Moreover, history reminds us all too well that the concept of nationalism is not always linked to liberty and high humanistic ideals and may also be associated with racism, totalitarianism, and destruction. Nazi nationalism, for example, was founded upon racism and waged war on democratic and liberal ideas. As a result, there is a tendency among political scientists and scholars of international relations to differentiate between negative nationalism and positive—usually called patriotism. Novelist and cultural critic George Orwell described patriotism as "devotion to a particular place and a particular way of life, which one believes to be the best in the world but has no wish to force upon other people";[28] and nationalism as patriotism gone sour—"power hunger tempered by self deception."[29] Scholars in political and social sciences have usefully distinguished between nationalism that is benign and civic and that which is malignant and authoritarian.[30] There is also a close link between the concept of ethnicity and the concept of nation when the nation in question is composed of an ethnically homogeneous group of people. When Greece was "born" in the early 1830s, for example, it officially incorporated only ethnic Greeks; as citizens, therefore, the members of this nation-state were connected by the specificity I have described above as the province of ethnicity, and the outside world, except for ethnic Greeks living outside of the new nation-state, was "other."[31] The main general distinction to be made between a nation and an ethnic group is that nation implies political autonomy and established borders, or at least organizations that establish roles, positions, and status.[32]

But, as I have suggested, ethnicity properly refers to a category more basic than nationality. Indeed, it seems that nationalism's day may now have passed; after the retreat of the European empires and the collapse of the Soviet Union, we may very well be living in an "Age of Ethnicity."[33] As historian Norman Itzkowitz and I have written, however, a focus on ethnicity, although not identified as such at the time, was present in earlier eras:

> It would certainly be amiss not to recognize the role of ethnicity in Cromwell's conquest of Ireland, and equally wrong-headed not to see the subsequent impact of that ethnic conflict in the New World. Many of the leading colonists, such as John Smith, had had their baptism of fire in the conquest of Ireland. They brought the lessons of that ethnic conflict with them. For them, the indigenous populations were often the Irish in other guises.[34]

Theories of modernization suggested that industry and trade would replace agriculture as the foundation of economy; industrial society would require universal values that would replace tribal and local values; and new forms of communication would lead to cultural assimilation and the eventual disappearance of ethnic identities.[35] The opposite seems to be the case, however, since "ethnic identities have gathered strength in the face of dehumanization engendered by modernization":

> In many ways, the fate of modernization theory is similar to that of the Leninist notion that the classless society that would be ushered

in by socialism would form a bulwark against war that was the ultimate product of capitalist society. The unfolding of history undermined both modernization theory and the classless society.[36]

Whereas ethnicity is not a category of nature, the related category of race, starting in the eighteenth century (according to the *Oxford English Dictionary*), was based on the idea that human beings can be divided into "subspecies" according to their respective variations in skin color, hair texture, facial features, and other physical phenomena of "nature." Racial distinctions have taken on the character of racism when assumed to reflect different stages of human development and used to support the systemic granting or withholding of rights and privileges. Racial divisions persist throughout the world, but its collective expression varies from one situation to another. Of course, Western Europe and its white colonies in North America, Africa, and Australia have experienced malignant racism, in which the target group—while in fact innocent—is perceived as dangerous by the destroying group.[37] Today, however, racism *per se* has substantially been replaced, especially in Western Europe, with the newer notion of neo-racism. Neo-racism is grounded not in biology but in anthropology and ideology. In some circles in Europe, for example, some people invoke the distinctions in religious custom, language, or value system specific to immigrants of African, Middle Eastern, or Asian origin to justify keeping those immigrant communities emotionally, if not physically, separate.[38] Neo-racism is similar to the concept of ethnocentrism, which denotes attitudes that uncritically or unjustifiably support the superiority of one ethnic group over others.

Even this brief review of the different categories of large-group identity suggests the need for flexibility in defining group-identity concepts—the historical details of the actual situation at hand must be taken into account in assessing the substance and functioning of any particular large group. The Christian Copts of Egypt, for example, proudly identify themselves according to their religious difference from most people in their region. But they also believe that they are the direct descendants of the ancient Egyptians who were governed by pharaohs. Thus they separate themselves ethnically from the majority of Egyptians, who are ethnically Arab. In order to feel secure in Egypt, however, they also consider themselves to be part of the Egyptian nation. Depending on the circumstances facing them at a particular historical moment, then, Copts may define themselves as a group by religion, by ethnicity, or by nationality and feel secure or insecure accordingly.

There is one last way of defining the identity of a large group: ideology. Some ideologies, such as Kemalism in Turkey after the Turkish war of independence (1919–1922), are confined within the boundaries of a specific large group or nation, and neither make nor aspire to make an impact elsewhere.[39] Others, such as Soviet communism, press for an international audience. I want to emphasize, however, that ideological identity is of a different type from ethnic, national, and religious identities. It is not durable or integral in the ways that the other identity categories are; a political ideology may be modified or given up without destroying the basic sense of core sameness among the members of a large group. Russians and Czechs, for example, continue to perceive themselves as Russians and Czechs even though they no longer ascribe to communist ideology.

Before we can understand why ethnic, national, and religious collective identities exercise such a powerful hold on people, subject them to political propaganda and other forms of manipulation, and sometimes make them follow their leaders blindly, we first need to review the psychoanalytic understanding of *individual* identity. The term "identity" in psychoanalysis is relatively new; Sigmund Freud himself seldom used it,[40] and those who took up the discipline he had established tended to follow his example. Among the psychoanalysts who first brought the term to general attention was Erik Erikson, who, in 1956, seminally described a person's identity as "a sustained feeling of inner sameness within oneself ... [and at the same time] a persistent sharing of some kind of essential character with others."[41] Following Erikson, it is now generally agreed that "identity" refers to a person's subjective experience of him or herself and therefore should be distinguished from other, related concepts, such as "character" or "personality": these latter terms delineate the collected impressions that other people gather of an individual's emotional expressions, modes of speech, and habitual ways of thinking and behaving. Unlike character and personality, then, identity designates the individual's inner working model of him or herself[42] and an individual's integration of his or her past, present, and future into a smooth continuum of remembered, felt, and expected existence. An individual with a crystallized core identity therefore has a realistic body image, an inner sense of physical solidity, a subjective clarity about his or her gender, a well-internalized conscience, and, most importantly for our purposes, "an inner solidarity with one's group and its ideals."[43] Thus, an individual's core identity and large-group identity develop alongside one another.

Adults can typically identify various aspects of what they perceive as their unique identity related to social or professional status—one may simultaneously perceive oneself as a physician and someone who plays handball, or as a carpenter and someone who enjoys reading. On the surface, these elements of one's "identity" seem to fit within Erikson's definition, but I do not believe that such manifestations truly reflect the sustained sense of basic sameness within oneself that Erikson identified. If a person's social or career identity is threatened, he or she may or may not experience anxiety in response—though anxiety is more likely if the threat is connected (mostly unconsciously) to one or more of the four fundamental internal danger signals identified by Freud: losing a loved one, his or her love, a body part, or self-esteem.[44] By way of contrast, consider an adult decompensating into schizophrenia: his or her basic sense of self-identity over time is fragmenting; he or she may feel like a star exploding into a billion pieces.[45] Such a person is certainly experiencing anxiety—anxiety so extreme that it is unspeakably terrifying.[46] In order to escape this terror, as soon as he or she is able, he or she creates a new sense of identity, albeit a false (psychotic) one; such a person might "reinvent" him or herself as Jesus Christ or Mother Teresa. The sense of identity that such individuals are terrified of losing and are driven to replace is what I call their "core identity." The loss of one's core identity is intolerable—it is psychological death.

For our present purposes, it is crucial to differentiate core identity from less-essential social or professional "identities" since, as I will detail later in this chapter, an individual's large-group identity is intimately connected to his or her personal core identity. As a result, serious threats to large-group identity, such as shared helplessness and humiliation, are perceived by members of that large group as *individually* wounding and *personally* endangering, psychologically speaking; they induce a collective response of anxiety or terror and shared defenses against the fragmentation of the self above and beyond each individual's specific personal defenses.

Each individual's core identity develops primarily through completing two mental tasks that must be accomplished early in life: "differentiation" and "integration." At the beginning of life, the infant, for practical purposes, does not know where he or she ends and where others (i.e., the mother or other primary caretaker(s)) begin.[47] *Differentiation* is the psychobiological task of separating what belongs to oneself from what belongs to other people and things (both called "objects" in psychoanalytic parlance). Before self-images are differentiated from object-images, however, they are organized by their emotional and sensory content as positive or negative—the pleasurable, satisfying, "good" images and the unpleasant, unsatisfying, "bad" ones. We can, therefore, visualize normal development of identity and perception of others as a rather complicated highway interchange.

Imagine a highway (see Figure 1). For the first few miles of the highway—representing the first month of life—there is no dividing line. The infant does not fully comprehend where he or she ends and where others begin. At the present time, we know that an infant's mind has certain autonomy and the capability of sensing who he or she is.[48] But, for practical purposes, the infant "fuses" him or herself with his or her caretakers. This is why I say that in the first few miles of the highway, there is no line dividing the highway into "me" (self) or "caretaker" (other) lanes. However, an infant soon begins to experience both pleasant ("good") and unpleasant ("bad") sensations. At this point—from the second month to around the sixth month of the infant's life—the highway divides into two lanes: "good" self/other and "bad" self/other. Soon, each lane becomes a road in its own right. As the infant's mind develops further, at about six to eight months old, each road begins to divide into two lanes, marking the beginning of the infant's ability to separate positive self-images from positive images of others and negative self-images from negative images of others. Eventually, the "good" and "bad" roads each separate into entirely distinct "self" lanes and "other" lanes; *integration* occurs when the two "self" lanes converge into a single road and the two "other" lanes meet in a separate single road. That is, integration begins when the child not only knows where he or she ends and others begin, but also is able to recognize 1) that he or she is comprised of both positive and negative parts and 2) that his or her mother (or any other person in his or her environment) remains the same person over time, regardless of whether he or she is experiencing that person as satisfying or frustrating at any given moment. This integration for all practical purposes is completed when the child is approximately thirty-six months old.

Naturally, integrating what we call "split" self-images—"good" and "bad"—is easier when the emotions the child attaches to those images are not very intense; the same is true for the infant's "split" images of others. Integration becomes more and more difficult to achieve if the opposing images are connected with more and more powerful feelings. By the age of 36 months, however, a child has, for practical purposes, integrated his

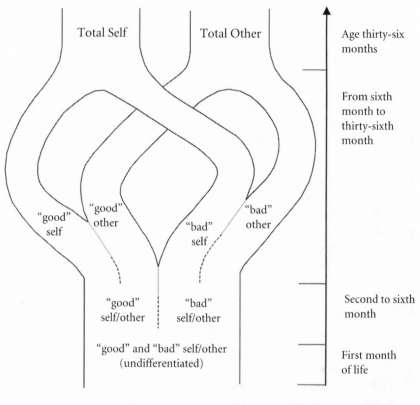

Figure 1. The "highway" model of normal identity development.

or her self-images as well as his or her object-images. At this point, the child should be able to tolerate *ambivalence*—that is, to simultaneously love and hate a person at any given time and still recognize and experience that person as consistently the same person. Though, as we shall see, the process of integration is never total, the three-year-old child's subjective experience of a sufficiently cohesive sense of self represents the foundation of his or her core identity.[49]

Once the child begins to know where he or she ends and others begin, the child becomes involved in another developmental task that, as we will see later in the chapter, is crucial for large-group affiliation: *identification*.[50] In identifying with others, the child unconsciously takes into his or her own sense of self the images and functions of significant people in his or her environment. The child thus enriches his or her core identity—for example, by identifying with the parent who controls and tames the child's temper tantrum, the child can perform the same function for him or herself.[51] Though the precise nature of identifications—with the image of a mother's loyalty, a father's masculinity, or a teacher's honesty—is different at each step on the developmental ladder, the child continually absorbs identifications into his or her self-image all the way through adolescence, the period in which an individual unconsciously re-examines and crystallizes his or her core identity. After the adolescent passage, an individual develops many new attachments and makes new identifications that change personal identity, but these changes are at the periphery of the sense of inner sameness that remains, for practical purposes, unchanged.[52]

As I began work on the psychology of political, ethnic, and religious conflict, I noted a need to expand the psychoanalytic conception of large-group psychology in order to understand what makes a large-group identity *specific* in its underlying psychological processes. Freud had theorized that large-group psychology reflects each member's Oedipal issues: an individual becomes loyal to the leader in the same way that an Oedipal boy sublimates his aggression against his father and identifies with him; the group forms as individuals who identify with and become loyal to the same leader band together.[53] Over years of observation, however, I have shifted the study of large-group psychology from the individual's perception of what a large group means to him or her to the structure of large-group psychology in its own right. When I think of the classical Freudian theory, I visualize people arranged around a great maypole, which represents the group's leader, as if in a May Day dance of identification with each other and of idealization and support of the leader. I have since built upon this metaphor by imagining a large cloth over the people, a "tent-canvas" of large-group identity; the people surrounding the pole are determined to keep the pole upright so that the canvas remains taut, a protective cover for the individuals beneath. That is to say, large-group activities center on maintaining the integrity of the group's identity; follower-leader interactions are just one element of this effort. In my experience, the leader's and followers' efforts to maintain, repair, and sometimes modify the large-group identity "contaminate," or accompany and affect, all "real world" issues, from legal to economic to military. Large-group rituals (see Chapter 3) exist to maintain and/or to strengthen the fabric of large-group identity and to repair any wear and tear in it. Thus, I began to focus on the various efforts of the leader *and* his or her followers—from propaganda to massive aggression—to keep their tent canvas upright, rather than on members' perceptions and expectations of the leader's role alone.

This does not mean, of course, that the psychology of individuals should be ignored. The scores or thousands or millions of people who live under the tent also wear individual clothing—their individual core identities—as well as the garments of family, clan, or professional subgroupings. But all of the people under the tent—men and women, rich and poor—wear the collective large-group identity as if it were a shared skin. At times of collective stress—such as economic crises, social upheaval, war, terrorist attack, or drastic political change—the tent's covering can take on greater importance than the various garments worn by the individual group members. The leader's and followers' activities to protect their tent covering can be put in a spectrum, from nondestructive to destructive, depending on the nature and level of regression that a leader and/or the followers experience.

I have identified seven "threads" that, when woven together, compose large-group identity:[54]

1) Shared, tangible reservoirs for images associated with positive emotion
2) Shared "good" identifications
3) Absorption of others' "bad" qualities
4) Absorption of (revolutionary or transforming) leaders' internal worlds
5) Chosen glories
6) Chosen traumas
7) Formation of symbols that develop their own autonomy.

The last four "threads" especially represent specific processes in the development and maintenance of large-group identity itself. Examining the first three illuminates how closely individual core identity and large-group identity are intertwined. Though the formation of large-group identity is often simply characterized as "acculturation," we are now able to delineate the specific unconscious but shared psychological processes involved in its evolution.

Shared reservoirs: The first thread of large-group identity is woven into the core of the individual quite early in life through the child's growing contact with the external world. Both individual and large-group identity begin to form in earnest (and become intertwined) at around the age of 36 months, when the child has accomplished the task of integrating his or her sense of self, as described in the last section;[55] until then, when frustrated or satisfied, the child experiences him or herself as two warring selves—the "good" and the "bad." Though this milestone is unquestionably a crucial one, it is important to recognize that "integration" is a relative term; the process is by no means complete at this point. Some images of the self and of others ("objects")—both "good" (associated with the child's own sense of peak pleasure) and "bad" (associated with his or her sense of peak aggression)—remain unintegrated at this early age. Because these fragments and the emotions associated with them threaten to destabilize the child's recently established core identity, they must be discarded; if the child does not rid him or herself of them, he or she will be unable to perceive his or her identity realistically.

Because these stray elements can create problems for the child, he or she must develop ways of coping with the threat.[56] Among the various psychological mechanisms children employ for this purpose, *externalization* (an early form of the more-familiar mechanism of projection, or putting unwanted images from one's own mind onto outside objects[57]) is both critical and ubiquitous. For example, a very young child falls down but does not want to be thought clumsy; the child says, "I didn't fall down— it was my doll that fell." This child has externalized his or her injured self-image onto the doll, and the doll thus becomes a reservoir for some component of the child's own image. Subsequently, an uncle or aunt may become a reservoir for the child's unintegrated "good" images and affects, and the child will therefore idealize his relative rather than him or herself. Later in life, the child may re-internalize and integrate some of what was externalized onto the uncle or aunt and thereby develop a more realistic view of him or herself as well as of the uncle or aunt; some childhood externalizations are temporary, whereas others may persist for years.

The special significance a child places on a person or thing by externalizing unintegrated "good" images of the self or of others does not necessarily create a bond with the child's large group or establish any particular aspect of large-group identity. It is, rather, simply a part of the personal developmental experience, formally mutable and changing frequently. For example, a special doll or cherished relative may be replaced by something or someone else, even though the child may keep the original item as a memento for many years or may develop a lifelong friendship with a person from his or her childhood. There are certain conditions, however,

under which externalization actually *initiates* a very early, crucial investment in large-group identity and a sense of alliance with the other children in a large group.

Though many of the reservoirs a child may use to promote and protect
his or her developing core identity do not offer a connection with historical events, others are imbued with special meaning for the specific group
into which he or she is becoming acculturated. Children are at first "gen-
eralists" in their large-group identities, to borrow Erik Erikson's term;[58]
although they remain individuals with their own specific psychic compo-
sitions, the large-group component of identity becomes more specific as
the child's internal world becomes tied to the external world through tangible shared items and experiences that are culturally and historically significant to their parents and other significant caretakers. Core individual
and large-group identity thus become inextricably intertwined when the
repositories that receive children's unintegrated positive self- and object-
images and associated peak pleasant or unpleasant affects are 1) shared by
all children in the large group and 2) constant. I have called such culturally significant image-containers "suitable reservoirs" for externalization.[59]
For example, going to a sauna is an experience that links together all
Finnish children, even those who will never meet during their lifetimes. As
adults, they use this practice as an ethnic marker; note the Finnish saying:
"*Paiva ilman saunae on nunkuin paiva ilman aurinkoa*" (A day without a
sauna is like a day without sunshine).[60] There are countless other examples
we could adduce; every ethnic, religious, national, or other large group
shares a set of recognizable suitable reservoirs. Though a child cannot be
forced to use certain items and experiences as reservoirs, he or she often
receives conscious and unconscious guidance from parents and others in
choosing things that hold commonly held significance for members of the
large group.[61] Without the individual child's conscious awareness, then, he
or she is subtly initiated into the large-group identity (or identities) by
becoming allied with the other children in the large group through the
common *material* items that permanently absorb the unintegrated "good"
self- and object-images of all group members.[62]

Because it develops so early, then, large-group identity exists
through and depends upon *external phenomena* before it is clearly felt
as an *internal feature* of the individual. As the child's mental capacities
enlarge, interacting with the adults in his or her environment and identifying with these adults' images help the child to form more sophisticated ideas about large-group membership. For example, more-abstract
concepts, such as "Scottishness" or "Finnishness," become associated

with the suitable reservoirs that are, indeed, at the foundation of a large group's identity.

A Scottish boy, for instance, becomes aware that a kilt or bagpipe represents and is associated with many things: masculinity, clan and national history, specific heroes, battles for independence won and lost, songs and poems, language and dialect, and other specific features of the large group's history. Projections of "good" thoughts, perceptions, and feelings—more sophisticated than mere externalizations of "good" self-images and/or internalized "good" object-images—increasingly accompany externalizations into suitable reservoirs. Concurrently, the boy internalizes specific aspects of an abstract Scottishness; these aspects are now felt or sensed, both consciously and unconsciously, as a part of the individual's core identity. A persistent sense of "we-ness" eventually becomes established as something inside the person. Still, suitable reservoirs remain as significant external links to the individual's internal sense of sameness, though at times the reservoirs may revert to a kind of "ordinariness." Thus, a Scot away from home may listen to a recording of bagpipe music when he is homesick or when he otherwise feels that his core identity needs "patching up," but he does not necessarily need or want to listen to bagpipe music every day.

Under stressful conditions, the members of a group may return to using tangible articles in a developmentally regressive (externalized) way, or may establish new suitable reservoirs in order to refortify group bonds. During Israel's occupation of the Gaza Strip, for example, many Palestinians carried in their pockets (where they could not be seen by Israeli soldiers) small stones painted with the Palestinian colors. These stones were an adult version of a shared reservoir—keeping parts of Palestinian large-group identity safe and creating an invisible network of Palestinianness. Under ordinary circumstances, the large-group identity that is located in shared reservoirs is abstracted and internalized by the individuals that comprise the large group; in this case, however, the threat that the large group collectively perceived caused it to reactivate the need to use shared reservoirs for externalization.

"Good" identifications: Shared reservoirs are closely related to the second thread of which the cloth of large-group identity is woven. Identifications with individuals in the immediate environment who belong to specific religious, ethnic, or national groups also play a significant role in incorporating elements of large-group identity into each child's personal core identity.

Robert Emde's study on the evolution of the infant mind suggests the existence of a psychobiological potential for "we-ness" and group-related behavior.[63] Because the environment of an infant or a young child is restricted to parents, siblings, relatives, and family friends, the extent of "we-ness" in infancy does not *directly* include a dimension of large-group identity. The adults in any child's environment do, obviously, belong to specific large groups. But the infant or young child, mentally unready to comprehend large-group affiliation or to differentiate any one such affiliation from any other with which it has no intimate contact, identifies with whatever he or she sees, touches, hears, smells, experiences; because the child identifies with his or her caretakers as individuals, he or she comes to identify with the specific set of cultural practices—including, especially, the language—that the caretakers observe and share with others outside the child's immediate surroundings.

Even before reaching the crucial milestone of integrating his or her core identity (for practical purposes) at roughly 36 months of age, a child begins to absorb overt and covert aspects of his or her fellow group members' shared attitudes, culture, and values via early identifications with his or her caretakers. Of course, not all developmental identifications relate to large-group identity; many identifications function, for example, to teach the child to do things as his or her parents do—to be a mother or father in the future and to sustain the family's ideals and values. Over time, individual children within a large group tend to acquire inclinations and capacities shared by all children in that group: the same language, similar food preferences, and shared nursery rhymes, songs, and dances. During the Oedipal phase of life—as well as during later phases—more-sophisticated identifications enlarge the child's mental life and his or her associations with large-group identity. Especially in adolescence,[64] identifications with teachers, religious authorities, peer groups, and community and large-group leaders cultivate children's investments in religion, ethnicity, and nationality and nurture their sense of differentiation from those who are unlike the group and/or inimical to it.

A child's investment in his or her large group depends substantially on what factors the adults in the large group collectively perceive as most important: ethnicity ("I am an Arab"), religion ("I am a Catholic"), nationality ("I am a German"), or a combination of these. It is important to recall that, as a large-group organizing principle, ideology is less durable than religion, ethnicity, or nationality because it is less basic, more intellectual. A child born in Hyderabad, India, for example, would be focused primarily on religious and cultural issues as he or she developed a large-group identity, since adults there define their dominant large-group identities according to religious affiliation—Muslim or Hindu.[65] A child born in Cyprus would absorb a dominant large-group identity defined by ethnic and nationalistic sentiments, because what is currently decisive in this part of the world is whether one is Greek or Turkish, not whether one is Greek Orthodox Christian or Sunni Muslim.[66] Though they may become important later in life, questions of investment in ethnicity versus religion, or nationality versus race, are not as essential to understanding large-group identity as are the psychodynamic processes of linking the individual's core identity to the large-group identity that is historically primary at the time of the child's development.

As a result of certain relatively uncommon circumstances, such as having parents belonging to different races, religions, or nationalities, a child may come to identify with more than one ethnic, national, or religious group. As psychoanalyst Edith Jacobson noted, simultaneous identifications with various others "may be in sharp conflict with each other, so that reconciliation and integration may present extraordinary problems."[67] W.C. Booth reports the poignant story of a young man of Navajo descent who seemed thoroughly steeped in his two cultures: traditional Navajo and mainstream American. When paralyzed in an accident, however, he did not know whether to turn to the Navajo medicine man or to the Western doctor for treatment.[68] In my own work in Transylvania in 1993 and South Ossetia in 1998, interviews with individuals born to "mixed marriages" (Romanian and Hungarian in the former case, South Ossetian and Georgian in the latter) revealed that identity difficulties were especially acute when drastic sociopolitical changes occurred or when wars broke out between the groups. In my clinical work in the United States, I have treated individuals born in the South to wealthy white families and raised primarily by African American servants; individuals who could put their "two mothers" on a continuum fared better than those with unloving mothers and emotionally satisfying nannies, who tended to have internal difficulties responding to interracial incidents in external reality.[69]

As I have suggested, adolescence is a crucial time for crystallizing the first two elements of large-group identity. As the adolescent unconsciously re-examines both childhood investments in the images (whether realistic or not) of people he or she has known and attachments to culturally appropriate suitable reservoirs, he or she unconsciously "decides" which aspects of large-group identity will become the fixed and permanent means of connecting him or her with others in the large group with which he or she is affiliated. The sauna, for example, may remain as a tangible item that connects a young Finn to his or her fellow Finns. But it is also during adolescence that his or her persistent, abstract sense of Finnishness, beyond any specific traditional practice, takes shape as an object of emotional allegiance that the individual shares with his or her peers.

After the first and second threads of large-group identity have been interwoven into an individual's sustained sense of self in adolescence, it is very difficult—if not impossible—to change the original sense of "we-ness" associated with his or her large-group identity. However, under exceptional circumstances the original sense of "we-ness" might be milder. I once worked with a young woman in analysis whose Jewish father had settled in a conservative city in the southern United States. The father had changed his Jewish-sounding name because he thought his business would benefit, and he had married a Christian woman. His daughter, my patient, had been raised as a Christian and never consciously saw herself as having any connection to Jewishness. She knew of her father's history, and reported that he had passed as a Christian because it was good for his business. When, six years into her analysis, Israeli athletes were murdered at the 1972 Olympics in Munich, she underwent a change in religious and cultural identity; the shock of the event caused her to sense her heretofore repressed investment in her father's heritage. At the same time, she became aware that, in spite of his overt behavior, deep down her father had kept his emotional investment in Judaism. Though she never formally converted to Judaism, she now felt comfortable joining her Christian and Jewish selves in an adaptive manner. In general, though, the individual cannot *truly* escape the fundamental childhood emotional investment in his or her original large-group identity, but can only repress or deny it, rationalizing that he or she now belongs to a higher entity (i.e., that the individual belongs not to his or her original large group, but to the "human family").

In the case of immigration, integration into a new country is generally smoother if the immigrant arrives voluntarily rather than as a refugee (subjected to forced immigration). If the immigrant still feels accepted in the country left behind, he or she, upon completion of the work of mourning, may become bicultural, resulting in a sense of belonging to both cultures. But, in short, a change in his or her identity occurs. From history we know that large groups of people, like individual volunteer immigrants, also can change their collective identity over the course of decades or centuries, especially if they gain something in the process, such as economic benefits. In fourteenth-century Bosnia, for example, many southern Slavs became Muslims within the first century of Ottoman Muslim rule over this part of the world; by converting to Islam, they avoided paying certain taxes which the Ottomans demanded from non-Muslim subjects. These converts were the ancestors of modern Bosniaks, who have emerged as a separate "ethnic" group from Serbs and Croats, who are also southern Slavs.

Absorption of others' "bad" qualities: Although the two "threads" we have examined so far link an individual's personal core identity with his or her primary large-group identity, a group's identity never exists in a vacuum—it always adjoins the identity of another group. Thus the third thread in the canvas of an ethnic, racial, national, or religious identity is produced by the interactions between two neighboring groups. Like a child who identifies with the way his or her mother (mostly unconsciously) perceives him or her,[70] members of a large group may themselves weave into the fabric of their shared identity a thread originally placed there by a dominant opposing group. In order to understand this third thread, picture two large-group tents side-by-side. Individuals in the first tent throw mud, excrement, and refuse—that is, externalize their "bad" images of themselves and others and project their own unwanted thoughts, feelings, attitudes, and expectations—onto the canvas of the second tent. For example, a child of Polish-Jewish peasant origins living in America, far from the dangers of the old anti-Semitic world, is taught to spit three times when passing a Catholic Church: "This may be dismissed simply as superstition, but it also partakes of the notion of the church as a suitable target of externalization. It is easier to give up targets of externalization in an atmosphere of comparative safety, but memories of them linger on."[71]

If the individuals in the first tent dominate those in the second, and if their externalizations and projections are backed by economic or other physical force, what they throw onto the second tent to some extent saturates its fabric and is absorbed into the existing threads of the second group's identity. That is, the negative externalization and projection may evolve as a permanent part of the subjugated group's identity; because the "stain" is composed of "bad" or undesirable elements originally belonging to the dominant group, the recipient group may experience anxiety over this large-group marker and may develop defensive signs and symptoms to conceal it.

U.S. psychiatric literature in the twentieth century provides an example of this phenomenon in the delusion of whiteness often reported in

African American patients suffering from psychoses. For decades, this delusion was misunderstood. John Lind's pioneering 1914 studies of the "color complex" asserted that this delusion reflected African American patients' simple desire to be white.[72] Subsequent publications suggested various other explanations referring to a variety of external factors, but not one publication mentioned white racism as a precipitating factor.[73] These researchers tended to place responsibility on black parents, minimizing the role of the dominant group in creating a thread of inadequacy, humiliation, and denigration in both the individual and group identities of these patients. For instance, one researcher stated that because African American parents knew that preferential treatment had been given to slaves of mixed ancestry, they wanted light skin for themselves and their children and passed on this desire to their children in early mother-child interactions.[74] By the late 1960s and 1970s, African American psychiatrists such as Charles Pinderhughes and Charles Wilkerson had begun to publish on the experience of being a reservoir for white people's externalizations and projections.[75] In my own work at the segregated, state-owned Cherry Hospital in Goldsboro, North Carolina, in the early 1960s, I observed that many black patients who expressed the wish to be white simultaneously experienced anxiety about the idea of bearing "white blood." That whiteness was desirable on one level and dreaded on another reflected the fact that, by "wanting" to be like those who denigrated them, African Americans were both identifying with their oppressors and denying the pain of being reservoirs for the "bad" elements those oppressors had consigned to them, such as "sexual aggressiveness" and "intellectual inferiority."[76] Similarly, assimilated Jews living safely in America sometimes joke about the possibility of hiring someone to beat up their children for being Jewish as a means of communicating to their children what it has meant, and may mean again, to be Jewish.[77] Thus, they simultaneously deny the pain of the Jewish experience throughout history (by telling a joke about anti-Semitic violence) and identify with the perpetrators (by becoming the agent of such violence).

Absorption of leaders' internal worlds: The fourth thread is woven into the cloth of large-group identity by certain types of leaders. A "transforming" or "charismatic" leader,[78] such as Vladimir Lenin, Mahatma Gandhi, Mao Tse-tung, and, most recently, Osama bin Laden, brings hundreds of thousands or millions of people out of political isolation and into a new kind of political participation, which can either be adaptive or destructive.

Such leaders often do something else as well: driven to meet the requirements of their own internal worlds, they reshape the external world and
the psychosocial and political identity of their large group. In order for
large-group identity to bend to the psychic organization of its leader in
this way, however, the large group must be in a state of what psychoanalysis terms "regression."

Transforming or charismatic leaders reflect the group's sentiments in
the opinions that they express, their public appearances, the speeches that
they deliver, their avowed likes and dislikes, and even the way that they
dress. Combined with externalizing and projecting aspects of their personal psychologies, these elements influence followers; create new political ideologies; inflame or tame religious, national, or ethnic sentiments;
and sometimes create "new" or modified suitable reservoirs for externalization. A small example from the historical relationship between Mustafa
Kemal Ataturk, the founder of modern Turkey, and the Turkish people
illustrates this process.

Until 1925, Turkish men did not wear Western-style hats; hats
belonged to "the infidel," and so were not a suitable reservoir of "we-ness."
Some Turkish men in villages and cities wore various sorts of turban-like
headgear; Turkish intellectuals and public servants wore fez. Previously
worn in North Africa and by the Greek Christians who inhabited
Ottoman-held islands in the Mediterranean, the fez had been introduced
as a new headcovering for the Ottoman military in the mid-1820s; in
1829, the fez was decreed compulsory for all classes of Ottoman officials.
As its use spread beyond the government corps, it became a symbol of
Turkishness and, indeed, a universal symbol of Islam. After a full century
of assimilation, then, the fez was to be extirpated from Turkish society
because it symbolized the Ottoman past, not the new Turkish Republic
Ataturk wished to establish.

In our extensive study of Ataturk's life,[79] Princeton historian Norman
Itzkowitz and I concluded that Ataturk's insistence that the new Turkey
should be secular and Westernized derived in part from an externalization
onto the nation, which had suffered greatly in the last years of the Ottoman
Empire, of his image of his grieving mother, who had lost three children
before Ataturk's birth and had been widowed when the future leader was
only seven years old. In reality, his mother, who had turned to religion for
solace from these losses, had smothered the young Ataturk, so he had much
unconscious personal motivation to make her happy, and thereby to enable
her to be a better mother to him. By extension, this personal motivation may
have prompted him to guide the new Turkey away from what he perceived

to be the "smothering" influence of religion. For Ataturk, fez were associated with religion and thus had to be purged from his new, superior state.

On August 25, 1925, Ataturk traveled to Kastomonu, north of the capital city of Ankara, which had been described to him as one of the most conservative districts in Turkey. When he arrived, he appeared in a gray linen suit, its cut decidedly Western. He wore a tie and carried a white Panama hat in his hand. As though on signal, all the assembled men shed their Muslim-associated headgear—fez, turbans, kalpak—as Ataturk stepped into the crowd. By the time that Ataturk returned to Ankara nine days later, he had destroyed the fez as an appropriate symbol of Turkishness; for Ataturk's Turkey, the Western-style hat was the new suitable reservoir.

While this example illustrates the influence of one leader's actions on a large group and his ability to express large-group identity in a relatively benign fashion, there are other examples of leader influence that can encourage large-group regression. We will return in detail to the crucial question of how the personality of the leader is a significant factor in the life of a large group in Part Three.

Chosen glories and chosen traumas: Understanding the fifth and sixth threads that compose large-group identity—what I call "chosen glories" and "chosen traumas"—requires collaboration between psychoanalysts and historians, for these two elements play by far the most important roles in particularizing each large group's identity and connecting the group with its past—whether realistically recalled or modified by wishes, fantasies, and mental defenses. Large groups tend to hold on to mental representations of events that include a shared feeling of success and triumph among group members; heavily mythologized over time, such events and the persons appearing in them become elements of large-group identity. Chosen glories are passed from generation to generation through caretaker-child interactions and by participation in ceremonies that recall the past success. It is not difficult to understand why parents and other important adults pass on the mental representation of chosen glories to their children; saturated with self-esteem-enhancing feelings, they are pleasurable to share. Likewise, chosen glories link a group's children to each other and to the group by enhancing individual self-esteem.

In times of stress or war-like situations, leaders often reactivate chosen glories in order to bolster their group's identity. During the Gulf War, for instance, Saddam Hussein depended heavily on chosen glories to galvanize the Iraqi people's support, even associating himself with Sultan Saladin, who defeated the Christian Crusaders in the twelfth century. By reviving a past event and a past hero, Saddam aimed to create the illusion that a similar triumphal destiny was awaiting his people and that, like Saladin, he was a hero. Saddam, like Saladin, was born in Tikrit, but it did not matter to Saddam that Saladin was not an Arab but a Kurd, or that he ruled from Egypt rather than Iraq. It did not matter to his people either, for the emphasis was principally on the ancient hero's religious identity; the idea was that, like Saladin, Muslim Saddam would also defeat the infidel United States and its allies. As we know more than a decade after the Gulf War, Saddam's expectation did not materialize and he was toppled by the United States and its coalition partners. A leader's reference to chosen glories excites his followers simply by stimulating an already-existing shared marker of large-group success.

The role of the chosen trauma—the collective mental representation of an event that has caused a large group to face drastic common losses, to feel helpless and victimized by another group, and to share a humiliating injury—in sustaining large-group identity and its cohesiveness is more complex than that of the chosen glory.[80] Clinical investigations of members of groups that have suffered a massive trauma at the hands of an enemy group reveal that although each individual has his or her own unique identity and personal reaction to the trauma, all (or almost all) group members have developed injured self-images as a result. Studies of the second and third generations of a group that has suffered such a trauma (such as the children and grandchildren of Holocaust survivors) clearly show that the mental representation of the shared tragedy is transmitted to subsequent generations in varying levels of intensity.[81]

There is far more to this transgenerational transmission of massive trauma than children mimicking the behavior of parents or hearing stories of the event told by the older generation; nor is it a matter merely of transgenerational sympathy, powerful as that emotion may be. Rather, it is the end result of mostly unconscious psychological processes by which survivors *deposit*[82] into their progeny's core identities their own injured self-images. In order to gain relief from feelings of shame and humiliation, the inability to be assertive, and the inability to mourn, a Holocaust survivor, for example, deposits his or her image of him or herself as a damaged person into the developing personal identity of his or her child; thus, the parent's self-image "lives on" in the child. Then the parent unconsciously assigns to (the image of him or herself that is now in) the child specific tasks of reparation that rightfully belong to the survivor: to reverse shame and humiliation, to turn passivity into activity, to tame the sense of aggression, and to mourn the losses associated with the trauma—the actual deaths of relatives and friends in the original tragedy, the loss of self-esteem and prestige, and the loss of land and other valuable things. What is passed to the offspring is not the traumatized person's memories of the event, then, for memory can belong only to the survivor of trauma and cannot be transmitted; deposited parental self-images are the only elements by which the representation of traumatic history can be passed from person to person. Since all the injured self-images that various parents in a traumatized group transmit to their children refer to the same event, a shared image of the tragedy develops. By sharing this image of their ancestors' trauma, a new generation of the group is unconsciously knit together. Over time, the mental representation of the original tragedy becomes a crucial marker of large-group identity.

Once the mental representation of a shared traumatic event becomes a chosen trauma, the actual history of the event is no longer especially important; what is essential is this marker's unseen power to link the members of the group together in a persistent sense of sameness through history. As a result, a chosen trauma may assume new functions as it passes from one generation to the next. In some generations, it may support a shared and sustained sense (and idealization) of victimhood;[83] in others, it may be used to construct the group as avengers. In the Protestant Reformation, historian and psychoanalyst Peter Loewenberg discovers an example of the crucial bridge between massive shared trauma and historical processes:

> [It] was a trauma of major proportions ... whose effect took centuries to work out to a new and secure equilibrium. One response of European religion, culture, and politics to these traumata was a new piety, flagellation, widespread practice of torture, and epidemics of demonic possession, which seized groups in the late fifteenth century for the first time. In this period we see the emergence of the witch mania that tortured and killed thousands. In one year the Bishop of Wurzburg killed nine hundred, the Bishop of Bamberg over six hundred; in Savoy eight hundred were burned in a festival. In 1514 three hundred were executed in the small Diocese of Como.[84]

A chosen trauma also may remain dormant in a group's "collective memory" over many generations. At times of stress, when the group's identity is threatened, an inactive chosen trauma can be revived through propaganda or hate speech and may be used by leaders to inflame the group's shared feelings about themselves and their enemy (or enemies). In what I call a *time collapse*, the chosen trauma is then experienced as if it has happened only yesterday: feelings, perceptions, and expectations associated with the past heavily contaminate those connected to current events and current enemies, leading to irrational political decision-making and destructive behavior.

As unlikely as it may seem, for example, the chosen trauma critical for understanding the tragedies in Bosnia in 1992 and in Kosovo in 1999 is the Serbian people's defeat at the Battle of Kosovo in 1389.[85] Despite the fact that the leaders of both sides—Ottoman Sultan Murat I and Serbian Prince Lazar—were both killed, and despite the fact that Serbia remained autonomous for some 80 years after the battle, the Battle of Kosovo evolved as the major chosen trauma marking the end of a glorious period of Serbian power and the beginning of their subjugation to the Ottoman Empire. In some periods, Prince Lazar's image was used to cement a shared sense of victimization and martyrdom under Muslim rule; at others, his image became a symbol of Serbs' desire to reverse the humiliation of the loss by reconquering Kosovo. Though the province was "taken back" from the Ottoman Turks in the late nineteenth century, Lazar's "ghost" still was not put to rest; after the collapse of communism, he and the Battle of Kosovo were resurrected by Slobodan Milosevic and Radovan Karadzic to reactivate the 600-year-old "memory" of humiliation and the accompanying desire for revenge. The time collapse that they facilitated through sophisticated as well as base propaganda prepared the Serbian people emotionally for the atrocities they would eventually commit against Bosnian and Kosovar Muslims, whom modern Serbs came to perceive as extensions of the Ottoman enemy of distant history. Thus the Serbian large-group identity was reinforced and reinvigorated by the lasting emotional power of this ancient event—at terrible cost to non-Serbs.

Though eyes untrained in human psychology may not see the relationship, Loewenberg observes, "[t]rauma is the theoretical link from individual to group, cohort, population, nation, the world."[86] When representatives of "enemy" groups face each other across a negotiating table, each group's chosen traumas are easily revived—and, without an appreciation of the psychological mechanisms at work, it can be very difficult for would-be mediators to interpret the responses generated by reactivated chosen traumas. Between 1994 and 1996, I served as a member of a facilitating team that brought together Estonian, Russian, and Russian-speak-

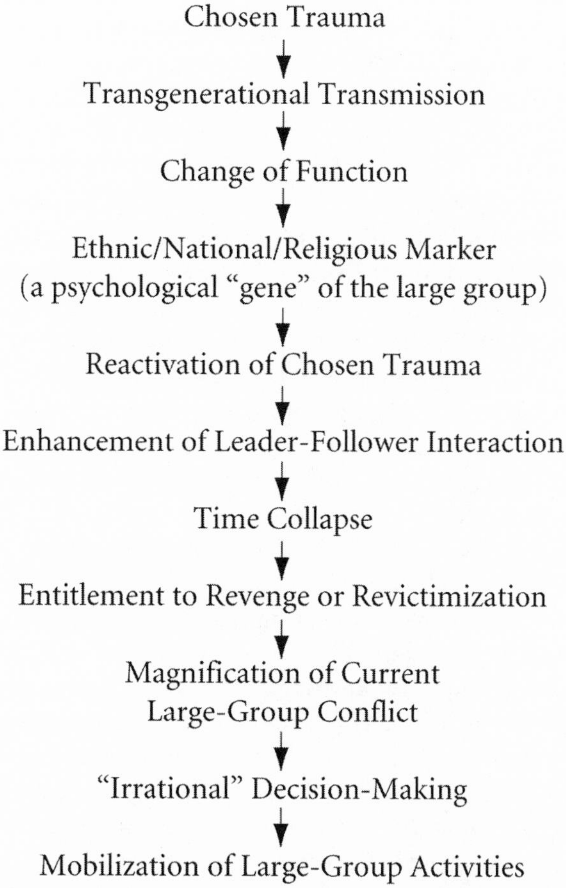

Chosen Trauma
↓
Transgenerational Transmission
↓
Change of Function
↓
Ethnic/National/Religious Marker
(a psychological "gene" of the large group)
↓
Reactivation of Chosen Trauma
↓
Enhancement of Leader-Follower Interaction
↓
Time Collapse
↓
Entitlement to Revenge or Revictimization
↓
Magnification of Current
Large-Group Conflict
↓
"Irrational" Decision-Making
↓
Mobilization of Large-Group Activities

Figure 2. Many present-day conflicts cannot be fully understood without first understanding how historical hurts and grievances survive from generation to generation as "chosen traumas." These psychological "genes" exist within many large groups and can be manipulated by leaders in subsequent generations to mobilize the group. The reactiviation of a chosen trauma may contribute to irrational decision-making and inhumane acts.

ing Estonian leaders for a series of unofficial dialogues aimed at easing the many political, social, and diplomatic tensions that afflicted Russia and Estonia after the latter regained its independence in 1991. In such a discussion, participants tend to become spokespersons for their large groups, and this situation was no exception; each "wore" the canvas of his or her group identity as his or her primary garment instead of personal clothing. At one point in the discussion, the ethnic Estonians refused to show appreciation for Soviet support against the Nazis or for Soviet capital investments in Estonia; the ethnic Russians responded by asserting that Russia had defended all of western civilization against Tatar and Mongol assault. To an untutored eye, this exchange would perhaps seem at best irrelevant, perhaps a non sequitur: what have the medieval "Golden Hordes" to do with Soviet expenditures? The connection is, in a word, humiliation. The Russians, the sons and daughters of an empire, felt humiliated by the Estonians, the sons and daughters of a people who had lived under the domination of others for almost a millennium. Russians turned to centuries-old "memories" of victimization at the hands of thirteenth- and fourteenth-century invaders in order to hold on to the thread of collective identity that strengthens their sense of "we-ness" in the Russian large group. Collapsed into Russia's relationship with Estonia in the mid-1990s, the revived mental representations of shared historical trauma naturally complicated any attempt at negotiation of current conflicts.[87]

Symbols: The seventh thread of a group's identity is the symbol that functions to tie together some or all of the other threads. Though such a symbol may originally stand for any one of the six threads already described, it eventually develops its own autonomy as a component of the large-group tent. Before we observe how symbols function as part of the fabric of large-group identity, however, let us review briefly the classical psychoanalytic understanding of the symbol more generally. In everyday life, certain symbols—such as the red octagon that symbolizes "stop"—function on the force of convention. In psychoanalysis, the concept of a symbol is rather narrower; psychoanalysis is most concerned with how and why symbols originate in an individual's unconscious and function in his or her internal conflicts. Freud, in *Interpretation of Dreams* and many other subsequent writings, argued that symbols repress unacceptable wishes and ideas and therefore function to reduce anxiety;[88] an individual is aware of the symbol itself, but unaware of what it symbolizes. If someone dreams of a snake, for instance, he or she actually sees an image of a snake, but does not consciously perceive the penis that the snake may represent. Initially, Freud believed that symbols representing body parts, body functions, birth, death, sexuality, and childhood intimate relationships with parents or siblings are universal, included in a kind of phylogenetic memory. This belief "has now been largely replaced by the assumption that the recurrence of such symbols across cultures has to do with the similarity of human beings' experiences and interests from infancy onward and of the cognitive processes involved in symbol formation."[89]

In considering the function of symbols in large-group identity, I focus here not on those that signify similarly across many cultures, but on those that are valued in specific ways by only one large group. Large-group symbols tend to be unique, but when many groups deploy the same symbol, each tends to attach minor or major differences to it to specify the common object's particular significance to that group. For example, stars appear as symbols on numerous national flags, but the Star of David only signifies Jewishness. Composed of two overlapping triangles creating a six-point star, this symbol was traditionally interpreted cross-culturally as representing male and female bodies joined together. For Jews, however, this symbol was associated with the biblical King Solomon, son of David and Bathsheba. With it, it is said, Solomon exorcised demons and summoned angels; Jews subsequently understood the symbol to represent YHWH ("Yahweh," or God).[90] Because of its association with Solomon for Jews, the two overlapping triangles came to be known as the *sigillum Salomonis* (Solomon's seal) or *scutum Davidis* (David's shield). Today it is usually known as the Star of David.

The image of Prince Lazar, as I mentioned earlier in this chapter, was used for centuries as a symbol of Serbian identity in folksongs, religious icons, paintings, sculpture, and other shared cultural forms. Upon close examination, it becomes clear that Lazar's image became an element binding some of the other threads of Serbian ethnic identity together: it not only became a suitable reservoir for Serbian children's unintegrated "good" images and projected idealizations, but also evoked the Serbian chosen trauma, which was transformed into a chosen glory when the Serbs succeeded in battle in the nineteenth and twentieth centuries. During the communist period, the Yugoslavian government officially denigrated Lazar's image as a "symbol of reactionary nationalism"[91] as part of its efforts to amalgamate Serbs, Croats, Bosnian Muslims, and others into "brothers and sisters" united under a higher Yugoslavian ideal. But the various ethnic group identities remained very much alive, as did the image of Lazar, whose name was affixed to a brand of red wine during this period (another was named after Princess Milica, Lazar's wife); we might even imagine that, when Serbs in communist Yugoslavia selected this wine to drink, they were unconsciously continuing to identify with the symbol of Lazar as national hero.

The respective evolutions of the Star of David's association with Jewish identity and Lazar's connection to Serbian identity are relatively clear, but often the original significance of a symbol for an ethnic, national, or religious collective is difficult to pinpoint because its significance generally develops over long periods of time and by unconscious, though shared, psychological processes. Take, for instance, the animal symbols that frequently represent national and ethnic group identities, a phenomenon that goes back to the beginnings of human history. The symbolic significance of certain animals, such as those associated with fertility, warfare, wisdom, or specific behaviors, is obvious; in other cases, animals are used to represent complex and abstract ideas. For still other groups, certain animal symbols were adopted by particularly important leaders and thereby elevated (or resurrected) as unifying symbols. Adolf Hitler's fascination and identification with the wolf, for example, has been well documented: "As a boy, he had been pleased to find that his given name was derived from the Old German 'Athalwolf,' meaning 'noble wolf.'"[92] Hitler named his favorite dog "Wolf" and generalized his identification with this predatory animal by calling the SS his "pack of wolves." At times, he also believed that the German people followed him because they realized that "now a wolf ha[d] been born."[93]

Other large-group symbols have assumed their representational status by explicit and intentional agreement. In cases of purely ideological identity, the large group's history does not belong to the distant past, so the history of the symbol, such as the Soviet hammer and sickle, may be well known. Today, symbols displayed on flags are often chosen through a vote or general consensus, as are the birds and flowers of each U.S. state; sometimes such choices are the subject of intense debate, competition, and rivalry.

Even when the process of such selection assumes apparently irrational proportions—indicating that large-group symbols are psychologically powerful things—in the end, the link between signifier and signified is clear, like the red octagon that signifies "stop." When a large group is under stress, however, that clear relation between signifier and signified may be lost, and its symbols may come to be perceived as what psychoanalysis calls *protosymbols*—that is, no longer as a symbol *representing* the group identity, but as the thing itself.[94]

Large-group members and their leaders are constantly engaged in the work of protecting their shared identity and keeping the seven "threads" described in this chapter securely woven together. Often we are not even aware of this work, for it is, as we will see, part of the everyday lives of a large group. When a large group's tent-canvas is shaken by conflict or humiliation or begins to show wear, the members become keenly aware of their group identity and of their collective efforts to maintain, repair, and stabilize it. At all times, though, these collective efforts take the form of shared rituals. In Chapter 3, we will look closely at the large-group rituals of identity from which political propaganda and political decision-making, whether used for poisoning or healing, derive their power. First, however, we must examine the psychological condition under which large groups become susceptible to political propaganda,[95] maladaptive political decision-making, and massive destructive behavior: large-group regression, the experience I call "plunging back into a world of fear and desire."

2 / regression: plunging back into a world of fear and desire

When I was a child I used to wonder
if our Greek neighbor's cat
was also Greek.
One day I asked my mum
and she said cats were Turkish
dogs were Greek
and dogs attacked the kittens.

Much later one day
what should I see?
Our cat was eating
her own kitten.

—Mehmet Yasin, "Our Cat's Tale"
    translated from Turkish by Taner Baybars

That regression is a response to anxiety is one of the key concepts in the mental health field. Anxiety is an internal signal that something dangerous is about to happen, and is thus distinguishable from fear. *Fear* is what one experiences when one faces an actual danger; for instance, a person will experience fear if, while visiting a zoo, he or she sees an escaped lion approaching. By contrast, if that person experiences uncomfortable sensations, racing heart, or sweaty palms while visiting a zoo where all the dangerous animals are safely contained, he or she is feeling *anxiety*—because the lions locked in their cages symbolize some psychological danger for that individual, not because they actually pose a threat to life and limb; one need not be in real peril in order to experience anxiety. Since anxiety is an unpleasant feeling, people develop various mental mechanisms for avoiding it, one of which is *regression*.

Regression is not intrinsically bad or good; rather, it is an inevitable and necessary response to certain levels of trauma, threat or stress.

Regression followed by progression also usually accompanies and enables creativity. In our daily lives, we continually alternate between regression and progression. Imagine going home after a hard day at work, sitting in front of a fire on a cold night, and "expecting" to be taken care of the way your mother took care of you as a child (regression). In a sense, regressing gives us psychological nutrition, for the next day, we go back to work and meet the demands placed on us as adults, making critical decisions and being responsible (progression). Now, imagine an adult who, after hearing of the accidental death of an acquaintance, goes home at the end of the day, imagines dangers lurking under the bed (regression). The news of the death awakened certain childhood internal dangers in him, we say, and for a while he behaves like an anxious child who avoids looking under his bed in order to control his anxiety. Regression and progression are part of normal daily life for most of us. It is only when regression becomes stubborn and long-lasting that we speak of psychological difficulties.

Imagine an adult who behaves in ways that reflect a sense of entitlement to be nurtured whenever he or she desires; this person behaves like a child, not seriously considering the give-and-take required of normal adult relationships. Or imagine another adult who, like an emotionally unprotected child, is preoccupied with threats lurking around every corner, the metaphorical monsters beneath the bed. Both of these people—the one who is extremely dependent and the one who hears thunder on a clear day, so to speak—exist in states of regression. There are two possible explanations (or a combination of them) for these individuals' mental conditions. First, each may have been fixed, from childhood on, in a regressed state: though they exhibit some adult functions, they also possess childhood desires and fears and want to satisfy or protect themselves as a child would. Alternately, they may be adults whose childhood fears and desires have been revived by recent events in their external environments—the unexpected death of a loved one, a business failure, or some other shame-inducing event—that have become unconsciously and symbolically connected with danger signals from childhood, such as losing parental love or expecting punishment; the current event has induced anxiety and, in turn, regression.

In our everyday lives, major regressions are temporary—unless, of course, what produces anxiety in us initiates a stubborn, or even malignant, psychological process within us. How long a person will remain in a regressed state depends on a number of factors, particularly on his or her psychological make-up before regression and on the severity and the length of the threatening event or events. Sometimes an individual internalizes the impact of an external event and continues to respond to it even after the circumstances change. I have a close friend—a university professor, well respected by his students and the community—who was once mistakenly accused of committing a crime and had to sit in jail for over nine hours before his innocence could be established. His brief stay in jail, where he felt helpless, was a threat to his self-esteem that echoed in his quotidian life long after the incident itself. Indeed, for many years he could not watch any television program that included scenes of imprisonment: as soon as he saw a person in jail on the screen, his heart would begin to pound, his palms would sweat, and he would feel very uncomfortable.

Like individuals, groups, from demonstrating crowds to religious cults to whole nations, can also regress—temporarily or for a long time, mildly or malignantly. We often see large-group regressions, for instance, after natural, man-made accidental, or ethnically, nationally, religiously, or ideologically motivated disasters. After such catastrophes, the surviving community tends to remain "in the basement" long after the storm has passed, metaphorically speaking; survivors often become preoccupied with images of death and destruction and may exhibit what is known as "survivor guilt," condemning themselves for having lived while loved ones perished. While working with families of World Trade Center victims in the fall of 2001, a colleague of mine who lives in New York City experienced such feelings compounded by a long-repressed personal sense of survivor guilt. Now in his fifties, at the age of six he had lost a sibling one year younger than he, of whom he typically thought only rarely. After the Twin Towers tragedy, however, he began to have nightmares and to wake suddenly in a state of high anxiety, all related to the image of his dead sibling. Eventually he realized that surviving the attacks on New York had reactivated his childhood survivor guilt; he responded to the new, shared tragedy by mentally returning to the past, personal one.[96]

The focus of this chapter is on *regression in large groups* (such as ethnic, national, or religious groups), which takes place when a majority of group members share certain anxieties, expectations, behaviors, thought patterns, and actions that can be explained by the concept of regression. Large-group regression after a society has faced a massive trauma—involving drastic loss of life, property, or prestige, and sometimes humiliation by another group—reflects the efforts of a group and its leader to maintain, protect, modify, or repair their shared group identity. As in individual regression, many survivors in a traumatized society continue to function like mature adults in some ways, even as they are experiencing regression in others: Regression is not an all-or-nothing experience and is typically accompanied by attempts to adapt; sometimes these efforts to cope with the trauma will take the shape of artistic creativity.[97]

When looking at large groups in regression, the role of the leader is a crucial factor. When a regressed large group has a strong leader, the signs and symptoms of its regression express themselves differently that when there is no such leader. A strong leader and his or her entourage reinforces the group's symptoms and may encourage the followers either to remain in a regressed state or to make attempts at progression. By contrast, when a large group *without* a leader becomes regressed, *chaos* ensues. Malignant large-group regression under a central leader can occur only where there is (or has been) individual regression on the part of the leader *as well as* regression of the group. By "malignant," I mean that the regression results in ruining the lives of many people, or killing people. A reparative leader, on the other hand, devotes him or herself to bringing the followers out of regression and promoting progression.

In this chapter, I will not dwell on political leaders' psychological states. Rather, I will ask: What precisely constitutes large-group regression? However, I want to be clear that my point here is neither to demonstrate some mental primitivism intrinsic to particular large groups nor to blame either the large groups living in poverty or the nations conventionally referred to as "Third World" or "developing" for bearing psychological "defects." I should explain what I mean by the term "mental primitivism." In a clinical setting, psychoanalysts have a tendency to differentiate between routine neurotic analysands and those patients who are "difficult" cases. The latter extensively utilize certain mental maneuvers, such as introjection, projection, denial and splitting of images, in dealing with their mental conflicts. Obviously such maneuvers exist in everyone's repertoire, but "difficult" cases use them more. When we speak of large-group psychology, we can not categorize societies as "primitive" or "advanced" according to their shared mental mechanisms. All large groups use shared "primitive" defense mechanisms regularly, just as all large groups are subjected to regression. In regression, large groups will use, as I will describe soon, certain shared thoughts, feelings, and activities to protect their large-group identity and differentiate their identity from the identity of "others."

Because the psychoanalytic developmental model is a universal one, *any* large group is subject to episodes of regression under certain historical conditions. Furthermore, to be in a regressed state is not the "natural" or necessarily permanent state of any society or identity group. I focus here on situations of political indoctrination or war (or war-like conditions) that have induced particular masses of people to change their existing shared patterns of feeling, thought, and behavior in order to illustrate how a large group can regress to—and may be kept in—a collective state of developmentally primitive psychological functioning.

The following is a list of the typical signs and symptoms of large-group regression under a central authority. In describing large-group regression, I focus on observable shared processes after a traumatizing event—whether destruction by war, war-like conditions, terrorism, or oppression by a dictator.

1) Group members lose their individuality.

2) The group rallies blindly around the leader.

3) The group becomes divided into "good" segments—those who obediently follow the leader—and "bad"—those perceived to oppose the leader.

4) The group creates a sharp "us" and "them" division between itself and "enemy" (usually neighboring) groups.

5) The group's shared morality or belief system becomes increasingly absolutist and punitive toward those perceived to be in conflict with it.

6) The group uses extensive "taking in" (*introjection*) and "putting out" (*projection*) mechanisms and may experience accompanying massive mood swings, from shared depressive feelings to collective paranoid expectations.[98]

7) The group feels "entitled" to do anything to maintain its shared identity.

8) Group members experience increased magical thinking and reality-blurring.

9) The group experiences new cultural phenomena or adopts modified versions of traditional societal customs that are intended to protect the group identity.

10) The group's chosen traumas and glories are reactivated, resulting in a time collapse.

11) The leadership creates a break in the historical continuity of the group and fills the gap with elements such as: "new" nationalism, ethnic sentiments, religious fundamentalism or ideology, accompanying "new" morality, and sometimes a "new" history of the group purged of unwanted elements.

12) Group members begin to experience some of the group's shared symbols as protosymbols.

13) Shared images depict and dehumanize enemy groups with symbols or protosymbols associated with progressively more subhuman traits: demons, insects, germs, human waste.

14) The group experiences geographical or legal boundaries as a "second skin."

15) The group focuses on minor differences between itself and enemy groups.

16) The leadership ruins basic trust within the family and creates a new kind of family hierarchy and morality that interferes with roles within the family (especially women's roles), with normal childhood development, and with the adolescent passage.

17) Group members become overly concerned with the notion of "blood" and an associated homogeneous or purified existence.

18) The group engages in behaviors symbolizing purification.

19) Group taste has difficulty differentiating what is beautiful from what is ugly.

20) The group turns its physical environment into a gray-brown, amorphous (symbolically fecal) structure.

Not all 20 signs and symptoms need be expressed for a society to be considered regressed, and I can not, therefore, say how many signs and symptoms need be present to definitively diagnose a society as regressed. Rather, the determination must be made on a case-by-case basis.

In order to illustrate these signs and symptoms of large-group regression under a central leader, I will provide sketches of these various symptoms, drawn from history as well as from my own observations around the world. I will not dwell much here on the psychological (especially unconscious) explanations of why these signs and symptoms emerge. I will also not detail the historical context of each example. Rather, I will focus on how a particular leader and his or her followers strive to maintain, protect, modify, and/or repair their shared large-group identity.

Group members losing their individuality and rallying around their leader: The first two signs of large-group regression have been known for a long time. For example, when Freud outlined his theory of large-group psychology in 1921, he described the rallying around a leader[99] as one of the crucial elements in the process of synthesizing followers into a cohesive group of "equals" under a leader. The regressive aspect of this phenomenon was noted by later psychoanalysts, and some have concluded—correctly, in my view—that Freud's theory of large-group psychology is applicable only to large groups in a regressed state.[100]

Since Freud made a reference to the army in describing his theory of large-group psychology, I illustrate the first two signs or symptoms by looking at the military in a regressed society. In Nazi Germany, a regressed society, it was difficult for an outsider to differentiate between one SS officer and another—but, more importantly, it also became difficult for each SS officer to differentiate *himself* from others. Of course, members of any well-established army share certain tasks and function as a unit, so there is an element of regression in any army deployed for specific military purposes. But, in the army of a (nonregressed) democratic country, soldiers do not lose their individuality altogether; for example, an officer can easily maintain an allegiance to a dissenting political party without compromising his or her military role. Further, in nonregressed countries, those who are not members of the military can openly express opinions that may not be favorable toward the military or government.

In regressed societies, the social and political hierarchies among followers (military or civilian) who do not belong to the governing cadre are erased. This leveling of the social structure is related to blind rallying around the leader. In such societies, members experience exaggerated dependence on the leadership and threats to basic trust. With his or her power, the leader can "make or break" a member of the group; he or she is perceived as omnipotent, and is therefore feared as well as loved—to tweak Machiavelli's infamous declaration. Michael Sebek, a Czech psychoanalyst who personally experienced life in a totalitarian regime, has posited the existence of "totalitarian objects," which, once internalized, force individuals into total compliance and obedience. Totalitarian objects block the individual's normal development, but paradoxically they also bring some sense of safety to the immature persons they create—who, through merging psychologically with the strong authority, achieve a feeling of false importance and wholeness. [101]

The stories of the birth of the Taliban in Afghanistan and its leader, Mullah Omar, consolidating his power, tell us a great deal about regressed groups and members' blind trust in the leader. From 1996 to 2001, the Taliban was the *de facto* government of Afghanistan, controlling as much as 90 percent of a country that has been a highly contested crossroads for at least two and a half millennia. The area now known as Afghanistan was previously called Khurasan, a region divided between Safavid Iran to the West and Mogul India to the East. In 1747, Afghan tribesmen were consolidated under the rule of Ahmad Shah Durani (or Abdali) into the country of Afghanistan. But the real power in central and south Asia rested with the British, who in fact coined the name Afghanistan. Throughout the nineteenth century and into the early twentieth, the British used Afghanistan as a buffer zone between their empire and that of the Russians. Not until the 1880s did Afghanistan emerge as a modern nation-state under Amir Abdur Rahman, who came to power with British support.[102] In order to maintain control of the area's ethnically heterogeneous population, which includes at least eight distinct groups, Rahman turned to cruelty and genocide.[103] Rahman's grandson, King Amamullah (1919–1929), who identified with Turkey's Ataturk, planned to institute a constitutional monarchy with an elected National Assembly, emancipate women, and introduce compulsory education. But his attempts at modernization resulted in an uprising in which he was overthrown. Both of the next two rulers were assassinated in rapid succession, but Mohamed Zahir Shah, who took the throne at age nineteen after his father's assassination, ruled the country from 1933 until 1973, when he was exiled after a relatively bloodless coup by his cousin Mohamed Daud.[104] Daud remained in power, however, only briefly, and a series of coups followed until the Soviet invasion of 1979. After the Soviets withdrew ten years later, civil war broke out between the former guerrilla resistance groups (*mujahidin*).[105]

Though reliable statistics about Afghanistan are difficult to come by (even the total current population of the country is not definitely known, estimated to be somewhere between 15 and 22 million), it is unquestionably true that the damage and suffering of its last several decades have been massive. During the ten-year Soviet occupation and the civil war that followed, there were an estimated 1.5 million war casualties. Between 1992 and 1996, according to a UNICEF survey, 72 percent of Afghan children lost at least one family member, and 40 percent of them had lost a parent: "The grief," as one journalist has written, "is almost inconceivable."[106] Just before the British and American air strikes on Afghanistan began in the fall of 2001, it was estimated that in the capital Kabul alone there were 25,000 to 50,000 street children, largely war orphans. Land mines continued to kill and maim many people daily. Drought and hunger added to the misery, and the country was at the end of its resources.[107]

Into Afghanistan's post-Soviet wretchedness came the Taliban, originally recruited mostly from young Pashtuns, Afghanistan's largest ethnic group. The Taliban, whose name means "religious students," first came to notice when, in late 1994, they successfully drove a local bandit group away from a thirty-truck convoy trying to initiate a trade route between Pakistan and Central Asia. Eventually, it grew from that original core group of only one hundred into a cohort of 35,000 men from forty-three countries. In its power base, the southern Afghan city of Kandahar, the Taliban demonstrated its power with draconian public punishments for crime and stringent controls on the actions of girls and women. As they refused to deal with warlords and fought local police forces as well as roving bandits, the Taliban applied a strict interpretation of Islamic law to combatting the corruption and chaos that plagued post-Soviet Afghanistan. Within two years, the Taliban had taken the capital, Kabul, capping its seizure of power with the brutal castration and hanging of the last Soviet-allied president of Afghanistan.[108]

The Taliban leader Mullah Mohammad Omar is a figure of considerable mystery. It is claimed that Mullah Omar was born in the very poor central Afghan province of Uruzgan in 1962, but a true biography cannot be definitively established. All that is known for certain about his early life is that his father died when Omar was very young, and that he seems to have been given the task of looking after his mother and extended family. Some claim that he has studied in several Islamic schools, whereas others state that he is illiterate; it is known that he did not study in Pakistani reli-

gious schools, though most of his followers would be drawn from such schools.[109] He is said to have had a dream in which Prophet Muhammad appeared to him and instructed him to bring peace to Afghanistan; Mullah Omar's dream-experience has apparently given him what he and his followers think of as a divine task.

In 1996, Mullah Omar put on the cloak supposedly worn by the Prophet Muhammad—brought to Afghanistan some 250 years ago and kept locked in a marble vault in the city center of Kandahar—for a rally of his followers on the occasion of his selection (by about 1,000 clerics, mostly Pashtun) as *Amir-ul-Momineen*, "Commander of the Faithful," the first since a nephew of Prophet Muhammad to publicly accept the ranking, which is "nearly second to the Prophet."[110] The cloak, which some of the people of Kandahar reportedly believe can cure the sick and heal the lame, had only been removed from its vault on two previous occasions: in

1929, when King Emanullah invoked it to unify the country, and again in 1935, when authorities turned to the relic to stop a cholera epidemic in the city.[111] In 2001, the keeper of the Shrine of the Cloak of the Prophet Muhammad, Qari Shawali, reported that in his lifetime only two people have asked to see the relic in its silver box, and one of them, former Afghan King Mohamed Zahir Shah, became too anxious to look at the cloak when the time came.[112] A remarkable post-Taliban *New York Times* interview with the forty-eight-year-old Shawali reveals Omar's act as both an act of propaganda aimed at legitimizing his leadership but also, because of his own religious beliefs, an apparently difficult personal task for the mullah.[113]

When Mullah Omar first came to see the cloak in the spring of 1996, the keeper asked him if he was properly ready to see the cloak. It would be sinful to do so if Mullah Omar had not ritually washed certain parts of his body. Mullah Omar was not ready and he had to leave. But some days later, Mullah Omar returned accompanied by some of his men, and he boldly told the keeper, "'Here I am, I have taken a bath and I have put on new clothes. Let me see the robe.'"[114] But Shawali recalls how Omar trembled when he laid eyes on the sacred robe and indeed became so disoriented that he mistook the direction of Mecca as he prepared to pray. A week later, a more confident Omar appeared at the shrine once more, removing the robe to an old mosque in the center of Kandahar. "For the next 30 minutes, he held the cloak aloft" from the roof of the mosque, "his palms inserted in its sleeves."[115] The assembled crowd cheered, and many reportedly lost consciousness.[116]

Donning the cloak publicly was certainly a gamble: as journalist Jeffrey Goldberg notes, the act could have easily been seen as blasphemous.[117] But, by successfully inflecting his image in the minds of his followers with the image of the Prophet, Mullah Omar blurred the reality that he and the Prophet lived in centuries apart and that they are two (perhaps dramatically) different human beings and leaders.[118] Thus he was able to use the cloak to solidify the shared national-religious identity of his followers as well as his image as the commander of the faithful. This was true politically and militarily as well as religiously: the Taliban had swept across southern Afghanistan in 1994, but still had not defeated the government forces in Kabul and was divided as to what to do next. It was only a few months after Mullah Omar merged his own image with that of the Prophet that the Taliban captured Kabul and began to enforce their oppressive laws on the Afghan population, and allowed Osama bin Laden and his al Qaeda organization, with its unlimited funds, to thrive in Afghanistan.

Two types of splits: Splits are frequent within regressed groups. We see two types of splits when a large group regresses. The first one occurs within the society itself. Those who are the followers of the political leader separate themselves from those who are not the followers of the leader. Obviously, there are splits in every large group. For example, in the United States, the Democrats separate themselves from the Republicans. Such a separation becomes more visible during certain times, such as when there is a campaign for a presidential election. But when a society is regressed, the split within becomes characterized by excessive clinging (blind trust) to the leader by his or her followers, paranoid expectations from one side towards the other side, and eruption of aggression. Often the leadership itself plays a significant role in stirring up emotions about the split. For example, in Albania during the regime of Enver Hoxha, people were either considered "good" or "black spotted" (see Chapter 9). The latter group was subject to torture and/or exiled to remote locations in Albania. In short, there is qualitative and quantitative differences between a political split in a nonregressed large group and a societal split in a regressed large group.

The second type of split in a regressed large group is between the large group in question and its external enemies. Swedish psychoanalyst Marta Cullberg-Weston's extensive research in Yugoslavia (as it was collapsing) revealed "a strong tendency toward splitting" between neighboring ethnic groups:

> Images were split into good/bad and into we/them categories. Almost everyone idealized their own ethnic group and demonized others. If you were not seen as in favor of the group in question, you were seen as an enemy. The black and white thinking was further encouraged by nationalistic leaders who actively played on group antipathy, using propaganda aimed at creating fear, rage and insecurity about people's safety.[119]

New morality, massive introjections, projections and entitlement: A regressed society's morality posits rigid societal obligations to be obeyed at all times, but on the other hand permits behavior that would be considered antisocial or antihuman by "normal" communities. Regressed morality in the individual rationalizes thinking and actions that in reality protect him or her from perceived dangers and anxiety. In a large group, the shared regressed morality helps to cement the place of the individual in the group and not only gives him or her permission to behave in ways unacceptable under ordinary circumstances, but obliges him or her to exhibit aggressive behavior in order not to be alienated from the group. Thus an SS officer in Nazi Germany would not have thought of stealing a watch from a fellow officer, but participating in the extermination of Jews was not merely acceptable but was expected under Nazi "morality." When group ideology becomes "sacralized," held to be beyond question or error, it leaves no room for flexibility or negotiation in relation to outsider (or internal dissenter) groups or individuals. When a group's identity itself is dependent on a shared ideology or religious belief held to be infallible, real or perceived threats to the group identity are frequently met with righteous violence.

Members of a regressed large group do not need to have an authority physically present in order to obey the "new morality," for by obeying, they can perceive the world as a place in which one's intense wishes can be gratified instantly. Jealousy and envy, which develop when people perceive others' wishes to be gratified while theirs remain unmet, are avoided, for obeying the dominant morality enables regressed followers' most basic desires to be met: to be loved by the leader-parent. At the same time, members of a regressed society perceive the world as a place of lurking dangers connected with childhood expectations and fantasies, for the threat of failing (intentionally or unintentionally) to be fully obedient is always there. To cope with childhood desires and fears, group members develop certain psychological defenses. Preeminent among the developmentally prior—or "primitive"—psychic defense mechanisms that regressed populations tend to use are introjection and projection. Collective "taking in" helps the assimilation of new ideas and the identification of followers with one another while blindly following the leader. The collective "dishing out" forces the group to become "obsessed" with its enemy or enemies; the group may imagine that it can read the enemy's minds. In extreme situations, whole "paranoid societies," like Albania under dictator Enver Hoxha, may be created.[120] On some occasions, shared paranoia tends to create a certain feeling of absolute entitlement to the shared identity and to generate behaviors imagined to preserve that entitlement. Such activities may include not only expressions of aggression toward others but also, paradoxically, shared "suicidal" behaviors, which can range from actual self-killing to idealizing victimization. It is easy to understand why a regressed group, if it has power, may try to destroy another group when the first group experiences the latter as dangerous to its identity. It is harder to conceptualize why a large group at times turns aggression toward itself in order to enhance its large-group identity.

Identity enhancing massive suicides usually occur in religious groups when the members develop a shared conscious or unconscious fantasy that through death they join a divine power. Members of such a group physically die when they kill themselves, but, paradoxically (and illogically), just before their deaths they contaminate their group identity with omnipotence and believe that an omnipotent group identity will survive. In Part Two, I will return to this theme and refer, for example, to Old Believers in mid-seventeenth century Russia who performed massive suicides by burning themselves inside their prayer houses. The idea of protecting one's group's identity by expressing aggression toward "others" as well as toward oneself echoes the actions of today's modern suicide bombers. I will turn my attention to them also in Part Two.

There are also societies where collective victimization is idealized in order to enhance the shared group identity. One of the best historical examples of this phenomenon occurred within the Serbian large group when they were under Ottoman occupation.

Magical thinking and blurring the reality: Accompanying the shared excessive use of introjection and projection in a regressed society is an increase in collective magical expectations and beliefs. During wars and war-like situations, for example, we often observe the development of certain myths. Marie Bonaparte, who played a key role in helping Sigmund Freud and his family escape Vienna to settle in London in 1938, collected much of the mythology born during the World War II period. She found, for example, that among some Germans, Hitler was said to be a reincarnation of Siegfried, the heroic figure of ancient German literature and protagonist of Richard Wagner's *Ring* cycle. Odd but strikingly similar stories circulated among people not in contact with one another, including one about a gypsy's clairvoyance and the projected end of the war.[121]

In a personal communication to me, the late psychoanalyst William Niederland, who coined the term "survivor syndrome," wrote that he found the myth of a secret or uniquely effective weapon was shared by many of the Holocaust survivors he had interviewed in his decades of work on the subject. I observed a similar phenomenon among Cypriot Turks when I visited their Nicosia enclave in 1968, when a bloody conflict between Greeks and Turks on the island severely regressed the Cypriot Turkish society. Children's play and adults' half-joking remarks at moments of anxiety revealed that this population shared the fantasy of a "great weapon" (in children's drawings it was depicted as a huge cannon) on a mountaintop near the ancient St. Hilarion Castle. A site already associated with heroism, sacrifice, and victimhood—a queen was said to have jumped from one of its windows rather than surrender to the enemy—the castle was also strategically important at the time, for it was the highest geographical point under Cypriot Turkish control and was crucial for access to the sea. Thus the kernel of truth in the modern myth—the castle probably was an important gun emplacement—combined with the castle's storied past made it a psychologically appropriate site for the fantasized secret weapon.[122]

Such magical thinking can infect rational, intellectual disciplines as well. After the Soviet Union collapsed, there was much interest in psychoanalysis among Russian intellectuals, many of whom I had met while studying the psychology of Soviet-American relations during the last years of the USSR. It is not surprising that many would want to taste what had been a forbidden fruit; perceived (and rightly so) as a tool for personal individuation, psychoanalysis was banned by the Soviet regime because it ran counter to the official ideological preference for the collective over the individual. In the early 1990s, as I listened to my acquaintances describe their efforts to form psychoanalytic study groups, I understood that for some of them, psychoanalysis was contaminated with magic; some spoke as if anyone who studied psychoanalysis would be miraculously transformed, freed from the felt and unfelt anxieties created by communist ideology.

New and modified cultural and societal patterns: Such patterns emerge in tandem with such shared myths and other "magical" patterns of thinking. After the 1986 nuclear disaster at Chernobyl, for example, many women of childbearing age in Belarus (a region only indirectly affected by the accident) dramatically changed their sexual and reproductive behaviors, imagining that any children they might have would suffer birth defects.[123] By avoiding a deformed generation, the society would preserve itself and its identity. In the economic collapse and societal regression that followed the 1992 South Ossetian–Georgian war, South Ossetian men revived a traditional courtship custom, but in an exaggerated, increasingly aggressive way. The old ritual "kidnapping" of brides began to take on a malignant cast as men actually began to kidnap women, not as a prelude to marriage but as a means of humiliating their victims. At the same time, South Ossetian men began to marry younger and younger women: In a culture that values bridal virginity very highly, but in which many young women had been forced into prostitution, the younger the bride, the more likely she was to be a virgin. These actions were an effort to assert that the society and its identity had not been damaged by the trauma of war.

Chosen traumas, chosen glories, and "new" history: Since the concept of chosen glories and chosen traumas and examples of them appear throughout this volume, I will refer to these concepts only briefly here. Regressed large groups are prone to reactivate what I have dubbed their shared chosen traumas and chosen glories. Many leaders know intuitively how to stimulate chosen traumas and glories as well as how to bring the emotions pertaining to these past events to present issues, thus magnifying both fears and the defenses against them.

Leaders of regressed large groups also may attempt to erase part of the large group's (or subgroup's) historical or cultural or religious heritage in order to replace it with a new history or belief system. Kurt Volkan describes how Soviet authorities emphasized Kazakh, Uzbek, Tajik, Turkmen, and Kyrgyz national identities as a kind of stepping-stone to Sovietization.[124] Though this tactic may on the surface appear contradictory, the aim of the Kremlin was first to defy an obstacle to the development of "New Soviet Man" that was more formidable than these various national identities: Islam. "The razing of institutions that 'pass' Islam from generation to generation was intended to create a vacuum in which Islam could be supplanted by other forms of identity, namely by national identities from which a broader, encompassing Soviet identity could spring."[125]

After World War II, Moscow instituted an "official" Islam. Perhaps in part a concession to the Muslims throughout the Soviet empire for their support during the war, this act brought Islam under the control of the Soviet authority that used extensive propaganda to undermine religion. In the early 1960s, under Nikita Khrushchev's "de-Stalinization" policies, many of the concessions that had been made to Islam were rescinded. Muslims were flooded with anti-Islamic films, plays, books, articles, and lectures; across the USSR, mosques were closed and Islamic clerics were deregistered. During the period of Leonid Brezhnev's rule, propaganda focused on the development of "scientific atheism," but the Soviet regime failed to erase Islam completely: to Central Asians in particular, Islam became "less important as a source and expression of religious spirituality, and more important as a source of group identity in response to the pressures and presence of the 'other'":

The rites of Islam that continued during Soviet rule effectively served as a reservoir for communal "psychological" bonding, in the absence of many visible markers of Islamic identity, and in response to an invading, imported, foreign culture attacking from above.[126]

In postwar communist Albania, too, there was an attempt to erase religion as well as to create a gap in the continuum of history. Here the attack did not come from without, but from within—from the Albanian leadership headed by dictator Enver Hoxha (see Chapter 9 for details). More successfully than the Soviet leaders, Hoxha effaced religion and replaced part of Albanian history with his own "purified" version of Albania's connection with its Ottoman past. After the death of the dictator, however, religion quickly returned, and Albanians began to wonder about their true history as well.

Protosymbols and dehumanization: As a large group regresses, some group symbols—especially those newly established to refer to collective experience, such as the Nazi swastika—may assume a more than symbolic significance. "Concretized" by those who use them as well as by their enemies, these protosymbols may in fact be included in an existing shared magical belief. The "great weapon" of the embattled Cypriot Turks, for instance, was not only part of a myth, but also an invisible symbol in its own right, representing the Turks' wished-for power. Indeed, the magical belief in its actual existence made it, at some level, a concrete symbol.[127]

A regressed group also changes the nature of its perceived enemies by assigning to others symbols or protosymbols. These often connect the enemy with body waste—the enemy is typically conceived as dark, malodorous, and foul—or, alternately, portray enemies as insects, rats, or germs that live on waste. Such symbols and protosymbols are certainly degrading, but they also reflect fear of the enemy. The process of demonizing the "other" occurs in stages. First, the other is made less human and more "evil-like," then its association with bodily waste such as feces makes it dangerous. As a last step, when regression becomes more severe, the enemy is dehumanized. During the 1994 conflict in Rwanda, for example, Hutus first described Tutsis as evil, and later began referring to them as *cafards* (cockroaches).[128] Individuals, such as serial killers, may dehumanize their victims due to their own personal psychological complexities. In conflicts at the societal level, however, people are perceived as less than human—or nonhuman—simply because they are members of a particular (other) large group. The dynamics of societal dehumanization cannot be understood unless we focus on the psychology of large-group identity and rituals.

Preoccupation with borders and minor differences: With regression, psychospatial borders and other tangible distinctions assume a new intensity of symbolic significance for the members of the group. The mental representation of dividing lines becomes like a second skin for large-group identity, thus threats to a border are perceived (in a shared fashion) as threats to the group's identity. In situations where the political borders of a large group are physically threatened by "others," the reality of such danger often makes it difficult to study the psychology of borders in a regressed group. Since preoccupation with borders is also a ritual, I will return to this topic in the next chapter.

Though there may be major differences of history, culture, language, and religion between a group and its enemy, the regressed group becomes preoccupied with the minor differences between them. When tension flares between Greece and Turkey, for example, even differences in the way each group makes the dessert dish baklava become an emotional issue (Greeks use more honey in their version of the pastry). Minor differences become the last frontier separating a regressed group's identity from the "other," and members must therefore maintain that difference in order to maintain their separate identity, which is perceived as their very existence.

Disturbances in the family system and ruining the "basic trust": These are crucial signs not always seen openly. Here I will illustrate these signs by giving some extensive examples of them. Picture once more the imaginary tent of large-group identity: in normal times, the people living under the tent are not especially preoccupied with the tent that covers them, nor are they intensely involved in supporting the pole that keeps the tent aloft. In their everyday lives, they are much more focused on the subgroups under the tent with which they are affiliated, of which the family and the clan are the most important. When the large group regresses severely, routine family relations—and, even more important, the unconscious mental images people hold about those family relations—are disrupted as group members turn their focus to the stability of the "tent." In order for a child to develop into a mentally healthy adult, he or she has to experience a basic trust-providing dyadic relationship with his or her parent (and other significant adults). In severely regressed societies, authorities and sometimes other external factors interfere with the crucial parent-child relationship by interfering with parenting or otherwise humiliating parents or nullifying parental authority in their children's eyes. The best example of this comes from Nazi Germany. Since there is considerable data to illustrate how the family system in Nazi Germany was ruined I will give a detailed summary of what happened there. Ruining the family system and child-parent relations is a crucial expression of severe societal regression (see also: Chapter 9 on Albania under Enver Hoxha).

Given the governing ideology of the *Volksgemeinschaft*, women were from the first a crucial cog in the Nazi machine, specifically in their roles as sexual partners and mothers. As historian Claudia Koonz, who has studied Nazi-era German women extensively, observes, Nazi propaganda created a male-dominated state in which women were, in a sense, a lower class, but "compensated" them with a role in the racial story: "Biology, which predestined [German women] to second-rate status vis-a-vis 'Aryan' men, elevated them above their 'racial inferiors.'"[129] In "racial science" courses in school, young women memorized "rules" for choosing a partner and, if they were deemed hereditarily fit, were exhorted to have as many children as possible to increase the supposedly superior Aryan population. If a woman had seven children, she received a gold medal for motherhood. A woman with six children would be given a silver medal, and one with five children, a bronze. From 1935 onward, Koonz continues, women had to accept a "double burden": not only serving as breeding vehicles, but also entering the labor market.[130] Koonz' statement is true, if we look at it from the standpoint of a modern, democratic, equal-rights position. But, on a conscious level, German women probably felt a sense of high self-esteem as long as they believed in the Nazi ideology. After all, they were idealized as breeders of the superior race. Further, working on the war effort may also have created a sense of self-reliance and self-esteem.

Hitler once called the German family the "germ cell of the nation,"[131] and this was to be true not only racially, but also ideologically. As early as *Mein Kampf*, Hitler had stated that children and youth would lead the National Socialist movement.[132] On the face of it, there is nothing extraordinary or original in this prediction; totalitarian, nationalist, and democratic movements alike often invoke children and youth, as we see in the rhetoric of practically every American political contest. What the Nazi regime actually did to children and youth in the process of forging a collective unity, however, was uniquely pernicious. Nazi propaganda before and during the war years crucially intervened in child-rearing practices and engineered a serious breakdown in routine parent-child relation-ships, such that, as Koonz suggests, "While the Nazi rhetoric evoked the nostalgic myth of a sheltering family, state policy promoted a submissive family that delivered up its members to the total state."[133] Of course, those subjected to it did not realize this effect: as long as they believed in Hitler, doing what he asked of them seemed to enhance their self-esteem.

As the NSDAP rose to power, it not only enlisted existing women's organizations to its cause, but, quite early, also formed its own official headquarters for "women's national work," the *Reichsfrauenfürung*. Established in the autumn of 1932, a new section of the *Reichsfrauenfürung*, the *Volkswirtschaft/Hauswirtschaft* ("National Economy/Domestic Economy Section"),[134] while training housewives to be frugal in support of the national economic interest, meddled in child-rearing practices. Nazi manipulation was facilitated by the fact that, tradi-tionally, the care and training of children for the first five years was "almost entirely in [mothers'] hands."[135] Though overtly concerned with children's physical needs, with raising strong, healthy "Aryan" children, the *Volkswirtschaft/Hauswirtschaft*, I will argue, covertly —and unintentional-ly, since authorities (and, in turn, German mothers) obviously believed that they were promoting collective unity, not psychological distur-bance—damaged German children's mental development.

Throughout the Nazi period, government propaganda directed ethnic German women to be politically aware, to be thrifty, and later to partici-pate in war-work. The *Volkswirtschaft/Hauswirtschaft* "took great care to investigate the properties of unusual new foods, to ascertain, for example, their protein content. The section's own research bureau carried out tests and devised palatable recipes using substitutes for items which were becoming unobtainable in some areas"[136]—a logical enough step into German housewifery, perhaps, on its own, but only the beginning of a larger pattern of intervention. Ethnic German homemakers were told, for instance, how much time to spend washing things, how to prolong the life of clothing, how to combat moths, and how to conserve energy.[137] As women became accustomed to learning such rational, useful information through the party channels, it must have seemed natural to follow the child-rearing instructions distributed through the same channels; in essence, they had been trained to obey Party orders, even when that "advice" was irrational indeed. Official guidance, summarized in Nazi physician Joanna Haarer's books *Die deutsche Mutter und hir erstes Kind* (*"The German Mother and Her First Child"*) and *Mutter, erzahl von Adolf Hitler! Ein Buch zum Vorlesen, Narcherzahlen und Selbstlesen fur kleinere und grossere Kinder* ("*Mother, Tell Me About Adolf Hitler! A Book for Reading, Retelling, and Self-Reading for Small and Older Children*"),[138] counseled parents to feed their children only on a rigorous schedule and not to rush to their children when they cried or encountered trouble with their surroundings; children were left to rely only on their own undeveloped coping mechanisms and not on parental care.[139] Further, parents were warned to reject the parenting advice of older generations and instead to consult the Nazi magazine *Mother and Child*.[140] Without being aware of doing so, I suspect, ethnic German parents—especially mothers—of the Nazi period ignored their children's natural dependency needs and ruined their sense of basic trust.

Because parents were taught to ignore their children's cries and desires, children were forced to experience the sense that there was no benevolent power in their surroundings and robbed of the opportunity to identify with a nurturing parent. Further, frustrated by their parents' behavior, children projected their own angry feelings onto the parents, imagining the elders to be more aggressive than they might actually be in reality. In turn, they felt that the only way to protect themselves was to become aggressors, tough kids. Indeed, they were "taught" that the whole world was populated with aggressors and grew up under an injunction to show no sign of weakness. Hitler himself called upon them: "We ask you to be hard, German youth, and to make yourself hard! We cannot use a generation of 'mother's boys,' of spoiled children."[141] Those children who exhibited such supposed self-assurance and self-reliance, in turn, received official approval as valued citizens through the party organizations for children and youth. They were to be "above" being hurt, omnipotent beings who would inflict aggression on others perceived to be weak; their own dependency needs as seen in "undesirable" groups and individuals would become their targets. They did not know that their self-assurance was defensive and false.

H.W. Flannery, an American correspondent based in Berlin before the war, noted that more and more youngsters were being physically removed from their parents by evacuation to the country, where they were stripped of their previous religious influences and "exposed to Nazi propaganda through schools, books, the press, radio, and motion pictures."[142] As he observed, "it was to be expected that the young were succumbing to the Nazi wishes."[143] Severed from the dependence on caretakers that they would naturally develop, youngsters came to rely instead on the local Nazi authorities who filled the children's "empty" self-esteems with defensive grandiosity, which made the youths exceptionally loyal and closely-bonded followers. As David Welch has observed, "Once they assumed power, the Nazis meticulously constructed an organizational network from which a child once caught had little possibility to escape.[144]

In a speech in Berlin on May 1, 1937, Hitler summarized what the Nazi regime sought for Germany's children and youngsters:

> We have begun, above all, with the youth. There are old idiots out of whom nothing can be made any more. ... But that causes us no concern. We take their children away from them. We bring them up to be new German human beings and we bring them up thoroughly. ... When a child is 10 years old it does not yet have any feeling about its birth and origin. ... One child is like another. At that age we take them and form them into a community until they are 18 years old. They enter the party, the SA and SS and other formations, or they march directly into the factories, the Labor Front, into the Labor Service, and they go into the army for two years.[145]

As Hitler's words reflect, Nazi propaganda also interfered with the normal mechanics of the adolescent passage. Ordinarily, character (or personality) crystallization occurs in adolescence as the young person reexamines his or her psychological investments in the important figures of his or her childhood, modifies these investments, and develops new investments in new figures, usually within his or her peer group and among idealized individuals in the public arena.[146] Normally, a youngster's investment in images of childhood parents, siblings, grandparents, and teachers do not altogether disappear, but are only modified; newly idealized persons or things thus remain unconsciously connected to the images of persons and things idealized in childhood, providing internal continuity within the family and supporting individual identity as it connects past to present and plans for the future. Nazi indoctrination and propaganda, however, sought to crush this internal, unconscious link between youngster and family: first local, then national Nazi figures—all, ultimately, under the shadow of the Fuhrer—were so idealized that connecting their images to "ordinary" early parental or teacher images had to be strained: the images of an omnipotent Fuhrer and idealized collective identity were separated from the images of "ordinary" older family members through denial, dissociation, or repression of childhood dependency needs. The ties between ordinary family bonds and the omnipotent Fuhrer and the collective identity he represented had to be broken—or at least repressed further. If a feeling of shame about parents or grandparents was induced in the youngsters' minds, breaking the link between

images of parents and grandparents and the images of idealized Nazi figures would be easier.

This repression created a particular character trait in these youngsters:
they had difficulty feeling remorse and experiencing mourning. Normally,
a person who loses a love object is psychologically obliged to mourn.
Mourning entails not only that the mourner gradually surrender the
investment one had in the person or thing that is no longer in the world,
but also that he or she internalize—in psychoanalytic terms, "identify
with"—some characteristics and functions that belonged to the lost person or thing. In other words, when a person loses a loved one in the real
world, the mourner unconsciously keeps aspects of that loved one as part
of his or her personality. (Individuals may also mourn for rather abstract
losses, such as the loss of ideals, belief systems, symbols, and images.)
Under the influence of Nazi propaganda, German youngsters could no
longer imagine their parents as loving caregivers. The idealized image of
Hitler and his representatives devalued any old image they might have had
of their parents. Therefore, they had no internal motivation to mourn; we
do not struggle with giving up valueless images. Of course, many parents
became Nazis themselves; under these conditions, youngsters "loved"
their parents as members of the idealized group, but could not mourn or
feel remorseful about losing the images of their parents simply as
parents.[147]

The *Hitlerjugend* for boys and *Bund Deutscher Madel* for girls sought
to incorporate two crucial elements of Nazi ideology into each
adolescent's crystallizing permanent character structure: 1) by removing
parental influence and creating inner security by stressing allegiance
toward a solid group identity; and 2) by emphasizing previously existing
anti-Semitic racist sentiments and devaluing "anti-socials." The young
people went on excursions, sang songs, and participated in exercises not
only to enhance their group sense of belonging, but also, in accordance
with the Nazi ideology, to exclude devalued and/or dehumanized individuals, such as Jews, Gypsies, homosexuals, the mentally ill, and the physically handicapped: no person belonging to an "unwanted" group was
allowed to become a member of the Party. During this period, the local
youth leaders initially did not seem to teach Nazi ideology directly,[148] but
rather prepared the youngsters to be obedient to the requirements of the
group, for example, through shame tactics. A "non-proper" male adolescent would be beaten up by the other members of the group while his
head was covered by a sheet. Meanwhile, the youngsters' grandiosity, given
to them through Nazi propaganda, supported their efforts to erase any

threat to their basic sense of trust, their *innere schwinehund* ("inner pig-dog"): their "soft," humane aspects and/or laziness. Later, they would expand their horizons to be obedient to higher Nazi authorities and ultimately to the Fuhrer. Slogans, modes of dressed, salutes, expressions of difference from unwanted "others," and other nonverbal messages and symbols shaped the nature of their group identity. Systematic manipulation of the Nazi youth saw that the youngsters externalized and projected their defensively-evolved grandiosity onto the "holy nation of Germany," with Hitler as its God. In turn, they became an extension of this omnipotent body. Meanwhile, they projected their helpless and shamed parts onto the devalued: no boomerang of the unwanted elements could take place. Safely separated from devalued, demonized, or dehumanized "others," the Nazi youngsters could "enjoy" their grandiosity; later they could feel entitled to eradicate those "others."

University of California at Los Angeles historian Peter Loewenberg (also a practicing psychoanalyst) suggests that German youths' particular receptivity to Nazi ideology may have been unconsciously related to a shared historical trauma of their infancy. Loewenberg observes that the extensive mortality rate and low birth weights during the 1917-1919 economic collapse in Germany probably also indicates that the surviving children born during this period were deprived of physical nourishment. At this vulnerable and developmentally crucial age, the children of that period may have experienced their undernourishing mothers and environment as "bad," or traumatizing, much as a child with an earache may experience his or her mother as "bad" despite the fact that the mother is not responsible for the earache and may not be able to ease the child's pain. According to Loewenberg, these children, now teenagers, may have responded to the Nazi ideology of grandiosity in order to deal with the continuing influence of the shared childhood trauma of paucity and loss.[149]

As David Welch describes, the initial enthusiasm of youth was carefully exploited through the concerted coordination of the mass media; "In particular, the Nazis chose to use the cinema to disseminate their political and cultural outlook: partly because they appreciated that the cinema was unexcelled in its ability to play upon the emotions, and also because it was the perfect medium for combining both entertainment and propaganda."[150] Starting in April 1934, the Hitler Youth sponsored "Youth Film Hour" (*Jugendfilmstunde*) for its members; Welch estimates that 300,000 youth attended Youth Film Hours in their first year, by 1937-1938 attendance was almost two million, and by 1942-1943, it topped 11 million.[151] Interestingly, the *Jugendfilmstunde* films were not always overtly political (by contrast with *Der Ewige Jude*); in many, uniformed men do not appear at all. Nevertheless, all of the films were deliberately coordinated by the Ministry of Popular Enlightenment and Propaganda, the Ministry of Education, and the Hitler Youth to communicate National Socialist themes and values to the members of the official youth organizations. A film about euthanasia, for example, was about a very ill woman who wishes to die. Those who watched her on the screen might identify with her. Only during the last minutes of the film is a parallel drawn between her story and the "need" to kill mentally ill individuals.

Nazi propaganda continued to reinforce this large-group identity as the children grew into adolescence and adulthood. When a young man joined the SS, for example, the police's code of behavior continued to insist that he be "tough" and that he subordinate himself to the morality propounded by the regime; thus a man could remain a "decent" individual—or, better, an extension of collective identity—while participating in the "Final Solution," but was forbidden to steal even a cigarette or a comb from one of his colleagues. On some occasions youngsters who were selected to be trained as SS officers were given puppies, and, after they had become attached to their pets, were ordered to kill the animals; this story parallels what they were asked to do with their internalized images of their parents. One can imagine the lingering or hidden guilt, remorse, and mourning, but belonging to an idealized group would help to repress or deny feelings that would make these youngsters more human; thus they became obliged to remain in the group in order not to feel painful emotions. Though relatively little psychoanalytic attention has been paid to the period of late adolescence,[152] psychoanalysts characterize this as the age at which the sexual couple begins to emerge; if a partner is chosen from the same large-group background, there is a tendency to invest further in shared symbols, emblems, traditions, and slogans belonging to the large-group identity. Nazi propaganda thus sought to ensure that late adolescent ethnic Germans would choose only their "own kind" as mates by promoting the increase of the Aryan population as a national priority.[153]

Of course, Hitler and Joseph Goebbels did not think of what they were doing in psychoanalytic terms. But *Mein Kampf* evinces an uncanny awareness of what was necessary to create what I am calling a malignantly-regressed society. Consciously, they planned for "Aryan" youth to join the *Volksgemeinschaft*, to be tough, to be absolutely loyal to the Fuhrer, and, when necessary, to kill (or to be killed) for him. First, children and youth were made to remain dependent and helpless by being severed from their natural objects of love and attachment. Then, this vacuum was filled with collective grandiosity and National Socialist "morality." Finally, propaganda and political persuasion reinforced these "values" at every turn as these youth entered adulthood.

More recently, Michael Sebek has observed that, under the communist ideology of the former Czechoslovakia,

> [W]omen are allocated the same hard [physical] work as men, and this latently and unconsciously damages the family structure. Not only does it ignore the difference between men and women, but it also establishes an assumption about the right to make decisions concerning the lives of the children living in the state; education in the collective is elevated above education in the family. False "improvement of the family position" was revealed in the new definition of *family* that appeared in [Czechoslovakia] in the 1950s[:] the family was [re-]defined as a "collective."[154]

Thus the developing foundation for children's future adult behavior and thought patterns does not follow a normal pattern of development.[155]

Even in societies whose regressions are initiated by enemy groups, such as Kuwait in the wake of the Iraqi invasion, we can detect some disintegration in the family system. In 1993, under the directorship of Ambassador W. Nathaniel Howell (ret.)—who, as U.S. ambassador to Kuwait during the invasion, kept the Embassy open for seven months during the Iraqi occupation of Kuwait City—I was part of a team that interviewed more than 150 Kuwaitis from divergent social backgrounds and age groups to learn how the mental representation of the shared disaster echoed in their shared mental life.[156] As in much of my work with large groups around the world, the technique of these conversations was based on clinical psychoanalytic diagnostic interviews, in which the analyst "hears" the subject's internal conflicts, defenses, and adaptations; as the subject reports fantasies and dreams, this material adds to the interviewer's understanding of the patient's internal world. After interview data is collected, we look for common themes in the interviews that indicate shared perceptions, expectations, and defenses against conflicts created by the traumatic event. These "common themes" may or may not register in the public consciousness as represented in news or cultural production but come to light as we observe them in many interviewees' internal worlds.

As can easily be imagined, we found that many Kuwaitis suffered from undiagnosed individual post-traumatic stress disorder. Beyond this observation, though, we discovered significant shifts in Kuwaiti social conventions and processes. We learned, for example, that young Kuwaiti men's perceptions of Iraqi rapes of Kuwaiti women during the occupation had become generalized. We found that many young men who were engaged to be married wanted to postpone their marriages, and that those who were not yet engaged wanted to postpone seriously considering finding a mate: because women who have been raped are traditionally devalued in Kuwaiti culture, the generalization of perception was threatening conventions about the age of marriage. While this shift did not pose an actual danger, it did reflect a loss of trust in women, however unwarranted.

We found even more direct expressions of societal "maladaptation" in post-liberation Kuwait. During the invasion and occupation, many Kuwaiti fathers were humiliated in front of their children by Iraqi soldiers, who sometimes spat on Kuwaiti men, beat them, or otherwise rendered them helpless while their children watched. In cases where humiliation or torture had occurred away from their children's view, the fathers often wanted to hide what had happened to them. Fathers, without necessarily being aware of it, began to distance themselves from certain crucial emotional interactions with their children, especially with their sons, in order to hide or to deny their sense of shame. Most children and adolescents, though, knew without explicitly being told what had happened to their fathers, whether they had personally witnessed it or not.

Many school buildings in Kuwait City had been used as torture chambers during the Iraqi occupation. When I visited Kuwait City during this project, however, from the appearance of the schools and the other buildings, it was hard to believe that catastrophe had struck there only three years earlier; except for several buildings with bullet holes which were intentionally left as memorials, the rest of the city appeared completely renovated. Adults did not speak to the children about what had happened in the schools during the invasion, but the children knew; when they returned to their renovated schools, that "secret" quite naturally caused them psychological problems. The very young—without, of course, knowing why—began to identify with Saddam Hussein instead of with their own fathers; in one telling instance observed by our team during an elementary school play staging the story of the Iraqi invasion, the children applauded most vociferously for the youngster who played the role of Saddam Hussein.[157] "Identification with the aggressor" is the psychoanalytic term for a period in which a child identifies him or herself with the parent of the same sex with whom the child has been involved in a competition for the affection of the parent of the opposite sex.[158] In childhood, this process results in a child's emotional growth: a little boy, for example, through identification with the father whom he perceives as an "aggressor," makes a kind of entrance into manhood himself. In other situations, however, like those of many Kuwaiti elementary school children, identification with the aggressor—in this case, Saddam Hussein—can obviously create serious problems.

The repetition of this "distant father" scenario in many Kuwaiti families set in motion new processes across Kuwaiti society. Many male children, who needed to identify with their fathers on the way to developing their own manhood, responded poorly to the distance between themselves and their fathers—resulting, for example, in gang formations among teenagers. Frustrated by the distant and humiliated fathers who would not talk to their sons about the traumas of the invasion, they linked themselves together and expressed their frustrations in gangs. Of course, a type of gang formation is a normal process of the adolescent passage, as youngsters loosen their internal ties to the images of important persons of their childhood and expand their social and internal lives through investment in new people (movie or rock stars, or sports heroes, for example) as well as in members of their peer group. In the ordinary course of events, however, this "second individuation"[159] maintains an internal continuity with the youngster's childhood. For example, a "new" investment in the image of a movie star is unconsciously connected with the "old" investment in the image of the mother; a "new" investment in a friend remains somewhat connected to the "old" image of a sibling or other relative. Images of humiliated and helpless parents necessarily complicated the unconscious relationship between the Kuwaiti youngsters' "new" and "old" investments as they entered adolescence. Indeed, as we have observed in other situations, when many parents are affected by a catastrophe inflicted by others, the adolescent gangs that form after the acute phase of the shared trauma tend to be more pathological. In Kuwait, the new gangs were heavily involved in car theft—a new social process, the emergence of a crime that essentially had not existed in pre-invasion Kuwait.[160]

Kuwaiti society might well have split along any number of lines during this period—for example, it might have divided into those who escaped to safety during the Iraqi invasion and those who stayed to suffer and/or fight. Once Sheikh Jaber al-Ahmed al-Sabah, Emir of Kuwait, re-established his traditional leadership, however, the incipient fragmentation within Kuwaiti society eased, and the country gradually moved out of its regressed state.

Preoccupation with "blood," contamination, and group homogeneity: Such a preoccupation may emerge under either "good" or "bad" leaders, especially when the group regression is severe. If the group regression is malignant, this preoccupation may lead to the worst human horrors: ethnic cleansing, even genocide. In the individual, the preoccupation with "blood" is connected with a developmentally very early sense of identity and its distinctness from the identities of others. A regressed large group's fixation on blood is thus connected to the very conditions of its existence as a group with a specific shared identity. According to French psychoanalyst Janine Chasseguet-Smirgel, blood is seldom truly symbolized, in the strict psychoanalytic sense. We are unable to find unconscious equivalents; at most, we discover allegorical representations of it, such as blood in the Christian Eucharist. Chasseguet-Smirgel argues that the ability to find symbols (such as effigies) to substitute for the body or body parts of others substantially protects others from our direct attack. However, when group identities are associated with unsymbolizable blood, the attack one group wishes to make on another cannot be transferred to a symbolic substitute; the urge to attack is the urge to annihilate.[161] Though I agree with Chasseguet-Smirgel's proposal that blood cannot be truly symbolized, I must add that, as a protosymbol, it is intertwined with the concept of identity. Observations of young children show that they are interested in what comes out of their bodies—feces and urine—but are not necessarily interested in blood. Through injuries that bleed, however, children gradually become aware that there is something "alive" under their skin, at a time when their core identity is developing. The child's sense of self, which, like blood, is also "alive" within him or her, becomes intertwined with the idea of blood: blood and identity become linked. Thus, later, under conditions of regression, blood may become a protosymbol.

When large groups and adult individuals regress severely, they tend to utilize blood as an equivalent to—rather than symbolic of—identity. They see it as the bearer of their very mental and physical existence. After the massive earthquake in Armenia in 1988 that killed more than 25,000 people and devastated the countryside, the regressed Armenians refused to accept blood donations from Azerbaijanis, for they were the "others," and accepting their blood was felt as a psychological threat to Armenian identity. It is when intense concern with blood as identity is shared by the members of a large group—as in Nazi Germany—that drastic and sometimes deadly societal and political processes may result.

Purification: Related to concern with blood and other kinds of homogeneity is the urge toward purification. This process of purification may be benign, as when a group discards an outmoded shared symbol, or malignant, as in ethnic cleansing. It is the activity of a group in transition, a ritual, the group seeking to crystallize a new identity when both threatened by regression and attempting to move out of regression. I will look at purification as a ritual further in the next chapter.

Environment: I turn now to the typical environmental impact of regressed societies. By way of example, I recall a visit to Vladimir, Russia, in 1991. Founded in 1108 C.E., Vladimir is one of Russia's oldest cities, the cultural and political predecessor to Moscow, and its splendid instances of early Russian architecture have been well preserved. Among these magnificent buildings, the most famous is the Cathedral of the Assumption, which was built in 1158 and has been rebuilt and repaired several times. On a cold and foggy day in November 1988, I entered Vladimir near its twelfth-century Golden Gate and saw Vladimir's magnificent buildings choked in yellow-brown smoke pouring from the tall, ugly chimneys of industrial plants, some of which were built almost alongside the city's centuries-old marvels of architecture. Under Soviet administration, the Vladimir that had been a major center of medieval cultural and religious life had developed into an industrial hub with numerous huge manufacturing and chemical plants. I was shocked at what I perceived as a forced equivalence of the beautiful and the ugly, an expression of large-group regression under a totalitarian regime. Everything in Vladimir lay in a yellow-brown shroud, creating an artificial sense of sameness among all its structures. This forced association paradoxically created a gap between modern Russians and their ancestors; ruined distinctions of sense, value, and hierarchy; and erased the unique contributions of history, the arts, and industry to the life of the city. When a society regresses, the physical environment may actually begin to resemble the psychologically-regressed society's human condition. Indeed, Michael Sebek has argued specifically that "[t]he polluted air, dirty rivers, devastated landscape, decadence of language, and deterioration of 'good' behavior that we associate with [the physical environments of former Soviet and Soviet-dominated cities] are symbolically very close to fecal material."[162]

Regressed large groups tend to express symbolically what psychoanalysts call in the individual "anal sadism" toward their environment: they pollute their surroundings with debris and junk, as if they were befouling "mother earth" with their bodily wastes.[163]

These signs and symptoms of regression vary from group to group, and the degree to which they are present and discernible depends not only on the degree and extent of the regression, but also on the particular historical circumstances of the group. In regressed societies where the political leadership cannot maintain its authority (by inspiring either fear or love in its followers), chaos ensues. Envy and jealousy come to dominate what is perceived as permissible or "moral." Aggression and sexuality merge and become exaggerated, leading to sexual promiscuity, criminal behavior, and sadistic pleasure in atrocities. I observed such phenomena in South Ossetia, after the 1992 war between South Ossetians and Georgians that devastated this society. In 2003, after Saddam Hussein's forces were defeated and the dictator disappeared, we observed a severe form of leaderless societal regression in Iraq, including looting, murders, change of morality and loyalty, multiple splits and lawlessness. Women and children especially suffer in regressed societies without a leader. If aggression turns inward, there are increased rates of suicide. The chaos may end if a new leader emerges and attempts a new "revolution." If the new leader is under the influence of his or her own regression, however, the new revolution may lead to the perpetuation of the existing regression, or even make it worse.

I also should point out the signs of progression used to reverse regression in a society. Sometimes in a society particular signs and symptoms of regression co-exist with signs and symptoms of progression. The latter include the following:

1) Preserving individuality and the capacity for compromise without damaging one's integrity;

2) Raising new generations of children with intact basic trust and maintaining existing family structures;

3) Halting the devaluation of women;

4)   Re-establishing family and clan ties and forming steady sub-groups, such as medical organizations or workers' unions, which are more important than ties to political or religious ideologies or to the personality of the leader;

5)   Valuing freedom of speech;

6)   Just functioning of existing civic institutions (including a fair legal system, prisons without torture, and mental hospitals with humane care);

7)   Maintaining the ability to question what is moral or beautiful;

8)   Separating fantasy from reality and past from present;

9)   Wondering about human aspects of the enemy groups and caring about the enemy's psychic reality; and

10)   Not dividing the world into idealized "us" and evil "them," while continuing to evaluate the realistic dangers of the enemy and protecting one's own group's safety.

Finally, it is important to remember that a regressed large group can move out of its regression under the guidance of a "good" leader, though the identity of the "progressed" group does not return to what it was before the regression. Elements from the time when regression dominated need to be discarded. Thus, a large-group "progression" also involves "purification," but in this instance the purification does not become malignant and destructive, as we will see in the next chapter.

3 / rituals that bind people together

Out, damned spot! Out, I say! ... What, will these hands ne'er be clean? ... Here's the smell of the blood still. All the perfumes of Arabia will not sweeten this little hand. Oh, oh, oh!

—William Shakespeare, *Macbeth*

Those who are in mental health professions often cite Lady Macbeth's notorious hand-washing as a literary instance of obligatory ritualistic behavior. Typically associated with obsessive-compulsive persons, ritualistic activity functions as a defense against the anxieties produced by internal psychological conflict; Lady Macbeth's ritual, then, is meant symbolically to wash away her feelings of guilt associated with the regicide that clears the way for her husband to seize the crown.

Clinicians often observe ritualistic behavior among their patients. One of my young male patients always, upon entering my office, counted the number of books on my bookshelf to find out if the total count would lead to an even or an odd number. He felt relaxed when he "discovered" each time that my books totaled forty: an even number which, for him, symbolically balanced the opposing forces of his ambivalence toward his brutal father, whose image he had projected onto me, his analyst. If the total count of my books had reached an odd number, the symbolic balance would have disappeared and my patient would have experienced the tension of simultaneously loving and hating his father.

Another of my analysands adopted the ritual of recounting every negative physical and mental experience from the previous day at the beginning of each session with me. Invariably, something bad had happened that would account for his pessimistic outlook—the roads were full of potholes, a local store had been robbed, he had stubbed his toe. Then he would list the "causes" of the misfortunes: the county did not have enough money, the store owner had not installed a security system, he had care-lessly left a brick on the path in his garden. In fact, as his analysis revealed, this ritual recalled his past experience. As a child, he had been poorly treated by his mother, and had often been left alone in his basement room, where he explained his unhappiness to himself by denying his mother's mistreatment, thereby preserving the hope of having a "good mother." By similarly recounting bad events and repeating the same kind of intellectu-alized excuses for them, he avoided confronting his internalized conflict with his mother, whose image was now transferred onto me. But there was still another aim—or at least another effect—of this ritual in his analysis. When the patient was immersed in listing negative events and enumerat-ing their "reasons," he was excluding me from his activity. I found myself in his childhood role of loneliness, and I came to feel empathy for his pain.

The ritualized behavior that a psychoanalyst observes among his or her analysands mainly reflects the patient's anxiety about unconscious con-flicts, even though such rituals may indirectly give other messages too, as illustrated by my second example. But ritualized activity is not a patholog-ical behavior *per se*; indeed, as Erik Erikson observed, rituals are essential to "normal" development.[164] In response to the ethological view that ritual practices in the animal world and in "primitive" cultures are designed to prevent fatal misunderstandings by transmitting unambiguous signals, Erikson posited that ritualization is fundamentally a positive phenome-non. Everyday ritualization, he argued, is a variation of the greeting with which a mother acknowledges the presence of her child, thereby fostering the child's sense of self while supporting her own identity as a mother. To explain how everyday ritualization develops from a mother's repeated greetings to her child, Erikson followed forms of play from childhood through and into adulthood, describing how they become irreversible action. One of the manifestations of playfulness is the everyday use of rit-ual, which, according to Erikson, "in a viable cultural setting, represents a creative formalization which helps to avoid both impulsive excess and compulsive self-restriction, both social anomie and moralistic coer-cion."[165]

What Erikson observes of the individual is also true of the members of a large group. "The microsphere of play table and sports field," he observes, is continuous with "the macrosphere of 'political' conflict."[166] Of course, he also sees some negative outcomes of those ritual activities, par-ticularly the categorical division of others. Erikson notes that a newborn is potentially able (within certain limits) to "qualify" for any one of a number of ethnic or religious societies. Yet an infant also needs, for his or her own developmental reasons, to be coached by family ritual for adult life in one specific society, inevitably absorbing prejudices in the process. As Erikson observed, it is in adolescence that everyday rituals of confirmation act as "a second birth" by integrating all childhood identifications into a wider view of the world and crystallizing as ideologically foreign all images, belief systems, and wishes that have become undesirable. In this mechanism, Erikson sees the origins of potential biological and cultural racisms, as undesirables, including one's own feelings of unworthiness—consciously or not—are assigned to "lower" species of man or foreign "others."

Though psychoanalysts generally agree on this picture of adolescence, I have argued for a much earlier phase of human development as the foundation-point for "us" and "them" psychology (see Chapter 1 for details). In this chapter, we will focus not on the rituals that individuals develop in response to personal conflict—such as wishing to express aggression against a parent, but also fearing to lose her love, but rather on collective rituals that exist primarily to protect the borders of identity[167]—specifically, those that aim to protect the boundaries between two large-group tents standing side-by-side and *thereby* consolidate the group identity shared by those underneath each tent.

Large-group rituals can be divided usefully into two general categories: 1) rituals that occur within a society that do not involve an active relationship with a contemporary "other" large group and 2) rituals that occur through and depend upon the interaction with an opposing or enemy large group, usually a neighbor or an "unwanted" subgroup, such as a minority ethnic group within a state. In practice, however, it is difficult to make a definite distinction between the two types. Both are intensified or modified when large-group regression sets in, and thus provide the foundation of signs and symptoms of large-group regression.

A society need not be either in the throes of "hot" conflict with an enemy group or regressed in order to participate in group identity-affirming rituals. Indeed, the display of symbolic markers reinforces large-group identities almost daily—though group members may not be conscious of it. Portraits, photos, statues, and other representations of past and present leaders and chosen glories are displayed in government offices, schools, banks, and at other significant sites; national anthems are sung at ceremonial events. Important symbols are featured on money and stamps, and nearly every manufactured item is imprinted with its country of origin.

But seeing the flag of one's own group every day, hearing the national anthem in peaceful times, or buying a product labeled "Made in USA" or "Made in Hungary" does not necessarily induce deep feelings of collective pride or belonging—unless and until the large-group tent is shaken. Then a political leader (or his or her followers) may deploy shared symbols, such as flags, to shore up the group identity or otherwise stir up emotions. When a large group perceives a threat to its identity (such as the Palestinians when they were displaced from their ancestral lands) and/or regresses, members of the group may begin to feel differently invested in the group's existing large-group symbols. Sometimes, the group trans-forms certain symbols into protosymbols—that is, things that actually *represent* the group identity, such as flags and cultural artifacts, come to seem to group members to be *constitutive* of that identity. In such a case, if "others" attack the group's symbol in any way, it is perceived as a shared injury to the group's shared self-esteem and, in turn, to the individual group members' personal self-esteem. The propaganda machines of large groups in conflict almost always disparage the opposing group's symbols in order to injure the enemy's self-esteem. Those whose protosymbols are injured may react violently, and the leader of the group may end up mak-ing maladaptive decisions led more by emotions than by logical thinking.

In addition to enhancing its expression of chosen glories, a large group that feels its identity threatened or that is in regression creates new and sometimes highly idiosyncratic symbols that nurture hope for the group's survival of the perceived or existing danger—again, sometimes without being aware of what it is doing. In the spring of 1990, I observed a most unusual example of this phenomenon in the North African city of Tunis, where the PLO had established its government in exile. There, a young Palestinian woman had become the symbol of an idealized Palestine, and though the people who had created her as a "living symbol" were not con-scious of what they had done, the young woman understood the role she had been given.

At that time, PLO headquarters was the focal point for a significant population of Palestinians, including Chairman Yassir Arafat, who lived mostly in Tunis during this period. As a group, the Palestinians in Tunis seemed to be in a state of perpetual alert against secret attacks by Israeli commandos. In fact, this fear was grounded in reality; prior to my visit, one of Chairman Arafat's closest associates had been assassinated in his home during an Israeli raid. Chairman Arafat, I was told, never stayed long at one location but moved around constantly for security reasons, and the PLO's "souped-up" civilian cars sped through the streets in seemingly perpetual motion. I had the impression that most of the Palestinians never had a good night's sleep; they would call or visit each other at all hours of the night just to ensure that nothing was amiss. Even though the Tunisian government had given the PLO a certain autonomy, almost all Palestinians in Tunis considered themselves refugees of a sort; they felt that they had been forcefully exiled and yearned to return to a peaceful homeland. Through group regression, they had created an intense sense of togetherness and had rallied around their leader and the rest of the Palestinian governing class.

My task in Tunis was to interview children at a Palestinian orphanage called *Biet Atfal Al-Sommoud* (the Home of Children of Steadfastness).[168] Administered by the PLO, the orphanage was located not far from PLO headquarters and housed fifty-two children under the age of eighteen who had lost one or both parents in the Middle East conflict. Chairman Arafat, we were told, often spent time in the orphanage and sent the children gifts; interestingly, many of the children in the orphanage had been given the family name Arafat because their fathers' identities were unknown. The children at *Biet Atfal al-Sommoud* spontaneously sang songs about Palestinian victimization and identified with the children and youngsters of the first *intifada* in the Israeli-occupied territories, whom they saw on television. They frequently expressed their hope for a "free Palestine" and their desire to return there. There was a general feeling among the Tunis Palestinians that the orphanage represented the group's historical suffering as well as their hope for the future.

The PLO had given me permission—along with two American colleagues of Palestinian descent, psychiatrist Dr. As'ad Masri and psychologist Dr. Nuha Abudabbeh—to study the psychology of these war orphans. Despite this prior approval, however, we were forced to wait in Tunis for three days before being allowed to visit the orphanage, presumably for further background checks. During our "waiting period," we visited many Palestinian homes and several offices of high-ranking officials. At times I felt that I was being questioned, albeit indirectly, to ensure that I would present my findings in a neutral way. It was not a secret that I planned to publish my findings and to speak about these orphans at an upcoming meeting in Israel titled *Children of War*, which was sponsored by the Freud Center at the Hebrew University in Jerusalem and organized by Boston-based psychiatrists Bennett Simon and Roberta Apfel.[169] When asked during one of my visits why I was not planning to interview Palestinian orphans older than eighteen, I replied that the idea had not occurred to me, since from the outset the project had focused on younger children. I let them know, however, that I would be willing to interview an adult candidate if one were interested.

And so, at a luncheon with senior PLO officials, I came to meet an extraordinary young woman, twenty-five years of age, who asked to be interviewed. For four evenings, she came to the hotel where my colleagues and I were staying, and we talked late into the night; when we finished, we had more than sixteen hours of taped interviews. When I tell her story here, her identity will be clear to anyone familiar with the Palestinian hierarchy. Although she gave me permission to use her name and write about her full story, I will refrain from using her real name and will only refer to those parts of her personal story that illustrate how she became a "living symbol" for Palestine, as I do not know her present circumstances. Let us call her "Radiant." She introduced herself to me, in perfect English, as the daughter of an airplane hijacker who in her eyes was a hero and a martyr. She was also one of Chairman Arafat's secretaries.

Radiant recalls waving good-bye to her father—whom she remembers as a handsome man with long dark hair and perfect teeth and as a very good father who loved his wife and four daughters dearly—from the balcony of their home in Beirut, Lebanon, when she was seven years old. On that day in 1972, her father flew to Belgium; he was the mastermind behind plans for hijacking a Sabena Airlines plane traveling from Belgium to Israel in order to force the release of 150 Palestinians imprisoned by Israelis. Her father was not scheduled to take part in the actual hijacking, but when one of those expected to participate did not arrive, he decided to head the team of hijackers himself.

After the Sabena plane landed in Israel, according to Radiant, her father was "tricked" by the Israelis: while the Israelis had agreed to send Red Cross workers to the plane, an Israeli anti-terrorist team dressed in Red Cross uniforms came to the plane instead. When Radiant's father opened the door to receive the Red Cross team, he was shot and killed. It is now known that Ehud Barak, later the prime minister of Israel and then a young soldier, headed that antiterrorist squad. The other male hijacker was also killed, and both female hijackers were wounded. During the skirmish, two passengers also died, one a pregnant woman.

The Israelis kept the corpse of Radiant's father in refrigeration for two years. Radiant now believes that releasing his body quickly would have initiated riots in the occupied territories since her father immediately became a martyr to Palestinians. Radiant's own childhood memories of learning of her father's death are vivid and poignant. As a child, Radiant dreamt of her father's return, talked to his picture as if the picture were a person, and exhibited other signs of being unable to mourn. At the time of his death, her father was thirty-three and her mother twenty-five, left with three young daughters and a baby only six months old. Neither the young widow nor her daughters could emotionally accept losing the man they loved. Radiant's mother would never remarry. No one in the family saw Radiant's father's body during the two years in which he was "on ice"—a fact that furthered the family's illusion that he still might be alive. When finally Radiant's father's body was released for burial, his older sister sent word from his birthplace of Hebron (then an Israeli-occupied territory) that she had seen her brother's corpse. This led even the family members living in Lebanon—who could not attend the funeral in Hebron—to accept the reality of his death.

Radiant believed that her father, a true patriot, had never intended to kill anyone and wanted only to save the Palestinian prisoners; whatever the truth of this belief, her idealization of her dead father was plain. According to Radiant, her father had been the keeper of the key of the Church of the Holy Sepulchre, the site at which, according to the belief of many Christians, Jesus was crucified by the Romans, was buried, and rose from the dead. According to tradition, it is two Muslim families in Old Jerusalem who keep the key for this sacred Christian place. Radiant recalled that, when she was a child, her father went each morning to unlock the huge doors at the Gothic entrance of the Church. I do not know whether her recollection is accurate, or whether it only reflects this young woman's idealization of her dead father.[170] By the time I met Radiant, Arafat had clearly "replaced" her idealized father. She made statements during our interviews such as "he [Arafat] is the real father," "He is a good and pure father," or "he is a good listener." Because she felt that the Chairman was very busy, Radiant was careful not to bother him with her personal problems, but reported that, when he once found her crying, he gently consoled her. As a member of Chairman Arafat's entourage, she was present at many official and social gatherings of PLO authorities and accompanied the authorities on various trips. For example, I attended a long luncheon given by Chairman Arafat, at which Radiant functioned as the implicit hostess, the traditional role of an adult daughter in a Palestinian home.

In 1987, fifteen-year-old Radiant was allowed to travel to Hebron to visit her father's burial place; it was during this trip that she first truly understood herself as a symbol even for Palestinians who had never met her. Of course, Radiant was already a significant person for many influential Palestinians. After her father's death, she had been, in a sense, "chosen" to be raised in the best possible ways. She had been sent by her father's friends (who were PLO officials) to the best schools, where she excelled, and later was sent to the United States for further education. And she was engaging and beautiful. When Radiant visited what she called "the most beautiful grave" at the Muslim cemetery in Hebron, though, she faced a new sense of herself as a special being. At first, because she was dressed in a "modern" style—in jeans—she found herself mistaken for a Jewish girl; other Palestinian visitors became angry that a Jew was sightseeing in a Muslim cemetery. But then someone shouted her father's name, adding that Radiant was the martyr's daughter. Suddenly, she recalls, everyone surrounded her, smiling and touching her as if she were a sacred icon.

Radiant became even more aware of her unique role in Palestinian history after moving in her late teen years to Tunis, where every Palestinian knew her by sight. Early in the interviews, in one of many psychologically revealing moments, she told me that she wanted me to know that she was still a virgin. Despite the pursuit of many of her fellow exiles, she had remained, as she put it, "pure." I later learned that although many men at PLO headquarters found her very attractive, she remained distant and unapproachable, much like the independent Palestinian state for which the exiles longed, and which at that time was unreachable. Even visually she represented the concept of purity; she wore a white dress every night that she came to be interviewed. In a sense, this young woman felt that she needed to remain like an untouched flower on the bloody Arab-Israeli battlefield that had been her whole world since childhood. And she was even aware that she represented the unreachable, idealized nation to which her fellow exiles yearned to return; she was conscious that her role among the Palestinian men who longed for her was to be "untouchable," unreachable.

As our interviews were coming to an end, I asked her why she had volunteered to come to our hotel to tell her story late into the night, to reveal her wishes and fears—in short, why she would open up so completely to a stranger. She responded that, though she was aware of (and attached to) her role as a "flag" for the Palestinians in Tunis, she also knew that she was made of flesh and blood. She had dreams of finding a husband, marrying, and being a regular person, she said, and she knew that it was impossible to be both a symbol and a woman: in order to be one, she would have to give up being the other. Having no solution for her internal struggle, she had developed a daydream in which she lost both identities. In the daydream, she imagined being in an airplane with Chairman Arafat, her living hero/father figure, when the plane exploded in mid-air, killing both of them. Psychoanalysts may impute additional meanings to her daydream, including unresolved Oedipal issues and a wish for reunion with her father's image. At the time of our interviews, she was the same age that her mother had been when her father was killed; perhaps Radiant was identifying with her mother by recreating in fantasy the tragedy that had befallen her mother, who in a sense had been psychologically "killed" by the death of her husband. Whatever other meanings may accurately be attached to it, however, I think this daydream also represented her fantasized escape from the tension of wanting to be both symbol and woman. Radiant's fantasy, unsurprisingly, had bothered her. But she was well-read and knew something about psychoanalysis, so when I, a psychoanalyst, appeared in Tunis, she wanted to share with me her internal dilemma, thinking that disclosing it might help. Interestingly, she knew in advance that, in keeping with psychoanalytic convention, I would not respond to her with any advice.

To this day, I do not know whether my empathic understanding of her internal struggle was helpful to her. I never met her again, though she often comes to my mind whenever I am professionally involved in Palestinian issues; she has become a symbol of "Palestine" for me also. Of course, dramatic changes in the PLO's political situation have taken place since I met her. Perhaps the return of formerly "exiled" Palestinians from Tunis to their ancestral lands, the Gaza Strip and the West Bank, removed the external pressure on this young woman to serve as the corporeal symbol of an idealized Palestine and the collective nostalgia for it. As the second *intifada* and Israeli military response turn that part of the world into a pool of blood once again, I wonder where Radiant is, whether she is safe, and how her self-image is being affected by the renewed intensity of the conflict.

Few, if any, historians of the PLO will probably ever mention the role that this young woman—as well as, to a lesser degree, other orphans at *Biet Atfal al-Sommoud*—played at PLO headquarters in Tunis in the late 1980s and early 1990s. Few will understand how a group of people in the midst of political maneuvering, terrorism, death, anxiety, and regression made this person a living symbol of their aspirations. But, as a representation of their idealized state and what it meant to them, her image, tinged with shared nostalgia, was perhaps crucial to helping her fellow Palestinian exiles tolerate other painful emotions associated with being deprived of their statehood and keep alive the hope of regaining it.[171]

Large groups also tend to exhibit symbols exaggeratedly during collective "anniversary reactions" to significant past events that ritualistically confirm its identity. The term *anniversary reaction* mainly comes from clinical observation of individuals in mourning who, often unconsciously, exhibit signs and symptoms around the anniversary of losing a loved one. Once more, I will first examine this phenomenon as it appears in individual psychology and then describe its analogous large-group process. While staying in Israel as an Inaugural Rabin Fellow at The Yitzhak Rabin Center for Israel Studies in Tel Aviv in the spring of 2000, I worked on several occasions with an Israeli high school teacher, an extroverted and happy woman in her forties who helped me observe a project that brought together a number of Israeli and Palestinian teachers. When I met with her on May 2, "Holocaust Day,"[172] however, I thought that I was meeting a different person: she was irritable, "paranoid," and even suicidal. Her behavior lasted only a couple of days, and then she returned to her usual self. Interestingly, she was aware that she was having an anniversary reaction since for many years she had experienced these symptoms on Holocaust Day.

This teacher's anniversary reaction is triggered by her response to the experience of her relatives during World War II. Her family had lived in Ukraine; they had been rich, and many Ukrainians had worked for them. During World War II, the head of the family (my friend's grandfather) was taken away by the Nazis and killed. Shortly thereafter, the rest of the family—including the teacher's mother—along with other Jews from the town in which they lived, had to hide in a forest near their town. A Ukrainian woman who had worked for the family knew that either Nazis or Nazi sympathizers would find this refuge and kill them. Since she was fond of my friend's mother, then only a child, the Ukrainian woman found a way to lure the child out of the forest on the day that the rest of her family—including her mother and sister—was killed. The teacher did not know the exact days on which her grandfather, grandmother, and aunt had been killed, but on each Holocaust Day, she "remembered" her murdered family members by identifying with them.

Less drastic anniversary reactions are common. As Chicago psychoanalyst George Pollock, a specialist in the psychology of mourning, observes: "For the vulnerable individual a specific time of day, a specific day of the week, a specific season of the year, or a specific holiday can serve as a trigger or activator for the appearance of a symptom related to anniversary reactions."[173] Aware of a link between traumatized personal identity and anniversary reactions—which are a kind of ritualistic behavior—Pollock notes that anniversary reactions are fundamentally based in a "sense of absolute helplessness which can result in a nothingness or destruction to the self."[174] It is for this reason, Pollock concludes, that anniversary reactions are so frequently connected with the death of a loved one and with the process of mourning such personal losses; the anniversary reaction represents the re-emergence of repressed conflicts and related symptoms associated with loss, helplessness, and difficulty in mourning. Age, season or holiday may resurrect repressed symptoms, reactions, behavior, or emotions connected with the original conflict; time itself seems to be the agent activating pre-existing vulnerabilities.[175] Some psychoanalysts, such as I. L. Mintz, have theorized that certain anniversary reactions reflect what Mintz calls an "unconscious sense of time" that initiates the anniversary reaction so that the individual can repeat efforts to master the anxiety associated with the event. Mintz is certainly right to observe that there seem to be two kinds of anniversary reaction: one in which the individual is conscious of a specific time that produces symptoms pertaining to a trauma that does not preoccupy him or her most of the time; and one in which there is no known conscious stimulus.[176] Though Mintz's notion of "unconscious time" is only a theory, and the psychology of time in the unconscious is a matter for much further study, practically every clinician has observed an anniversary reaction of some sort and some degree of intensity and complexity.

We know, too, that cultures and religions develop practices to help individuals to deal with the crises that may be precipitated by anniversary reactions. In Mexico, for example, November 2 is commemorated as the Day of the Dead. Based on the belief that something of dead persons' souls remains in the grave for three years after death, families traditionally gather shortly before midnight at the gravesites of recently deceased relatives to put flowers on the graves, eat, and talk about the deceased. At midnight, bells toll for the dead, women kneel down, and men recite funeral eulogies.[177] Orthodox Jewish practices, "characterized by periodic, continually ongoing obligations, both public and private, which continue throughout life ... as a cult of the dead ancestors with some form of deification," provide a different and more permanent ritual means of confronting anniversary reactions.[178]

As collective rituals, culture- and religion-sanctioned anniversary reactions, in addition to helping individuals to cope with difficult circumstances, also support a society's shared identity; they bring—and bind—people together. Some shared rituals are related to anniversary reactions involving political events, and are therefore susceptible to being used as fuel for political manipulation and propaganda. This is especially true of rituals pertaining to a group's chosen trauma, to its "need" to re-examine and re-invest in this thread in the cloth of the group identity. Perhaps unsurprisingly, accounting for a large group's anniversary reaction is even more difficult and complicated than explaining the reaction of an individual.

Most individual anniversary reactions, as I have mentioned, belong to people who have suffered a traumatic loss—even if, like my Israeli teacher friend, the sufferer is removed by one or more generations from the original event. In large-group anniversary rituals, when decades or even centuries have passed since the traumatic event, all of the group's members are temporally removed from the calamity that has become the group's chosen trauma. Yet feelings for and defenses against helplessness, humiliation, and complications of mourning remain very much alive, since members of the previous generations have passed down—"transgenerationally transmitted"—a mental representation of the event to the current members of the group. Elder generations give their children conscious and unconscious directions on how to respond to that shared mental representation of the original trauma, which then becomes a defining aspect or marker of the large group and links its diverse members together. Thus a group's anniversary reactions can be described as ritualistic reactivations of large-group markers (such as the chosen trauma) that direct the members to behave collectively in certain ways, and thereby enhance their shared sense of sameness.

It is not difficult to find numerous examples of this process among "victimized" ethnic, national, and religious groups that have experienced drastic losses, helplessness, and humiliation at the hands of other large groups. It is important to note, however, that that a sense of shame and guilt may be passed from one generation to the next within the "victimizer" group as well, as has occurred in post-Nazi Germany.[179] However, members of the victimizing group typically have difficulty openly experiencing an anniversary reaction, usually denying their shame and guilt until social or political change allows for a clearer examination of the past, or until members of a later generation begin to observe that the derivatives of shame and guilt are manifesting in maladaptive ways, as in the case of the "skinhead" movement in Germany.[180]

Large-group anniversary reactions are conscious events—the time of the original traumatic or (in the case of chosen glory) celebrated event is officially recorded, its history is documented, and the society and its leadership prepare deliberate ceremonies to recall it. In the past, folk tales, songs, plays, and other artistic creations splendidly recounted real or mythologized victories or defeats and images of idealized dead leaders and heroic achievements, while today, CNN, Al-Jazeera, and the Internet dramatically activate and document anniversary reactions to chosen traumas, chosen glories, and dead heroes. Still, significant aspects of the need to enhance large-group identity through such ritualistic ceremonies remain unconscious. In peaceful times, a large group's anniversary reactions are tame. When a large group regresses, however, an anniversary reaction may turn into an emotionally invested event filled with intense feeling at both the individual and group level; all members truly feel that they are living under the same tent. When a large-group tent is threatened, the repeating rituals used to recall shared history, destiny, and identity tend to become exaggerated. Under stressful circumstances, people do not wait until anniversaries to reactivate mental representations of past shared glories and traumas or the idealized leaders associated with them; sometimes they are shared or recalled on a daily basis. Often, political leaders intuitively focus on such reactivations and use them in propaganda. Hate speech directed toward contemporary enemies may accompany the remembrance of chosen traumas. During the year preceding the 600th anniversary of the Battle of Kosovo, for example, Slobodan Milosevic and his associates encouraged the Serbian people to experience frequently and intensely the shared mental representations of the Battle of Kosovo, the Serbian chosen trauma, and of Prince Lazar, the Serbian leader killed in this battle.[181]

When we think of the large-group anniversaries of chosen traumas and chosen glories, or the ritualized display of important symbols, the first things that come to mind are grand and often elaborate events, such as the Fourth of July, Cinco de Mayo, Veterans' Day, Bastille Day, Bloody Sunday, and countless others around the world. But large groups turn to many less-obvious identity-enhancing rituals, which are practiced virtually every day when they feel threatened or under stress. Rather than resurrecting or reinvigorating a chosen trauma, as occurred among Serbs, large groups may instead modify or exaggerate certain aspects of traditional rituals to help repair the canvas of the large-group tent. For example, soon after Croatia gained its independence following the collapse of Yugoslavia, a period in which there was much shared anxiety about what would happen in this part of the world, Croatian wedding ceremonies began to look different. As is the custom, the bride and groom wear traditional Croatian costumes and are accompanied by musicians and singers as they go to the church and then to the civil ceremony; family and friends continue to join the traditional entourage as it makes its way through the town or village. But today, unlike in the past, this procession includes the display of numerous Croatian flags, prompting an outsider to mistake a wedding for a national holiday parade.

In addition to defining themselves on the basis of the history, language, culture, customs, tradition, and religion that their members share, and in addition to ritualistically enhancing the fabric of their shared identity with symbols, chosen traumas, and chosen glories, large groups define themselves by ritualistically differentiating themselves from other groups. In other words, a large group, like an individual, defines itself not only by what it is, but also by what it is not. For some time, I have observed that these other-based rituals of differentiation are governed by two fixed and intertwined essential rules of behavior: 1) maintain nonidentity between the groups and 2) establish and/or preserve a psychospatial border between them.[182] That these two governing principles of inter-group relations are intimately bound up with large-group identity itself is amply demonstrated by the high degree of shared anxiety that large groups evince when their ability to perform these tasks is threatened for any reason. In fact, the purpose of the two rules is to protect large-group identity from contamination by the other.

The preoccupation with "minor differences"[183] in groups in conflict clearly illustrates the first principle. Though enemy groups are certainly aware of their major differences, regressed large groups obsess about minor differences as a last-ditch effort to maintain the all-important differentiation from the enemy group. Though Freud thought that such preoccupations were relatively harmless ways of satisfying the inclination for aggression and of maintaining group cohesion, we know today that when large-group identity is threatened, the fixation on minor differences no longer remains harmless. For example, Duke University political scientist and law professor Donald Horowitz reports that, in 1958, Sinhalese mobs methodically victimized only men bearing earring holes in their ears and wearing shirts over their vertis. These features identified people as enemy Tamils in the absence of differentiating skin color or other dissimilar characteristics. When large groups regress, members of each group do not wish to acknowledge consciously that the enemy, to some extent, is like them. It is for this reason that minor differences between enemy groups often figure so prominently in the propaganda that a political leader uses to shore up group identity around him or herself. Of course, minor differences can be found practically everywhere—food, clothing, architecture, leisure, sporting activities, and so forth. Diplomats, especially those in nonaligned teams facilitating negotiations between enemy groups, rightly attempt to learn as much as possible about the players, politics, and policies of the parties in conflict. They tend, however, to think chiefly of clearly observable, major differences; many minor differences escape their attention, or are disregarded as "unreal" or insignificant. It is precisely this sort of minor difference, however, that may become the locus of the most stubborn and unalterable investment by disputing groups. Emotional attitudes attached to what appear to be trivia easily become "real world" problems and, then, ritualistic preoccupations. Diplomats and other makers of foreign policy would do well to consider that, although individual and large-group responses may seem to reflect ridiculous preoccupations, those responses are deeply connected with core self-esteem and identity issues and therefore cannot be ignored.

This need to differentiate is closely related to the second principle I mentioned above, the need to maintain psychospatial distance between the groups. Although demarcating borders has always been vital to international and large-group relationships, closer examination indicates that physical borders are effective only when they represent psychologically sufficient ones as well, as I have observed while visiting exaggerated physical borders such as the Cold War-era Berlin Wall, the Israeli-Jordanian border in 1986, and the Green Line that divided the northern, Turkish sector of Cyprus from the southern, Greek one for decades until Spring 2003, when Northern Cyprus leader Rauf Denktash and his government decided to open the borders. Like the valorization of minor differences, the border, perceived as a gap, clearly separates the two groups in conflict, enabling the illusion of noncontamination between them. This gap also stabilizes one large group's externalizations and projections onto the other. Elaborate rituals—including ceremonial changing of guards, constant monitoring and maintenance, and complex protocols and practices—are common along such borders, and define and strengthen the separation of large-group identities as if the boundaries have formed a thick, symbolic skin protecting the collective identity. Like the barrier of minor differences, geographical boundaries between opposing groups distinguish the groups psychologically as well as materially.[184]

The celebrated mid-twentieth century British psychoanalyst Donald Winnicott observed that some political divisions, such as the border between England and Wales, are natural, based on mountain ranges or other topographical features; in contrast, he saw the man-made Berlin

Wall as an ugly, unnatural barrier erected solely by international conflict. Nevertheless, even Winnicott acknowledged that a boundary such as the Berlin Wall might have a *positive* function, suggesting that a dividing line between opposing forces "at its worst postpones conflict [but] at its best holds opposing forces away from each other for long periods of time so that people may play and pursue the arts of peace. The arts of peace belong to the temporary success of a dividing line between opposing forces; the lull between times when the wall has ceased to segregate good and bad."[185]

When the Berlin Wall came down in 1989 and later Germany's reunification took place, Germans' adjustment to "binding together" all Germans again did not quickly occur. When the symbolic skin protecting the collective identity was removed, the stability of externalizations and projections was removed and such mental mechanisms could be then easily seen in routine daily life. A few months after the reunification of Germany, I visited a friend who lived in a town on the west side of the former East German/West German border. He asked if I would like to see the former border and then drove us to a grassy area not far from Gottingen that, prior to 1990, had been on the boundary between the two German states. My friend described how the trees had been cut down to aid the border guards in apprehending defectors. That day, of course, there were no soldiers, and the watchtowers were empty. I was, however, struck by the eerie silence of the place, and also by the fact that my friend was whispering. It was as though there was still danger in this former border region. We then drove across the old border and into former East Germany, something my friend had not done since before Germany's division. Though they had been reunited, the physical disparities between the two former countries were immediately obvious: the roads were poorly maintained and designed and even the shape of the electric poles was different. It was indisputable that we were now in a different "country."

As we rode through the countryside, leaving heavy traffic behind, my friend took a deep breath and asked me if I smelled something foul. I could not detect anything out of the ordinary, and told him so, but he did not accept my answer. He pointed to a car that was quite a distance in front of us and said: "You see that car? It's communist-made. Those cars smell." I was certain that he could not have realistically smelled anything emanating from the car because it was too far away. It seemed that since he "knew" communist-made cars had an offensive odor, his senses were playing a trick on him. Seeing the car stimulated his smelling the car. As a psychoanalyst, I also came to another conclusion: My friend was externalizing and projecting some unacceptable elements of his own onto East Germans. He was "clean"; East Germans "stunk." I did not verbalize my deduction but sensed that my friend, also a psychoanalyst, had come to a similar conclusion about his experience. He seemed embarrassed and quickly changed the topic of conversation.

This story illustrates how political borders are associated with large-group identities. Even though the people from both sides of the border between East Germany and West Germany belong to the same group, their respective histories during Germany's separation had led to the evolution of two "ethnic" groups. Thus, reunification—at least initially—induced anxiety about mixing the two "ethnic" identities. The psychological reverberations of German reunification still continue. In 2003, Irene Misselwitz, a psychoanalyst based in Jena, in the former East Germany, wrote about the influence of processes of social and political transformation on the human psyche. Looking at her own and other German's feeling and thinking patterns, she noted that more than a decade after the fall of the Berlin Wall, the wall "resides in people's minds" and "remains robust and it is not easily overcome."[186]

When clear physical demarcations are perceived by bordering large groups as ambiguous or indistinct, anxiety may easily develop. The tension between Romania and Hungary over the region of Transylvania, which is home to people of both ethnicities, is representative of this phenomenon. Today, the region lies within the national borders of Romania, but at various times in the past, it has been part of Hungary; it is geographically separated from the rest of Romania by the high and vast Carpathian Mountains. Because of ambiguous physical, historical, and political factors, then, both Romanians and Hungarians maintain an intense emotional investment in the region, a source of recurring friction between the two nations.

Preoccupation with borders and border rituals became a necessity in the United States after September 11. "Borders" began to appear in many places besides their legal and physical boundaries. Anyone traveling through U.S. airports (and now airports almost anywhere in the world) cannot help but experience a kind of "concretized" border crossing, and the efforts underway to "perfect" such security checks can only increase this feeling. Because there is the reality of danger, it becomes difficult for the people to understand that there is also a "border psychology" that accompanies these necessary activities—a psychology that reflects an aspect of large-group regression. While passing through such borders, in our minds, we face the possibility of meeting the "enemy" who is intruding into our space, creating a stress for our personal and large-group identity. Knowingly and unknowingly, our sense of basic trust is disrupted.

When there is a realistic danger and "borders" have to be erected to protect the population, it becomes very difficult to notice and study the psychology of borders.[187] In Israel, policed "borders" are more obvious than those in the United States. Israel's "borders," by necessity, are everywhere: at shopping centers, movie theaters, amusement parks and other public places. The following story from Israel illustrates that even when there are realistic reasons to erect "borders," such actions induce deep psychological reactions in people. In driving along the recently removed border between East and West Germany, my German friend had a need to separate himself from the "other." In the following story from Israel, we will see how erecting "borders" was experienced as an intrusion into personal identities.

Israelis create "borders" to protect their schoolchildren: they put fences around their schools, some of which, like one in the affluent neighborhood of Petach Tikva near Tel Aviv, appear to be part of the design of the building: only when I sought entrance to the school did I realize that the fence had a significant security function as well. Students and visitors alike underwent careful scrutiny whenever entering or departing the school; a guard had to open the locked door before anyone could enter or exit. This is typical of practically all Israeli schools.

One school that was not elaborately protected when I visited it in May of 2000 was Ramot Hefer, a combined junior and high school at Kibbutz Maabarot, near the center of Israel. The road from Tel Aviv to Kibbutz Maabarot goes through Hashoron (in Arabic, Beit Lid) Junction, about ten miles away from the West Bank. At this junction, there is a small monument, surrounded by neatly kept flowers, that honors the victims of a terrorist attack about two years prior to my visit. On this site, a bomb had exploded, wounding and killing young Israeli soldiers waiting for rides home. When people arrived to help the soldiers, a second bomb exploded. Two miles after passing this junction, one enters Kibbutz Maabarot through a gate. Ramot Heffer is inside this kibbutz, though its students come from outside the community.

Until a few months before my visit, the school had only a fence across the front, perhaps because it was in the middle of a kibbutz with its own security measures. By the time I arrived, however, an additional fence enclosing the school's campus had gone up: there was an iron gate at the entrance and a security guard, and one could see a fence disappearing into the woods at both sides of this gate. What was interesting was that, despite the huge expense of erecting this iron door and fence, there were "holes" in the school's borders of which many persons were aware. There was, for example, another gate entirely without obstacle just to the left of the entrance, open for any visitor to pass through on foot or by car. It led to a small dormitory for the students who were children of Ethiopian Jewish immigrants, which was only a few unobstructed steps from the school campus proper, the administration building, and the huge and beautiful garden that served as the school's courtyard. I was told that there were at least two more unguarded "holes."

Israeli insurance companies will not reimburse schools, school administrators, or teachers for any type of accident that may befall a student if a court finds that the school was not securely surrounded by a fence. Indeed, it was under threat from an insurance company that Ramot Heffer installed the huge iron gate and fence surrounding the school. Some Israelis told me that the insurance companies demand these impenetrable fences for protection against drugs and antisocial behavior, which is no doubt part of the story; when some teachers spoke of the fence around Ramot Heffer, though, they directly referred to the possibility of terrorist attacks. What is important for us here is the resistance to the insurance company's demands that I observed among some of the teachers: "Our school perhaps is one of the few places where we are not fenced in. We do not wish to be fenced in." Not having a fence meant some sort of internal freedom to them. Thus it is perhaps unsurprising that when they built the fence system, "holes" somehow remained. The teachers that I spoke with knew about this "secret" and were delighted by it: psychologically speaking, they were not completely confined.

Since there is a monument a couple of miles away reminding everyone of the reality of danger, the teachers' (and, I was told, some students') resistance to the new fence (and satisfaction with its deficiencies) requires psychological explanation. These teachers and students were resisting the large-group regression hidden behind obvious realistic concerns expressed in Israeli society's highly rigid border rituals. When forced to conform, they felt irritated. As long as they were not "fenced in," they felt, they had kept their individuality and maintained their sense of basic trust. And when they discovered "secret" holes in the security system, they took pleasure in feeling that they had been able to keep their individuality after all. This response was relatively atypical, however; Israeli children are exposed very early to a truly dangerous world and unconsciously many of them adapt to this environment by developing certain character traits: lack of a sense of humor, lack of patience with niceties, a need to be on guard at all times, and a sense of entitlement. In general, Israeli security concerns are highly institutionalized and widely embraced without much conscious awareness that there is a psychological price to pay for that normalization.

Interestingly, many Israeli psychologists and psychiatrists, as well as others, are aware of the negative effects of border psychology. But security concerns, obviously, come first and dealing with such negative effects will be postponed until peace is finally established in Israel—as difficult as that is to imagine in a time of seemingly unending suicide bombings and severe and often brutal Israeli responses.

As long as the rituals that serve to separate groups are not rigidified by large-group regression, they function positively to protect and enhance large-group identity and to keep expressions of each group's aggression under control. When the tension between competitive groups increases, however, each group's existing rituals of self-definition grow less flexible, and new rituals develop: rituals in which we can detect signs of magical thinking and blurred reality. The enemy is increasingly perceived as a conglomeration of every undesirable quality; in such negative stereotyping, the enemy is often thought of as a lower class of human, and, at worst, as actually less than human. As the late Israeli psychoanalyst Rafael Moses observed, each group loses its own humanity in dehumanizing the other, for otherwise it could not act so savagely toward other human beings.[188] I would add that the behavior of groups that dehumanize other groups very much resembles that of a child toward a nonhuman or inanimate reservoir of "bad" externalized images. Of course, a threatening large group dehumanizes its enemies in order to avoid guilt for injuring and killing them and to protect its sense of shared (if regressed) morality. There is a deeper motive, however: the dehumanizing group is setting up psychological borders, first for the group and then for individual members, in order to avoid anxiety deriving from the unconscious expectation that what it externalizes and projects will "boomerang" on itself. It imagines that its projections will be unable to traverse the great psychological distance between the human (themselves) and the nonhuman (the other).

Demonization and dehumanization, of course, set the stage for terrorism, war-like conditions, and wars, and leaders may manipulate this dynamic in order to support their own political decision-making. Nevertheless, the symptoms of regression usually remain hidden behind realistic strategies and exercises of logic. After all, enemies are real, security concerns are real, and leaders, governments, and organizations certainly need to deal with genuine dangers. But a large group may become so regressively fixated on real dangers that there is no room to deconstruct the shared fantasies that the group has attached to security concerns and its images of the enemy. Because the enemy has become the repository of all "bad," devalued, and dangerous elements in the group's psyche, it becomes very difficult to develop any empathy either for the enemy group's positions and concerns or for any losses it has suffered. This behavior, in turn, creates many obstacles to finding adaptive solutions to the basic conflict, and thereby magnifies the actual danger posed to each group—as the continuing Israeli-Palestinian hostilities amply demonstrates. Indeed, the extensive logistical planning and analysis that are involved in preparing for and waging war or terrorism can easily deflect attention from the psychological processes that accompany them.

After a nation or large group emerges from a crisis such as war, the break-up of a political system, or drastic revolutionary change (whether "good" or "bad"), a period of restabilization typically ensues and the group remains, for some time, in a regressed state. During this time of reassessment and redefinition—when the large group in a sense collectively asks, "Who are we now?"—a new type of ritual often develops. Like a snake shedding its skin, a large group will cast off certain elements—symbols, ideologies, leaders, even subgroups or neighbors—that no longer seem useful or appropriate, or that seem to impede or threaten the growth and revitalization of identity. Such *purification rituals*,[189] some of which begin to emerge while the group is still engaged in war or war-like conditions, represent attempts to modify or "recreate" identity, to increase cohesion, and to foster a sense of sameness among members that is more durable, relevant, and effective. These rituals involve a spectrum of practices, policies, propaganda, and ideologies ranging from benign to malignant. In benign purification rituals, what is shed or discarded is not projected onto an enemy; in malignant rituals, a specific "other" is targeted and is attacked.

As a result, purification rituals are not always reasonable, or even politically expedient, and some of the most malignant forms may seriously inflame a group's relations with others. After Latvia regained its independence in 1991, for example, a bill was sponsored in the Latvian parliament to remove the bodies and gravestones of Russian soldiers from the Latvian national cemetery. This attempt to purge Latvia of unwanted "non-Latvian" elements was met with strong resistance from Russia, and relations between the two countries became increasingly tense over this and other issues. The tense relations fortunately caused the proposal to be dropped.[190] In some cases, when one large group's projections onto another are extensive and intense, policies of "ethnic cleansing" will emerge in order to eliminate not only the signs of an unwanted and threatening "foreign" influence on the society, but also any individuals associated with the enemy group. In India in 1992, the sixteenth-century Babar Mosque in Ayodhya was destroyed by Hindu extremists, and those of Muslim faith were subjected to increased pressure to "return" to Pakistan. After the collapse of the Soviet Union, Serbs, Croats, Bosniaks, Slovenes, Montenegrins, and Macedonians all faced some version of the question, "Who are we now?" As Serbs sought to "re-create" their identity, cultural and ethnic cleansing shockingly reminiscent of the Third Reich took place in Bosnia-Herzegovina and later in Kosovo.

Next, I will examine the psychological processes that exist in extreme religious cults. An understanding of cults such as the Branch Davidians under David Koresh can serve as windows onto the psychological aspects of much larger extreme and militaristic movements, such as al Qaeda.

/ part two: psychology of religious fundamentalism

4 / from waco to the bamian valley

With the success of scientific theories in describing events, most people have come to believe that God allows the universe to evolve according to a set of laws and does not intervene in the universe to break these laws. However, the laws do not tell us what the universe should have looked like when it started–it would still be up to God to wind up the clockwork and choose how to start it off. So long as the universe had a beginning, we could suppose it had a creator. But if the universe is really completely self-contained, having no boundary or edge, it would have neither beginning no end; it would simply be. What place, then, for a creator?

—Stephen Hawking

Almost immediately following the April 1995 bombing of the Alfred P. Murrah Federal Building,[191] speculation centered on the notion that "Islamic fundamentalists" were responsible. In many ways, this was an unsurprising – if entirely unfounded, as it turned out – supposition. In recent decades, before September 11, 2001, and the Iraq war of 2003, the American news and entertainment media have typically come to associate the word "fundamentalist" with all religiously-affiliated militant groups in the Middle East, Africa, and South and Central Asia. Indeed, many Americans have developed a tendency to think of "fundamentalist" as the usual sequel to the word "Muslim," and to associate both with acts of terrorism.[192] In mainstream American discourse, then, "fundamentalism" and "fundamentalist" are almost always pejorative words. But there are, of course, fundamentalist groups within practically every faith tradition—Christianity, Judaism, Islam, Hinduism, Sikhism, Buddhism, and Confucianism included—and these movements share certain traits "despite the substantive differences among them in terms of doctrine, cosmology, social composition, size, organization, and scope of

113

influence."[193] In this chapter, we will be considering their psychological commonalities through several recent instances of violence associated with religious fundamentalism and, more generally, identity issues, regression, and rituals in such groups. Before turning, in Chapter 6, to the radical attacks of September 11—we must first try to discern the psychological "shape" of religious fundamentalism more generally.

As the nation eventually learned, it was not radical Islam but another fundamentalism altogether that underlay the Oklahoma City attack. The date of the bombing itself was no coincidence; Timothy McVeigh, the man executed in the summer of 2001 for organizing and carrying out the attack, planned the bombing in Oklahoma City, Oklahoma, to coincide with the second anniversary of the Federal Bureau of Investigation (FBI) raid on the Waco, Texas, Mount Carmel Community Center. McVeigh, a disaffected ex-soldier affiliated with a right-wing anti-government subculture, had been so infuriated by the FBI's behavior during the six-week "Waco siege," which resulted in the deaths of 81 members of the Branch Davidian religious sect, that he was inspired to launch a direct attack on the federal government of the United States.

Of course, McVeigh was not the only person who had perceived the government's actions at Waco as problematic; the so-called "Waco hearings" co-sponsored by the House Judiciary and House Oversight and Reform Committees in 1995 reflected a wider public concern with the way that the FBI had handled its confrontation with the Branch Davidians. But the Oklahoma City bombing had definitively shown that the FBI's responses to critical situations like the one at Waco could trigger volatile social situations which might reverberate in subsequent poisonous "aftershocks," in turn creating further societal fragmentation. It was with pleasure, then, that in late 1995 I accepted the invitation to chair a Select Advisory Commission to the FBI's Critical Incident Response Group charged with examining behavioral sciences insights that could enhance the agency's ability to respond to crises such as the one at Waco.[194] Indeed, the expertise of the psychoanalyst offers particular insight into the dynamics that resulted in these two tragedies. As I will show, expressions of the severe regression that existed in the Branch Davidian group induced counter-feelings and counter-reactions among the law enforcement officers ranged against the group; in this relation we can see something analogous to the patient-therapist relationship in which the regressed patient on the couch, insisting that the analyst misunderstands him or her, sometimes induces negative feelings in his or her analyst. But analysts are trained to react in a therapeutic fashion to such feelings; that law enforcement officers at Waco were not so trained substantially contributed to the eventual disaster.

Though the Branch Davidians and their leader, 33-year-old David Koresh, were generally little known when the Bureau of Alcohol, Tobacco, and Firearms (ATF) first raided their Texas compound to serve arrest and search warrants alleging illegal possession of firearms and explosives,[195] they were not actually an entirely new sect. In fact, the movement dated to the late 1920s, when Victor Houteff (1885-1955), a Bulgarian immigrant to the United States, was expelled from the Seventh-Day Adventist Church for claiming to be its new prophet; in 1935 Houteff bought the 189 acres of land in Texas on which the Mount Carmel community was established. In this lineage, the Branch Davidians represented an especially fundamentalist strain of one tradition in American Christian millennialism. The Seventh-Day Adventist Church traces its origins to William Miller (1782-1849), a farmer born in Western Massachusetts, who was convinced that Jesus would return to earth in 1843 or 1844. When the dates proposed for the return passed and Christ did not appear, the followers of the "Millerite Movement," approximately 50,000 in number, experienced what became known as the "Great Disappointment." Even after this "failure," however, many Millerites held that Christ's return was still imminent, and Seventh-Day Adventism, with Ellen G. White as its prophet, grew from the theological wrangling necessitated by the "Great Disappointment." Among the elements that eventually separated the Davidian movement from the established Seventh-Day Adventist church was the Davidian belief that the prophecies and statements of the King James version of the Bible could be deciphered to interpret present events and to predict the end-time. For them, this specific version of the Bible was the true word of God, and other translations were filled with falsehood. This special, literalist devotion to a particular text was one of the elements that most clearly marked the Branch Davidians as a fundamentalist group.[196]

But, of course, the Branch Davidians were hardly alone in this sort of literalist devotion: Michael Barkun, political scientist and expert on Protestant culture in the United States, estimates that fully 25 to 30 percent of the current population of the United States is fundamentalist Christian.[197] After all, the term "fundamentalism" was actually coined in the United States as a term of Christian self-definition in the 1920s.[198] Barkun suggests that, dating from the 1870s or 1880s, certain social tensions have led many Americans to Protestant fundamentalism. The gradual shift of socioeconomic power from rural to urban areas, the transition from primarily agricultural to primarily industrial organization, immigration, and other ethnic shifts have all generated shared anxieties among certain segments of the American population. According to Barkun, as these changes and others complicated the demographic scene, American Protestants responded in two ways: some Protestants took a "modernist" approach by living agreeably with Catholics and non-Christians, Jews especially; others became anti-Catholic and anti-Jewish "traditionalists." Initially, more traditionalists lived in the North; in time, however, more traditionalists came to be found in the South.

The advances of science, especially Darwinian evolution, also placed significant strains on American Protestant culture. About two centuries after the Enlightenment and the beginning of scientific experimentation, Charles Darwin's *Origin of Species* (1859) exercised a dramatic effect on scientific thought and popular culture alike in the English-speaking world. Among its other effects, the theory that all existing forms of life were lineally descended from those that lived long before the Cambrian Epoch, about 545 million years ago, drastically challenged the biblical creation story. In the United States, one of the best-known events that dramatized the deepening traditionalist-modernist dichotomy was the Scopes "Monkey Trial" (its moniker derived from the supposed Darwinian idea that human beings evolved from monkeys), later memorialized in the play and movie *Inherit the Wind*. In 1925, Tennessee became the sixth southern state to criminalize the teaching of evolution; an instructor teaching "any theory that denies the story of the Divine Creation of man as taught in the Bible, and [teaching] instead that man had descended from a lower order of animal" could be fined.[199] John Scopes, a 24-year-old Dayton, Tennessee, general science teacher, agreed to participate in a test case challenging the law. Commanding international attention, the twelve-day trial created a circus-like atmosphere in the town, with vendors selling food, toy monkeys, and Bibles to the hordes of spectators. In the courtroom, American Civil Liberties Union (ACLU)-supported Clarence Darrow, a "militant" agnostic, faced off against William Jennings Bryan, a three-time presidential candidate nicknamed the "Great Commoner." Even some of the principals in the proceedings openly displayed personal commitments to fundamentalist thinking: under Darrow's questioning, Bryan admitted that he believed that Eve was literally made from Adam's rib and that Jonah was swallowed whole by a big fish; the judge arrived each day carrying a Bible and opened the daily proceedings with a prayer. Unsurprisingly, Scopes was found guilty and fined one hundred dollars.[200] Since the Scopes trial era, many American Protestant fundamentalists have chosen to withdraw from political participation (a tendency which began to reverse in the 1980s) and to reject shifts in the mainstream culture such as changes in sexual norms.

Of course, the debate over science and religion continues to this day, with modernists tending to believe that science and religion complement each other in useful ways, and traditionalists holding the position that religion has supreme authority over science. Fundamentalists continue to insist that there is no empirical evidence to support the theory of evolution: "We do not deduce Mother Teresa from nature. Human goodness is a rebuke to Darwin," George Roche—author, lecturer, and at one time the presidentially-appointed chairman of the National Council on Educational Research—wrote in 1987, well over a century after the publication of *Origin of Species*.[201] Perhaps the only other major thinker against whom Christian fundamentalists in the United States still fight so vigorously is Freud. In some ways, this opposition is unsurprising; Freud, after all, did declare religion "the universal obsessional neurosis of humanity":

> ... like the obsessional neurosis of children, it arose out of the Oedipus complex, out of the relation to the father. If this view is right, it is to be supposed that a turning-away from religion is bound to occur with the fatal inevitability of a process of growth. ... Our knowledge of the historical worth of certain religious doctrines increases our respect for them, but does not invalidate our proposal that they should cease to be put forward as the reasons for the precepts of civilization. On the contrary! Those historical residues have helped us to view religious teachings, as it were, as neurotic relics, and we may now argue that the time has probably come, as it does in an analytic treatment, for replacing the effects of repression by the results of the rational operation of the intellect.[202]

But Christian fundamentalist objections to Freud run rather deeper, too. "Darwinism, and a few decades later, Freudianism," Roche observes, "seemed to cement the case for Natural Man, cut loose from any metaphysical moorings and from the traditional Christian basis of Western Civilization. The last barrier to a pure and final equality of man had apparently fallen."[203] That this typical fundamentalist view of Freud is a misreading diminishes nothing of its force.

Barkun estimates that 20 percent of American fundamentalists (that is, 5 to 6 percent of the total population) are, as the Branch Davidians were, millennialists.[204] Though millennial movements are historically many and various,[205] the main theological position in Christian versions is that Jesus

Christ will return to earth and establish a kingdom that he will rule from Jerusalem for 1000 years. [206] Before this Second Coming, it is said, there will be a seven-year Tribulation. During the first half of this period, upheaval and violence will prevail; after the first three and a half years a charismatic figure will emerge who is in reality the Antichrist, Satan. He will rule for three and a half years until Armageddon, the final war between good and evil, which will take place in Israel. During Armageddon, most Jewish people will be killed; after Christ descends to earth, the remaining Jews will be converted and will accept Jesus as their Messiah.[207] One thousand years of peace will begin, during which Satan will be kept away, though not destroyed. During this, "the millennium," there will be no war, no hunger, and no suffering. After 1000 years, the Last Judgment will take place, and a new world and new heaven will appear.[208]

Millennialists maintain apocalyptic beliefs: they expect an imminent transformation on earth and look for signs suggesting the arrival of Tribulation and/or the Second Coming of Jesus Christ. For example, some millennialists have called the 1948 creation of the State of Israel "God's time-clock," designating this event a sign of the Second Coming. Some groups considered the 1986 explosion of the nuclear plant at Chernobyl a millennial event. For others, dramatic upsurges in mobility and education are divine signals because the Bible describes such conditions as indicators of the coming of the Messiah (see Daniel 12:14). Still others have interpreted an increased frequency of earthquakes as the birth pangs of the new creation (see Matthew 24:17), and still others view the increased centralization of world financial and political power systems as signaling a Satanic incarnation who will deceive most of the world (see Daniel 7:12; Matthew 24:115; Revelation 13).[209]

The 42 men, 46 women, and 43 children of various ethnic backgrounds living at Mount Carmel just prior to the Waco tragedy saw the world in just these kinds of terms. The Davidians had initially become involved in illegal gun trade to support themselves, but by 1991 or 1992 they had come to believe that Armageddon could begin at Waco rather than in Israel, and that keeping weapons on their compound was therefore a necessity. Following the ATF raid, Koresh interpreted the confrontation biblically: the Davidians came to associate their besieged position with the Fifth Seal of the Book of Revelation (6:9-11), a "waiting period" before godly people (in the Davidians' minds, themselves) would be killed as predicted in the Sixth Seal (Revelation 6: 12-17). Tape-recorded negotiations between FBI agents and the Davidians indicate that the blockade only fed the Davidians' existing view of the federal government as satanic; it is apparent from transcripts of the negotiations that the Davidians wished to save the FBI negotiators' souls. Unfortunately, the aggressive behavior of the authorities during the "siege" unintentionally fed the Davidians' millennial expectations of catastrophe.

The tragic end of David Koresh and the Mount Carmel community was foreshadowed long before the day that FBI agents drove a tank shooting rounds of chlorobenzylidene malonitrile (CS) gas into the community center, however.[210] In some senses, it is in David Koresh's troubled personality—and in the sad childhood which shaped it—as much as in the religious traditions and the cultural milieu of late 20th-century America that we must look for the roots of the Waco disaster. According to Peter Olsson, a psychoanalyst and scholar of cult leadership, Koresh's observable personality characteristics fulfilled the criteria of the American Psychiatric Association's definition of "narcissistic personality disorder" (NPD), which I will discuss at some length in Chapter 7.[211] Persons who suffer from this disorder exhibit a pervasive pattern of grandiosity and believe they are omnipotent. Preoccupied with fantasies of unlimited success, power, and brilliance, they display a sense of entitlement and require constant attention and admiration.[212] We also know from psychoanalytic studies of such personalities that, while exhibiting overt grandiosity, they hide a deep sense of vulnerability.[213] And David Koresh certainly bore a history that would leave a child dangerously vulnerable.

Born Vernon Wayne Howell in 1959 in Houston, Texas, to fourteen-year-old Bonnie Clark, Koresh later would say on tape: "I was only born because my Daddy felt something in his loins and lusted after my Momma."[214] Though Bonnie never married Vernon's biological father, she was briefly married to another man who was physically abusive toward the child, and Vernon therefore went to live most of the time with his maternal grandparents. When Bonnie divorced and remarried, this time to a carpenter named Roy Haldeman, Vernon returned to his mother's home, learning for the first time at the age of five that his "Aunt Bonnie" was in fact his biological mother. Not long afterward, she became pregnant with his half-brother, complicating this rather late "togetherness" between Vernon and his mother. Koresh's later comments about this time of his life reflect an entirely understandable reaction to such turmoil: "I was shocked! I was confused. ... Here I was, five years old and my whole world was turning upside down."[215] Further, Vernon suffered from "dyslexia" and performed poorly in school. Though I do not know whether his learning disabilities had any organic base, I would not be surprised, based on my own clinical work with traumatized children, if the learning disability diagnosed were in fact a cover-up for psychological problems. Whatever the reason for his difficulties with schoolwork, he was mocked mercilessly by other children as "Mr. Retardo."[216] We can safely assume that as a young child Koresh had low self-esteem.

Vernon and his stepfather, Roy Haldeman, did not get along well, and Haldeman did not provide a loving, caring male role model for Vernon. Instead, the child turned his attention to radio and television evangelists, and his grandmother often took him to the Seventh-Day Adventist church. The young Vernon became highly religious. We can easily imagine that, with identity difficulties and a lack of steady mother and father figures, he was seeking solace from divine parent-figures. It seems likely that associating himself with such figures from childhood helped Vernon to build a growing sense of omnipotence that helped him battle against his sense of helplessness in the real world, leading him eventually to believe that he possessed divine power.

Vernon Howell joined the Mount Carmel community in 1981, perhaps as a response to the loss of a girlfriend. When Howell was 18 years old, he impregnated a 16-year-old girl who subsequently had an abortion. When she became pregnant again by Howell, her father "ran Vernon off";[217] soon after, now 22, he joined the Branch Davidians. At that time the community's prophet was 67-year-old Lois Roden, who "apparently took [Howell] as her lover, and began to promote him as the prophet who would succeed her."[218] Howell's relationship with Roden angered her son, George Roden, who wished to be the next prophet himself. But George Roden was erratic, and Howell seemed to display omnipotence, so some influential members of the community supported the newcomer as their next prophet.[219] Within a couple of years of Lois Roden's death in November 1986, George Roden had been committed to the Big Spring State Hospital for mental illness after murdering a man and later died from a heart attack.[220]

In 1984, Howell legally married a 14-year-old girl; in January and February of 1985, he traveled to Israel with his new wife. It was during this visit that Howell felt that he received a "message" from God that he was indeed a prophet. This experience led him, five years later, to take the name "Koresh," the Hebrew version of the name "Cyrus"; Vernon Howell renamed himself after Cyrus the Great (590-529 B.C.E.), founder of the Archaemian dynasty and the Persian Empire, and, more significantly, the biblical conqueror of evil, pagan Babylon in the biblical Book of Revelations: "To Babylon you must go and there you will be rescued; there God will ransom you out of the power of your enemies" (Micah 4:10).

In August 1990, Howell legally took the name David Koresh and assumed leadership of the community, who thought him to be the Messiah or "Lamb." Koresh believed that he could not be Jesus Christ, since Jesus did not have children, and Koresh already had children. Instead, he modeled himself after a messiah referred to in Psalms 45, "'Who married virgins and whose children ruled the earth.' Koresh saw his marriage to young women and the birth of his children as fulfilling this prophecy."[221] Even before he emerged as "David Koresh," Vernon Howell had "married" another 14-year-old, Karen Doyle, in 1986, the same year that he "married" his first wife's 12-year-old sister. In 1987, Howell "married" three more very young women, aged 16, 17, and 20 respectively. The girls' parents consented to these extralegal "marriages," apparently believing that their daughters, by becoming pregnant by Howell, would give birth to children for God.[222]

Once his leadership at Mount Carmel was secure, Koresh declared that all women of any age at Mount Carmel were his "wives." Except for Koresh, men at the community were to be celibate. In the place of conjugal love with women, they could love and be loyal to Koresh since his character included a feminine element: the "Christ Spirit" in Koresh was dubbed "Shekinah," a feminine spirit. Thus both women and men at the community could be "married" to him. Breaking with routine family structures was explained by what Koresh called "New Light" interpretations of the Bible; a less divine explanation of Koresh's behavior would consider his troubled childhood, his search for an identity, and his disappointment with original mother and father figures. By becoming the lover/child of the 67-year-old Lois Roden, he was probably unconsciously searching for a satisfactory mothering experience. Later, becoming sexually involved with very young women also probably brought him symbolically closer to the 14-year-old girl who had been his actual mother; at the same time, he may have perceived his relationship to his young "wives" as nurturing, "mothering."[223] Further, by rescuing his own children from the corrupt Babylon of modern American culture, by securing them places in God's kingdom, Koresh was, symbolically and unconsciously, rescuing himself from his own childhood environment.[224] The child who had never experienced a stable family was now creating a "family" at Mount Carmel under his own strict controls; unlike his absent biological father and uncaring step-fathers, he seemed determined to become the loving "father" and "mother" of his Mount Carmel family.[225]

Clearly, however, the "family" itself was experiencing regression. Though I did not have the opportunity to study Koresh or any of his "family" members personally,[226] all available information suggests that, as under the Nazis, "basic trust" among the Davidians was primarily supplied by a leader who tightly controlled followers' activities and interfered in their familial relationships. My clinical work with former cult members and with other individuals attracted to strict ideological organizations suggests that such persons as individuals (and sometimes as families) are typically seeking to patch up wounded personal (or family) identities. By replacing their existing identities with the "second skin" of the cult identity, they imagine, they will escape anxieties associated with their individual (or familial) identities. And, temporarily, they do experience relief. In this sense, the psychology of the leader and the followers in such groups is interestingly similar: the leader seeks to parent others in an attempt to replace or repair the bad parenting of his or her childhood; the followers seek a new parent-figure in the leader in order to resolve childhood traumas. Sadly, followers most often end up re-experiencing relationships with "bad" parenting when the leader's internal world poisons his or her "parenting."

Well before the ATF raid, the regression within the Davidian community had created strong reactions among "outsiders" – what religious studies scholar Catherine Wessinger calls "cultural opposition"[227]—to Koresh and his community. Koresh and his followers' evangelical efforts and claims to be extensions of divine power had alienated local non-believers. In particular, the breaking down of familiar social regulations within the community had induced aggressive counter-reactions among people outside the Branch Davidian circle. Having sex with underage girls may have been Koresh's attempt to find a solution for internal conflicts stemming from a troubled childhood, but his attempt to "heal" himself was certainly pathological and poisonous, and naturally disturbed many who were not (or were no longer) under his spell.[228] While allegations of child abuse did not, of course, come under the jurisdiction of the ATF, this preexisting "cultural opposition" to the Mount Carmel community created a rationalization, an emotional motivation, for the ATF raid.

From a psychological point of view, the Mount Carmel community's behavior during the confrontation was dominated by regressive rallying around Koresh and loss of individuality. As the wounded Koresh prepared to surrender to the FBI, signs of malignant leaderless group regression appeared as some Davidians made a suicide pact. When Koresh did not surrender as expected on March 2, 1993, however, the Davidians returned to their "waiting period"[229] of millennial expectation. This, in turn, provoked the FBI agents to feel that the Davidians were "daring" them to attack. And the more overtly aggressive the FBI became, the more resolutely the Davidians clung to their expectation of catastrophic events to come.

When the FBI later examined its agents' behavior during the siege, a communication gap between the agency's behavioral scientists and its tactical commanders at Waco clearly emerged. The February 1996 report of the FBI Select Advisory Commission which I chaired[230] sought to bridge this gap with two new positions: that of the "Futurist" and that of the "Resource Analyst." Given clear direction regarding legal limits, including first amendment issues associated with individuals and groups, the Futurist would "scan the horizon" of domestic and international fronts and assist in developing an early warning methodology. The Futurist would thus help the FBI to be prepared for future possible critical incidents and to understand the psychological and social processes underlying critical events before they actually take place. The Resource Analyst, who would work with the Futurist, would serve as an "asset manager," a bridge between outside behavioral scientists and the FBI's Critical Incident Response Group.[231] Both figures would retain their academic or organizational positions and would work for the FBI on a part-time basis only, forming significant links between the FBI and outside expert communities. The FBI did in fact establish these two positions, both of which were first filled by members of the Commission: Gregory Saathoff, a psychiatrist and the director of the Critical Incident Analysis Group (CIAG) division of the University of Virginia's Center for the Study of Mind and Human Interaction (CSMHI), became the Resource Analyst; and Allen Sapp, a professor of criminal justice, became the Futurist.

The FBI's new commitment was put to the test almost immediately. By the time of the Montana Freemen standoff in March 1996, the bridge between FBI agents and outside scholars had been established and relevant analyses of the critical incident were now carried out systematically. The negotiations between the parties, as described to me by Dr. Saathoff, now incorporated techniques enhanced by the psychodynamic understanding of conflict and by psychotherapeutic maneuvers. For instance, FBI behavioral scientists met with Montana Freemen representatives for long dialogues, during which these scientists tried to understand the "psychic realities" of the group and to show empathy without threat. As a result, even though the Montana Freemen's views were even more aggressive than the Davidians—they viewed the U.S. government as illicit and wanted to destroy it in order to establish a millennial kingdom—this confrontation concluded without replicating Waco's tragic loss of life on either side.[232]

Of course, not all fundamentalisms—let alone all religions—bring their followers to such tragic, violent conclusions as at Waco. Religions can fuel humane ideals, transform and support individuals performing good deeds, and stimulate creative urges and artistic expressions. At the same time, throughout history people have initiated unspeakable human suffering in the name of religion. Religion *per se*, then, is neutral: religions can heal or poison individuals, depending upon specific psychological make-up and group influence.

Hence we find some fundamentalist groups that are peaceful and civil, and some that are violent. In the Russian Old Believers of Mustvee, an Estonian town at the shore of Lake Peipsi with a population approximately half ethnic Estonian and half ethnic Russian, we can observe a peaceful fundamentalist group. In the mid-seventeenth century, Patriarch Nikon of the Russian Orthodox Church reformed certain church rituals, but the changes were too much for some priests and churchgoers, who thought Nikon's reforms were a sign of the influence of the Antichrist and formed the Old Believer movement in reaction. Fiercely persecuted, Old Believers began to see the Tsar, who supported Nikon, as the Antichrist, and believed that he was ruining Orthodoxy. The reaction of some Old Believers, who performed group suicide by burning themselves inside their prayer houses when harassed by the authorities, was more masochistic than sadistic. Others fled Russia and scattered around the world, including the United States. Though some Old Believers who settled elsewhere retained a kind of clergy, Old Believers who migrated to the Lake Peipsi area more than three centuries ago came to believe that after the reforms introduced by Nikon the apostolic succession was broken: there are no more bishops and accordingly, no more priests to be ordained. This community of Old Believers has lived in relatively peaceful coexistence with their Estonian neighbors. Indeed, during the communist era, when authorities frowned upon religious practice, Estonians and Russians in Mustvee cooperated to keep valuable 16th- and 17th-century Old Believer texts and icons from being destroyed.

With other members of the Center for the Study of Mind and Human Interaction (CSMHI), I visited Mustvee several times between 1993 and 1996. After the collapse of the Soviet Union and reestablishment of Estonian independence in 1991, Mustvee's economy was in tatters: the main Soviet market for their products—onions, cucumbers, and fish—was now closed to them, and their textile industry was in ruins. Though there had been no major disturbances between ethnic Estonians and ethnic Russians living in Mustvee for centuries, the economic collapse in the town stimulated a split along ethnic lines. Whereas all Estonians could speak Russian, almost none of Mustvee's Russians could speak Estonian. After 1991, Mustvee Russians' economic concerns were aggravated by a wider perception that ethnic Russians were being "mistreated" by the Estonian government. We thought that, with the participation of members of both ethnic groups, building an ecotourism industry could help to re-establish peaceful coexistence between Estonian and Russian residents in Mustvee and its surrounding towns.

On one of our visits, we noticed some priceless Old Believer books in a house next to a church which had burned some years ago in an accidental fire—only its front wall and door still stood. We thought that these books as well as some ancient icons would interest tourists, and so, working with authorities at Estonia's Tartu University, we were able to secure the funding to create temperature-controlled rooms in the church house to maintain these books and icons in good condition. Also in the church house lived the bearded, smiling leader of Mustvee's Old Believers, Zosima Yotkin, who lived a life almost entirely devoid of worldly possessions. Adherence to centuries-old religious rituals and customs had not made Lake Peipsi's Old Believers a violent fundamentalist group. The only "aggression" that Yotkin exhibited was a "threat" to baptize me—someone had told him that I was not a baptized person—in Lake Peipsi, whether it was summer or winter. I always sensed that Yotkin's "threats" to baptize me were his gesture of affection; since I was his friend, he wanted to save my soul. Even though he was never able to dip me in Lake Peipsi and I remained an "infidel," Yotkin, who had worked to facilitate a good relationship between Old Believers and Estonians throughout a period of great upheaval, continued to treat me as a valued friend, and in turn I always responded to him in kind.[233]

At the other extreme of the spectrum, some fundamentalist groups become violent. Some seek to become what Catherine Wessinger has called revolutionary fundamentalist groups;[234] on the birthday of the Prophet Muhammad in 1980, for example, Kano, Nigeria, sect leader Alhaji Mohammadu (Maitatsine) Marwa, who had proclaimed a new era of anti-materialist reformed Islam, led his followers to the central mosque in Kano, charging Nigerian military though armed with little more than bows and arrows. As many as 8,000 people may have been killed during their uprising.[235] American right-wing "militias" such as the Montana Freemen—who are in fact motivated, as Michael Barkun argues, by religious fundamentalism, though their aims are avowedly political rather than religious[236]—also exemplify Wessinger's revolutionary category.

Other fundamentalist groups expect an Armageddon and become involved in creating violent signs of its approach. The leader of the Japanese Aum Shinrikyo cult, Shoko Asahara, who believed that he was Jesus Christ reincarnated as well as the first "enlighted one" since Buddha, declared that only his followers would survive an approaching global conflict in which a nuclear bomb would once more be dropped on Japan. Members of Aum Shinrikyo attempted several acts of biological terrorism in Japan between 1990 and 1995, including the release of a deadly nerve agent in the Tokyo subway in March 1995.[237] Some groups strike out because, realistically or no, they believe their survival is at stake—not the literal survival of individual members, who may be expendable, but the survival of the collective identity, which is perceived to be threatened from within or without. The militant fundamentalist group Hamas, an Islamic movement of Palestinian resistance established in 1987, for instance, was founded to oppose Israel as a threat to the very existence of the Palestinian people and to establish an Islamic state in historic Palestine.[238] The Islamic fundamentalist group that assassinated Egyptian President Anwar Sadat in 1981 claimed that his murder was "punishment for having corrupted Egyptian society with false non-Muslim values."[239] What Wessinger calls an *assaulted* group, such as the Mount Carmel community, reacts with violence to attacks on them by outside authorities: "The Branch Davidian community was not suffering from internal weaknesses that made the believers despair about the accomplishment of their ultimate concern. In 1993, the Branch Davidians were not a threat to the general public or to law enforcement agents."[240] Still others become violent in part because they believe it is their mission to save the souls of non-believers; as Iran's Ayatollah Khomeini once declared: "If an infidel is allowed to pursue his nefarious role as corrupter on earth until the end of his life, his moral sufferings will go on growing. If we kill him, and we thus prevent the infidel from perpetuating his misdeeds, this death will be to his benefit."[241] Some Christian fundamentalist groups have similarly felt obliged by God to convert others to "the truth," sometimes by force. Still other fundamentalist groups turn violence not on others, but on themselves; such groups are often what Wessinger classifies as *fragile*, in which the leader/prophet's power is threatened.[242] By the early 1990s, for example, the Order of the Solar Temple could be called "fragile." A full-time "spiritual master" since 1976, Joseph DiMambro had built his own temple, preparing for the return of Jesus Christ in solar glory. Since DiMambro thought that he did not possess enough charisma himself, physician Luc Jouret became the leader of the group, with DiMambro pulling the strings backstage. By the early 1990s, however, there were serious disagreements between DiMambro and Jouret, and DiMambro's son Elie, along with other members, was beginning to question his father's power. During the night of October 4, 1994, in two separate fires in western Switzerland and Quebec, Canada, 53 Solar Temple members, including DiMambro and Jouret, died as a result of mass suicide; some were probably murdered. In December 1995, another sixteen followed suit.[243]

To understand properly why some fundamentalisms become malignant and others do not, however, we must not only enumerate the various situations in which religiously-motivated violence erupts, but also consider the psychological roots of religious feeling and explain what differentiates extremist fundamentalism from routine religious belief. As I mentioned earlier in the chapter, Sigmund Freud considered any religious commitment, fundamentalist or mainstream, to be an expression of unresolved individual psychological issues from childhood.[244] According to Freud, the terrifying impressions of helplessness in childhood arouse the need for protection, which could be provided through the love of a father. The duration of one's sense of helplessness—overt or covert—throughout life, Freud concluded, makes it necessary to seek an omnipotent father, an image of God, to assuage the feeling of vulnerability; thus religion is related to shared illusion. In 1901, he famously rewrote the well-known text of Genesis, "God created man in His own image," as "Man created God in his."[245]

For a long time, psychoanalysts continued to interpret religious practice as one of the various behaviors that redirect immature, unruly impulses into mature and socially acceptable conduct (such as the creative work of building magnificent cathedrals) or as a remnant of regressive behavior (cutting off established relationships with others and adopting a monastic life, for example, as a mirror of infantile wishes to submit to a powerful father). As investigation began to shift from Freud's focus on the infant or young child's relationship with the mental image of his or her father to the child's relationship with his or her mother, however, the psychoanalytic understanding of belief-system formation also changed. It was the early 1950s work of British psychoanalyst Donald W. Winnicott on what he called *transitional objects* that most crucially enlarged psychoanalytic theory concerning the foundation of religious beliefs and feelings. His work—and subsequent elaborations on it by psychoanalysts such as Phyllis Greenacre, Arnold Modell and myself—has allowed us to see the progressive, healing, and creative aspects of religious beliefs and feelings as well as their regressive, destructive, and restrictive aspects.[246]

Winnicott saw the foundations of religious feeling as present in the *normal emotional development process* of the child, of which he understood the "transitional object"—the blanket that the "Peanuts" cartoon character Linus carries everywhere is an example of a transitional object—to be a universal element. During the early part of the first year of life, each infant or toddler chooses a transitional object from whatever is available to him or her (sometimes even an infant's own hair can become a transitional object) on the basis of texture, odor, and moveability. Usually, the child chooses a soft object, such as a teddy bear,[247] which is under the child's absolute control. Over the course of his or her first years of life, this object becomes the first item that is clearly "not-me" in the child's mind. Though this first "not-me" image corresponds to a thing that actually exists in the world, the transitional object is not entirely "not-me" because it is also a substitute for the child's mother, whom the toddler perceives to be under his or her absolute control (an illusion, of course). At this early stage of life, the child's mind is in a state of confusion; the toddler cannot fully experience where he or she ends and the mother or other caretakers begin. Through the blanket or teddy bear, the child begins to get to know the world around him or her. It is not part of the child, so it signifies the reality "out there" beyond the child's internal world, the "not-me." But it also bears another meaning for the toddler— as a substitute for the mother, whom the child's mind does not yet fully understand as a separate individual in her own right. This is why playing with a teddy bear or blanket or keeping it close by can soothe the child and, conversely, why on certain occasions the child can discharge aggression against the toy without fearing that it will retaliate when the child again treats it as a soothing object.

To clarify, let us consider an imaginary lantern with one transparent side and one opaque side located between the infant or toddler and his or her actual environment.[248] When the toddler feels comfortable, fed, well-rested, and loved, he or she turns the transparent side toward the real things which surround him or her, illuminating them and beginning to understand them as entities separate from himself or herself. When the infant feels uncomfortable, hungry, or sleepy, he or she turns the opaque side of the lantern towards the frustrating outside world, "wiping out" the surrounding real things. Most mothers have observed that, when their toddler is falling asleep, the child holds onto his or her blanket as if the child's whole world consists of himself or herself and the blanket; at such times, the transitional object is a mother-substitute that cuddles the child and "protects" him or her from the rest of the real world beyond. When the lantern is thus turned opaque side out, we imagine that the child's mind experiences a sense of cosmic omnipotence. In "normal" development, the toddler plays with his or her "lantern" hundreds and hundreds of times, getting to know reality in one direction and succumbing back to lonely, omnipotent (that is, narcissistic) existence in the other direction, until his or her mind begins to hold onto unchangeable external realities, such as having a mother separate from oneself who is sometimes gratifying and at other times frustrating. During such repeated "play" the toddler's mind learns both to differentiate and to fuse illusion and reality, omnipotence and restricted ability, suspension of disbelief and the impact of the real world, and so on. Using his or her blanket, teddy bear, or other transitional object, the child is involved in a watershed concept.[249]

If the child's development is normal, he or she eventually develops an acceptance of the "not-me" world, the indifference of the universe, and, accordingly, to logical thinking. However, people also need "moments of rest," if you will, during which they do not need to differentiate between what is real and what is illusion, in which logical thinking need not be maintained, and it is in these moments that the relation to the transitional object echoes throughout a lifetime. At moments of "rest," then, a Christian might know that it is biologically impossible for a woman to have a baby without the semen of a man, but also believe in the virgin birth. Rationally, we might know that no one really sees angels, but we may behave as if they exist. In other words, the function of the transitional object remains available to us for the rest of our lives, in support of the religious beliefs given to the growing child by family members and other adults in the child's environment. The need for what I am calling "moments of rest" varies from individual to individual, and from social subgroup to subgroup. Some people declare that they do not require such religious moments of rest, but perhaps they refer to the same function by different names. For example, they may "play" the game of linking magical and real in astrology, or paint abstract paintings that represent a mixture of illusion and reality.[250] As Winnicott wrote:

> Transitional objects and phenomena belong to the realm of illusion which is the basis of initiation of all experience... This intermediate area of experience, unchallenged in respect of its belonging to inner or external (shared) reality, constitutes the greater part of the infant's experience, and throughout life is retained in the intense

experiencing that belongs to the arts and to religion and to imaginative living, and to creative scientific work.[251]

Whatever form the transitional object function takes in an adult life, it plays a significant role in linking the individual to his or her large group; the "normal" range of religious belief, like the "normal" range of psychological health, is socially determined.

In summary, then, I consider religious beliefs and feelings to derive from normal developmental processes in early childhood and from the times when we require a moment of "rest" in adulthood from the struggle to differentiate between illusion and reality. Religion is not a "universal neurosis" responding *only* to mental conflicts of childhood associated with feelings of helplessness and the corresponding desire for an omnipotent father, as Freud thought. The image of God incorporates input from different sources as the child grows, and is modified according to an individual's own psychology, sociocultural experiences, education, and use of religious (proto)symbols. And, as an individual goes through his or her life cycle, he or she may use religion to gratify or to defend against various needs, wishes, and internal tensions and conflicts. For some people, Freud's original description of the emotional link between God and a father-image does indeed dominate. But, for each individual, the image of God becomes a source of various combinations of transitional objects and phenomena, maternal or paternal love, fear of punishment, hatred, omnipotence, and so on—including, very significantly, the sense of belonging to his or her family, "clan," and/or large group.

Though in normal child development a time comes when the child gives up his or her teddy bear or blanket and only its memory remains,[252] then, the *function* of "play" with such objects is available to us throughout our lives. Some of us use this function mostly for creative purposes, to get to know the world better and/or to enjoy a mental connection between magical and real in our fantasies and artistic creations. Thus a person who is non-regressively devoted to his or her religion can comfortably believe in seemingly magical and illogical aspects of religion, yet also comfortably be a rational, logical, and functioning member of society. Others, especially those whose early parent-child relationships were disturbed, or those who were raised in religious environments where religious "propaganda" had been internalized as real, have a tendency to reactivate the regressive aspects of transitional object play. In a sense, in their adulthoods they try to "wipe out" external reality and rational thinking in order to make the world center around themselves and their "teddy bears." For people whose "teddy bear" is an exaggerated investment in religion, their very identity and psychic existence accordingly depends upon the regressive use of religious belief and feeling. Returning to the lantern metaphor, the religious fundamentalist is preoccupied, whether mildly or severely, with keeping the opaque side of the lantern turned against a real world perceived as threatening and frustrating. Unlike the infant, who can probably block out the external world more thoroughly, however, the fundamentalist is an adult and therefore more unavoidably conscious of an environment which he or she perceives as threatening.

Thus extreme fundamentalist sects exhibit what theologian Martin Marty and historian Scott Appleby the "tendency of some members of traditional religious communities to separate from fellow believers and to redefine the sacred community in terms of its disciplined opposition to non-believers and 'lukewarm' believers alike."[253] Establishing absolute psychological (sometimes even physical) borders within which to live is one of the most important ways in which fundamentalist groups seek to safeguard their purity against those perceived threats from without. The Haredi community in Israel, for example, who share "an existential angst about the continuing survival of Judaism and the Jewish way of life,"[254] are preoccupied with the threat of Jewish secular society, and so "tend to raise barricades around themselves. ... They define themselves as a 'learning society': men seclude themselves in Yeshivot in which they study the holy scriptures without maintaining contact with general culture and knowledge."[255] Such psychological borders may take symbolic form; members may separate themselves from non-believers by wearing a specific color or style of dress, for example. Sometimes psychological "barricades" even take physical shape, such as the wall which surrounds South Carolina's Bob Jones University, an institution that champions Christian fundamentalist beliefs. The individuals who are attracted to fundamentalist religious groups often struggle with what is permissible and what is forbidden, and the submission to radical and non-negotiable religious ideas and a leader who "knows the truth" removes the need to make moral decisions. Inside the "safe haven," such individuals seek to escape anxiety, personal problems, or societal changes. Thus the emergence of fundamentalist sects is often a response to societal and religious crises provoked by modernization, secularization, and now globalization.

In understanding the mechanisms of fundamentalist group identity and violence, it is crucial always to remember that religion binds men and women not only to an image of the divine, but also to each other; it responds to the basic, normal human need for a sense of belonging. Once an individual is involved in the network of an extreme fundamentalist religious group, it becomes difficult to quit or escape. Most groups create tangible incentives or economic dependence to ensure that members do not leave the group. More importantly, all the actions and thoughts of believers are highly organized and institutionalized, and supported by shared magical belief in the leader. Thus the putative divine rule infiltrates members' everyday existence and intimate personal relationships, fundamentally changing them and thus creating psychological pressure to remain dependent upon, and obedient to, the organization. At Jim Jones' Peoples Temple, for example, ex-member Jeannie Mills reports, followers "had to admit that [they] were homosexual[s] or lesbians":

> We were forced to stop all sexual activities with our marriage partners. Pastor Jim Jones claimed that he was the only person who knew how to love, and frequently had the women and men he had had sexual relations with stand up and testify to what an excellent lover he was.[256]

The cumulative effect of these pressures is a psychological sense of "specialness" which acts as a shared badge in the present world as well as in the expected next life. Thus, as Peter Olsson remarks, "Cult followers are not merely passive victims of the leader. They have longed for, then merge with, the easy solutions, exciting apocalyptic scenarios and … spurious triumphs of a collective, deeply rebellious purpose."[257]

At the same time, such extreme groups expect intrusion into their self-established "lonely omnipotence." Perceiving their religion to be continually under attack by non-believers, scientists, or even rival fundamentalist groups that cite other texts as truly divine, fundamentalist religious groups are what Israeli historian Emmanuel Sivan calls "pessimistic" movements.[258] Since they believe that "others" outside their borders do not understand them and threaten their existence, the shared sense of victimization actually becomes an essential component of the collective identity. Paradoxically, because they anticipate threats from those without, they in fact play a role in inducing persecutory attitudes in others, for the severity of fundamentalist religious violence is correlated to the degree of danger the group perceives in the world beyond the "security blanket" of their religious identity. The sense of shared victimization in an extreme fundamentalist religious group reinforces, as we have seen in the case of the Branch Davidians, a special devotion to the prophet, who alone has the power to decipher divine messages and to find expressions of these messages in actual or expected events. Threats to the power and authority of the person considered to be personally divine, or at least an extension of the higher power, may cause intense anxiety and/or identity confusion. The more that the group perceives attacks from without, the more intensely it rallies around its central leader. In turn, as we have seen in other examples of regressed groups under a supreme leader, the hierarchy among followers tends to be minimal, effacing the significance—and eventually, if the regression is severe enough, the value—of each individual life within the group in favor of the group itself. The last words of Annie Moore, a 24-year-old nurse who was the last to die in the mass suicide at Jonestown, chillingly encapsulate the regressed collectivity's sense of threat and the violence with which it may respond: "We died because you would not let us live in peace."[259]

The degree of regression is individual to the group, depending on the specificities of societal, political, and historical elements, as well as on the particulars of leader-follower interaction in a given historical moment. A group regression has become malignant, however, when its members will tolerate extreme shared sadism and/or masochism in defense of the group's identity. Sadism leads to destroying "others" who are seen as threatening to the group, as in the case of Jewish extremist Baruch Goldstein's 1995 massacre of Muslim worshippers at the Cave of the Patriarchs mosque in Hebron. Masochism turns the malignant aggression inward on the group itself, as in the mass suicide of the Peoples Temple, an effort to bring to reality the illusion of merger with God and psychologically to preserve, in death, the infantile illusion of omnipotence. The combination of sadism and masochism yields a believer—a suicide bomber, for example—willing both to sacrifice himself and to do violence to others. Paradoxically, destroying oneself (whether in a suicide bomber's attack or a group's mass suicide) stands as an act of assertion because it emphatically separates the identity of the group willing to sacrifice themselves from that of the "others" perceived as threatening them.

Because religious identity is often intertwined with ethnic or national identities, the psychodynamics of religious groups are thus structurally similar to those governing ethnic alliances, which I described earlier. Indeed, religious fundamentalist violence is most often amplified when closely associated with ethnic or nationalistic sentiments. It is this dynamic that has so powerfully delineated some conflicts around the globe, for example, the conflict that is now raging in the Middle East, a conflict with which I have worked, on and off, over several decades. In the face of intense political conflict there, both Jewish and Muslim fundamentalisms have malignantly regressed in defense of their respective group identities.

Israeli psychoanalyst Rena Moses-Hrushovski has discussed that one effect of the 1967 Six-Day War was the transformation of Jewish religious fundamentalism into a militant movement.[260] Ultra-religious Israeli groups[261] tended to see Israel's defeat of the combined Arab armies as attainment of the "Land of Israel"—including the Temple Mount and the Western Wall—and the unification of Jerusalem "as a fulfillment of the prophecy that Israel would control and settle the full biblical extent of the Jewish land" and as heavenly signs that the age of the Messiah was nearing.[262] The Land of Israel is holy, according to this logic, and must be consolidated in preparation for the appearance of the Messiah. One example of Jewish extreme religious fundamentalism and its role in violence is described below:

After the Six-Day War, Jewish "settlers" moved into the newly-occupied areas—including the Sinai region, which Israel held as far as the Suez Canal. Three years after a major Jewish settlement was established in the Yamit region of the Sinai, Anwar Sadat's Egyptian forces carried out a carefully planned attack on Israeli forces in the Sinai during the holiday of Yom Kippur, 1973.[263] Though Sadat was not immediately able to "liberate" the Sinai, and Yamit remained under Israeli control, Sadat had won the psychological war by bringing a new understanding of the Arab-Israeli conflict to the world diplomatic scene. As a result, the Israelis eventually withdrew from the entire Sinai peninsula, including Yamit, the largest and most prosperous of the Sinai settlements. The turmoil of the 1982 withdrawal received worldwide media coverage, unlike the withdrawal from Sharm El-Sheikh—at the southern tip of the Sinai peninsula, a few miles from the Straits of Tiran— around the same time, which received little attention outside the region. The Israeli army clashed with protesters,[264] and in the end the Israeli authorities bulldozed the settlements at Yamit, close to the Israeli border. A closer look at the events at Yamit reveals that there were actually few Yamit settlers among the protesters; the larger contingent, which included settlers from the West Bank and others from elsewhere in Israel, had been organized by *Gush Emunim* ("The Block of Faithful"), a national religious subgroup. For Gush Emunim, to give up areas that were included in the "Land of Israel" violated God's command; in a crucial broadening of religious Zionism, religion and nationalism had become intertwined for them.[265] As Moses-Hrushovski observes:

Israelis sat glue[d] to their television sets as Hesder Yeshiva students battled Israel Defense Force soldiers in an effort to prevent the hand over [of Yamit]. The split deepened, and dialogue became even more strained eleven years later as the Rabin government began to implement the Oslo II Accords.[266]

The propaganda created as a result of this shift among extremist religious/nationalist groups played a significant role in poisoning the sociopolitical atmosphere and, as a result, in Yigal Amir's assassination of Israeli Prime Minister Yitzhak Rabin, whose territorial concessions were perceived by some Jewish fundamentalists to contravene God's commands.[267] More than a decade before a fundamentalist Jew took the life of the Israeli leader, an extremist fundamentalist Muslim group played the key role in the assassination of a Muslim political leader, Egyptian president Anwar Sadat, during a 1981 military parade commemorating the Yom Kippur War of 1973. In the next chapter, I will look closely at extreme Islamic fundamentalism. But first, I would like to highlight what I have said about the psychology of religious fundamentalism so far.

Are all religious fundamentalisms and fundamentalists regressed? My answer is yes—but, equally important, as I observed in Chapter 2, regression is not always a bad thing: in order to cope with the challenges of progressive everyday actions and creative living, people may find comfort in the transitional function of religion or gain new strength from the symbolic images of nurturing parents native to an earlier developmental stage. So a person with literalist beliefs about the Bible or Koran should not be considered an extremist if he or she functions more or less normally in the world. A religious fundamentalist possessed by anxiety, a sense of uniqueness and omnipotence, and fantasies of external threat (or violent responses to actual external threat), however, displays a severe regression that disables his or her ability to act in and relate to the heterogeneous real world; by contrast, a fundamentalist such as the Old Believer leader Zosima Yotkin, who is obviously able to relate comfortably to a non-coreligionist such as myself, cannot be said to be dangerously regressed. It is most useful to think of different religious fundamentalisms as occupying various positions on a spectrum of regression, from mild and adaptive to extremist and malignant. Small extreme religious cults are a model to understand basic psychodynamics of massive extreme religious movements such as the Taliban or al Qaeda.

In summary of what we have seen in this chapter's survey, then, I offer a list of the psychological elements shared by extremist forms of religious fundamentalism, whether they are small extreme religious cults or massive large-group movements:

Absolutist belief in possession of the "true" divine text and/or rule.

A supreme leader as the sole interpreter of the divine text.

Exhibition of "magical" beliefs.

Pessimistic attitude.

Coexisting paradoxical feelings of omnipotence and victimization.

Construction of psychological (and sometimes physical) barricades between the group and the rest of the world.

Expectation of threat or danger from people and things outside the group's borders.

Altered family, gender, child-rearing, and sexual norms, often including degradation of women.[268]

Changed shared morality, which may eventually be accepting of mass suicide, murder, or the destruction of monuments or buildings perceived as threatening to the group's beliefs.

As we can see from this list, though the psychology of leader-follower interactions in extremist religious groups resembles that of other regressed large groups examined earlier in this book, religious fundamentalisms emphasize a particular constellation of certain signs and symptoms of large-group regression. Indeed, that particular constellation of symptoms is one especially liable to induce negative—and at times outright hostile—feelings in "neighboring" groups because of its challenges to some of the most basic elements of social organization: sexual norms, interfamilial relations, and a sense of the basic validity of one's way of life.

Purification rituals of extreme religious fundamentalist groups can be most devastating since "permission" to purify one's large-group identity is given by a divine power and since what is destroyed by purification (people and/or things) are perceived as the protosymbols of the devil.

The Taliban has become known by the American public because of its association with Osama bin Laden. But, prior to the World Trade Center and Pentagon attacks, an outcry arose from much of the world, including many Islamic countries, when the Taliban's cultural/religious purification policy toward two tremendous statues of Buddha in the picturesque Bamian Valley, about ninety miles north of Kabul, became known. Though now solidly Muslim, Afghanistan was once a region where Buddhism flourished. Between the third and fifth centuries A.D., followers of this religion chiseled a 175-foot-high sandstone statue of Buddha on a cliff overlooking the valley. Another 120-foot-high Buddha was hewn from a rock nearby. On February 26, 2001, Mullah Omar ordered the statues destroyed. This followed the news that more than fifty pre-Islamic artifacts in the Kabul Museum had already been destroyed in the preceding month.

The Metropolitan Museum of Art in New York City offered to remove the two Buddha statues, which were described by the Dalai Lama—the exiled Tibetan Buddhist leader—as "world treasures," from the Bamian Valley at the museum's expense and show them at the museum. This offer was rejected. On March 3, 2001, the Taliban militia blasted away the legs and heads of the two Buddha statues. The Taliban information minister, Quadratullah Jamal, announced that "They were easy to break apart and did not take much time."[269] The complete destruction of the statues took some days, however, and required dynamite. After ten days' work, the Taliban authorities slaughtered 100 cows and distributed their meat to the poor in an Islamic ritual of atonement "meant to seek Allah's forgiveness for having taken several days more than expected to destroy [the statues]."[270]

Of course, the Taliban is not the only group to be involved in such acts of religious-cultural purification. Before and during the "ethnic cleansing" in Bosnia-Herzegovina, for example, Serbs and Croats (both Christians) actively sought to purge the region of the cultural and religious heritage of Bosnian Muslims.[271] Great mosques, the famous Gazi Husrev Library in Sarajevo, and a well-known Mostar bridge dating back to the great days of the Ottoman Empire were all destroyed. Remarkably, many of the Bosnia-Herzegovinian Serbs who bombarded Sarejevo were from the Bosnian capital itself;[272] in their collective regression, they bombed their own city to "purify" it of Muslim connections. There are, of course, many other examples of such religiously-motivated "purifications." Much earlier in history, Martin Luther denounced the "false idols" of the Catholic Church. Most recently, the Americans and its coalition partners could not protect the National Museum in Baghdad and priceless items were stolen by Iraqis themselves. The National Library was burned. We have no choice but to become curious about multiple reasons—including psychological ones—for the Western forces permitting such a crime to take place. While the items that were stolen were pre-Islamic, one wonders if they were perceived by the invading Westerners as Islamic—belonging to Muslim Iraqis—and if this played a role in "allowing" the tragedy to take its course.

Returning to Afghanistan, the Taliban's motivation for this destructive act—on a surface level—included religious-political considerations and a wish to express aggression toward "others" who did not understand the Taliban's sense of victimization. Taliban spokespeople frequently talked quite reasonably of the world caring more for the pieces of stone and wood of which the statues were made than for starving Afghan children. But destroying the statues also responded to a need to enhance the group's identity and served to purify the Taliban identity. As the Taliban's regression deepened, the Buddha monuments increasingly became protosymbols, which, in turn, "needed" to be destroyed. As art historian David Freedberg observes, "Images are feared not because they are dead, but because they seem to be, and are often believed to be, alive."[273] In regression, the transitional object aspect of art may not be tolerable; the art may emerge as a fear-inducing "not-me" item with which the regressed people cannot "play." The Taliban behaved like the disturbed child who directs his or her frustration and rage against a teddy bear to express the feeling that he or she is not in a safe and psychologically nurturing environment. Freedberg suggests, too, that perhaps ordinary Afghans—in their regressed state—might have been so impressed by the size and beauty of the statues that they saw them as "new" gods, like the omnipotent, fear-inducing teddy bear of a disturbed child. As Freedberg writes, "[t]his may seem a preposterous idea; but it is surely a kinship—not the difference—between such primitive notions and our own susceptibilities to art that is the source of at least part of our shock at what happened in that remote and beautiful valley."[274]

5 / from the bamian valley to iraq

Remove your veil and illuminate the earth and skies
Make this elemental world more brilliant than any paradise

—Zeyneb Hatun (late 15th century female Ottoman poet)
    translated by Walter G. Andres, Najat Black, and Mehmet Kapakli

The suicide attackers of the World Trade Center and Pentagon were *not* psychotic. For anyone touched, however distantly, by the horror of September 11, 2001, this may be a difficult fact to grasp. How can human beings capable of such impersonal, indiscriminate violence be called sane? Surely, one may feel, madness is the only explanation.[275]

In the wake of the attacks, the already close association of the word "fundamentalist" with the word "Muslim" that I mentioned in the last chapter has become even more thoroughly crystallized in the minds of most Americans. And the idea of Islamic fundamentalism is itself now more thoroughly coupled with the impression of violent insanity than ever. But the truth, for good and for ill, is much more complicated.

Of course, Islamic fundamentalism, like any other religious fundamentalism, by no means necessarily entails violence, and, as Ambassador (ret.) W. Nathaniel Howell, who has closely observed Islam in the Middle East during a long foreign service career in that part of the world,[276] reminds us,

[In examining Islamic Revivalism w]e are not in fact concerned with Islam *per se*, but rather with competing interpretations and visions which tend to narrow, simplify and constrict Islamic doctrine and experience. The movements of the Islamic Awakening that attract our attention are no more reflective of the full sweep and richness of Islam than "Branch Davidians" or "Liberation

139

Theology" are of Christianity. … [T]he serious observer should not accept at face value any claims that one group is singular and the authentic voice of the Moslem world.[277]

It is clear, however, that in some circles what Howell has called the "nostalgia movement"[278] of the Islamic Revival has been poisoned. Taking up a certain dualistic strain common to Islam, Judaism, and Christianity, some regressed fundamentalist subgroups have projected the West—or, more generally, the "House of Unbelief"—as the enemy of the "House of Islam."[279] When religion, the influence of certain leaders, and ethnicity or nationality become intertwined and associated with absolute good, any enemy group can appear to be the embodiment of evil; feared, it must be destroyed.

But whence the psychological need to associate Islamic identity with the absolute good? After the terrorist assaults on the Twin Towers and Pentagon, journalist and commentator Christopher Hitchens pondered the significance of the date of the attacks:

Believers in propaganda by deed, like Gavrilo Princip and Timothy McVeigh, usually choose to invest themselves with portentousness by selecting an anniversary that will freight their murder with meaning. Often, it is a date that only meant something to a very limited or arcane circle until its true value was unveiled to a stunned world. Thus Princip chose the date of Serbia's 14th century defeat in Kosovo and McVeigh chose the anniversary of Janet Reno's bloodbath at the Branch Davidian compound in Waco, Texas.[280]

On September 11, 1683, Hitchens continues, the armies of the Muslim Ottoman Empire were met, held, and turned back at the gates of Vienna. Though I consider it rather unlikely that Osama bin Laden and his entourage chose the date of September 11 in order to reverse symbolically a centuries-old Ottoman defeat (and, in any case, the Siege of Vienna actually concluded on September 12, not September 11),[281] Hitchens nevertheless touches on an important historical-psychological truth here. It is in certain senses true that, despite various Ottoman successes in subsequent centuries, Islam as a military and political entity had a hard time recovering from the defeat at Vienna. This defeat became a kind of "chosen trauma" for the Ottomans. The Ottoman Empire had come into existence in the early 1300s and in a sense became the heir of Muslim power, following the great days of Arab Islamic culture and dominance.[282] Most Arab lands eventually came to be subject to the Ottoman Empire, but the greatness of Islam lived as long as the Empire was powerful. As the Ottoman Empire began to shrink, and became especially humiliated during the last 100 years of its existence, the Western influence on the Muslim world began to grow. When the Ottoman Empire ended after World War I, most Arab countries freed from the Empire found themselves ruled by the European powers. In fact, the modern borders of the Middle East were basically designed by French, British, and Italian leaders, who literally sat around a table drawing borders for the Arabs according to Western plans and interests. Under secularizing founder Mustafa Kemal Ataturk, the new Turkish Republic, born out of the ashes of the Ottoman Empire, abolished the Caliphate, which had in some senses been Islam's papacy.[283] And, even before the Caliphate was eliminated, the British authorities and some Arab elites played around for some time with the idea of who should be the next Caliph, stimulating political divisions and competition between Arab and Indian Muslims and so on. In the end, nothing came of it except a bad taste in the mouths of many Muslims.[284]

The new Turkey was hardly alone in minimizing religion in historically Islamic societies: Soviet Central Asia and most of the Balkan states marginalized Islam, and the elites in many other Muslim countries (including some Arab states) secularized while avoiding outright legal separation of religion and state. And Muslim political losses have been accompanied by the rise of non-Muslim rulers over Muslim societies and invasions of foreign ideas, laws, and ways of life—including the emancipation of women and rebellious children in some Islamic societies. It may well be the shared psychological representations of these successive stages of military, political, and cultural defeat that, reactivated, were reflected in world affairs of the late 20th century as a desire to reassert Muslim values, or at least certain versions of "Muslim values," again not in all countries where the population is mostly Muslim, but in some of them. In certain countries, Pakistan, Malaysia, and Iran, the political powers depended on Islam "as an integrative and distinguishing force"[285] and modern Islamic revivals did not challenge the state "but rather [sought] to control the state."[286] In the Arab world, many attempted to link nationalism and Islam and at times tried hard to distinguish themselves from Muslims living in non-Arab lands. For example, during the formative years of Arab nationalism, "the Egyptian thinker al-Tahtawi treated the Turks as the 'internal and external other,' questioning their understanding of Islam and arguing that 'national brotherhood is over and above the brotherhood in religion.'"[287]

By identifying the West as the enemy, concludes historian Bernard Lewis,[288]

> Islamic fundamentalism has given an aim and a form to the otherwise aimless and formless resentment and anger of the Muslim masses at the forces that have devalued their traditional values and loyalties and, in the final analysis, robbed them of their beliefs, their aspirations, their dignity, and to an increasing extent even their livelihood."[289]

The varieties of religion professed by those regressed Muslim fundamentalists who turn to violence are apocalyptic and militant versions of Islam. Lewis identifies Islam, rather than any other element, as the ultimate basis of identity, of loyalty, and of authority[290] . Certainly many elements from poverty to oppression are crucial elements in the appearance of massive threats against large-group identity. Nevertheless, some groups tended to put religion as the dominant identity to be protected against outside dangers. In order to understand the Islamic awakening in the second half of the 20th century, let us begin by looking, through a psychological lens, at the Prophet Muhammad and at certain crucial points in the history of the religion. Certain facts, legends, and military and political strategies concerning the birth of Islam and its quick expansion are part of the foundation for Islamic large-group identity for such fundamentalist groups. When regressed, Islamic movements of today return to the "memories" of the birth and expansion of Islam as something to be copied in a wished-for geopolitical revival.

From the Koran and the anecdotal *hadith* combined with the several other primary sources available, scholars have pieced together a fairly complete picture of the life of the Prophet Muhammad.[291] Indeed, as Subhash C. Inamdar, a scholar of the life of Muhammad and the rise of Islam, suggests, the Koran itself "in many ways might be considered autobiographical."[292] Born in Mecca in 569 or 570 C.E. into a turbulent tribal society, the child Muhammad apparently had a traumatic early life indeed. His father died some weeks before the future prophet was born into the mercantile Quraysh tribe, which claimed descent from Ishmael, the biblical Abraham's first son. In accord with governing tradition, the infant was sent to a Bedouin wet nurse. After about two years the child was returned to his mother, Aminah, but Muhammad's grandfather,

Abd al-Muttalib, became his main caretaker. When he was six, on a journey with Muhammad to his father's tomb in Medina, Aminah died suddenly, and his grandfather died only two years later. At this point, the
orphaned Muhammad was placed in the care of his uncle, Abu Talib. This
experience may well be reflected in certain parts of the Koran that urge
charity to orphans and other outcasts, or denounce those who treat them
poorly:

> As for the orphan, oppress not,
> As for the beggars, refuse not,
> As for thy Lord's mercy, expatiate. (Surah 93, Verse 9)

> You respect not the orphan,
> urge not feed the destitute,
> savour the heritage greedily,
> love wealth ardently. (Surah 89, Verse 18)

There is little information about Muhammad's adolescent and teen
years, though we do know that he began to work at different jobs as a
child, including sheep-herding, and traveled to Syria with his uncle on
trading journeys. By the time he reached the age of 25, he was known as a
businessman of integrity and honesty. A rich widow and businesswoman,
Khadija, hired him, and they soon married. Around the age of 35, he
began to be absorbed in spiritual meditation, and had a vision during a
solitary retreat to Hira at the age of 40. As Muhammad reported it, the
angel Gabriel came to him, informing him that God had chosen him to be
His messenger; unlike Jesus, Muhammad did not claim to be divine himself, but presented himself as the prophet of God. The vision made
Muhammad anxious, however, and it is apparently through Khadija's
reassurance that he accepted the mantle of Prophet. Khadija was thus the
first Muslim believer.

Indeed, all sources refer to Khadija as a highly influential figure in
Muhammad's life; Ibn Ishaq touchingly describes how Muhammad "used
to tell [Khadija] of his troubles."[293] Said to have been 40 at the time of her
marriage to the 25-year-old Muhammad, Khadija was the mother of four
daughters, all of whom would live long enough to become Muslims themselves, and a son who died at a very young age, another significant loss that
perhaps reminded the Prophet of earlier losses. Muhammad remained
loyal to Khadija until her death in 619, not long before the Prophet was
forced to leave Mecca for Medina. In the older woman, it seems, he had

found the stability of a nurturing maternal figure which he had signally lacked as an orphan. After her death, he reversed the role and became, in a sense, the nurturer or mother-figure for the numerous wives he collected[294]—at least one of whom was a child when they married, and some of whom were widows of his followers—who may be seen as representatives of his orphaned childhood self. But, as a messenger of God, Muhammad became, psychologically speaking, the voice of his lost father-figures as well. As the Prophet, then, he combined masculine and feminine in a total parent-image for his followers. It is clear from his revelations, which include injunctions to love children and animals and to protect the weak and the poor, that he had begun to assume this identity even before Khadija's death, and it was Khadija who, through her support, apparently enabled him to evolve into this charismatic figure.

With Khadija's early encouragement, then, Muhammad started to preach his mission secretly among intimate friends, and began to speak publicly around 613, three years after his first vision, all the while slowly beginning to win converts. For the rest of his life, he periodically received "revelations": messages on a range of topics said to come directly from God, though it was not until almost 30 years after Muhammad's death that the various revelations—many of which had been maintained by oral transmission—were codified as what we now know as the Koran. The revelations that Muhammad relayed not only prescribed rules for behavior, but also provided commentary on historical events in which God's messenger was involved, explaining the Prophet's own behavior. Some of these events were quite personal, such as Muhammad's marriage to the former wife of his adopted son, Zayd, a former Christian slave who was given to Muhammad by Khadija. According to the story, one day Muhammad saw Zaynab, the adopted son's wife, scantily dressed and was taken by her beauty, but declined to enter her house. Zaynab told this story to her husband, who offered to divorce her for the Prophet. Though Muhammad refused his offer, they divorced anyway, and Muhammad married Zaynab after the prescribed period of time. The Koran comments: "When Zayd divorced her [Zaynab], we gave her to you in marriage, so that for the believers there may be no guilt in [marrying] the wives of their adopted sons when they divorce them."(Surah 33, Verse 37). When Muhammad's marriage to Zaynab was criticized, revelation granted him permission to have many wives, though all other male believers were restricted to four wives. Given the historical conditions of the Koran's production and preservation, then, it is perhaps unsurprising that it contains many apparently contradictory[295] revelations, which, I believe, have made it easy for later Islamic leaders, including but not limited to extremist fundamentalist leaders, to elevate certain sections of the Koran and ignore others, and thus to interpret "God's intentions" in almost any way.

When Muhammad first began to report divine revelations in his home city of Mecca, however, the first response of most people in his own tribe was ridicule: some accused him of being possessed by *jinns* (spirits) and threw feces on him while he was praying. It was at this point in his career that Muhammad reported the *mi'raj* (ascension): in a vision, he was taken to heaven and received by God, and there witnessed all the marvels of the celestial region. After the *mi'raj*, he instituted the ritual prayer of Islam, during the last part of which the faithful repeat the greetings between the Prophet and God on the occasion of the mi'raj: "The blessed and pure greetings for God!—Peace be with thee, O Prophet, as well as the mercy and blessing of God!—Peace be with us and with all the [righteous] servants of God!" Reports of the *mi'raj* escalated the conflict between Muhammad's followers (called the *umma*) and the non-believers of Mecca; with the death of his uncle, also in 619, Muhammad had lost his main protection against the majority of Quraysh who had not converted. Finally, Muhammad and the *umma* had to migrate to Medina in order to escape persecution; 622 C.E, the year of the *hijra* to Medina, now marks the beginning of the Muslim calendar.

In Medina, Muhammad the businessman and prophet would become Muhammad the military innovator and political leader as well. Fused with religious fervor, the tribal practice of *razzias*, the usually non-fatal raids on enemy caravans, evolved into the sometimes deadly *jihad*, which also brought economic gains for the *umma*. The term *jihad*, in fact, refers to two kinds of struggle: the spiritual struggle of each individual against vice, passion, and ignorance as well as holy war to convert non-believers.[296] Muhammad exhorted his men with the promise from God that those who were slain would go to a heavenly paradise, achieving a kind of immortality: "It was the promise of martyrdom and paradise that was probably the most potent factor that Muhammad brought to the annals of warfare."[297] (Indeed, the battle cries he devised may even be seen as the first examples of modern political propaganda directed to one's own people.) During this period of armed conflict, revelation often commented on behavior during or after battles and even addressed possible feelings of guilt among the Muslim combatants. After the Battle of Badr, for example, which was fought between Muhammad's forces and non-Muslims from Mecca in 624 C.E., the Koran observes: "You did not kill them, but God killed them;

you did not shoot when you shot, but God shot, to let the believer experience good for himself" (Surah 8, Verse 17). Concerning those who were captured, God commands:

> O Prophet, say unto those captives who are in your hands: "If God knoweth any good in your hearts, He will give you better than that which hath been taken from you, and He will forgive you." (Surah 8, Verse 70)

The Koran similarly reflects Muslims' changing relationships with neighboring groups. It acknowledges other religions, venerates Jesus, Moses, and other Jewish and Christian prophets, and recognizes other "people of the Book." But, as historical conditions changed, the Koran's attitude toward "others" changed as well. After the *hijra*, Muslims' feelings toward the large Jewish community in Medina, for example, were initially very positive; God reveals that before the Koran "there was a Book of Moses, given as a guide and an act of mercy" (Surah 11, Verse 17). When tensions began to develop between Muslims and Jews, God forbids Muslims to feel close to Jews:

> O you who believe, do not choose those outside your community as intimate friends. They will spare no pains to corrupt you, longing for your ruin. From their mouths hatred has already shown itself and what their breasts conceal is greater. (Surah 3, Verse 118)

In 630 C.E., backed by a thousand followers, Muhammad finally returned in triumph to his birthplace, but forgiving rather than punishing the Quraysh who had not yet accepted Islam.[298] Entering the Kaaba, believed by the Quraysh to have been built by Abraham, he knocked each of the Kaaba's 360 idols with his spear, causing them to smash on the ground. He then ordered all of the wall paintings of false prophets to be washed away with water from the Zamzam well, which was known in the pre-Muslim period as the oasis that saved Ishmael and his mother Hagar from dying of thirst. With these acts, concludes Middle East commentator Sandra Mackey, "Muhammad raised the Kaaba to the central point of Islam. But he retained Medina as his political capital."[299] As Mackey's observation so concisely reflects, Islam has, almost from the first, assumed an authority both spiritual and temporal, not only ordering the believer's relationship with God but also regulating social and legal relationships among believers.

Muhammad died on June 8, 632, with his head in the lap of his favorite wife, Aisha, just two years after conquering Mecca. In the short span of slightly more than two decades, Muhammad had accumulated a substantial following and created new shared mental structures—providing for the basic needs of his followers, changing the simple forms of tribal life, establishing a patrilineal culture, strengthening the sense of individuality in a society where there had previously been little, establishing standards of law and justice, providing models for settling disputes, and laying the foundations for future Islamic cultural and military successes.[300] Now the relatively young *umma* in Arabia searched for a successor to the remarkable leader. Abu Bakr, Muhammad's father-in-law, was elected *Kalifa* (Caliph), which means "deputy" or "successor" of the Prophet. Assuming control over the Islamic army, Bakr exercised not only theological authority but also political power over the *umma*. Any tribe that rebelled was militarily subjugated. Already an old man, however, Bakr lived for only two years after Muhammad's death. From this time on, the office of the Caliph would be based on the model created by Bakr. Less than a century after the death of Muhammad, Arab Muslim armies had established a huge empire, stretching from India to Spain, and everywhere Islamic culture bloomed. But, after the fourth caliph's move from Mecca to a location in the northern part of the Arabian Peninsula and eventually to a site in modern-day Iraq, the governing body of Islamic power never returned to Mecca or Medina.

Theologians and historians divide the history of the Arab Caliphate from 632 until 1258 into several phases. The first four caliphs, from 632 to 661, belong to the Patriarchal Caliphate or the *Rashidun*, the "Rightly Guarded" caliphs, as they are sometimes called. They were followed by the Umayyad Caliphate (661-750), and then the Abbasid Caliphate (750-1258), whose capital was Baghdad. The Mongols killed the last Abbasid Caliph upon conquering Baghdad in 1258. During the reign (1512 to 1520) of the Ottoman Sultan Selim I, "the Grim, " the Turks took over Syria and Egypt, where another Abbasid had established himself; in 1517, the Arab Caliphates came to an end as the Ottoman sultan assumed the title and "inherited the role of the defender of the holiest places in Islam, the cities of Mecca and Medina, which were the cradle of Islam."[301] This double role of the Ottoman sultan as religious leader and political defender of the Islamic world lasted until the end of the Ottoman Empire. After World War I, the sultan escaped from Istanbul for his own safety, and the title of Caliph was passed to one of his relatives. This last caliph was stripped of his title when the Turkish Republic was established in 1923 as a secular, westernized nation. But the unity of Islam had actually been broken long before; there had been factions, bitter divisions, and regional power struggles almost from the very beginning.

The most important division had occurred after the fourth Caliph, Ali, Muhammad's cousin and son-in-law, was killed. A group of Muslims known as *Shi'ites* (from the Arabic *shiat Ali*, "the party of Ali") rejected the legitimacy of the first three Caliphs in the line of Muhammad. They accepted Muhammad as the Prophet and the Koran as divine revelation, but proposed their own interpretation of Koranic law. As Islamic studies scholar Denis MacEoin writes, Shi'ism "began as a politico-religious movement centered on the question of true authority within the community," further proof of the fact that there is little, if any, substantive "distinction between religion and politics in Islam."[302] Today, Shi'ites make up some 10 to 15 percent of the world's Muslim population, including most of Iran's Muslims. The majority of Muslims worldwide, however, are Sunni Muslims, whose traditions were established by the first Caliphs. Thus the Ottoman Turks had seized spiritual leadership only of Sunnis, about 88 to 90 percent of the Muslim world; when the Caliphate was abolished, the main head of the Sunni world was gone, though many regional and factional heads remained.

As a result, when, after September 11, the Western media searched for an authoritative voice from the Islamic world to condemn terrorism, it searched in vain. In some ways, it is because the religion lacks a central authority. As Emmanuel Sivan observed in 1985, "the Islamic establishment stands powerless ... subservient to governments, looking only for ways and means to justify the latter's actions."[303] Looking back, one wonders whether a Caliph or other transnational religious authority would have been able to respond to Islam's political decline since 1924 in ways that would have enhanced Muslim self-esteem and, therefore, left Muslims less vulnerable to various extreme fundamentalist movements. In fact, Islam experienced a sort of leaderless regression as described in Chapter 2: leaders would appear at various times, but none of them could capture the leadership role for the majority of Islam. The 1979 Iranian revolution was a reaction to this lack of leadership in Islam, as a group of Shi'ite Islamic reformers, whose ideas reflected nostalgia for an earlier period of Shi'ism, sought for religion to assume political power in that country. The *Dar al-Tabligh al-Islami* (Institute for the Propagation of Islam) was established in 1965,[304] fueling the development of a "religious counter-culture" in Iran[305] that intensified throughout the 1970s, as the U.S.-backed repressive Shah of Iran attempted westernization. By 1979, the Shah had been deposed and exiled, and the Ayatollah Khomeini had taken power in Iran with apocalyptic, millennial plans for a perfect theocracy.[306]

But the prestige of the Iranian revolution among other Muslims (especially among Sunnis) declined in the late 1980s as a result of economic mismanagement, widespread torture, executions, human rights violations, and the war between Iran and Iraq: "Iran was no longer a role model for Sunni radicals,"[307] who began to search for their own means to deal with both actual and perceived humiliations, frustrations, and felt or denied jealousy of the economic and technological riches of the West. Many Arab governments felt unstable in view of growing grassroots Islamic revivalist movements and their fundamentalist branches, such as the militant Egyptian Muslim Brotherhood organization. In Algeria, Egypt, Jordan, and Turkey, fundamentalists began to show electoral strength. Thus, when fundamentalists began to turn their aggression toward the United States, Israel, and the West in general, there appeared to be support—some direct, mostly indirect—for their actions from above: those in shaky government or royal offices preferred that the developing aggression did not turn toward them. Of course, the unresolved Palestinian issue continued to be a festering and humiliating wound that did not help to tame these aggressive feelings.

When we examine the group regressions of today's extremist, militant Islamic fundamentalists, it is immediately evident that they focus on the strategic prowess of the warrior Muhammad rather than the nurturing deeds of the caring Muhammad. In this choice, we may suppose, extreme fundamentalists feel like the "orphan" Muhammad: they want to strike out at those perceived to be the cause of their victimization and return to Koranic passages such as Surah 8, Verse 17, in order to imagine themselves as divine agents and thus not to feel remorse or guilt. They set aside, or even deny, the Prophet's ability to integrate various peoples into a new large-group identity, to love others, to show mercy, to believe in justice, to respect women, and to coexist with those holding other beliefs in favor of selective, absolutist readings of the Koran that emphasize an "us against them" psychology. These regressed groups pursue purification rituals such as the Taliban's destruction of the Bamian Valley Buddha statues (discussed in the last chapter), an echo of Muhammad's destruction of the idols in the Kaaba. They denigrate real women as perilously seductive, desiring women to exist only as caretakers of (orphaned) children. Female sexuality has to be hidden or appear only in the idealized angels (*houris*) of paradise.[308] They reinvoke the Prophet's promise of immortality to urge members to give their lives in "defense" of the group against perceived threats from without.[309] But, for those in malignant Islamic fundamentalist regressions, this time "the battle is not merely conquest, but annihilation of the enemy."[310]

In my 1997 book *Bloodlines: From Ethnic Pride to Ethnic Terrorism,* I reported that ethnic terrorist leaders about whom I had significant available data seemed to share an experience of early childhood mental or physical abuse.[311] Because of their flawed personal identity formations, I found, those who seek to become leaders of terrorist cells are also seeking to use their ethnic identities to patch up their personal identities. For such persons the canvas of the ethnic identity "tent" compensates for the wear and tear of their personal identity "garments." As leaders—the pole of the large-group identity tent—they want to be sure that the canvas remains in its proper place and does not collapse. For their own personal psychological reasons, then, such persons become preoccupied with their large-group identities instead of their own personal identities in order to hide the vulnerability of their personal identity formations: "Terrorist leaders [and] their lieutenants have a psychological need to 'kill' the victimized aspects of themselves and the victimizing aspects of their aggressors that they have externalized and projected onto innocent others."[312] I will not be surprised to discover that Osama bin Laden had a personal past similar to those I found among these ethnic terrorist leaders, though I must emphasize that at this point we can only speculate on the structure of his internal world.

Two biographies published prior to September 11, 2001[313] give us a glimpse of Osama bin Laden's developmental years; several facts suggest a strong possibility of chronic trauma in his early life. Bin Laden was born in 1956 or 1957, the son of a Saudi millionaire of Yemeni origin who had some 50 children with at least 10 wives and other partners. A poor man when he immigrated to Saudi Arabia in 1930, Mohammed bin Awad bin Laden became the extremely rich owner of the largest construction company in Saudi Arabia and eventually established ties with the members of the Saudi royal family. Osama was his father's 17th child, but this fact would not necessarily have been traumatic; rather, Mohammed bin Awad bin Laden's relationship with Osama's mother may have been one source of personal trauma. An article in the Spanish newspaper *El Correro*[314] claims (on the basis of an interview with a Spanish woman who participated in a summer program abroad with the 14-year-old Osama) that bin

Laden's mother was a concubine, rather than a wife, of his father;[315] this claim was confirmed to me in January 2002 by a source in American intelligence. A Saudi scholar I have interviewed, however, told me that bin Laden's mother should not be considered a concubine,[316] as a Muslim man in Saudi Arabia can have up to four legitimate wives: according to this informant, the elder bin Laden had divorced one of his four wives when he married Osama's mother, Hamida, which would have made her a "legitimate" wife. Nevertheless, Hamida's background and her relationship with her husband and his other wives indeed made her different, even if we cannot call her a concubine. It is not fully clear whether the elder bin Laden married 22-year-old Hamida because he had heard of her beauty or because such a marriage would help his business affairs in Syria:

> while visiting Damascus, Mohammed had come across her (Hamida), the daughter of a Syrian family with whom he had business links. Although Mohammed usually married Saudi women, entrenching himself within a society that he always felt looked down on him for his Yemeni roots, Hamida was stunning and her family were happy to marry her off quickly.[317]

The marriage quickly soured. In Mohammed's Saudi Arabian household, the Syrian wife was perceived as a stranger. Isolated, Hamida was known as *"Al Abeda"* (the slave"), and Osama, the only child of the marriage, was branded *"Ibn Al Abeda"* ("son of the slave").[318] We can easily imagine that, as a child, Osama was humiliated as his mother was humiliated. We can also surmise that Osama felt further traumatized when his father exiled his "concubine" or "slave" wife to a distant place in northern Saudi Arabia, while Osama, stayed in his father's main household in Saudi Arabia among other "mothers" and their natural children. I have no data about how the young Osama related to his surrogate mother, his father's first wife, or how he handled his probable humiliation or the separation from his biological mother. My hunch is that, since his father was a strict disciplinarian—there is evidence that Mohammed often beat his son and forced him to follow a strict religious and social code—Osama had to repress or deny any rage he likely felt in the midst of this personal upheaval.

When Osama was about 10 years old,[319] his father died in an air crash, bringing the 17th child an estimated 80 million dollars in inheritance.[320] After his father's death, a young uncle took over the bin Laden clan and Osama was sent to live with Hamida. Adam Robinson describes the prepubertal child's ambivalent reunion with his biological mother; soon Osama was writing to his uncle, asking to return to the more privileged household, even though he was probably still perceived as the "slave" woman's son there.

Osama's oldest brother, who was also involved in running the family business, tragically followed in Mohammed's footsteps when he died in a plane crash over San Antonio, Texas, in 1988. Though we lack information concerning Osama's reaction to this event specifically, there is some evidence[321] that, as a teenager, Osama drank a great deal and visited prostitutes before finding a surrogate father in Sheikh Abdullah Yusuf Azzam, a Palestinian Arab from the West Bank whom Osama met while the younger man was a student and the elder a teacher at Jeddah's King Abdul-Aziz University. The year after Osama's older brother died in a plane crash, Azzam, his "spiritual father," who had helped to crystallize Osama's fundamentalist religious beliefs, was assassinated in Pakistan.[322] We can easily imagine that bin Laden's "slave" or "distanced" mother, tyrannical father, and the violent deaths of his biological and spiritual fathers as well as his older brother have all played significant roles in setting the psychological foundations—including possible unconscious fantasies in which he identifies himself with the orphan Muhammad—that enabled him to become the leader of a terrorist organization and a hero to millions of extremist Muslims.

Though the specifics of those roles can only remain speculation until further information becomes available, Osama bin Laden obviously demonstrates a preoccupation with "getting even," often speaking publicly of historical events that he feels, on the conscious level, have hurt him personally. Bin Laden's public pronouncements clearly reflect what we know from clinical work as the almost unvarying psychological pattern of absolutist, pathologically vengeful people: "grudging, unforgiving, remorseless, ruthless, heartless, implacable, and inflexible ... liv[ing] for revenge with a single-mindedness of purpose."[323] Clinical research indicates that such individuals' capacity for love has been damaged in early childhood so that, instead of developing love for childhood caretakers and receiving pleasure from them, the child comes to wish for their pain and destruction. As adults, such individuals are especially sensitive to losses and tend to feel aggressive and vengeful, rather than sad or depressed, in response. At other times a sense of personal failure (which is also a kind of loss) may trigger the same feelings. As New York psychoanalyst Charles Socarides has written:

Passionately he moves toward punitive or retaliatory action—above all other desires is the one to "get even" (in effect, to get more than "even"). Whether he feels and acts from the conviction that he is engaged in "just retaliation" or "malicious retaliation," the clinical picture is identical.[324]

Even the least powerful of such individuals tend to unconsciously experience political leaders (in their own countries or elsewhere) as depriving and persecutory parent images. Accordingly, those leaders (and their countries) often become targets for revenge-driven individuals.[325]

Though we cannot yet determine bin Laden's personal unconscious motivations with certainty, we can nevertheless begin to situate his extremist ideology and the development of his career in psychohistorical context. Above all, bin Laden perceives the world as turned upside down by the victories of the West. Though he does not openly say that he feels humiliated, we know from clinical practice that vengefulness is one side of a coin, humiliation the other: from his open expressions of resentment, anger, and entitlement to revenge, then, we can deduce that bin Laden and those who share his views feel humiliated by the encroachment of Western culture and power across the globe.

Thus he has taken as his mission "getting even" in the name of God. Illuminating the specifically apocalyptic character of bin Laden's pattern of thought, historian Richard Landes notes, "[b]in Laden's narrative is not a story of the tides of civilization, but relentlessly cosmic in scope and urgent in rhetoric."[326] Indeed, it is clear from his various videotaped messages to the world that, in his role as an agent of God, bin Laden feels omnipotent, "a central player in a cosmic battle that pits the warriors for truth against the agents of Satan and evil in this world."[327] Bin Laden has repeatedly cited three historical events deserving of his divinely-sanctioned vengeance: the U.S. military "intrusion" into holy places in Saudi Arabia, U.S.-led United Nations sanctions upon Iraq (of course, prior to the U.S.-led invasion of Iraq) and subsequent suffering of Iraqi civilians, and U.S. support for Israel against Palestinian Arabs.

But he also goes back more than 80 years to the end of the Ottoman Empire and the abolition of the Caliphate—when (as he is reported to have said) "the Islamic world [fell] under the banners of the cross"[328]—as the symbol of his humiliation and that of the Islamic world.

Azzam, bin Laden's university mentor, had not only been a major supporter of the Afghan *mujahidin* resistance to Soviet invasion, but also had advocated a *jihad* to unify the Islamic world in a new empire under one ruling Caliph, which we can see as a millennial urge not unlike the Nazi dream of a "thousand-year Reich." After Azzam's death, bin Laden emerged as a leading propagandist for both causes. Azzam and bin Laden[329] were not alone in the desire to restore Islamic world leadership, it must be said. In Germany in 1995, Metin Kaplan, the leader of an Islamic cult of Turkish origin, declared himself the "Caliph of Cologne" after the death of his father. In 1998 Kaplan supporters tried to anticipate—unsuccessfully as it turned out—the perfect horror scenario of using a manned airplane to destroy a hated symbolic building, an idea that became a ghastly reality in September 2001: Turkish security forces foiled their attempt to fly an airplane into the Ataturk mausoleum in Ankara. According to the German Federal Office for the Protection of the Constitution, Metin Kaplan's organization has been associated with Osama bin Laden's for some time; Taliban representatives evidently visited Cologne in August of 1998, but the German authorities could find no evidence of money transfers between the groups, nor evidence of discussions about strategies of terrorist attacks. At the very least, Kaplan and bin Laden's goals were overlapping: while Kaplan was calling for a "liberation struggle" to create a "divine Islamic state," bin Laden sought to unite the most radical Islamist forces to establish his own worldwide Muslim community.[330] The money available for Kaplan's activities was limited, but bin Laden's seemingly unending financial resources permitted him wider range of action.

For extremist Islamists, Landes suggests, Muslim humiliations at the hands of the West are brought to "an unbearable intensity" by Israel's mere existence: "[being] conquered by a great power is one thing, [being] conquered by a subject people is intolerable."[331] Further, however, Israel is a key figure in the millennial imagination of bin Laden and those who think as he does: to this view, "the Nakbah (Catastrophe of 1948 [the founding of Israel]) was the Dajjal's (Satan's) forces at work. The West at a distance may have presented a threat, but Israel represented a desecrating cultural invasion."[332] The attack on the U.S., therefore, struck at the other pillar of Western evil; indeed, in the Islamist apocalyptic literature, "New York is the Whore of Babylon."[333]

How did bin Laden's millennialist Islamic fundamentalism come to hold such power in the nation of Afghanistan—whose people, British journalist Louis Palmer has written, "are not fanatics and never have been"[334]—that its leaders would rather suffer the full force of the mightiest military on earth than extradite him? (The Taliban, the *de facto* government of Afghanistan from 1996 to 2001, had twice rejected U.S. and UN requests to hand over bin Laden, rationalizing that bin Laden was considered their "guest."[335])

Foreign powers—including the U.S. and Britain, who, alarmed by the Soviet invasion of Afghanistan, were willing to foment Islamic fundamentalism in this part of the world in order to drive the communists from Afghanistan and weaken the USSR—were supporting the fundamentalists as their numbers grew along the border between Pakistan and Afghanistan. Under Zia-ul-Haq, American- and British-supported dictator of Pakistan from 1977 to 1989, the number and character of religious schools (*madrassahs*) grew dramatically from the 900 registered in 1971 to 8,000 registered (and thousands more unregistered) schools in 2000,[336] serving up to some one million students, mostly Pakistani and Afghan;[337] London-based journalist Tariq Ali calls "[t]he ascendancy of religious fundamentalism [Zia-ul-Haq's] legacy."[338]

Up to this point, such establishments had usually remained in the background while non-religious elites ran the government, military, and economy. The new *madrassahs*, however, produced a different kind of student, a "soldier-politician" devoted to a "purified" form of Islam. Most of these schools appeared in isolated, rural areas of Pakistan, close to the border camps of refugees from the war in Afghanistan, and were the primary sources of education for sons of poor families.[339] In the interest of fostering "pure" Islam, many wealthy Saudis also funneled money into Pakistan's madrassah system, matching the U.S. support drawn from the estimated 4 to 5 billion dollars it spent between 1980 and 1992 to aid the *mujahidin*.[340] Thus the *madrassahs* of Pakistan combined elements of the extremely conservative official religion of Saudi Arabia, Wahhabism,[341] and anticolonial Deobandi[342] ideology to create an extreme form of militant Islamic fundamentalism conveyed through even the most basic lessons: "The primers taught that the Urdu letter 'jeem' stood for jihad; 'tay' for tope (cannon), 'kaaf' for Kalashnikov, and 'khay' for khoon (blood)."[343]

The Taliban leader, Mullah Omar, was not a graduate of a Pakistani religious school, but the vast majority of his followers were: eight ministers in Omar's government, formed in Kabul in 1999, were graduates of the Haqqania *madrassah*, the most popular school of its type in Pakistan, which journalist Jeffrey Goldberg visited in 2000.[344] That year, it enrolled more than 2,500 students; the previous year it had turned away two-thirds of applicants for want of space.[345] Room and board was free at the Haqqania *madrassah* to a student body drawn mainly from the dire poor of Afghanistan and Pakistan as well as Kazakhstan, Tajikistan, Uzbekistan, and Chechnya. There Goldberg observed at close range the dissemination of extremist and militant fundamentalist propaganda to students ranging in age from 8 and 9 to 30, sometimes 35, concluding that "[t]he Haqqania madrasa is, in fact, a jihad factory."[346]

Students spend much of their day seated cross-legged on the floor in airless classrooms, memorizing the Koran. Since Arabic is the original language of the Koran, fundamentalists believe that it has to be studied in its original language as it was revealed by God. Thus, the Koran the students study is in Arabic, a language that they do not know, so they simply memorize the text without applying any critical faculty to evaluating it. This rote learning lasts up to three years. Older boys are in an eight-year course studying the interpretation of the Koran, the sayings of the Prophet Muhammad (the *hadith*), and religious rulings (*fatwas*), including the rules governing the waging of holy war. There are no science courses or studies in world history. Computers and television are absent. Students who are separated from their families never see a woman since there are no females present at the madrassah complex. In a sense, a "wall" is erected around these young people as they are taught that non-believers— Hindus, Jews, and especially Americans whose policies are supposedly dictated by Jewish Americans—are victimizing Muslims around the world. Goldberg writes that, strictly speaking, there were no weapons at the Haqqania *madrassah*, and no one there taught the students how to make bombs. What is taught, however, is a deep sense of victimization at the hands of "non-believers" and the corresponding *jihadist* ideology. This indoctrination is accompanied by rallying around images of "Talibanized" leaders and Osama bin Laden. When Goldberg asked the students, "Who wants to see Osama bin Laden armed with nuclear weapons?" every hand in the room is raised; some students applaud.[347] The students told Goldberg that bin Laden, the "guest" of Omar, "is a great Muslim ... wants to keep Islam pure from the pollution of infidels ... wants to bring Islam to all the world."[348] It was from such schools that the Taliban arose (the name of the movement itself meaning "students") to fill Afghanistan's post-Soviet power vacuum.

It seems to me that in Afghanistan there was a particularly "good fit" between a hurt and victimized country and a man whose extreme hate may be a reflection of personal pain and sense of victimization. Bin Laden first became interested in Afghanistan through his spiritual mentor, Azzam—who, impressed by the devotion and heroism of the *mujahidin*, had moved his family to Pakistan just one year after the Soviet invasion.

Already a father-figure to bin Laden, Azzam founded the *Bait-ul-Ansar* (*Mujahidin* Services House) in Peshawar, Pakistan, and supplied help to the Afghan opposition cause, including volunteers to fight. With his almost endless funds, Bin Laden followed Azzam's lead, becoming a leading financial supporter of the mujahidin and various other militant fundamentalist groups throughout the world. In the mid-1980s he and Azzam co-founded *Maktab al-Khidamat* (MAK), a group that sponsored bringing Muslims from many countries to fight the Soviet invasion of Afghanistan. After Azzam's death, bin Laden lived for five years in Sudan, from which he was expelled under Saudi pressure in 1996, the same year he publicly declared holy war on the United States: "We—with God's help—call on every Muslim who believes in God and wishes to be rewarded to comply with God's order to kill the Americans and plunder their money wherever and whenever they find it."[349] He then returned to Afghanistan, where he and Mullah Omar eventually became "friends." In this country utterly devastated by war and drought, the financial resources that bin Laden could provide must have been nearly irresistible to the ideologically sympathetic elite he had helped to create during the Soviet occupation as well as to those merely looking for any means of survival.

But how does a pathologically vengeful individual such as Osama bin Laden persuade other individuals to die *intentionally* for his politico-religious cause? Certainly the psychology of the suicide attacker is extremely puzzling, not least because he or she appears to choose suicide out of a seemingly very *high* level of self-esteem, whereas in routine clinical work mental health professionals see people who wish or attempt to kill themselves because they have low self-esteem and suffer from intense feelings of guilt.

Suicide attacks have been carried out by people who are not Muslims. For example, the Tamil Tigers are Hindus and they have carried out more suicide missions than Muslim extremists. Kamikaze pilots of Japan were not Muslims either. I first began to consider the psychology of Palestinian suicide bombers when, at a Palestinian orphanage in Tunis, I met five children who were survivors of the Sabra and Shatila massacre in Lebanon.[350] On September 15, 1982, Israel Defense Forces encircled Sabra and Shatila, two adjacent Palestinian refugee camps, in West Beirut. In the late afternoon of the following day, the Lebanese Christian Phalangist militia, allied with Israel, attacked the camps, indiscriminately killing civilians trapped in the cramped streets. It is estimated that 2,750 refugees were killed that day in what is surely one of the most barbarous events of recent decades. Subsequently, the Israeli government arranged a commission of inquiry which found eight Israeli political leaders, including then-prime minister Menachem Begin and Ariel Sharon, the present prime minister, guilty of "indirect responsibility" in the massacre.

As my colleagues and I entered the walled yard of the converted gyne-cological hospital that now housed the *Biet Atfal al-Sommoud* orphanage in Tunis, I noticed many children playing soccer; five younger children, however, huddled near the entrance to the main building. They appeared to be a "team" and were so intensely involved with one another that they failed to notice the visitors. We soon learned their story: they had been infants living at Sabra and Shatila when the carnage occurred. From what I could gather, their mothers or other adults had saved their lives by hid-ing them—one under a bed, the other four in trash cans. Their real iden-tities were unknown, so they had all been given the last name "Arafat," after the PLO chairman, who was a regular visitor to Biet Atfal al-Sommoud. Over our several visits to the orphanage, I observed the five Sabra and Shatila children as often as I could. The "Arafat" children appeared "normal" when they were all together, but if one were separated from the group and addressed as a separate individual, he or she would become destructive and agitated: when we attempted once to interview one of the five alone in the director's office, he literally attacked the direc-tor's furniture. They did not know how to be individuals. To me, these five children came to be emblematic of the process of replacing a person's individual identity to a great degree with the large-group identity.[351]

But I observed a milder version of this phenomenon in all of the 52 children housed at the orphanage. Those who had some connection with the image of their dead parents, such as specific memories or objects, fared better.[352] For those who lacked actual contact, their large-group iden-tity tended to supercede their individual identities. Whether or not they were Aysha or Hamid with specific desires and fears had become a lesser fact hidden behind the main fact that they were part of "one unit" or "a team" of victimized Palestinians.[353] The children's individual interests took a backseat to the group's feelings of revenge against its enemy, and they became preoccupied with raising their large group's self-esteem. Their lives at night as separate individuals—replete with nightmares and bed-wetting episodes—were more tragic than their lives during the day, when they were all together singing songs of victimization, watching trauma-tized Palestinian children in occupied territories on television, or playing soccer.

Let me be clear: this orphanage was not a "*jihad*-factory," and the children who lived there were not subject to propaganda promoting military or paramilitary violence. The director, herself badly traumatized, was a kind woman, and the orphanage's sole purpose was to provide a loving home for abandoned and orphaned children. But the orphanage was nonetheless a symbol of Palestinian suffering, victimization, and anger, and the children living there responded to this fact: the most common "when I grow up" fantasy among them, especially among the boys, was the desire to become pilots who could bomb Israel. Through no fault of their own or of their caretakers, the internal psychological mechanisms by which these children's large-group identity overcame their personal identities mirrored those by which German youngsters became bound to Nazi ideology and identity, as I described in Chapter 2: they had little or no basis for basic trust. They had no personal family images (except, possibly, fantasized images) with which to identify in the process of developing solid core personal identities; they had only group images to internalize and so community identity dominated their core identities.[354] What the Nazi regime had done intentionally to its children, historical trauma had done to these youngsters.

Nevertheless, this is precisely the main factor, I have found, in successfully "creating" suicide attackers: to replace or suppress the person's individual identity and to replace or dominate it with the large-group identity. In clinical practice, we sometimes see a similar phenomenon in isolated individual cases: a youngster who cannot maintain a cohesive sense of personal identity may become psychotic and have religious hallucinations, such as believing he or she is the reincarnation of an old religious leader. In such cases, the psychotic person replaces their damaged personal identity with an identity that is "made up" and obviously false to outsiders. But suicide bombers are not psychotic: in their cases, the created identity fits *well* with the external reality and is *approved* by outsiders. Thus, future suicide bombers feel normal, and often experience an enhanced sense of self-esteem. They become, in a sense, spokespeople for the traumatized community and assume that they, at least temporarily, can reverse the shared sense of victimization and helplessness by expressing the community's rage.

But precisely *how* can a person's large-group identity be made to supercede his or her individual identity? In the past, *before* suicide bombing became endemic to the second *intifada*, the technique for creating suicide bombers in the Palestinian territories typically included two basic elements: 1) finding people whose personal identities are already disturbed and who are seeking a second identity to stabilize their internal worlds; and 2) forcing the large-group identity, whether ethnic or religious, into the cracks of the persons' damaged or subjugated individual identities.[355] Once people are "educated" for suicide attacks, the ordinary "rules and regulations" of individual psychology no longer apply to their patterns of thought and action. Killing one's self (one's personal identity) and others (enemies) does not matter; what matters is that the act of terrorism brings self-esteem and attention to the group: the psychological priority is the repair and/or enhancement of the large-group identity (through a sadistic and masochistic act), which actually enhances the suicide bomber's modified personal identity because other members of the traumatized community have come to see him or her as the carrier, the agent, of the group's identity. Though Islam expressly forbids suicide, there is no lack of conscious or unconscious approval of Palestinian suicide bombers from at least some other members of their communities: in early 1996, only 20 percent of Palestinians supported the practice; recently, about 70 percent do.[356] A poll conducted by the Palestinian Center for Public Opinion (PCPO) after the May 2001 Netanya suicide bombing showed that 76 percent of the Palestinians participating in the survey supported this act.

Most Palestinian suicide bombers in the Middle East are chosen as teenagers, "educated," then sent off to perform their duty when they are in their late teens or early to mid-twenties. It appears that the "education" is most effective when the individual can replace personal senses of helplessness, shame, and humiliation with religious elements of the large-group identity, as internalizing the divine makes a person feel omnipotent and supports their self-esteem. Typically, the "education" of the young Palestinian candidates for suicide attacks was carried out in small groups.[357] Sometimes good candidates are educated quickly, but more often these groups read the Koran together and chant religious scriptures. Unlike most of the Pakistani and Afghan students in Pakistani *madrassahs*, Palestinian suicide attack trainees were able to understand what they are reading in the Arabic Koran, but for this reason their readings are carefully curtailed. For example, here is a passage from the Koran that seems to justify turning what historian Lewis has called "Muslim rage"[358] on a Western world perceived as ranged against Islam:

> Allah does not forbid you to deal justly and kindly with those who fought not against you on account of religion nor drove you out of your homes. Verily, Allah loves those who deal with equity. ... It is

only as regards to those who fought against you on account of religion, and have driven you out of your homes, and helped to drive you out, that Allah forbids you to befriend them ... (Surah 60, Verses 8 and 9)

The "teachers" also supply mystical-*sounding* phrases to be repeated over and over in chant, such as, "I will be patient until patience is worn out from patience." These kinds of "mystical" (but actually nonsensical) sayings, combined with selective reading of the Koran, create an alternate reality.

Meanwhile, the "teachers" interfered with the "real-world" affairs of their students, mainly by cutting off meaningful communication and other ties to students' families and by forbidding things which may be sexually stimulating, such as music and television. Suicide bomber candidates are instructed not to inform their parents of their missions. No doubt parents in this part of the world often surmise what their children's missions are, but, regardless, keeping secrets from parents and family members helps create a sense of power within the youngsters: such secrets induce a false sense of individuation and symbolize the cutting of dependency ties, which are supposedly replaced as the youngster becomes a "flag" for the large group.[359] The "teachers" then turn the trainees' attention to the heavens and convince them that their sexual and dependency needs will be fulfilled by houris (angels) in paradise once they become martyrs. Sex and women, the students are promised, can be obtained after a kind of passage to adulthood—but in this case the "passage" is killing oneself. The death of a suicide bomber was honored at a "wedding ceremony," a celebration at which friends and family gather to proclaim their belief that the dead terrorist is in the loving hands of angels in heaven.

Repeated actual and expected events humiliate youngsters and interfere with their adaptive identifications with their parents when they are humiliated as well. Feelings of helplessness and dehumanization help to create cracks in individual identities, and those who select "bomber candidates" develop a certain expertise in determining when personal identity cracks are most suitable for filling with elements of the large-group identity. In the Palestinian context, youngsters who have experienced immediate, concrete trauma—a beating, torture, loss of a parent, and so on—are thought to be more suitable candidates than those suffering more generalized trauma.[360] I have already shown how the more the large group identity-tent is shaken—the more stress is placed on a large group—the more the people under that tent will be inclined to wear the shared canvas as their main identity garment. Therefore, the more a community feels under stress, humiliated and helpless, the more easily "normal" people can be pushed to become candidates for terrorism. I believe that this has taken place among Palestinians. Mohammed Dahlan, former head of Palestinian Preventive Security in the Gaza Strip, reflected this process when he told an Israeli reporter, "I can put out a table to sign people up at the Rafah roadblock and in two minutes I'll have 200 suicide bombers. Once it was difficult to persuade people to commit suicide. Today everyone wants to. Don't you people understand that?"[361]

As the American press reported in the wake of September 11, the attacks seemed to upset the existing "profile" of the standard Palestinian suicide bomber. Those belonging to this supposed "new breed" of suicide bomber were generally older and well-educated, and generally came from wealthy, educated families exposed to a Western style of living, whereas the standard suicide attacker is a young, uneducated malcontent who comes from a poor family. In many ways, the hijackers of September 11, such as the alleged ringleader Mohammed Atta, do appear to belong to a group distinct from the Palestinian suicide bombers described above. But I believe that the mechanisms I have described apply to these better-educated, wealthier men as well. Of course, we cannot be certain until more data becomes available about the lives of Atta and the other hijackers, but I suspect that, despite their apparent privilege, they too were subject to psychological traumas that cracked their personal identities, and that historical conditions led them as well to choose to fill those cracks with large-group identity (extremist fundamentalist Muslim, specifically al Qaeda), and to submit to an absolute leader (bin Laden) whom they perceived to be the spokesperson for this identity and for the "true" Muslim faith.[362]

Bin Laden's al Qaeda—meaning "base," as in military base—appears to share most of the basic elements of extremist fundamentalist group regression listed at the end of the last chapter. But there are at least two major differences between bin Laden's organization and other, more "routine" extreme fundamentalist groups. The main difference is the vast amount of money that was (and presumably still is) available to al Qaeda, making the group more like a giant transnational corporation with a CEO, directors, technical assistants, and associated "companies."[363] As a result, though al Qaeda maintains symbolic and psychological borders against others, the "infidels," its physical borders are hard to define: the organization apparently has quasi-independent "cells" of followers in at least 43 countries around the world. We now know that, in the past, followers from many countries came to be trained in camps in

Afghanistan;[364] the followers returned to their homelands or elsewhere, primed for terror and sometimes given selected signature operations. The second difference is that the strong pessimism that characterizes most extreme religious groups is repressed, probably as a result of the string of "successes" it has accumulated.[365]

Excerpts from a rough translation of a four-page document left behind by some of the September 11 hijackers illuminated at least one small corner of al Qaeda's training and command practices.[366] Besides matter-of-fact advice about concealing their true identities, the document also contained selected references from the Koran that seem to give permission for suicide and to sanction killing enemies in the name of God as well as "religious" instructions that referred specifically to a happy afterlife with the angels. Between the lines we can see how these instructions create a ritual that mixes "God's words" with practical instruction in mass murder. "Tightening one's shoes," "washing," and "checking one's weapons"—above and beyond their functional aspects for mission preparations—are easy tasks to perform without much internal conflict; the instructions for "cleaning" and removing grime, filth, mud, and stains (above and beyond their religious significance as requirements before praying to—or meeting—God) balance against the instructions for the actual "dirty work" of killing oneself, the passengers and crew aboard the plane, and the people in the target building. Thus the steps from leaving one's apartment to hijacking and crashing an airplane have been ritualized and made psychologically easy. Of course, we do not know how consciously the hijackers' trainers strategized the instruction of their underlings, but to my mind these instructions alone demonstrate a certain mastery of psychologically effective ritual.

As I have discussed in prior chapters, shared anxiety may lead to societal regression and the use of shared psychological defenses. And, as we saw in the example of the Branch Davidian-FBI standoff, the psychological interactions between groups in conflict can bear powerfully on the escalation of those conflicts. So we must examine the American public's psychological responses to the terrorist attacks on New York and Washington, D.C.

As expected after such a tragedy, there would be an obligatory "average expectable" regression and this initially happened as the shared sense of vulnerability set in. U.S. citizens rallied dramatically around the central leader, as evidenced by the extraordinarily high approval ratings accorded George W. Bush in the weeks and months following the disaster. Within hours of the attacks an American chosen trauma, Pearl Harbor, had been reactivated to help make sense of the one at hand. The slogan "United We Stand" appeared on popular bumper stickers and common billboards across the country; the flag became somewhat protosymbolic. We also developed an emotional sensitivity regarding physical borders, especially the borders of the nation itself. In certain circles, especially among Christian fundamentalists, magical thinking appeared that read the tragedies as divine punishment for the "sinful acts" of homosexuals, feminists, and civil libertarians in the U.S. In some segments of the populace, the tendency to erase differences between Muslims and lump them all into the same category increased. Some Americans even became involved in acts of violent "purification" against those who supposedly resembled the enemy.

But in this "average expectable" regression, despite the specter of additional attacks, there has been no massive interruption of family relations or basic trust. Any loss of individuality remained well within the realm of the non-pathological, as it did not exceed feelings of patriotism, emotional closeness to others, and preoccupation with the tragedy. Nor did Americans, as a group, remained helpless and passive in the face of the attacks. Indeed, the U.S. government has responsibly made a number of efforts, including President Bush's early visit to a Washington, D.C., mosque, to stem any malignant impulses toward acts of racist "purification" directed toward people who simply looked like the enemy. And the President's appeal to American children to donate one dollar each to Afghan children probably not only minimized "purification" impulses in children, but also alleviated a sense of helplessness in society's most psychologically vulnerable population by involving them in actively helping others.

Still, the anthrax cases (not yet resolved) and ongoing warnings of possible terrorist attacks continue to make it difficult for the public to differentiate between legitimate fear of actual danger and fantasized anxiety, an inability which can especially poison a society's atmosphere. The rally around the President Bush and his administration has made it difficult to question the leadership's methodology in the "war on terror," which has reflected (above and beyond realistic security measures) a rigidified "morality" (another sign of regression, as we have seen in earlier chapters) that has surfaced most prominently around civil liberties questions. Following the September 11 attacks, the U.S. Department of Justice detained hundreds of immigrants, refusing to identify them, and instituted a "voluntary interview" process of Middle Eastern and Arab men living

here legally; debates about secret military tribunals for the trial of suspect-
ed terrorists, rather than open court trials come to our attention. Before
the Senate Judiciary Committee, Attorney General John Ashcroft defiant-
ly testified that "criticism of the Administration's investigative methods is
designed to 'scare peace-loving people with phantoms of lost liberty.'"[367]
President Bush has repeatedly demonized bin Laden as "the evil one,"
linking the enemy with Satan, and the rhetoric of other members of the
Administration has periodically dehumanized the hijackers as well as
Taliban followers. Bush's ill-advised initial branding of the "war on terror"
as a "crusade" and his advocacy of prayer as a "shield of protection against
the evil"[368] have in a sense brought religion into the political realm. Such
speech and policymaking unfortunately reflect an "us-and-them" division
that not only interferes with attempts to understand the terrorists' psychic
reality, but also mirrors extremist Islamists' union of religion and politics.
Moreover, such "us-and-them" divisions are unnecessary to effectively
prosecuting the necessary security and military responses to the attacks.

Such actions and language at home had considerable impact around
the globe. Some Muslim media report that the United States perceives
Islam as a pack of self-contradictory absolutes and in turn emphasize that
Western post-industrial society itself juggles two irreconcilable absolutes:
democracy and capitalism. While democracy strives for human equality,
they argue, capitalism thrives on a non-democratic inequality, and U.S.
democracy has been hijacked by the maneuvering of capitalists for their
own selfish interests.[369] The further devastation of an already ruined
Afghanistan and the deaths of an estimated 3,767 civilians (as reported in
Pakistani newspapers in late December 2001) in American bombing raids
on Afghanistan received relatively little attention in the U.S. media, but
made headlines in newspapers around the world. Especially in Pakistan
and the Middle East, some were only too happy to point out that this is
roughly the same number as were killed in the September 11 terrorist
attacks. Others pointed out that the U.S. government actions to curtail
civil liberties may seem to license undemocratic leaders who will not hes-
itate to declare their political opponents "terrorists."[370] We even heard
vague threats of using nuclear weapons on "undesirable/terrorist/others"
and rhetoric such as "axis of evil."[371] These could be considered examples
of a powerful nation's use of propaganda to scare its enemies, but they
also reflect U.S. leadership's support for societal regression. This is, in my
opinion, unfortunate: a different approach, one that acknowledges and
addresses the complexity of world affairs while still realistically protecting
Americans would enrich humane values and promote nonviolence.

Then came the preoccupation with Saddam Hussein and an emphasis on his weapons of mass destruction and statements directly or indirectly connecting him with al Qaeda. Through political propaganda, a formidable enemy was created. This, in turn, began to be a steady source for anxiety among the American population. A "wounded" superpower needed to strike out again, after the war in Afghanistan. "Islam" also became, in general, a word to define an enemy like a dark cloud which may come over the skies of the United States with deadly lightning power. The image of September 11 and the vulnerability it created have become a "psychic reality" that could not be put into the past. Since such a vicious and dramatic event *did occur* in reality it became very difficult to differentiate fantasy from reality for future disasters on American soil. The American leadership, instead of helping to separate what is real from what is fantasized, did the opposite. The reality of the need to protect the American borders completely discarded the poisonous effects of the border psychology I described earlier. As a superpower we needed to make our security measures "perfect."

Concurrent with all this, the "Bush doctrine" evolved, crystallizing the pre-existing theories in favor of preemptive strike. September 11 became a catalyst for putting this "doctrine" into practice. Since Saddam Hussein in reality was a horrible dictator with bloody hands he was an excellent target to attract hostility and the American's wish for revenge. Meanwhile "Islam" as an abstract dehumanized concept became equal to "evil" in the minds of the common man in the street. The idea of losing our sons and daughters in a war and killing thousands of civilians became acceptable. The rationalization was that it was alright to destroy a large group of people and induce unbearable grief to give them "democracy" and change the political nature of the Middle East, secure Israel's existence, and of course protect the flow of the oil.

The initial "average expectable regression" in a slow and silent way became similar to the regressive philosophy of Islamic religious fundamentalists: "We are absolutely right and thus special, divine and omnipotent. But we are under attack. Therefore, we are entitled to attack those who are 'evil.'" I will illustrate this analogy by referring to well-known psychoanalytic terms: the id, ego, and superego. If we consider bin Laden's and Saddam's activities as an expression of primitive impulses (id), the American response can be considered as divinely and omnipotently punitive (superego). What was lost was the ego functions that attempt to tame emotions and do not dehumanize and divide people into categories. In short, ego functions work for furthering the evolution of civilization.

Certainly, the terrorists are a real threat—and there are dangers still to come. One has to be deaf and blind not to know it. Still, a purely superego response derails any possibility of advancing civilization.

When "Gods" are involved in human group conflict, tragedies follow. Because "Gods" do not negotiate, "they" give permission to destroy the "evil." The war on terror and the war in Iraq have raised many questions not only about the personalities and psychological make-up of Osama bin Laden and Saddam Hussein, but also the personalities of Western political leaders, such as President George W. Bush. We must first wait for the tread of history to take its course; when the dust settles, the role that President Bush's personality has played in the setting of Administration policy will be seriously studied. But in Part 3, I will raise the question: "How much of a role does the personality of a political leader play in poisoning or healing large-groups and the human condition?"

/ part three: leadership and personality

6 / "a decisive trifle"

Cell growth and multiplication are normal processes which can advance to the point of malignancy. Ambition and power can similarly grow wild and proliferate, as much out of control as a malignant tumor into the body or a mushroom cloud into a placid atmosphere. Mastery and control can range from benign to oppressive, from a good master to an evil dictator.

—Leo Rangell, *The Mind of Watergate*

David Ben-Gurion, considered the "father" of the state of Israel, once asked Israeli historian Yehoshua Arieli whether the personalities of political leaders were important in history. Thoughtfully, Arieli began to answer: "Well, it depends on many factors: the times, historical conditions, the social and political system, and, of course, the individual's stature in government." If the leader possessed the drive to be a leading figure in public affairs, Arieli continued, "if he concentrated his influence into political power that was welded to his leadership, and if, in this way, he arrived at the highest position in public affairs during a period of crucial decisions ... then, yes, the personality of the leader would play a crucial role in shaping his nation's fate." But even before Arieli could finish his answer, Ben-Gurion brusquely interrupted: "I disagree! History is made by the nation, not by leaders!"[372]

By now, it may go without saying that I would have taken Arieli's side in his dramatic encounter with the legendary Israeli leader; as Israeli historian Tuvia Frilling once remarked to me: "A leader like Ben-Gurion may be compared to a locomotive that not only pulls the whole train but also determines its direction."[373] As to why Ben-Gurion would wish to diminish the influence of his personality on the creation of the state of Israel, I cannot say. Among other factors, his thinking was probably influenced by the theory of *Realpolitik* (the politics of real things), which focuses on "practical politics" in the balance of power between opposing parties, and

171

by its intellectual progeny, so-called "rational-actor" models of international and domestic politics, which analyze political decisions as "deduced from evidence and inferences made with minimum emotion" and political processes as "dominated by logical reasoning."[374]

Leaders do rationally process a great deal of data and information—including what they perceive to be the national interests, the will of the public, the designs of foreign enemies, and domestic opposition—in the process of making decisions about policy and propaganda in international and domestic affairs. In fact, on many occasions, when there are few alternatives before the leader and the available information is concise and accurate, the issues at hand may be handled without the interference of psychological factors; when the decision-maker's internal world is calm, rational-actor models can be sufficient to explain his or her choices, and there is little need to probe hidden psychological influences. However, when political decisions are made under especially complex or stressful conditions for the leader or for the large group he or she leads, rational models of political decision-making often fall short of satisfactory explanation. At such times, the leader consciously or unconsciously is forced to focus on the protection and maintenance of the large-group identity. Thus the leader inflames or tames large-group regression and mobilizes old large-group rituals or initiates new ones, some of which—such as purification rituals—may lead to destructive events.

Furthermore, when leaders' internal worlds are agitated, their macropolitical decisions can become "personalized"—that is, leaders may unconsciously equate the political or diplomatic circumstances at hand with an unresolved personal conflict, or may otherwise be influenced by personal desires and inhibitions, strong emotions, and unconscious fantasies. Indeed, in certain critical moments, a single person's psychological make-up can definitively shape historic decisions with long-ranging consequences—even in countries such as the United States, where governmental systems of checks and balances substantially protect political processes from being influenced by individual leaders' personalities.[375] It is in such moments that a leader's personality proves to be what the distinguished political theoretician Robert Tucker has called "a *decisive* trifle."[376]

Since psychology-ignoring Realpolitik and rational-actor models do remain the dominant way of looking at international relationships, however, let us consider in a bit more detail what is meant by these terms before turning to how a leader's personality influences mass processes.

The origins of modern political "realism," or Realpolitik, can be traced to those who reacted against Romantic idealism in the mid-nineteenth century, including German anti-liberal commentator August Ludwig von Rochau, who advised politicians to base their decisions on what an enemy or ally *really* wanted, not what they *said* they wanted, and to use force when necessary to support one's own objectives or to thwart someone else's.[377] Following the spectacular success of Realpolitik practitioner Otto von Bismarck (1815–1898), architect and first Chancellor of the German Empire, realism dominated political thinking for the next century. International relations scholar John A. Vasquez suggests that Realpolitik's tenacity in the twentieth century was a direct result of the failure of Woodrow Wilson and other "idealists" to prevent World War I:

> [I]dealists were perceived as exaggerating the influence of reason by assuming a fundamental harmony of interests, when in fact, according to realists, there are often conflicts of interest that can only be resolved by a struggle for power.[378]

Though the idealist-realist debate persisted through the decades between the wars, the 1940s saw that dispute decisively resolved in favor of realism, which would dominate much Cold War-era theory and practice. Hans J. Morgenthau's 1948 work, *Politics Among Nations*, is especially noted as widely influential in this period.

Generally classified as "rational-actor models," mid-twentieth century Realpolitik-influenced theories of international relations shared the premise that policy decisions and propaganda efforts are based on the logical calculation of interests, costs, benefits, and potential outcomes. These models also generally held that such calculations result in the greatest good. Dominant in political analysis in the United States at the height of the Cold War, this conceptualization of political decision-making was even nicknamed the "American Model," and most American political analysts assumed that other developed countries also used this paradigm.[379] Although its name implies cool, logical, and clear thought processes, the rational-actor models actually made a number of working assumptions about human behavior. The first was that decision-makers develop preferences and make choices based on circumstances that they perceive rationally. Second, it assumed that variation in outcomes depends solely on the options available to the decision-maker—that cultural differences do not affect the options that appear "available" to the decision-maker. Its third assumption was that the state or political entity behaves as a single actor, and that neither modifications in personnel—including leaders and members of the leaders' entourage—nor previous patterns of decision-making or bureaucratic politics come into play in the decision-making process.[380] Over time, all of these assumptions have been disputed from within the discipline itself, but these initial challenges still gave little weight to psychological factors. In 1959, for example, political scientist and economist Charles Lindblom introduced the "incremental model," which tried, without reference to depth psychology, to explain how a decision-maker deals with uncertainty and complexity in approaching promising alternatives.[381] In 1967, Amitai Etzioni proposed what he called "mixed scanning," a combination of rational-actor and incremental models.[382]

Graham T. Allison, another powerful early dissenter, noted in 1971 that during the Cuban Missile Crisis, neither John F. Kennedy's decisions nor those made by Soviet leaders appeared to follow a standard rational-actor model. Allison recognized that decisions could be based not only on rational calculation, but also on bureaucratic politics and organizational and "intra-national" processes.[383] He and Morton Halperin observed

> not only … that individuals within nations do the acting, but also … that the satisfaction of players' interests are to found overwhelmingly at home. Political leaders of a nation rise and fall depending on whether they satisfy domestic needs. Individuals advance in the bureaucracy when they meet the standards set by political leaders or by career ladders.[384]

Allison and Halperin concluded that an "organizational process model" best explained U.S. decision-making during the Cuban Missile Crisis: although major decisions were made collectively by the Executive Committee of the National Security Council, actions were determined substantially by standard operating procedures and established routines. Acknowledging that different organizations have different modes of customary performance, Allison and Halperin noted that some organizations make decisions by "fractionating" them—such that problems are not seen in their entirety or context—rather than by re-evaluating new input. The presence of a Soviet submarine found lurking close to U.S. shores, for instance, had been handled according to the Navy's standard operating procedures, applicable to a variety of circumstances concerning a hostile presence, rather than in the larger context of United States–Soviet relations.

Although Allison and others sought to reconceptualize political decision-making processes, the rational-comprehensive/rational-actor model remained the preferred framework of political analysis during the 1970s and 1980s and beyond. The so-called "deterrence" theories characteristic of Cold War-era scholarship and practice depended on the assumption of rational calculation; since they seemingly prevented nuclear war and generally helped to manage relations between sovereign states, there seemed to be little reason to change.[385] But policies based on deterrence also have failed on occasion, especially in regional conflicts. On Yom Kippur (October 6) 1973, for instance, Egyptian President Anwar Sadat surprised both Israeli and U.S. military intelligence by launching a massive attack on Israel across the Suez Canal. Based on rational calculations of deterrence, policy analysts did not believe that an Egyptian offensive could be launched before 1975, and so regarded the Egyptian troop movements reported in September 1973 as mere exercises. Thus Egyptian forces were able to overrun poorly manned Israeli defenses and drive deep into the Sinai, though Sadat's army ultimately suffered heavy losses before a ceasefire was declared later that year. Israel's air superiority and credible commitment to engage fully any attacker "should" have provided an effective deterrent,[386] but Sadat was not deterred. In the long run, the Yom Kippur War initiated the process of returning the Sinai to Egypt.

The profound influence of the rational-actor assumption naturally has made collaboration between political and behavioral science difficult. However, in the late 1970s and early 1980s, as the shortcomings of various rational-actor models became increasingly evident, some political scientists—and even some government decision-makers and diplomats— began to borrow concepts from cognitive psychology to explain "faulty" decision-making. They did not look to psychoanalysis for insights, despite the significant precedent in the pioneering work of Harold Lasswell, who had closely linked psychoanalysis with political science as early as 1930 in his formulation *P=pdr: political behavior* equals *private motives* becoming *displaced* onto public causes and *rationalized* in the public interest.[387] Eventually, the influence of cognitive psychology expanded studies of political analysis, political decision-making, propaganda, and techniques of influence by recognizing the significance of "molding experiences" and belief systems in both governance and diplomatic decisions as well as in public opinion.[388] According to this view, leaders and other political decision-makers—like all other human beings—are limited by their own experiences and by the way their perceptions are structured; they cannot possibly engage in complete evaluations of all possible options. In other words, humans interpret new information in the context of a particular cluster of values, ideas, and historical memories, and the inherently partial nature of such belief systems often results in distorted logic and defective causal reasoning.[389]

As they do today, cognitive psychologists of the 1970s and 1980s sought to "scientifically" study political decision-making and methods of mass influence, searching for "hard evidence" of the nature of propaganda and the causal factors behind political, diplomatic, and military decisions. It was almost immediately clear, however, that cognitive psychologists had difficulty achieving the desired level of "scientific" precision because they focused so exclusively on conscious processes. As far back as 1977, Irving Janis and Leon Mann acknowledged the relevance of *unconscious* motivations in their application of cognitive concepts in understanding decision-making:

> For ethical as well as technical reasons, the investigator is rarely able to introduce into a laboratory setting a decisional conflict sufficiently intense to trigger deep-seated unconscious motives. If the study of unconscious motives and defense mechanisms that affect decision-making is to proceed, it is necessary to take account of other types of research, including psychoanalytic observation in intensive case studies.[390]

It was during the same year that Janis and Mann published this observation that Anwar Sadat's Knesset address implicitly summoned psychiatrists and psychologists to investigate the psychology of Arab-Israeli relationships, which I mentioned in the introduction to this book.[391] Psychoanalysts, however, generally ignored such "invitations" until the American Psychiatric Association (APA)'s Committee on International Affairs initiated its series of unofficial psychopolitical dialogues between Arabs and Israelis. Though each delegation included psychoanalysts and psychoanalytically-influenced psychiatrists, many representatives came from diplomatic and political backgrounds, and there were two former diplomats among the American facilitators as well.[392] Thus a handful of psychoanalysts came to work side-by-side with diplomats and political scientists as well as with individuals of great political clout and high-level military authority.

After this brief review about rational-actor models, I can now return to examine the influence of leaders' personalities on massive movements.

Until this chapter, I have concentrated on the concept of identity in order to analyze the intertwining of personal and large-group affiliations in relations between nations and other large-group communities. As I turn to the question of how an individual leader's personal psychology can play a role in political processes, however, I will be using the concept of *personality* instead of identity. Think of identity and personality as two sides of the same coin: when an individual perceives him or herself, it is called "identity"; when another person observes the outward expressions of this identity, it is called "personality." Whereas identity is the individual's subjective sense of his or her own inner sameness, personality comprises an individual's habitual behavior, thinking and feeling patterns, modes of speech, and physical gestures: the observable and predictable patterns that an individual uses regularly—consciously or not—to maintain harmony in relationships with others and to create a routine and stable existence. In order to understand how a person perceives his or her own consistent internal sameness (identity), one needs to develop an intimate and meaningful relationship with that person, such as the relationship that develops between analysts and their analysands. This is, for obvious reasons, difficult to achieve with most political leaders—although, when sufficient data is available, psychoanalysts can write sophisticated psychobiographies of leaders whom they have never met.[393] On the other hand, an outside observer can "see" another person's personality without needing to know specifics about the person's personal history and internal world.[394] In this chapter and the following ones, then, I will not be providing a full examination of leaders' internal worlds: I am not offering in-depth psychobiographical investigations. Rather, I will note a number of leaders' observable personality characteristics and investigate limited areas of their psychologies that may explain their effects on international relations and on the lives of many.

At the same time, we must remember what political theorist and Stalin biographer Robert Tucker observes: in considering the role of personality in leadership, it is insufficient "to examine [the leader's] personality in as systematic and insightful a way as possible":

> It is [necessary], in addition, to delve into those linkages and interactions of personality with social milieu and political situation which alone made it possible for the personal factor to become historically important in a given case.[395]

Thus, for Tucker, comprehending the events of Joseph Stalin's Soviet Union requires considering the complex relationships among an array of elements: not only Stalin's personality, but also Bolshevism as a political movement, the nature of the early Soviet regime, the international histor- ical situation of the 1920s, and Russia as a country with traditions of repressive rule and popular acceptance of autocracy. Clearly, for a thor- ough understanding of any given leader's role in influencing large groups, we need to go beyond the study of the leader's personality. But the litera- ture of diplomacy, politics, and international and domestic relations usu- ally tells us much about political movements, actual events and old tradi- tions; what it typically fails to consider is the degree to which it is in the individual person of the leader that political movements, historical situa- tions, cultural traditions and large-group identity issues and rituals con- verge. In totalitarian regimes and democracies alike, the "power" that gives direction to political propaganda, political decision-making, how the large-group identity will be supported, and what rituals will be initiated, is located in the leader; the leader's personality, to a great extent, deter- mines the expressions of this power.

Of course, most people possess some aspects of various personality types and therefore cannot be easily or quickly classified as strictly one personality type. In some people, however, a specific type of personality is dominant. Typically, when we face a situation that makes us anxious, we hold ever more tightly to our personality characteristics (except in situa- tions in which the regression is so severe as to make us actually crush our personality altogether). Thus political leaders—who tend to have a strong dominant personality type—will usually react in a specific habitual man- ner to danger or will repeatedly prepare particular types of strategy and propaganda to protect or remove themselves (and by extension their fol- lowers) from dangerous situations. Realistic dangers that a political leader may face (or wish to avoid), such as the possibility of losing an election, meeting the leader of an enemy nation, or going to war, are practically countless. But they can be reduced to only a few types when we consider how such realistic dangers may be unconsciously linked with the major childhood dangers first identified by Sigmund Freud, which I mentioned in Chapter 1.[396]

To help us begin to understand propaganda, decision-making and international relations associated with large-group identity issues, regres- sion and rituals from this more-complicated, but necessary, perspective, we will explore what is known of the personalities of several leaders. Since my focus is on the personality of the leader, I will limit my examples to brief sketches of the historical situations in which these leaders have been involved.

Just as in the population at large, some leaders are more flexible in their responses both to others and to events, exhibiting diverse patterns of behavior, thought, and feeling; others' responses are more predictable. We call a person "obsessive," for example, if this person is habitually and exaggeratedly preoccupied with the smallest details of a task at hand, strictly controls his or her emotions, intellectualizes a great deal, is opinionated, and exhibits certain rigid physical gestures. Looking at the behavior of an obsessive man, we may see that he is preoccupied with an event for hours or days. He's extremely ambivalent—he keeps trying to balance things, but always something in his mind tips the balance. His face reveals when he is angry, but he keeps smiling as if always in control of his emotions. Unless this individual's personality becomes a source of continuing problems, we typically do not understand it as something psychologically "bad." When an obsessive individual begins to suffer from the various consequences of his or her habitual way of reacting to others and to events—such as losing his or her friends or job as a result of becoming aggressively stubborn—clinicians begin to speak of *personality disorder*.[397] Every individual has a personality, so the term does not necessarily imply a psychopathology, but personality disorders are on a recognizable continuum with the nonpathological personality types that psychiatrists, psychologists, and even lay people readily recognize.

Obsessional people may win elections or move up the ladder of leadership because they appear to have moral vocations and can articulate their missions compellingly. Indeed, it is this sense of vocation that makes obsessional people seek political power in the first place. But obsessional leaders are stiff and rigid in manner; they tend to behave like living machines. They search for the one "right answer" to problems and thus may overvalue bureaucracy, stifling creativity. And after considering their options in great detail, they often make decisions rather abruptly, sometimes alienating their colleagues and constituencies. Even those decisions that seem technical, rational, or intellectual may actually bear hidden emotional and ambivalent motivation. Despite their appearances of bureaucratic rationality, then, obsessional leaders must engage in a constant struggle to control their aggressive (what psychoanalysts call "sadistic") impulses. When a leader's obsessionalism becomes exaggerated, the constant need to control people and events—and the anxiety surrounding the possible loss of that control—may counteract the effect that brought him or her to power in the first place.

And when such a leader loses control, he or she may become agitated or even depressed.

Woodrow Wilson, the twenty-eighth president of the United States, was a spoiler of his own success. Wilson demonstrated the adaptive qualities of a well-functioning obsessive-compulsive person throughout his adult life. He demanded perfection in himself and in the communication of his ideas, and he paid a great deal of attention to detail: Wilson's speeches are considered among the best of American presidents. But his obsessionalism also caused problems: from time to time, the healing aspects of his personality became poisonous. Wilson biographer Arthur S. Link notes that Wilson's problems while Governor of New Jersey in 1912 (Wilson had been elected governor in 1910) did not stem simply from external events and partisanship, although these elements contributed to his problems. They were the result of Wilson's personality characteristics, which first became apparent when Wilson was president of Princeton University. His obstinacy contributed to the demise of his university presidency. Link writes how Wilson, as governor, exhibited:

[t]his temperamental inability to cooperate with men who were not willing to follow his lead completely; he had not lost his habit, long since demonstrated at Princeton, of making his political opponents also personal enemies, whom he despised and loathed. He had to hold the reins and do the driving alone; it was the only kind of leadership he knew.[398]

During Wilson's U.S. presidency, his clinically obsessive habits once more appeared. Link states:

What striking similarities there are between the Princeton and the national periods! During the first years of both administrations, Wilson drove forward with terrific energy and momentum to carry through a magnificent reform program, and his accomplishments both at Princeton and in Washington were great and enduring. Yet in both cases he drove so hard, so flatly refused to delegate authority, and broke with so many friends that when the inevitable reaction set in he was unable to cope with the new situation. His refusal to compromise in the graduate controversy was almost Princeton's undoing; his refusal to compromise in the fight in the Senate over the League of Nations was the nation's undoing. Both controversies assume the character and proportion of a Greek tragedy.[399]

Like obsessionalism, the paranoid personality need not be pathological. Consider a woman with a paranoid personality in the "normal" range: she is habitually alert, does not trust others easily, and checks and rechecks the motivations of the people around her. Her eyes may constantly seem to be checking the horizon, even when she is speaking with you directly. Such "normal" suspiciousness and caution combined with "normal" obsessionalism could be an asset for this person if she is, for example, the chief executive officer (CEO) of a company that is developing a new, revolutionary technology coveted by other companies. If this individual suffers from a paranoid personality *disorder*, however, her suspicion will be raised to a delusional level: such a leader will spend her energy fighting, like Don Quixote, with imaginary foes. Thus a CEO with paranoid personality disorder would not function well as a corporate leader. Her hyperalertness and suspicion would become exaggerated, causing her to become accusatory and fearful of everyone, eventually losing contact with reality and probably ruining the company in the process.

Mild paranoid characteristics may help political leaders to protect their followers and sometimes even to create an extraordinary and charismatic image for themselves. A leader with "normal" paranoid personality characteristics is typically able to arouse followers' identification with the goals he or she espouses as well as with the leader him or herself. In addition, hypersuspicious leaders may be effective in creating followers who, energized by emulating the leader's alertness at the grass-roots level, abandon their own feelings of apathy, indifference, and helplessness. Leaders with paranoid personality characteristics are often quite industrious, driven, mistrustful, arrogant, and aloof, but inwardly timid, frightened, naïve, and gullible. They may seem moralistic and prone to religious and ideological fanaticism. They tend to lack a sense of humor, and are apparently without romantic interests, although they may at times become crudely humorous about sexual matters. They typically strive for absolute reliability in their environment as a way of avoiding the particular anxiety produced in their personality type by the threat of betrayal. Though they are highly vigilant, paranoid leaders—once their personalities reach a *disorder* level—may spend so much energy searching for clues that fit their pre-existing idea of the world that they may miss the "big picture" of an event. Suspicious, they continuously look for "evidence" of others' hostile intentions, transferring their own undesirable thoughts and characteristics to others. Similarly, such leaders consistently portray themselves as continuously beleaguered, and thus always at center stage in any situation. This grandiosity yields delusions of world-historical uniqueness. The belief that outside threats are ever-present and the accompanying vigilance and readiness to act against these dangers tend to require enemies as targets for hostility.[400]

There is an essential difference between the perceptions of "enemies" held by an obsessional person, such as Woodrow Wilson, and those held by a person with paranoid personality characteristics. The obsessional person can realistically evaluate the feelings of the "other," but actually creates the "enemy" in order to hold stubbornly onto his or her own "perfect" position. He or she may attack the perceived enemy, but has no fantasy that the enemy is malignant. On the other hand, people with paranoid personality—in varying degrees, depending upon the severity of paranoid traits—are unable to have any empathetic understanding of the "enemy." In their view, the enemy actually is malignant and threatening. When the paranoid personality becomes pathological, he or she loses the adaptive elements of paranoia and becomes destructive. Thus the pathologically paranoid leader projects his or her aggression onto an enemy, which magnifies his or her perception of the enemy's danger.

One of history's most famous leaders with paranoid personality disorder was Joseph Stalin (1879–1953), who once remarked: "The greatest delight is to mark one's enemy, prepare everything, avenge oneself thoroughly and then go to sleep."[401] Stalin's personality is described by Nikita Khrushchev: "Stalin was a very distrustful man, sickly suspicious; we know this from our work with him. He could look at a man and say: 'why are your eyes so shifty today?' or 'why are you turning so much today and avoiding to look me directly in the eyes?' The sickly suspicion created in him a general distrust even toward eminent party workers whom he had known for years. Everywhere and in everything he saw 'enemies,' 'two-facers,' and 'spies.'"[402]

I had the opportunity to talk with Stalin's two personal interpreters, Zoya Zarubina and Valentin Berezhkov. I met Berezhkov, then a senior researcher for The Institute for the USA and Canada Studies, of the USSR Academy of Sciences in Moscow,[403] and Zarubina, then a professor and translator at the Diplomatic Academy in Moscow, during joint studies of the Center for the Study of Mind and Human Interaction and the Soviet Academy of Sciences and Diplomatic Academy. During the days of Mikhail Gorbachev's *glasnost* and *perestroika*, each reminisced with me about their time with the long-discredited Stalin. Their recollections reflect not only how Zarubina and Berezhkov, as young individuals, experienced a powerful leader, idealizing and fearing him as well as wishing to be liked by him, but also how a leader with a paranoid disorder was even capable of kindness—when he was in control and unthreatened. (I will return to Zarubina's and Berezhkov's recollections later in this book.)

There are personalities, which clinicians call "borderline" or "psychotic," that are always pathological. A person with a borderline personality will experience his or her surroundings in a rigid "black-and-white" fashion: he or she unrealistically experiences things and especially people, including him or herself, as either absolutely "bad" or absolutely "good." A person with a psychotic personality will be less capable of differentiating between the real and the unreal and will, as a result, repeatedly exhibit behavior that seems bizarre to others. For our purposes, I will omit personalities that are that absolutely pathological, for those who possess them cannot, for example, manage an effective campaign and therefore be elected as leaders, or capture established leadership in other ways, because they are unable to engage effectively with even the basics of reality.[404] Any person who attains leadership must be able to manipulate his or her environment and, in order to do so, must have a basic grasp on reality (though, once in power, such a person may deteriorate and become "sicker"; a person with a "normal" paranoid personality, for example, may evolve a true and even malignant disorder once he or she gains a leadership position). Therefore, I will discuss people whose personalities may have been either "normal" or "pathological," but were in any event sufficiently nonpathological or reality-oriented enough to allow them to capture leadership by election or by other means. The degree of "normality" or pathology in their personality characteristics varies, according to their ability to create a better living environment for their followers and to build peaceful relationships with others.

Observing a person's habitual reactions in a clinical situation naturally is far easier than accessing a political leader's expected reaction to various types of situations, if for no other reason than because leaders are difficult to access, being surrounded by their entourage, cronies, and technocrats.[405] Further, the pressure to consider political and diplomatic demands coming from the large group's political system and from international opinion leaven the appearance of the leader's personality in political decision-making; this is especially true in the United States and other established democracies. Though this is also true to some extent even where political leaders—such as Cuba's Fidel Castro, the PLO's Yassir

Arafat, and Northern Cyprus' Rauf Denktash—have stayed in power for decades, the leader's personal characteristics may play a more obvious political role in such states.[406]

Anwar Sadat, a long-term leader of Egypt (he was president from 1970 to 1981, and would have remained in power longer had he not been assassinated), for example, had a personality infused with high self-esteem and self-reliance, which was reflected in his behavior in the political and international arenas. In a sense, Sadat was a loner; he depended only on himself. Before making major decisions, Sadat would go to the village where he was born and raised—Mit Abul Kom, forty miles north of Cairo—don a *galibia*, smoke a pipe, think, and reach a decision. His decisions came not from discussions with other people, but from his own "inner voices." Certainly he was not modest: he considered his mind to be superior to the minds of those who might give him advice about political matters, and he easily discarded reports given to him by his own policy advisors. He believed that he could predict how political events would progress and once told Israeli historian Shimon Shamir, who became the Israeli ambassador to Egypt after Sadat's death, that his mind worked like a Swiss clock.[407] We can say that Sadat was a "rational actor" while he was thinking, calculating and predicting future events, but we can also see Sadat's personality at work in the predictable, almost ritualized, way he made decisions. In Sadat's case, his personality gave him the courage to take bold and unusual steps. For instance, within hours of ascending to power after the previous Egyptian president Gamal Abdel Nasser died in 1970, Sadat removed Nasser's elite followers from power positions. In a major reversal of traditional Egyptian diplomacy, Sadat turned to the West, and especially to the United States, for allies. Once he had decided that the Soviet experts brought to Egypt during Nasser's time had to go, about 20,000 Soviets left Egypt within a week. He went to war with Israel in October 1970, an act that Shimon Shamir has said initiated the political and international process that returned the Sinai to Egypt.[408] And, of course, one of his most celebrated decisions, again a result of listening to his "inner voice," was to travel to Israel in 1977 to speak at the Knesset, an act which shifted the diplomatic momentum, leading to the 1978 Camp David Accords and the final peace treaty with Israel in 1979. In many ways, Sadat's "Swiss clock personality" worked well.

Even in states where governmental structures limit the degree to which a leader's personality may pass unmitigated into governmental decision-making, public reactions to the leader's personality traits may echo in political and social processes. After most Americans began to perceive

President Bill Clinton's sexual affairs as part of a habitual behavior pattern, for instance, "morals" and "family values" became a more visible campaign issue in the 2000 presidential contest between George W. Bush and Clinton's vice-president, Al Gore. Former German chancellor Helmut Kohl's political fortunes provide a similar example.

The first post-World War II German leader untainted by the Nazi past, Kohl ruled Germany for more than fifteen years until he lost an election to Gerhard Schroeder in September 1998. Overweight and folksy, his public persona was easygoing and nonthreatening. A strong supporter of European integration and the father of German reunification, he was perceived as one of the most powerful political figures in Europe until, in 1999, the treasurer of Kohl's political party revealed that secret party financial accounts were being fed by clandestine donations. A scandal erupted: Kohl acknowledged that he had taken money illegally, but he refused to name the donors. The German people did not perceive in his "silence" a man honorably protecting the reputations of those who had helped him, but a man covering up more-serious political misdeeds through a stubborn secrecy: the "bad" characteristic of a "dishonest" personality. Some members of the German parliament began to suspect that Kohl and his party received cash from a French company that had taken over a former East German oil refinery with the permission of Kohl's government.[409]

The public usually becomes fascinated with political leaders' personality characteristics when expressions of them peak, such as in President Clinton's affair with Monica Lewinsky, or when their previously held perceptions of the leader drastically change, as happened in Germany. But the personality of the leader, like that of any other human being, is always there.

We also must recall that behind personality traits are the mostly unconscious processes and motivations that have shaped the leader's observable personality. What is crucial in the crystallization of personality traits is not the actual experience that a child faces, but the intertwining of the influence of that experience with the child's own perceptions and fantasies about it: "I am being punished because I have this or that wish that angers my father," for instance. The "meaning" of the actual event that settles in the child's mind—not the event itself—is what can become a factor in motivating him or her to carry out certain behavior patterns. It is for this reason that a traumatic childhood does not necessarily entail a pathological personality disorder in adulthood. The child or young person's own adaptive capacities and the adults in his or her environment with whom he or she can identify positively can help a person to deal creatively with the effects of childhood trauma in adulthood. But it is also true that whenever we examine someone with personality disorder in a clinical setting, we invariably find out that he or she had a traumatic childhood.

I must add that "traumatic" can refer to a range of actual experiences: some childhood traumas are concrete, as in the case of a child who is beaten again and again by a brutal father, but others are less tangible. Consider, for example, a young boy who has a new sibling and, perceiving the sibling to be an unwanted intruder into his special relationship with his mother, wishes the sibling dead. Feeling guilty about the wish, such a child may imagine that his father will beat him as punishment for his aggressive thoughts. As a result, the more the boy wishes for his sibling's disappearance, the more he will perceive his father as a potential tormenter. In this case, the child's "trauma" is not real; it is pure fantasy. Nevertheless, reality and fantasy are often intermingled in creating childhood traumas. Such traumas are usually associated with the hidden but powerful psychological motivations that psychoanalysts call unconscious fantasies.

Simply put, in an unconscious fantasy, the small child, using the immature mental tools available to him or her at his or her early stage of development, interprets certain experiences and understands them in illogical, fragmentary ways.[410] This "understanding," connected with feelings about the experience, remains in the child's mind without being represented in words. In the classic example, a small child witnesses his or her parents making love and "interprets" it as a physical fight between them. Later, as the child gets to know the world, the "story line" of his or her unconscious fantasy is usually repressed effectively. When an unconscious fantasy is not successfully repressed, however, it remains "alive," though of course not in the awareness of the individual who has it. It continues to exert an unconscious influence on the individual's thinking, actions, and personality characteristics.[411] So, if the child who understood the adult lovemaking as a fight keeps the fantasy alive in his or her unconscious, for instance, he or she may have sexual difficulties as an adult or may develop personality characteristics to cope with this difficulty, such as avoiding sexual encounters.

Sometimes, an individual's active "unconscious fantasy" is very specific. For example, Mohammed Reza Pahlavi, who ruled as the Shah of Iran from 1941 until he was "dethroned" by Ayatollah Khomeini in 1979, had clear "flying fantasies." As an adult, the Shah was preoccupied with flying and heights; he acquired his "wings" (learned to fly) two days before his twenty-seventh birthday. As head of state, he invested in a massive expansion of the Iranian Air Force, and a 1976 Senate report observed that "[i]t has been said that [the Shah] reads *Aviation Week* before he reads the Iranian press."[412] According to Marvin Zonis, the Shah's biographer, Pahlavi unconsciously linked his father's great height with that of the mighty Elburz mountains, and Zonis suggests, further, that the Shah's interest in flying might be connected to a childhood ambivalence about his very tall and powerful father. In 1946, two years after he learned to fly, the Shah was at the controls when his single-engine plane crashed; though he and his passenger survived without a scratch, Zonis suggests that the accident helped revive the Shah's youthful, anxious "flying fantasies."[413] His expansion of the national air force beyond a rationally necessary size may have been a reflection of a personality for whom it was important to dominate the heights.

One of the most common unconscious fantasies is known as the "repairing fantasy." People who carry such fantasies usually have had significant losses in childhood and grieving or depressed mothers. Psychologically speaking, as children, such people felt threatened with the loss of their mothers and, more generally, the loss of love. Their repairing fantasy is a defense against this sense of loss, which becomes habitual. In one form of such a repairing fantasy, the individual develops an unconscious "story" in which he or she can bring dead siblings back to life.[414] When such an individual reaches adulthood, still under the influence of the fantasy, he or she tends to exhibit repeating behavior patterns, symbolically erasing sadness or creating "life" in his or her environment. For example, he or she may become a gardener, creating life when his or her flowers grow; as the leader of a troubled country, such a person may repeat acts meant to cultivate hope and diminish followers' shared depressive feelings and increase their shared self-esteem by idealizing their large-group identity. Of course, since the fantasy is "unconscious," the individual is aware not of the reason for his or her repeating behavior patterns, only of the urge to repeat such patterns.

A reparative leader lifts the self-esteem of his or her followers by helping them to idealize their large-group identity. By doing so, however, he or she raises his or her own self-esteem and increases his or her self-love. There are also leaders who exaggerate their own self-love by hurting others; they are destructive. Some leaders who possess a personality with exaggerated love (narcissism) therefore can be both reparative and destructive. Leaders with exaggerated self-love are, in my mind, true mobilizers of large-group identity issues, rituals, and massive regressive or progressive moves. I will examine such leaders in the next chapter.

7 / force of narcissism

Man, as an individual, is condemned to death. To work, not for oneself, but for those who will come after, is the first condition of happiness that any individual can reach in life. Each person has his own preferences. Some people like gardening and growing flowers. Others prefer to train men. Does the man who grows flowers expect anything from them? He who trains men ought to work like the man who grows flowers.

—Mustafa Kemal Ataturk

The term "narcissism," of course, comes from the Greek myth of Narcissus, a young man who sees and falls in love with his own reflection in a pool of water; in psychoanalysis, it has become a technical term for "love of self." As with regression, narcissism is not pathological in and of itself, and is as normal in human psychology as having sexual or aggressive desires and anxiety about internal conflicts. Indeed, healthy narcissism is necessary for anyone to survive, work, and maintain a solid identity. But narcissism is also subject to frustrations, which may lead to unhealthily weakened or inflated self-love.[415] It is when people have *exaggerated* love of self that they exhibit the repeated thought, behavior, and feeling patterns that in combination are called *narcissistic personality*. Such individuals think that they are unique and grand, which causes them to feel omnipotent and to act as though they are better than anyone else. But people with narcissistic personalities live in a paradox: while they overtly love themselves too much and feel grandiose and omnipotent, they also covertly possess an aspect that is devalued and "hungry" for love; periodically, the latter aspect pushes itself into awareness and overwhelms the person. The fact that such individuals have an overt grandiose self and a covert hungry self reflects a lack of cohesive identity.[416]

189

Let us create a model of the mind of a person with narcissistic personality. Imagine serving a freshly baked apple pie: in placing the pie on the dinner table, a bottle of salty salad dressing spills and soaks a small section of the pie. In order to protect the edible and larger section of the pie, we cut off the spoiled section and push it to the periphery of the serving plate. The large, edible piece symbolizes the part of the person's identity that is invested with exaggerated self-love; the smaller, spoiled piece stands for the individual's devalued aspects. Because narcissistic people are unable to integrate the inflated, grandiose part of themselves with the devalued, humiliated aspects, it becomes essential that the "good" piece not touch the "spoiled" piece.

Exaggerated narcissism tends to develop defensively in people who have experienced repeated frustrations, humiliations, and deprivation (especially in childhood)[417]—though, of course, the level of exaggerated narcissism varies from one individual to another. An outside observer often sees expressions of habitual contradictory behavior, thought, and action in a person who has narcissistic personality organization. How the mind of a person with narcissistic personality works depends on how well the dominant identity is maintained, how it responds to the threats against it, and what the person does to protect and exhibit the good part of the pie for everyone to adore while attempting to hide the spoiled piece from everyone, including him or herself.

Acknowledging only the "good" part of their identities, people with narcissistic personalities behave as if they are "God's gift to the world": "number one" in beauty, intelligence, power, and so on.[418] They often collect what they consider to be "unique" achievements, whether they are substantial or trivial, such as winning a tennis match or being the first person to leave a boring conference—extra chocolate chips sprinkled over the ice cream on the pie, if you will. A narcissistic woman, for example, looks in the mirror in the morning and thinks, "Move over Julia Roberts: I am more beautiful than you are!" One such individual whom I treated developed the fantasy that, if she modeled naked in Washington, D.C., the city would experience the worst traffic jam in its history as everyone stopped their cars to see her "most beautiful body." Such people frequently use words like "fantastic," "unbelievable," and "earthshaking" when describing events that they are involved in, regardless of whether they are really of consequence. Most of their sentences start with "I," since they need whatever they do to be recognized before they can acknowledge others; in extreme cases, the thoughts, feelings, or activities of other people are not emotionally recognized at all. For the typical person with narcissistic personality, to be "average" (like most of us, who do quite well in our "average-ness") is to live in a kind of horror. So, whereas the usual young man dates one woman at a time, an analysand of mine with narcissistic personality dated three: He took Patricia out to a movie. He found an excuse to leave her at the theatre to go have coffee with Jennifer. He stopped by Beverly's house to have sex after coffee, and was back at the theatre to meet Patricia just as she was leaving the show.

The large, good part of the pie has to be protected at all times. Individuals with narcissistic personality characteristics often have fantasies of living gloriously alone under what I call a "glass bubble,"[419] pushing the spoiled slice even further away, and covering the large piece with a transparent protective dome. One such person literally referred to herself as a beautiful flower under glass, but the "glass bubble" often appears in symbolic ways, such as in the case of an individual who repeatedly fantasized himself as Robinson Crusoe *without* his Man Friday. There was no need to have Friday around since the patient believed himself omnipotent; the sea surrounding the Island of Juan Fernandez functioned as a "glass bubble."[420] At the same time, narcissistic individuals also may be aware of the spoiled, devalued part of themselves, the part that reflects their "hunger" for love and wish to be nurtured and "fed." Thus, the man who dated three women at once and called himself the "world's greatest lover" also had to have a huge supply of canned food in his cupboard, "in case of a rainy day." If his supply dwindled to a certain number, he would begin to sense his devalued aspect, the threat of shame and humiliation would appear, and he would rush to the store for more canned food in order to quell his anxiety. The food he hoarded symbolized the emotional nutrition for which he strove.

If the spoiled piece of pie can be put onto someone else's plate—if the narcissistic individual can develop the illusion that what is unwanted in the self no longer actually belongs to him or her, but to someone else— that individual will feel better, at least in the short run. But the narcissist must spend a great deal of psychic energy placing the unwanted piece onto someone else's plate, ensuring that the bad piece is not returned to his or her plate, and blurring the reality of the rightful ownership of the unwanted piece. This process of *externalization*,[421] as we shall see, plays an especially important role in the behavior of some political leader with narcissistic personality organization.

Individuals with narcissistic personality characteristics typically experience a rather limited repertoire of feelings. Because such people basically see others as existing only to adore them, they generally fail to appreciate others as freestanding individuals with lives of their own. Further, if the narcissist has externalized his or her devalued identity onto another, he or she often mentally renders that other person worthless. Accordingly, narcissistic people have great difficulty genuinely exhibiting emotions such as remorse, sadness, and grief when they mistreat others or lose their friendship. The narcissistic person living in his or her lonely kingdom watches others through the "glass bubble"; considering those who do not look upon the kingdom with adoration and jealousy to be disloyal, he or she remorselessly consigns them to "nothingness," absolute emotional insignificance. Accordingly, people with narcissistic personalities easily experience envy when faced with the possibility that someone else might preempt their stellar role.[422]

There is a type of personality that displays what psychoanalysts call *malignant narcissism*, which is contaminated with paranoid expectations and often to some degree with psychopathic tendencies. For such a person, it is not sufficient to separate the large, unspoiled piece of pie from the smaller, spoiled part, nor is it enough to put the unwanted piece on someone else's plate. Rather, the small, unwanted piece has to be completely ruined or destroyed to protect the malignant narcissist from experiencing anxiety, depression, and especially humiliation. Because malignant narcissists perceive the other individuals or groups who represent the devalued aspects of themselves as threats to the stability of their own self-esteem, only the remorseless destruction and immiseration of the devalued others maintains the malignant narcissist's illusion of grandiosity and omnipotence. Such people are addicted to what Gabriele Ast and I describe as repeated "aggressive triumphs," through which they receive temporary pleasure.[423] In order to perform these "aggressive triumphs," these individuals infuse their exaggerated self-love with paranoid characteristics, psychopathy, and a developmentally primitive belief that they are entitled to be repeatedly destructive merely because they exist. Some serial killers, such as Ted Bundy, are believed to possess such a personality organization.[424] *American Psycho* (2000), a motion picture directed and co-written by Mary Harron based on the novel of the same title by Bret Easton Ellis, takes as its protagonist a character named Patrick Bateman, whom we can recognize as a person with malignant narcissism infused with psychopathy. A Harvard graduate and a broker on Wall Street, Bateman is preoccupied with becoming and remaining "number one" in many areas, including using the finest products to sustain his beauty, performing a thousand abdominal crunches daily, and wearing only the finest suits. He cannot tolerate a reservation refusal at the "best" restaurant, so he lies about this failure. In one humorous scene, Bateman competes with three other men, all of whom display exaggerated self-love, to see whose business card has the nicest typeface and most prestigious watermark. Behind his mask of sanity, though, Bateman is a serial killer at least in fantasy, imagining murdering a business competitor, a homeless person, and a number of women in the course of the film. He can not, however, fully differentiate his fantasies from the reality. What the victims represent for him is not revealed in the picture, but we can assume that they in some way represent the spoiled piece of Bateman's identity that "needs" to be destroyed.

The intensity of the thought, feeling, and behavior patterns in people with narcissistic personalities changes according to the degree of their grandiosity. Some have chronic difficulty relating to others and at times have a blurred vision of reality. Those who also possess areas of integrated identity—those who, alongside their belief in their superiority, know where to stop and what to pursue—are better adjusted to life and may become quite successful in the world's eyes. Indeed, for some narcissists who actually are very smart, handsome, powerful, and effectively manipulative, their inner craving for achievement and applause often will direct them to leadership positions in education, business, or social organizations. This person is what is called a *successful narcissist*.[425] A "successful narcissist" thinks he or she is superior to others but exhibits a false modesty: in reality, he or she values becoming "number one" in a group and being perceived and experienced by others as such. This person, if the external circumstances are favorable, is quite apt to become involved in politics and even to become a political leader.[426] By "successful," I am not referring to the moral worth of their individual deeds but to the fact that they each were able to find an echo of their personalities in the external world by which they achieved primacy in the eyes of others. For successful narcissistic leaders, a "fit" occurs between their internal demands and their followers' responses to them. Some such leaders are able to maintain that "fit" over an extended period of time, and some are not. Even though successful narcissistic leaders obviously do not typically become patients, clinical work with patients with narcissistic personality can illuminate a great deal about such leaders' internal worlds.

It is generally when a large group's identity is threatened and when the group is regressed that the "fit" between a community and an individual with exaggerated self-love is likely to be strongest: the leader's belief in his or her own omnipotence and power creates comfort for followers in search of a savior. Of course, political figures with exaggerated narcissism always try to achieve "number one" status and can manipulate their way to the top under a variety of circumstances. Some, in fact, may perform heroic acts and are perceived as heroes by their followers. In general, I believe that what Max Weber and others[427] have argued about the emergence of "charismatic leaders,"—the necessity of the large group being in a crisis—applies to the ascendancy of a narcissistic leader as well, but not all charismatic leaders necessarily have the narcissistic personality organization described here. Narcissistic leaders' biases, prejudices, and official acts (though subject to modifications in democratic societies) reflect the demands of the inner psychological structures discussed in this section of this chapter. Their personalities drive them to manage their followers by devaluing some in order to underline their own superiority, or by placing high value on those who pay them the homage for which they yearn. In their immediate environments, such political leaders deny full individuality to those who adore them; they use the adorer to shore up their own greatness.

A leader with excessive self-love may wish for his or her followers to achieve an imagined and hoped-for high level of functioning in order to reflect the leader's shining self-images and be extensions of his or her superiority. I call this type of narcissistic leadership *reparative*. Returning to our apple pie metaphor, the reparative leader tries to wipe the salad dressing from the spoiled piece, or attempts to sweeten it and perhaps improve it enough to remain on the same plate with the unspoiled piece and indeed touch it.

An example of a successful reparative leader is the founder of modern Turkey, Mustafa Kemal Ataturk. A brief summary of Ataturk's life as it appears in conventional history is as follows: Mustafa was born in 1881 in Selanik (now Thessaloniki, Greece), a port city of the Ottoman Empire. His father, a customs clerk and small businessman, died when he was seven years old. Mustafa left home as a young teenager to enter military school, where he received a second name, Kemal (meaning "perfection"), from a teacher. He graduated near the top of his class. Although he became an officer in the Ottoman military, he was critical of the Sultan and became active in anti-government organizations. After distinguished service in World War I, highlighted by his heroic leadership against Allied forces at Gallipoli, he was promoted to the rank of general at the age of thirty-five. As Allied forces threatened to overrun what remained of the Ottoman Empire after World War I, and the Sultan proved powerless to fend off Italian, French, British, and Greek incursions, Kemal sought to salvage Turkish independence. He left Istanbul for Anatolia, the "heartland" of the Turkish people, and organized an army to resist invading Greek forces. Fearing Kemal's growing power, the Sultan, under pressure from the Allies, ordered his dismissal, prompting Kemal to establish a provisional nationalist government in Ankara, to which he was elected leader. While in Ankara, then only a provincial town, Kemal planned campaigns against the Greeks, who had invaded Anatolia, and ultimately defeated them in 1922, leading to a peace agreement with the Allies. The Sultan went into exile, and modern Turkey was established in 1923 with Kemal at its head. Kemal adopted the surname "Ataturk," meaning "Father Turk," after coming to power.[428] Upon becoming the first president of the Turkish Republic, he instituted drastic political and cultural changes in order to modernize and secularize Turkey:[429] abolishing the Caliphate, dismantling Islamic law and curtailing religious influences over the state, instituting a legal system based on European models,[430] emancipating women, replacing Arabic script with the Latin alphabet, and instituting various economic modernizations. According to a generally held Turkish belief, Ataturk almost single-handedly inspired his war-weary country to reestablish its independence and created a new Turkish identity through cultural revolution. Though he died in 1938, he is venerated in an extraordinary way in Turkey as though he still lives. Even now, many people simply refer to him as Ata (father) or Atam (my father), and he is immortalized as "The Eternal Leader."

Some may object to my characterization of Ataturk's actions as reparative: some may see Ataturk as a micromanager of his followers' behavior, perhaps even a westernizer for westernization's sake. For instance, Ataturk's secularization program could be said to have interrupted existing family and child-rearing practices, causing a societal regression. But the Islamic law used in matters of marriage, divorce, and inheritance during the Ottoman period had been very unfavorable to women, and Ataturk believed that "[a] bad family life inevitably leads to social, economic, and political enfeeblement. The male and female elements constituting the family must be in full possession of their natural rights and must be in a position to discharge their family obligations."[431] Ataturk sought to remove existing burdens from his followers' minds so that they could function more creatively and productively. Though his innovations sometimes required legal enforcement, their intent and effects were always to enhance his followers' personal autonomy,[432] to turn the existing societal regression into progression.

As Itzkowitz and I discovered, Ataturk's personality and identity were perhaps most significantly shaped by the fact that he was born into a house of mourning. All three of the previous children born to his parents died at early ages while his family was living in an isolated and inhospitable area near Mount Olympus, close to the Greek-Ottoman border. A story about one of the dead male children was often repeated by the family when Mustafa was a child: the child had been buried in a grave by the sea, and a high tide had exposed the corpse, which was discovered after it was ravaged by animals. At the time of Mustafa's birth, the family had moved from the border to Selanik, and was experiencing a brief respite from hardship, leading us to conclude that his parents perceived him as "special," bringing some sunshine into the gloomy darkness of the family. But this time was not to last long, as one of his younger siblings died shortly after birth and his mother became a widow at the age of twenty-seven, with only a small pension on which to support herself and her only two remaining children. Itzkowitz's and my research has confirmed that young Mustafa received less than adequate parenting—particularly mothering—in this house of mourning.

Without delving into the details of Ataturk's life story, let us illustrate here, through Ataturk's *own words*, the leader's perception of emotional "hunger" in his childhood home and his subsequent development of an exaggerated love of self. In a 1930 essay, Ataturk clearly (though symbolically) refers to the deaths of his older siblings at the home near the dangerous border. The essay opens with a discussion of humanity's relation to nature:

> Man does not decide whether to be born or not born. At the moment of his birth he is at the mercy of nature and a host of creatures other than himself. He needs to be protected, to be fed, to be looked after, to be helped to grow.[433]

Here one can catch an echo of the family story about his older brother's body exposed by the tide and ravaged by animals. We can surmise that he may have condensed his fantasy of what can happen to little boys (death and body mutilation) with his experiences in a house of mourning where maternal love could not be good enough and began to develop narcissistic character traits in response. The following adult statement reflects his premature maturation, or the defensive inflation of his self-concept.

> Since my childhood, in my home, I have not liked being together with either my mother or sister, or a friend. I have always preferred

to be alone and independent, and have lived this way always … Because when one is given advice one has either to accept and obey it—or disregard it altogether. Neither response seems right to me. Wouldn't it be a regressive retreat to the past to heed a warning given to me by my mother who is more than 20 or 25 years older than I? Yet were I to rebel against it I would break the heart of my mother, in whose virtue and lofty womanhood I have the firmest belief.[434]

Ataturk saw himself as above others—and was perceived as such by his followers. He did not, however, seek fantasied enemies or subgroups to devalue or destroy in order to remain superior in comparison to others. His narcissism expressed itself quite differently:

Why, after my years of education, after studying civilization and the socializing processes, should I descend to the level of common people? I will make them rise to my level. Let me not resemble them; they should resemble me![435]

From one of Ataturk's adopted daughters, the late Sahiba Gokcen,[436] whom I interviewed in 1974 at her modest apartment in Ankara, I learned that Ataturk was preoccupied with turning his personal environment from the house of mourning of his childhood to a house of joy. He constantly told his adopted daughters to smile: there was no room in the presidential palace for the expression of grief or depression. In spite of (or perhaps in some ways as a result of) his overt preoccupation with "life" and "happiness," there were tragedies that befell some of the adopted daughters, including a suicide.

Perhaps he was a better father to the nation than to his immediate family, for Ataturk's main preoccupation was to create a "happy" Turkey: there are many funny stories about his efforts to remake the dusty little town of Ankara, the capital of the new Turkey, on the model of "Gay Paree." When Ataturk came to power, Turkey was overwhelmed with grief indeed. The Balkan Wars and World War I had left millions of Turks killed, maimed, displaced, or grieving. Most of the people now living in Anatolia were immigrants from lands lost by the Ottoman Empire, such as Macedonia, Greece, and Bulgaria. Ataturk identified his grieving nation with his grieving mother and regularly reactivated his rescue fantasies as a political leader. He developed a daily ritual, based on his earliest memory, to deal with the "hungry" part of his personality so that his "omnipotent" part could perform grand rescue operations. Ataturk's first memory was of his father, just before his death, tactfully standing up to Ataturk's devout mother in order to give the youngster a new direction in his life and thinking.[437] Secular, Western-style schools had sprung up during Ataturk's childhood, especially in cities such as Selanik, and his father wished him to attend such a school. Ataturk later recalled the "deep struggle" between his parents over the issue of his education. Ataturk's father had first registered his son in religious school, in accordance with the wishes of Ataturk's mother, and had the child stayed there he would have been on his way to becoming a traditional Muslim Ottoman. But then his father hit upon a solution to their conflict: to allow him to complete the ceremonies performed upon entering religious school, thus satisfying his mother (who appeared to have sought solace from her grief in religion), and then to withdraw his son from the religious school after a few days and enroll him in the secular school. In a significant sense, we can think of the young boy's educational opportunity as a special "gift" from his father, which he would in turn pass on to the modern nation he was eventually to lead.

During his presidency, Ataturk's mother came to live with him in Ankara. Ataturk would kiss his mother's hand every morning, similarly "satisfying" her wishes before going about his work of secularizing and westernizing Turkey. But this act was only half of his daily ritual. He often awoke late in the day, since he entertained dinner guests every night at the presidential palace until old age and illness caused his doctors to forbid such activity. He often invited politicians, scientists, and artists, but a group of cronies was also always present, serving as his "glass bubble."[438] Dining and drinking began early in the evening and would continue well into the early morning hours. Ataturk ate little at table and drank alcohol very slowly,[439] but he often ordered dishes that he remembered from his childhood, and would occasionally send food back if it was not cooked exactly the way his mother would have cooked it. All actions at the table were completely under his control, down to the songs sung by him and the guests: he frequently demanded that the musicians play music from his childhood. Thus he symbolically revisited his childhood every night—visiting the image of his mother, making this image "nurturing" through food and song, and repairing her broken heart.

Each morning, after again completing the ritual with his mother's image by kissing the hand of his real mother, he would turn to identify with his father's image, calling himself "Father Turk" and carrying on with his efforts to turn his regressed large group onto a progressive path.

Certainly there were discussions of his revolutionary ideas at the dinner table, but the dining room was more like a child's playroom than a state dining room. Ataturk and his guests, especially the cronies, would "play" together with songs, drinks, and jokes in between serious discussions of political and economic issues and the consideration of revolutionary ideas. They would "regress" nightly in the service of the next day's "progression." As we know from clinical work, this pattern of regression followed by progression is the very foundation of creativity.

Ataturk used his belief in his own superiority to create a new Turkey, and strove to raise the bar for his followers in order to "make" them more suitable to his own exalted overt identity. Perhaps he never consciously realized the relationship between his "hungry" self, his exaggerated self-love, his rescue fantasy, and the transference of this fantasy from his grieving mother to a grieving nation. However, he must have had some consciousness of this pattern. During a speech in August 1924 commemorating the second anniversary of victory over the Greeks, Ataturk suddenly spoke of the importance of "family life"—paradoxically, but symbolically, revealing the hardship of his family life during his childhood and the failure of his marriage: "the basis of civilization, the foundation of progress and power are in family life."[440] There are also indications that he was aware of the sublimated rescue urges that became altruistic behavior as he grew older.

Another "successful" narcissistic leader was Richard Nixon, the thirty-seventh president of the United States, who possessed a highly intelligent, analytical mind. Unlike Ataturk, whose image remained as the "savior" for his followers even after his death, Nixon could not comfortably maintain the grandiose part of his personality. At times, he experienced it to be under attack by "enemies." Eventually, his personality characteristics led to destructive acts, including the destruction of his political position.

Nixon's need to achieve remained constant throughout his adult life. He was elected president of the Whittier Alumni Association, the Duke University Alumni Association of California, the Orange County Association of Cities, and the 20-30 Club, all while still in his twenties. At the age of 33, he was elected to Congress; at 37, he became a U.S. Senator, and in 1952, at the age of 39, he became the second-youngest man to be elected vice president of the United States. He also collected "firsts," whether significant or trivial, from becoming the first U.S. president to visit the People's Republic of China to being the first candidate to visit a particular small rural town on the campaign trail. According to his aide, John Ehrlichman, "There was a running gag on a Nixon campaign; everything that happened was a 'historic first.'"[441] Accumulating such "firsts" was a sign of his need to collect emotional nutrition for his grandiose self, so that no one, not even himself, would know his anxiety concerning the spoiled, unwanted part of the apple pie in his mind.

What became known as the "Nixon Method" of presidency, I believe, reflected a "glass bubble" syndrome.[442] Some individuals in Nixon's entourage, H.Robert Haldeman and John Ehrlichman, for example, developed functions above and beyond their actual political duties that responded to Nixon's need for splendid isolation. It is no wonder that they were nicknamed the "Berlin Wall," surrounding the leader's lonely internal kingdom as they did. In *The Making of the President* (1968), Theodore White writes that he saw Nixon stroll down New York City's Fifth Avenue one day, "smiling as if amused by some inner conversation. His habit of great concentration lent itself to inner colloquy."[443]

It is clear that, under stress, personality became a factor in Nixon's decision-making, propaganda activities, and actions. Specifically—as political scientist and psychoanalyst Blema Steinberg first suggested in her detailed examination of the events surrounding the controversial U.S. bombing of North Vietnamese sanctuaries in Cambodia on March 17, 1969, and subsequent invasion of Cambodia in 1970—Nixon's personal response to shame and humiliation was often involved in significant decisions of his presidency.[444] My intention here is not to present a full psychobiography of Nixon. Norman Itzkowitz, Andrew Dod and I already published a detailed psychobiography of Nixon. Based on this work, the following is a bird's eye view of Nixon's life. I hope that this brief summary illustrates why he developed a narcissistic personality organization. I especially wish to prepare the reader to consider why Nixon was prone to extreme reactions when he sensed that someone or something humiliated him. He wanted to hide his "hungry self." When he noticed his "hungry self," he felt humiliated and, in turn, he became aggressive against those whom he perceived as humiliating him as well as those who symbolically represented his own "hungry self."

Born in January 1913 in the small agricultural community of Yorba Linda, California, Richard Nixon was the second child of a struggling family of ordinary means that frequently faced death, separation, and financial hardship. Even in his first year of life, young Richard faced numerous challenges. It took many weeks for his mother, Hannah, to recover from her pregnancy, and she took in a newborn nephew when Richard was only six-months old. A few months later, Hannah entered the hospital for a mastoid operation and returned to her parents' home to recover. Soon pregnant again after returning to her husband and sons, she again moved back to her parents to give birth to Don. Another son, Arthur, was born in 1918, followed by Edward twelve years later. From the first, then, Nixon's life was marked by interruptions in his relationship with his mother. As an infant, Richard cried long and loud. Yet young Richard apparently received little sympathy from his mother, nor could he turn to his father, who was a harsh and generally bad-tempered man. Recalling later her son's extended periods of crying, Nixon's mother considered his loud wailing a sign that he would become a great orator or preacher—not a sign of distress, frustration, or unhappiness with insufficient parental care.

With four young boys to take care of, Hannah had her hands full in the small house her husband Frank had built, and Richard Nixon's childhood and youth were characterized by circumstances that further deprived him of time with his mother. During Richard's early years, Frank Nixon's small lemon grove failed, forcing him to return to working on odd jobs or in the nearby oil field; Hannah went to work in the local lemon packing house. Her sons Richard and Don came with her, and sometimes worked as sweepers. A year later, when Richard was seven, he and Don worked as child laborers, picking beans and lemons at local farms. At the age of 12, he was sent to live for five months with an aunt about 200 miles from home in the hopes that he would improve his skills at the piano under her tutelage. Once more Nixon faced a "loss" and may well have felt that he was unworthy of staying with his mother. When Richard was 14, his older brother Harold contracted tuberculosis. After stays in two private sanatoriums, a cabin was rented for him in Prescott, Arizona, and Hannah moved there to care for her son and a few other tuberculosis patients she took in to make ends meet. They did not return to Whittier, where Harold died in 1932, until Richard was nearly 19. It is well known that as an adult Nixon more than once spoke and wrote of his mother's "saintliness." He (defensively) exaggerated the virtues of his mother in public, especially whenever he felt disgraced, to defend against an intense fury at the image of his mother from his early years. His own childhood's "misfortunes" and his mother's "saintliness" were the two sides of the same coin.

In this strained environment, Richard Nixon apparently sought approval and love through achievement, facilitated both by his own native intelligence and by his parents' encouragement. He learned to read at a young age, skipped second grade, played the piano before the age of seven, and otherwise developed as a quiet, self-reliant, and aloof boy who preferred reading in his room to being outside with his brothers. In a sense, he bypassed the playfulness of childhood. When the Nixon family moved to Whittier, California, when Richard was nine, he got his own room where he could read in private, while his other three brothers continued to share a room. Shortly after he returned home from the five-month stay with his aunt at age 12, his younger brother Arthur became sick and died only a few weeks later at the age of seven. Our study of his life shows that from that time on he studied even harder to protect himself from experiencing feelings about severe losses and to repair his parents so that, in the long run, he could get better parentage himself.

We can surmise, then, that from an early age, Richard sought to achieve something he desired and needed—he was considered "special" by his parents (and others). Yet this specialness remained fragile, depended upon specific types of achievements, and could not mask his deprivations and sense of shame. He "matured" too quickly and this "maturation" became the base of his narcissistic personality organization. Only being a special, superior being could he hide his "hungry self" and the humiliation and associated negative feelings.

Throughout adolescence, Richard continued to excel in his studies. He was an intense, serious, and dedicated youth. But life in his "motherless" home was hard and he learned more and more to take care of himself and be "number one." In his senior year of high school he ran for student body president—one of the few elections he would lose over the next forty years. He then attended Whittier College, where he was elected student body president, and Duke University Law School, where he graduated third in his class. I will focus on his decisions concerning Cambodia and give an illustration of how his narcissistic personality organization, especially when he was under stress, played a significant role in international and military affairs.

When a person feels constant or frequently-repeating anxiety about experiencing shame, he or she may develop certain habits and elements of personality that help to push that anxiety into the shadows of the mind. For example, in order to protect oneself from the experience of shame, such a person may limit self-exposure and shy away from love or other intimate interpersonal relationships in order to avoid becoming vulnerable to criticism or rejection. Such a person also may do something that on the surface appears to be the opposite of shying away from others: he or she may aim to become "number one" in some respect to protect him or herself from being shamed by others. If the person's defenses against shame break down, he or she may turn aggressively against him or herself, exhibiting depression and self-destructive behavior—in a sense, attempting to get rid of or "kill" the shamed image of him or herself. More often, however, the person discharges aggression against someone else. Such an individual can thus control the anxiety of experiencing shame because he or she unconsciously "chooses" to take actions that seem to increase self-esteem. The person who is prone to aggressive outbursts, however, creates other problems for him or herself: such behavior and efforts to devalue and destroy others or their property are (usually) not socially acceptable behavior patterns, and may even lead to legal problems.

In our biography of Nixon, Itzkowitz, Dod, and I described in detail how from childhood Nixon became prone to anxiety about experiencing shame and humiliation and to episodes of depression and aggression.[445] Nixon's nearly continuous anger, which in his day-to-day adult life manifested itself in the habitual use of curse words, served to hide from himself his anxiety about experiencing shame; as Steinberg observed, "Aggression and its control were central themes" in Nixon's personality.[446] Nixon apparently had no introspective sense of why he was angry. For him, there was always a stimulus for his anger "out there," and it was "natural" to him to accept his resultant anger. If something "out there" made him sense shame and humiliation, he would spontaneously strike out. Of course, the scandal which ultimately led to his resignation is perhaps the best-known of the episodes in which Nixon's political actions were angry "responses" to enemies "out there" whom he perceived as maliciously out to thwart and humiliate him. But Steinberg's and our work on Nixon, corroborated by the first-hand observations of then-Secretary of State Henry Kissinger, reveals that Nixon's actions before and during the Watergate scandal were not the only presidential decisions influenced by personality traits that were exaggerated when he sensed possible humiliation. Even geopolitical decisions, including ones related to the war in Vietnam, were shaped by this persistent personal anxiety.

Nixon thought that escalated military action was the key to a diplomatic solution in Vietnam. But that strategy had clearly not worked for his predecessor, Lyndon Johnson, and had in fact driven Johnson from the presidency. Why, then, did Nixon remain committed to it? According to Steinberg,

Nixon's preference for strong military action was dictated only partly by his conception of appropriate strategy and tactics; it was largely activated by his sense of outrage. Nixon was determined that the United States would not be "humbled by Vietnamese communists." … [H]e feared that "American credibility" in Moscow and Peking would be undermined—thus weakening Washington's hand in all future dealings with its "adversaries."[447]

In January 1969, a special task force prepared exit strategy options for Nixon, ranging from an open-ended and gradual withdrawal of U.S. forces to an indefinite presence in Vietnam. For Nixon, the unilateral withdrawal option would have been "a 'buy-out,' something Nixon could not tolerate viscerally or intellectually."[448] As Steinberg observes, decision-makers not prone to feelings of shame and humiliation could have been equally opposed to withdrawal at this juncture, but what followed clearly illustrates how Nixon's personality characteristics played a significant role in his decisions concerning the war in Vietnam.

Nixon's decision to order the first bombing campaign on Cambodia was, on the surface, a response to renewed North Vietnamese offensives on February 22, 1969. At the time, Cambodia, a monarchy with 7 million subjects, was trying to stay neutral, but the North Vietnamese had established sanctuaries in the border area between the two countries. Earlier, Nixon had examined research and intelligence that indicated that bombing these sanctuaries would drive the North Vietnamese further west, and deeper into Cambodia, perhaps eventually causing Cambodia to fall to the communist regime, and so he had decided not to attack the bases.[449] But Nixon took the February offensive as a personal assault. To him, the move "was a deliberate test, clearly designed to take the measure of me and my administration at the outset. My immediate instinct was to retaliate."[450] Further, the offensive had begun one day prior to Nixon's ten-day ceremonial visit to Europe: Nixon felt that the North Vietnamese had timed their offensive specifically to humiliate him,[451] and Kissinger also perceived the action as "humiliating the new president."[452]

Without consulting the relevant advisors, "in the absence of a detailed plan," Kissinger reports, Nixon decided to bomb the Cambodian sanctuaries as he flew from Washington, D.C., to Brussels the very day after the attacks.[453] He did, however, agree to Kissinger's request to postpone the order for forty-eight hours, then later cancelled the original bombing plan. He ordered another strike on March 9, only to rescind it a second time. The first B-52 raid on North Vietnamese bases in Cambodia finally commenced on the morning of March 18. He kept the bombing secret from the American public and told Kissinger: "[The Department of] State is to be notified only after the point of no return."[454] Only after ordering the retaliation on North Vietnamese bases in Cambodia did Nixon meet with some of his advisors, giving them the impression that their input would be considered, even though the attack was a *fait accompli*.

The mid-March attack, codenamed "Breakfast," was initially intended to be a single run. I do not know who came up with this code name; it certainly represents food (psychological support) for Nixon's hungry self; if his hungry self is fed, then his grandiose self will not be threatened. "Breakfast," however, was soon followed by "Lunch," a second attack in mid-April—again, according to Kissinger, based in part on another humiliating situation. This time, the desire was to retaliate against North Korea, which had recently shot down a U.S. spy plane: "But as always when suppressing his instinct for a jugular response, Nixon looked for some other place to demonstrate his mettle. There was nothing he feared more than to be thought weak.[455]" Steinberg summarizes the psychology of Nixon's displaced response:

> What the raid signaled at a personal level was that Nixon was incapable of tolerating weak and impotent feelings in the face of what he perceived to be a deliberate North Korean enemy action. His narcissistic need to be invulnerable and to identify with a powerful United States necessitated a forceful response somewhere, against someone. If the obvious target of a strike, North Korea, was deemed unsuitable, then another target would have to be found. Attacking Cambodian sanctuaries ostensibly enabled Nixon to demonstrate U.S. resolve; but his use of violence was a way of restoring his self-esteem.[456]

According to Steinberg, maximum secrecy was imposed in order to avoid potential humiliation for the president at home as well as to avoid the possibility of having to alter policies as a result of public pressure. The secrecy surrounding the Cambodian bombings may have been the origin of Nixon's preoccupation with leaks to the press and his practice of wiretapping. Nevertheless, as "Lunch" was succeeded by "Dinner," and eventually expanded into an entire "Menu," it became clear by the fall of 1969 that the strategy was failing to serve its overt purpose of weakening the enemy's will to fight and covert purpose of feeding the president's hungry self. Indeed, the North Vietnamese—as predicted in early intelligence—had begun to move deeper into Cambodia, whose ruler was eventually overthrown by military coup in March of 1970.

This dynamic of displacing a response to the threat of personal humiliation is one that Nixon would repeat many times, including in the actual invasion of Cambodia in May 1970. A series of domestic events beginning in 1969 threatened to humiliate Nixon from nearly every angle.[457] Ongoing student unrest placed pressure on Nixon personally as well as publicly, as the possibility of disruptive anti-war demonstrations prevented him from attending the graduations of his daughter Julie from Smith College and his son-in-law David Eisenhower from Amherst College. In April 1970, his nominations of Clement F. Haynsworth and G. Harold Carswell to the U.S. Supreme Court were rejected. Presidential historian James Barber underscores the linkage between these humiliations and revenge: "Nixon moved from April and Carswell to May and Cambodia, from defeat to attack."[458] Further, the Apollo 13 moon mission had been aborted only days after the defeat of the Carswell nomination, leaving Nixon additionally "frustrated, angry, and embarrassed."[459] The combativeness of Nixon's April 30 speech announcing to the public his decision to invade Cambodia illustrates his preoccupation at the time: "We will not be humiliated. We will not be defeated," he asserted, adding that America must not act like "a pitiful, helpless giant." When he declared, "it is not our power but our will and character that is being tested tonight,"[460] he unintentionally revealed the anxiety that he, the symbolic head of the American polity, was experiencing personally: anxiety about having his will and character tested.

Even in private, Nixon seemed like "a man angry and obsessed with the idea that the other side was trying to push him around" in Cambodia, according to Roger Morris, then a National Security Council (NSC) staffer, who reports that discussion of the invasion plans was relatively brief and limited.[461] In a lengthy NSC meeting, Vice-President Spiro Agnew expressed his own view on what should be done, apparently threatening Nixon's superiority, as Kissinger later recalled:

> If Nixon hated anything more than being presented with a plan that he had not considered, it was to be shown up in a group as being less tough than his advisors…I have no doubt that Agnew's intervention accelerated Nixon's ultimate decision to order an attack on all of the sanctuaries and use American forces.[462]

At the same time, the president was fortifying his narcissistic personality traits just before the invasion, watching the film *Patton*—which he had already seen at least four times—shortly before the invasion began.[463] As Steinberg has noted, this repetitive behavior suggests that Nixon needed to identify with the idealized general and thus, in a sense, to adopt the

World War II general's power as his own, to stand up to his enemies as Patton had done. Clearly, concern for the nation and concern for himself were intimately connected in Nixon's mind; unless he took national political action, he would feel personally powerless and humiliated, and such threats were intolerable. As Steinberg reminds us, Nixon's actions would have a powerful ripple effect indeed: the U.S. invasion of Cambodia on May 1, 1970, marked the beginning of a full-fledged civil war that devastated Cambodia and killed more than a million people.[464]

Massive student protests erupted following the invasion, and Nixon faced criticism from Congress, yet he did not waver in maintaining that the invasion was both necessary and effective. When Secretary of the Interior Walter Hickel sent Nixon a letter warning that history had shown that "youth in its protest must be heard,"[465] he was summarily fired. To Nixon's narcissistic personality, Hickel's criticism marked him as the spoiled piece of pie, to return to our metaphor, which had to be eliminated. Similarly, as Haldeman reports, when Nixon's cabinet refused to support his position on Cambodia, he ordered that the White House tennis court—which several cabinet members regularly used—be removed immediately.[466] Though he revoked the order three months later, the tennis court incident reflects how a person with narcissistic personality can use even trivia for the psychological satisfaction they "need." Taking away the tennis court was Nixon's revenge on those who had failed to support his grandiose self; by exercising his superiority over them, he could restore his internal sense of power, thereby erasing the humiliation.[467]

Though Nixon's personality eventually led to his own political downfall, its effects were absorbed in the vast democratic processes of the United States as well as by generalized public denial that a large-group's leader might be a troubled person, and therefore caused little permanent damage to the American public. I do not consider Nixon to be a typical destructive-type leader. It is well known that he also made many reparative attempts. During his presidency, Nixon embarked on one ambitious endeavor after another, including plans to consolidate the power of the executive branch, to mend the political divide between northern and southern conservatives, to reform welfare, to establish détente between the United States and the USSR, to resolve other diplomatic issues concerning China and the Middle East, and to end the Vietnam war with honor. He therefore combined reparative and destructive urges under the demands of his personality organization and according to support or threat he perceived for or against his grandiose self. But there are narcissistic political leaders who are truly of the *destructive* type. They may be imagined to seek the complete ruin of the small, damaged piece of the pie by sprinkling hot peppers all over it so that the two pieces—the good one drenched in ice cream and chocolate and the bad one covered with salad dressing and peppers—must stand absolutely apart from one another. If leaders of the destructive type have *malignant* narcissism, then they will be prone not only to devalue and mistreat a selected large group or subgroup onto which they have projected their own devalued aspects, but also to destroy it: the good part stays under the protection of a "glass bubble," preserved from the threat of ever being mixed with the bad one. By "malignant," I mean the deliberate destruction of "others" with a sense of entitlement to do so and with no remorse.

In some respects, the distinction between the destructive and reparative types of narcissistic leaders can be confusing, at least for a while, not only because one may turn into the other under certain circumstances, but also because both induce collective regression among their followers. Sometimes, narcissistic leaders who enter the political arena protesting injustice may display effective nurturing leadership for some time before their vulnerability becomes obvious and they evolve into destructive, even malignant, leaders.[468] Even Adolf Hitler was capable of protesting injustice and upholding an ethical ideal of some sort for a short time after appearing on the political stage. Overall, however, the reparative type can be seen to help the regressed group move out of its regression and to obtain a new level of functioning with a modified identity, whereas the destructive or malignant narcissistic leader, like Hitler, actually helps to keep his or her followers in a regressed identity.

There have been many attempts to understand the mind of the man who presided over the Holocaust. Scholars have reviewed the various possible psychological influences on the formation of Hitler's personality.[469] Since so much is known about Hitler and the Third Reich, I will not attempt to present a psychobiography of Hitler. I will simply refer to the personality patterns that are reflected in his writings, such as *Mein Kampf (My Struggle)*. What we do know is that his ideology, propaganda, and activities aimed to create two collectives: the first, the Nazis, who were supposed to be tough, grandiose, superior, and powerful; the second, Jews, "Gypsies," homosexuals, and others deemed sub- or even nonhuman. The idea alone that the latter group, the small piece of the pie, "had" to be destroyed leads to the conclusion that Hitler's personality fits well with our understanding of malignant narcissism.

Hitler had an especially talented confederate in Joseph Goebbels, whom he appointed head of Nazi propaganda in 1928 and who is credited with creating the "Fuhrer myth" while Minister of Propaganda and Public Enlightenment (*Propaganda und Volkssaufklarung*) under the Third Reich.[470] Austrian historian Victor Reimann—who was arrested by the Nazis in 1940 and spent the next five years in Nazi prisons—observes, "The Hitler/Goebbels combination is perhaps unique in world history."[471] Goebbels was the architect of the glass bubble in which Hitler could maintain and hide his grandiose self where it could stand uncontaminated and unconnected with Nazi cruelties, so that any atrocities that came to light could be blamed on others; "'If only the Fuhrer knew' became a byword in the Third Reich."[472] Goebbels forbade jokes about the Fuhrer and sought to conceal Hitler's personal weaknesses: a god does not have weaknesses. Hitler's drawings and watercolors from his days as a struggling artist were collected so that no one could critique Hitler as an artist. Goebbels banned even the use of quotations from Hitler's *Mein Kampf* without the permission of his Propaganda Ministry.[473]

It was Goebbels who was ultimately responsible for crafting Hitler's image and many of his signature gestures, Goebbels who made compulsory the use of the title "Fuhrer" and introduced the greeting "Heil Hitler," which, according to Reimann, "sounded more like an exorcism or magic formula than a greeting.[474] Within his glass bubble, Goebbels saw that Hitler was presented as a "god" to the post-1919 Treaty of Versailles Germans, who had been humiliated both materially and emotionally. Hitler's image in his glass bubble was that of a beneficent god, a friend of children and animals, a lover of nature, and a spotlessly clean person.

There were yet more explicit efforts to associate Hitler with God's image in German minds. Walter C. Langer reports German press notices "to the effect that, 'As [Hitler] spoke, one heard God's mantle rustle through the room'"; one German church group even passed a resolution stating that "Hitler's word is God's law, the decrees and laws which represent it possess divine authority."[475] The party adopted a creed that clearly echoed Christian professions of faith: "We all believe, on this earth, in Adolf Hitler, our Fuhrer, and we acknowledge that National Socialism is the only faith that brings salvation to our country."[476] At the Nuremberg rally of September 1937, the inscription below a giant photograph of Hitler read, "In the beginning was the Word ... ," the opening line of the Gospel of John.[477] On another occasion, a photographic portrait of Hitler surrounded by a halo appeared in the front window of each of the large art shops on the *Unter den Linden* in Berlin.[478]

But the Nazi regime's representation of Hitler as a substitute god was not simply iconic. An Israeli psychologist, Judith Stern, describes the various "Thou shalt nots" of the Ten Commandments as all following directly from the acknowledgment of the divine as a transcendental force. Hitler's usurpation of the "first commandment," his establishment of himself as the absolute authority, similarly became the basis of his twisted version of the sixth commandment: thou shalt not kill, except for those who represent the spoiled piece of the apple pie and do not accord with the Aryan ideal, whom thou shalt kill—Jews, homosexuals, "Gypsies," and those with mental and physical disabilities.[479] It was this structure of authority that enabled the paradox lived by Hitler's followers: they killed and tortured and yet returned to their families as apparently normal, loving individuals. Similarly, by investing his grandiose self with sole, divine authority, Hitler invoked the promise of the second part of the Bible's first commandment: the promise of freedom. As Stern reminds us, however, the people of Israel had to wander in the desert for more than a generation before being delivered to the Promised Land—in some sense, in order to develop a society fully organized around the Commandments, with individual freedom gained in accordance with the internalized Commandments. Thus the biblical story depicts a group whose members learn to respond not only to external strictures, but also to internal, non-situational structures of thought, feeling, and judgment that allow freedom of choice within boundaries. The Nazi version, by contrast, promised instant "freedom," but aimed to crush all internal liberty and responsibility; propaganda was their instrument of enforcement.[480]

Intriguingly, the propaganda engineered by Goebbels sought to deify the Fuhrer in ways that apparently accorded with Goebbels's personal experience of Hitler. On November 6, 1925, long before the National Socialists came to power, Goebbels wrote glowingly of his meeting with Hitler at Braunschweig three days earlier: "We go by car to see Hitler. He is at his table. He jumps up, there he stands before us, presses my hand like that of an old friend. And those large blue eyes, like stars ... ." Though Hitler must be tired from the other two speeches he has given that day, Goebbels continues, "he holds another speech here lasting half an hour, full of wit, irony, humor, sarcasm, gravity, and glowing passion. This man has everything to be the King. The born people's tribune. The coming dictator."[481] Reimann describes Goebbels as virtually "possessed by Hitler,"[482] and the propaganda minister remained faithful to his Fuhrer to the end, though not to the Nazi party. Plainly, Goebbels' own idealization of Hitler dovetailed neatly with the political expediency of presenting Hitler to Germans as a "god," as well as with Hitler's belief in his own destiny.

In addition to Goebbels's idealization of the Fuhrer, Rudolf Hess, Hermann Goering, Heinrich Himmler, Joachim von Ribbentrop, Robert Ley, and Alfred Rosenberg also played significant psychological roles in Hitler's entourage. From Zurich psychoanalyst Arno Gruen we have learned a great deal about how Hess and Goring were involved in supporting Hitler's glass bubble and thus protecting Hitler's narcissism, his lonely kingdom.[483] Hess, like Goebbels, was very impressed by Hitler when they first met in 1920; indeed, Hess's wife described her husband's instant attachment to Hitler as "almost magical." Upon returning from a meeting at which Hitler had spoken, she reported, her husband repeatedly shouted "The man! The man!"[484] In a 1934 address, Hess described his perception of Hitler and his own role in idealizing the leader:

With pride we see that one man remains beyond all criticism, that is the Fuhrer. This is because everyone feels and knows: he is always right, and he will always be right. The National Socialism of all of us is anchored in uncritical loyalty, in the surrender to the Fuhrer that does not ask for the why in individual cases, in the silent execution of his orders. We believe that the Fuhrer is obeying a higher call to fashion German history. There can be no criticism in this belief.[485]

Gruen also describes how Goring also surrendered himself to Hitler when he first heard Hitler speak in 1922 and provides details of how Goring's own personal psychology made him part of Hitler's "glass bubble."

Though Joseph Goebbels ensured that Nazi propaganda typically presented Hitler not as an aggressive person but as a good man who was personally completely ignorant of any violent atrocity done in his name, there were times when the satisfaction Hitler derived from his "aggressive triumphs" was publicly apparent:

Hitler's 1932 telegram to five Nazi S.A.[or "storm troopers,"—] murderers [imprisoned] in Potempa, Silesia, in which he congratulated the killers for hacking and kicking a communist organizer to death, was to demonstrate publicly his brutality, ruthlessness, and contempt for normative rules of political conduct. His wire to them read: 'I feel myself bound to you in limitless loyalty. From this moment your liberation is a question of honor.' Further examples of his trampling upon the normative values of German and Western conduct and culture were the burning of books and the banning of 'degenerate' art. He projected an image of barbaric, irresistible power and an extraordinary capacity for aggressive violence independent of moral norms. The message was that opposition was pointless and hopeless. Resistance was futile.[486]

It is clear, then, that even malignant narcissistic leaders need "cronies," who become the "glass bubble" around the leader and maintain their own self-esteem by becoming extensions of the powerful leader. In turn, they help the leader to protect the illusion that his grandiose self is safe and impenetrable. Followers carry out the demands of malignant destructive narcissism, as in Hitler's case, which "spares" the leader from feeling responsible for those acts of destruction. The malignant leader is afraid that the bubble will become penetrable; devalued or "dangerous" others threaten to enter the leader's lonely kingdom; he combines his exaggerated narcissism with pathological paranoid characteristics. But this statement itself needs further scrutiny. Even Hitler showed "reparative" qualities. Nazis themselves, in Judith Stern's terms, were made into "small gods" by their imitation of Hitler.[487] In a sense, Hitler attempted to enhance the self-esteem of his followers. But, as a malignant narcissist, this reparative activity could only be present at the expense of dehumanizing and destroying other groups. Those followers that were made "little gods" were not actually given their personal "freedoms"; they were used to enforce the leader's glass bubble.

Like Hitler, it appears that Joseph Stalin, whose paranoia was more visible than Hitler's, had created a glass bubble. Some years ago, as I already mentioned, I had a chance to interview Stalin's personal interpreter, Valentin Berezhkov.[488] I also had some friendly association with Zoya Zarubina, another interpreter for the Soviet dictator. She is especially known for being with Stalin, Winston Churchill and Franklin D. Roosevelt during the Tehran Conference in 1943.[489] Berezhkov's and Zarubina's descriptions of the Kremlin suggest that the compound's walls acted as a protective bubble around Stalin. Movement through the Kremlin gates was severely restricted. All of the *Politburo* members and secretaries lived in the Kremlin's very modest accommodations, except for Laurenti Beria, head of NKVD, the secret police.[490] According to Berezhkov, Stalin would start working in his office around eleven o'clock in the morning and work until about seven o'clock in the evening. From seven to ten o'clock, he would go to his apartment, and then would return to his office and work until around six o'clock the next morning. Berezhkov never undressed at night, because a call from Stalin could come at any time. Ministers, all members of the Politburo, sometime would call Berezhkov and ask if Stalin had retired for the evening. Berezhkov thought that the ministers' decision to stay in the Kremlin—and they certainly stayed if Stalin were awake—was connected with their "personal enthusiasm and striving to do the best possible work." He added, "on the other hand, they were also afraid."[491] They stayed within the Kremlin, Stalin's glass bubble, not as individuals in their own right but as an extension of the dictator and especially the protectors of the leader's narcissism.

Zarubina recalled how surprised she was when she met Stalin for the first time. Contrary to publicized newsreels and photographs, Stalin was a rather fragile-looking man, no taller than she, with pockmarked and pale skin. He was ugly. Clearly, Stalin was careful never to show any vulnerability; his smallpox scars would have been a weakness, they would make him a regular fellow. So his entourage kept his image handsome, tall, and grand: Stalin's pitted nose and cheeks were never seen by the public because either the photographs were touched up or makeup was used. The same cronies and propaganda machinery also presented Stalin as a "Genius of Mankind, "Father of the People," "Standard-Bearer of Communism," "Leading Light of Science," and "Transformer of Nature," among others.[492] All of the titles bestowed on Stalin protected his narcissism and strengthened the impenetrable invisible "wall" around him.

On the other end of the spectrum, some leaders with exaggerated love who are not destructive or malignant, who do not possess paranoid trends, and who are truly reparative, have openings in their "glass bubbles" and thus interact more intimately with the public. Because the reparative leader's goal is to increase the value of his followers, the "wall" of his or her bubble is more porous, so that those who enter become idealized along with the leader and followers are granted their individuality to one degree or another. A reparative leader supports his or her grandiose self by being loved by people who have their own self-esteem.

For example, although Ataturk, a reparative leader, was indeed a lonely man internally, he did not have paranoid characteristics; he did willingly expose himself and his "glass bubble" to the public. Like other reparative leaders, whether or not they exhibit exaggerated self-love, Ataturk served as a good teacher for his followers for some time. The next chapter will examine in greater detail his function as teacher of the nation and will consider other political leaders who have acted as teachers. Internal worlds of such teachers can be reflected in societal processes influencing large-group identity issues, rituals and regression or progression.

8 / leaders as teachers

How significant and how durable is the stroking that led to the sale of, say, a washing machine? If the salesman was relying on his sweet-talking rather than the quality of the product, will the washer wear out before the memories of the sweet talk wear thin?

—James MacGregor Burns, *Leadership*

While traveling in Europe in July 1998, I caught sight of an unusual photograph on the front pages of some local newspapers. In the photograph, a man dressed in a long-sleeved shirt was looking out of a car window and holding a shoe in his right hand; one finger of that hand bore a huge, expensive-looking ring. Oddly, the man seemed to be waving the shoe in greeting to his onlookers, as if it were a hat or a handkerchief.

The subject of the photo, Bacharuddin Jusuf "B.J." Habibie, was the new president of Indonesia; he had come to power a few months earlier when the autocrat Suharto was forced to resign after more than three decades as president. Though the Suharto regime had initially created economic growth in Indonesia, a country comprised of 17,670 islands spanning 3,500 miles from Southeast Asia to Australia, it was supported by a repressive military, and its tenure was riddled with human rights abuses. In the throes of severe economic crisis, the regime finally crumbled in May 1998. Habibie, an aeronautical engineer by training, had worked for his predecessor for more than twenty years before succeeding him.

The new president announced the establishment of a "Reform and Development Cabinet," but outside observers, and most Indonesians, expected Habibie's presidency to be brief because of his clear connections to Suharto. It did not take long for these predictions to be validated.[493] In

215

truth, Habibie had become president under dreadful conditions. Law and order had broken down terribly in the last days of Suharto's regime. Further, as the Suharto-era ideology of "*Bhinneka tunngal Ika*" (Unity in Diversity) collapsed, tensions had spread through the country's many ethnic and religious groups; economic collapse and the ensuing riots had induced shared anxiety and regression in Indonesia's population, deepening "us-and-them" divisions and a kind of destructive purification ritual. Many ethnic Chinese had lost their property in the riots, and approximately 168 Chinese women and girls were subjected to systematic sexual assault on the basis of their ethnicity.[494]

But Habibie did nothing to calm these conditions, declaring early in his administration that the ethnic Chinese who had fled in the face of such threats would not be missed. In September 1998, Habibie's armed forces commander and Minister of Defense and Security, General Wiranto, and the Minister for Women's Affairs, Tuty Alawiyah, stated that their investigation turned up no woman who claimed to have been raped, though the independent international organization Human Rights Watch continued to insist that rapes had occurred.[495] Though Habibie later began to speak of the importance of ethnic Chinese residents to the Indonesian economy, his flip-flop on anti-Chinese racism, the debate over the rapes, the country's economic chaos, and continuing anxiety and insecurity did not provide an atmosphere in which Indonesians could fully maintain a shared idealization for their new president. In 1999 elections, he was replaced by Abdurrahman Wahid.

Though Habibie's time as a political leader was short-lived, the picture of him waving a shoe lodged in my mind as an image of a leader engaging in a "show and tell" sort of activity, if ultimately an unsuccessful one. As the articles which accompanied the photo reported, Habibie had bought the shoes he waved for $2.70 (USD) in a market in Jakarta, the Indonesian capital. By showing the cheap shoes to his followers, he was offering himself as a figure with whom Indonesians could identify, attempting to "teach" his fellow citizens how to be thrifty. That Habibie failed as a teacher speaks, obviously, to Indonesia's historical circumstances as well as to his personality and personal history. But I think we can look once more to the image for insight: the juxtaposition of the cheap shoes and the expensive ring did not make for a consistent "lesson" to the Indonesian people and reflected his past association with the corrupt Suharto regime. The people did not rally around Habibie, even though chaos and regression prevailed in the country. So we must look elsewhere to find leaders who have been effective "teachers"—whether toward productive or counter-productive ends—whose "show and tell" and other propagandistic activities taught their followers new ways of thinking, behaving, or developing new skills, and, more important, modified their large-group identity and their rituals and effected their regressive or progressive movements.

I know of only two political leaders, Mustafa Kemal Ataturk of Turkey and Julius Kambarage Nyerere of Tanzania, who were officially called "teachers"—"*muallim*" and "*mwalimu*," respectively.[496] Both were, in fact, "virtuous" teachers who used teaching to elevate their followers' emotional and physical conditions and provide self-esteem for their identity. In Chapter 1, I related one instance of Ataturk's "show and tell" behavior, when he almost instantly changed Turkish headgear into a symbol of the group's "new" large-group identity. It was three years after this Panama hat episode, in 1928, that Ataturk took the nickname "muallim."[497] The same year, a cabinet regulation transformed the entire nation into a "School of the Nation," of which "every male and female Turkish citizen is a member." Further, this regulation states that "the chief instructor of the School of the Nation is His Excellency the President of the Republic, Ghazi Mustafa Kemal."[498]

This same regulation was the legal source for Ataturk's alphabet reform scheme, which began with a drama—a teaching session worthy of this exalted title. When the new Turkey rose from the ashes of the Ottoman Empire in 1923, 80 percent to 90 percent of the population was illiterate, and Ataturk sought to transform Turkey into a nation of literate people. Before many ethnic Turks settled in what is now Turkey, their language had used the thirty-eight character Altay alphabet, which is similar to Chinese ideograms, but when the Turks came under the influence of Islam, they adopted the Arabic alphabet (with the addition of some Persian letters), which is not the best vehicle for the Turkish language's complex vowel system.[499] Converting Turkish to the Latin alphabet would make reading and writing Turkish easier and would reduce illiteracy in Turkey; it also would suit Ataturk's general western orientation. Though his advisors predicted that the transition would require at least seven years, the leader held that the alphabet should be changed within three months. In May 1928, Turkey's numbering system was changed to conform to that of the West; two months later, a special commission, with which the leader worked personally, was established to devise the new alphabet. The public curtain rose on alphabet reform at an evening gathering in Istanbul that August. Mustafa Kemal rose with a paper in his hand and asked for someone to come forward and read it. One young man offered, but was baffled by the Latin characters on the page. The leader then gave the page to a member of the alphabet commission, who read aloud the message to the audience, a message to the Turkish nation from its "chief instructor" explaining why a new alphabet was needed. This stage drama was followed by cheers, after which Ataturk rose to his feet and lifted his glass of *rakı* (a Turkish "national" drink[500]) in a toast: "In the past," he said, "those two-faced impostors [the Ottoman elite] used to drink a thousand times more of this secretly in their dunghills. I am not an imposter. I drink to the honor of my nation."[501] His toast dealt another blow to Muslim tradition, for the consumption of alcohol is forbidden in Islam. But, since their leader drank openly, most of the audience followed suit.

The Latin alphabet became the official system for the new Turkey on August 1, 1929. One might have expected sharp and outraged resistance to such language reform; the adoption of the new letters could easily have been seen in religious terms as alignment with the "infidel" world, since the new law undermined the special status of religious teachers and the Arabic writing system they had traditionally used. Excepting one outbreak of religious fanaticism in December 1930—which was not explicitly a response to alphabet reform alone, but a general response to Mustafa Kemal's westernization program—the new alphabet was officially in place within approximately three months.

Ataturk took an active and highly visible role in helping the new alphabet take root. The nation's headmaster had blackboards set up around the Dolmabahce Palace in Istanbul, where the last sultans of the Ottoman Empire had resided; chalk in hand, Ataturk himself gave lessons in the new script to palace visitors. Parliamentary deputies were required to learn the new alphabet quickly, and then were sent to the countryside to teach the rural population. The headmaster himself traveled around the country in the service of alphabet reform; a huge blackboard was set up wherever he went for his "show and tell" lessons. One particularly famous photograph shows Ataturk standing before a blackboard set up under a tree, teaching the new script to adult "students." He would spend hours lecturing, and then, like a teacher, would question his audience to make sure that his "students" had absorbed the lesson. Interestingly, because children learned the new alphabet more quickly than adults did, it was not unusual during this period to see children instructing their parents, which I suspect was particularly gratifying to a man of Ataturk's personality: to see children not only relying upon their own inner strength as they surpassed their parents, but also "repairing" their mothers and fathers through education.[502]

If we revisit Ataturk's first memory of life—his father's insistence on giving him a secular education—we can identify yet another psychological motivation behind his role as the nation's teacher. After his father's death, young Mustafa transferred to his teacher his idealizations of his dead father and came to identify with this new father-figure, whose name was Semsi, a derivative of the Arabic word for the sun. But religious fanatics repeatedly attacked young Mustafa's "westernized" teacher verbally and physically, cursing and beating him and chopping his classroom furniture into pieces. Against great odds, the young teacher survived and kept his school open. In his later roles as military leader, reformer, and national teacher, Ataturk often returned to his identification with the besieged but ultimately successful Semsi by invoking the image of the sun. His speeches and a revolutionary song (which he adopted from a Swedish tune) frequently refer to his followers' shared grief and desperation in an enemy-occupied country as a dark cloud and depict himself as the sun that will dispel the darkness. Interestingly, his followers also perceived him in these terms, and often used the same symbols when talking and writing about him. When I later interviewed individuals who had met Ataturk, many reported that they could not look into his eyes for they "shone like the sun," too bright to look into directly.

Like Ataturk, Julius Kambarage Nyerere, the "co-founding father" and first president of the United Republic of Tanzania,[503] loved to teach and liked his followers to think of him as a teacher.[504] Indeed, Nyerere was trained as a teacher and idealized education. Born in 1922, Nyerere was the son of a chief of the Zanahi tribe, who lived on the eastern shore of Lake Victoria. Though he did not begin to walk the twenty-six miles to the nearest school until he was twelve years old, Nyerere's teachers recognized his intelligence almost immediately, and it is likely that young Nyerere received a great deal of praise and approval for his extraordinary efforts toward learning. Eventually, with the help of the Catholic Church, he was able to attend Makerere University in Kampala, Uganda, for teacher training. Some years later he received a Master of Arts from the University of Edinburgh in Scotland, where he was exposed to social democratic ideas, particularly Fabian thinking, which advocated that the negative effects of capitalism be remedied through social reforms.[505] Nyerere became a political figure when he returned to Tanganyika, but he remained a teacher at heart.

When Tanzania became a sovereign state in 1964, it was one of the poorest countries in the world. The British had left the country with an 85 percent illiteracy rate and only two engineers and twelve doctors. President Nyerere, the teacher, believed that formal education during the colonial period had served western interests and to enslaved its native students.[506] Nyerere's idea of learning advocated the liberation of the student; he scorned those who pursued education only to collect diplomas for their walls and considered such an attitude to be the disease of an acquisitive society. People learn in order to do something, he argued: education must become a part of life if it is to contribute to national development. So he sought to design an educational system that was oriented toward rural life and would engage teachers and students in productive activities that would improve their earning power and thus the economy. Children in the new Tanzania began their schooling at seven years old, but Nyerere's program also emphasized adult education. Education, he believed, would increase the mental freedom of all citizens and increase their control over themselves and their own lives.[507] At the end of Nyerere's presidency, Tanzania could boast a relatively low 9 percent illiteracy rate and thousands of professionals, such as engineers and doctors.

It is generally agreed that Nyerere's educational initiative in the early 1980s offered his people equal citizenship and new hope, especially for refugees who had escaped from conflicts in the Great Lakes region into Tanzania. Though he remained active in domestic and regional politics for the rest of his life,[508] Nyerere voluntarily resigned from the presidency of Tanzania in 1985, a marked contrast to the actions of many other African political leaders of his generation, even considering his two decades in the presidency. Whether he succeeded in his every effort is beyond the point:[509] the fact remains that Nyerere was a compassionate and reparative leader who advocated peaceful change, social equality, and racial harmony. The Mwalimu ("Teacher") Nyerere Foundation in Dar es Salaam seeks to perpetuate his legacy by promoting people-centered development and peace throughout Africa.

How does large-group "teaching," such as that performed by Ataturk and Nyerere, work? First we must consider what psychoanalysis has to tell us about teaching more generally.[510] According to the basic psychoanalytic model (developed mostly by observing children in therapeutic nursing schools and young adults in classrooms), the teacher emerges, in a safe classroom environment, as a person in whom the students invest various emotions; the teacher may be experienced as an extension of parents or others with whom the student struggles emotionally, or he or she may be idealized. When possible, teachers show symbolic representations of the intellectual concept or perform the skill as a kind of "show and tell." This performance affects the emotional state of the student, who begins to assimilate the meaning of the concept or skill while partly identifying with the teacher. Once the students come to identify with the teacher, they experience something similar to what psychoanalysts call the *separation-individuation process* of childhood:[511] the teacher is no longer needed once the student is able to use what he or she has been taught to control and relate more adaptively to his or her environment. Often, the younger the student is, the more prominent the emotional relationship between the teacher and student. When students are older, rational considerations and intellectual activities tend to be superimposed on increasingly hidden emotional aspects of teacher–student interaction and identification. The student also comes to use logical thinking to evaluate critically what he or she is being taught. Thus it is not necessarily an obstacle to education when students disagree with their teacher: a good teacher will track down hidden concerns and help the student discuss them in order to assist the student's intellectual and emotional development. "The teacher not only imparts knowledge, but also nurtures and empowers"[512] as the student assimilates the teacher's ways of thinking and behaving and love of the topic or skill that he or she is teaching.

As in a conventional classroom setting, the large-group leader is subject to the expectations of his or her followers, and followers may identify with the leader when he or she "shows and tells" a new concept or skill. But this sort of teaching differs critically from teaching in one-to-one or small classroom situations: the relationship between a large group and its leader is generally characterized by greater expectations—whether wishes or fears—as well as a greater tendency to distort the teacher according to those expectations.[513] Students' personal experiences with the reality of their classroom teachers tend to modify and lessen such distorted expectations. As followers of a political leader seldom know their leader personally, however, their processes of learning (and maintaining) what the leader seeks to teach depend greatly upon the large group's level of anxiety and regression and upon shared and intense perceptions of the leader that may have varying bases in reality.

The result tends to be that the individual follower is swept up with fellow group members toward accepting new information, especially when the teaching is accompanied by the systematic manipulation of official propaganda. The struggle against identification with the leader, which I described as an important part of the teacher-student relationship in the classroom, is bypassed to some degree, and the learner is often deprived of a *slow* process of mastering new concepts and skills and their meanings.[514] Hence no process analogous to the "separation-individuation" can take place in the members of a large group. Instead of being enriched as individuals, the members of a large group, following their quick identification with the political leader-teacher, tend to focus on their shared large-group identity as modified by the leader's teachings. In this process, we can catch an echo of Sigmund Freud's description of the dynamics of mass psychology that I have already described in some detail earlier in this book: the members of the large group identify with each other because they have all learned the new concept or skill, and they rally around the leader who has taught it to them. Symbolic representations of the leader's teaching provide new links among group members. Thus the Panama hat and the new alphabet in Turkey were visible symbols that linked Turks to one another and to their leader across vast distances.

Initially, the members of the group must preserve their shared idealization of the leader in order to maintain what they have learned; over time, they may even assimilate the changes they have been taught to make. Nevertheless, durable change in a society where new ideas have come from the top is no sure thing: new political doctrines or ideologies imparted to a large group by a teaching or "transforming"[515] leader may lose their staying power once the leader dies or otherwise ceases to be a magnet for his or her followers' shared idealization. Typically, political leaders are aware of this fact and create legal measures and other institutions to force or aid assimilation of new concepts or skills. For example, the fact that Turkish children were prohibited from using the Arabic script in school made the assimilation of alphabet reform possible. Legal measures and cultural institutions thus enforce a procedure analogous to slow-process teaching in the classroom.

If in the future the group ceases to idealize the image of the political leader, who may by then be dead, it may again struggle over the shared processes initiated by the leader's teachings. Some forty years after Ataturk's death, for example, some groups in Turkey, especially those with extreme fundamentalist religious affiliations, began to question certain aspects of the "Ataturk revolution." Still, a new doctrine or ideology can persist if the group shares the belief that to give it up would actually weaken the fabric of the large group's shared identity. Thus "Kemalism"[516] persists more than half a century after Ataturk's death because it has, with the aid of his successors' support and propaganda, become essential to modern Turkish identity.[517]

In the last decade of the twentieth century, two political leaders took opposite directions when their countries were, in a sense, "reborn" after drastic changes. Nelson Mandela in post-apartheid South Africa became a truly reparative leader; Slobodan Milosevic in post-communist Yugoslavia became a horribly destructive one. A comparison of their "teaching" styles illuminates how a leader can use his or her power to heal or to poison a society in crisis and influence large-group regression or progression.

It is a truism among researchers of Nelson Mandela's career that he developed the ability to make compromises and forgive his "enemies" without bitterness as a result of a transformation during his twenty-seven-year imprisonment.[518] As Mandela himself writes, "In prison, my anger toward whites decreased, but my hatred for the system grew. I wanted South Africa to see that I loved even my enemies while I hated the system that turned us against one another."[519] To his biographer Brian Frost, Mandela explains the development of his ideology of reconciliation as a transformation of "my hunger for the freedom of my people [into] a hunger for the freedom of all people, white and black. I knew as I knew anything that the oppressor must be liberated just as surely as the oppressed, for all had been robbed of humanity. When I walked out of prison, that was my mission, to liberate the oppressed and the oppressor both."[520] From a memory of childhood described in his autobiography, however, we can see that Mandela's ability to sympathize across a divide perhaps has deeper roots in his personality. Mandela recalls losing face among his friends after being thrown from an unruly donkey. Even though it was a donkey and not a person that had unseated him, he learned that to humiliate another person was to make him suffer. He told Frost that even as a boy, he defeated his opponents without dishonoring them.[521] In this single memory, which may be one of a set of more-complex memories of the same nature, he reflects not only his own youthful embarrassment, but also his capacity for empathy and his commitment to not humiliating others. It is a lesson that he has taught his followers over and over.

In "teaching" new ideas to his political entourage, Mandela could behave more like the teacher in a conventional classroom, since his close associates of course knew him personally. Early in 1994, for example, the executive committee of Mandela's party, the African National Congress (ANC), was set to discuss the question of the country's national anthem.[522] The country's first fully democratic election would be held in April 1994, and it was clear that the ANC would win. The existing anthem, *Die Stem*, seemed obviously unacceptable to the committee members, as it celebrated the triumphs of nineteenth-century Afrikaner trekkers as they fought and conquered the indigenous peoples. Mandela was slated to preside over the meeting in which the issue was to be discussed, but he was called away soon after the meeting began. During his absence, an overwhelming majority of the committee members expressed their wish to replace *Die Stem* with *Nkosi Sikelele*, which expressed the suffering of the indigenous people. Tokyo Sexwale, a leading ANC figure who had spent time with Mandela in prison, vividly remembered the mood at the meeting during Mandela's absence. "We were enjoying ourselves. It is the end for the *Die Stem* song, we said. The end. No more."[523] When Mandela returned to the meeting, however, he responded much like a correcting schoolmaster:

> Well, I am sorry. I don't want to be rude ... but this song that you treat so easily holds the emotions of many people whom you don't represent. Yet, with the stroke of a pen, you would make a decision to destroy the very—the only—basis that we are building upon: reconciliation.[524]

No one in the room protested; as Sexwale recalled, "we were all like small primary schoolchildren."[525] After the ANC victory in the April election, South Africa adopted *Nkosi Sikelele* as an additional anthem; both are always played in succession at official ceremonies.

In 1995, the year following Mandela's election to the presidency, South Africa hosted the World Cup Rugby Championships, the most significant international event to take place there since the fall of apartheid. South Africa had been barred from the first two World Cup Rugby Championships, in 1987 and 1991, because of its policy of apartheid. Indeed, the 1995 tournament would be a test for the new image of South Africa. What Mandela actually did, however, went far beyond ensuring an organized tournament that reflected well on the new government. Mandela created an emotional atmosphere that not only enabled the South African team to triumph on the field—beating the former world champion, Australia, in the opening match, prevailing over France in the semifinals, and winning the championship over New Zealand in overtime—but also helped to teach his fellow citizens a new way of thinking about each other and the nation.

Until the 1995 World Cup, rugby had been considered a white man's sport in South Africa; in fact, it had been "a symbol of white Afrikaner unity and pride dating back to the Boer War" at the turn of the twentieth century.[526] In 1995, the South African team was virtually all white, with only one nonwhite player on its roster; even its nickname, the Springboks, was a controversial symbol strongly associated with apartheid. Yet Mandela, playing the role of reconciler, was able to turn this team into one that truly represented post-apartheid South Africa. Donning a Springbok cap, he visited the team's training camp and shook hands with the players, telling them that the whole nation was behind them. In public speeches, he began to talk about a new image for the Springboks. The day before their match against Australia, the rugby team visited Robben Island, where Mandela had been imprisoned for some two-thirds of his twenty-seven years as a political prisoner. After visiting his former cell, they dedicated their efforts in the World Cup to their president. The whole country was galvanized.

The next day, under the spell of this emotional atmosphere, the Springboks defeated Australia 27–18. A high percentage of the residents of the black township of Soweto, on the outskirts of Johannesburg, watched the team that had been associated with the apartheid regime,[527] even though the single black player on the team was out with injury and did not participate in the game. On the eve of the match against France, Mandela continued to speak publicly about the Springboks' new image. In a speech given to the black community in the town of Ezakheni, he pointed to his cap—again, like a teacher doing "show and tell"—and said, "This cap does honor to our boys. I ask you to stand by them tomorrow because they are our kind."[528] After winning the championship, the Springboks participated in a public service campaign designed to encourage black township residents to pay their utility bills—many had refused to pay even after the fall of the apartheid government—so that the rebuilding of all South Africa could begin. Sports had merged with civic education and politics.

Using black South Africans' feelings and perceptions of him as an idealized figure, Mandela was able to use an unlikely symbol to modify existing societal attitudes about race, nation, and civic responsibility. Black South Africans' strong pre-existing identification with Mandela meant that his embrace of the national rugby team spread quickly without much critical evaluation. In turn, many black citizens projected onto the sport other positive connotations associated with this identification with Mandela. For instance, soon after Mandela's visit with the rugby team, a headline in *The Sowetan* boasted, "*Amabokoboko*," Zulu for "Our Springboks."[529] Black South Africans now felt a sense of "ownership" toward the mostly white team. Thus the sport of rugby became an important symbol of common ground between blacks and whites.

The thinking of Archbishop Desmond Tutu, chair of South Africa's Truth and Reconciliation Commission (TRC), paralleled Mandela's insistence on reconciliation as a paramount value.[530] In April 1996, the TRC began to investigate crimes committed during the apartheid era, often offering immunity from prosecution in exchange for testimony. There were critics of the TRC at times, including some blacks, who claimed that the TRC was partial to whites. When in 1997 the TRC granted amnesty to Dirk Coetzee, a confessed apartheid hit-squad leader, for example, some South Africans were incensed. It is my opinion that at such points it was Tutu's *personality* that enabled the work of the TRC to continue. I have occasionally heard talk of attempts to create organizations similar to the TRC in other traumatized societies; once I was asked to review a program designed by some German political scientists for Bosnia-Herzegovina. Though, from a psychoanalyst's point of view, TRC-style work is the best way to deal with chronic anger, helplessness, and difficulty in mourning in a traumatized society, its success is not guaranteed. My belief is that no such program will work as well as the South African TRC unless it is conducted under the leadership of someone like Desmond Tutu—a human being possessing intelligence, compassion, integrity, honesty, and humor in abundance—in an atmosphere like the one created by Nelson Mandela.

South Africa still faces serious societal problems, among which the most publicized is a high incidence of rape. One wonders if this behavior is in some way connected to the humiliation to which the indigenous black population was subjected under apartheid. I do not know the answer, but I believe that it is an important and valid question: in other traumatized societies that I have observed at close range, rape and intrafamilial violence increased, and previous family structures and values were destroyed, once acute ethnic war had concluded. Nevertheless, under the guidance of Mandela and his reparative leadership, violent civil war between whites and blacks was averted. Over the same period in another part of the world, another leader began to teach his people a quite different ideology, one that led finally to massive destruction and death.

In 1988, Slobodan Milosevic—supported by an organized propaganda effort that included his entourage as well as certain academics and Serbian Orthodox Church officials—was able to reactivate a Serbian chosen trauma concerning the 1389 military defeat at the Battle of Kosovo by engaging in a "show and tell" behavior. As I mentioned earlier, Milosevic ordered the disinterment of a Serbian battle-hero's ancient remains and toured with those remains from one Serbian village to another. At each location, political speeches were made by Milosevic's proxies and funeral ceremonies held as if the fourteenth-century Prince Lazar had been killed just recently. The next day, Lazar would be "resurrected" in order to be "killed" and waked in another location, creating the atmosphere for a "time collapse": the fantasies and feelings Serbs shared about the past event and hero became intertwined with shared perceptions and anxieties surrounding contemporary social and political conditions. During the last (and permanent) rituals of reburial on the 600th anniversary of the traumatic military loss, Milosevic himself performed the "show and tell," reactivating Serbian unity and sense of purpose.

As a helicopter descended onto the Kosovo field where the battle had taken place, delivering Milosevic to the gathered crowd, that "time collapse" put a sharper symbolic edge on the day's events. After Lazar's death at the hands of the Ottomans, the mythology that grew up around his image associated the dead prince with Jesus Christ himself: in heroic self-sacrifice, Lazar had chosen a kingdom in heaven. Now, on June 28, 1989, the symbolic message was that Milosevic represented Lazar's second coming. And the righteous kingdom on earth that this resurrected Lazar promised was one in which Serbs' present humiliation would be overcome by reversing the humiliation of the past. Lazar, like Jesus, had been killed, but his killers had been Muslims, not Jews. Thus, when Milosevic "took the podium from dancing maidens in traditional folk costume and transported the crowd to heights of frenzied adoration," it was "with a simple message: 'Never again would Islam subjugate the Serbs.'"[531] Accordingly, the targets of Serbian aggression under Milosevic were mostly Muslims: Bosniaks in the former Yugoslavia, and later Kosovar Albanians.[532] While we cannot reduce the rituals that centered on Prince Lazar's body—much less the genocidal events that followed—to an expression of Milosevic's personality alone, I suggest that we can nevertheless discern some evidence of the influence of Milosevic's personality in these events.

Milosevic came from a broken family and experienced severe trauma early in life. His favorite uncle, an army officer, committed suicide by shooting himself in the head when Milosevic was seven years old. Thirteen years later, his father would do the same thing, and his mother killed herself as well, when Milosevic was in his early thirties. It is difficult to imagine that these terrible events did not have a profound effect in shaping Milosevic's adult personality. He married his teenage sweetheart,

Mirjana Markovic, but that story also lacks a fairy-tale ending. Mirjana's mother, a Yugoslav partisan during World War II, was captured by the Nazis and surrendered crucial information under torture. After her release, the leader of her partisan group—who happened to be her own father—executed her.[533]

From clinical experience, we know that individuals who have experienced such drastic losses often become stuck in mourning, and that these "complicated mourners" sometimes try symbolically to "resurrect" the dead in order to find resolution. There are those who "succeed," who are able to "resurrect" and "repair" symbolic substitutes for their lost loved ones—or even, as in Ataturk's case, for losses suffered by a parent. Others who have conflicted feelings about their lost ones, who nurtured a great deal of aggression toward them or experienced humiliation at their hands, may not be able to turn their efforts into adaptive behaviors: their minds, at least unconsciously, may be preoccupied with repeated killings and resurrections without resolution. Milosevic's "show and tell" behavior involved such a "killing and resurrecting": a year-long public ritual involving the 600-year-old corpse of a Serbian hero. If Milosevic projected a preoccupation with his dead relatives onto the outside world, he may have been spared from feeling any internal ambivalence toward those lost figures, since his internal conflict was being reenacted externally, in the historical argument.

What differentiated Milosevic's curriculum of Serbian resurgence (and the propaganda campaign that supported and developed it) was its connection to the Serbian chosen trauma. It is when a new religious doctrine or national ideology is taught as being connected to a sense of shared victimization—or, though to a lesser degree, to a sense of shared domination over an enemy—that the leader's teaching may become a poisoning force of destruction. Unlike Milosevic, reparative leaders do not focus on their followers' grievances at the hands of others: Ataturk, for example, did not teach his people that the Western world was an enemy to be destroyed—even though, in fact, Ataturk's new Turkey was the successor state to the Ottoman Empire, which had been defeated by a Western alliance. Rather, Ataturk's "enemies" were illiteracy and ignorance among the people and the old Ottoman elite's poor treatment of ordinary citizens. His changes sought to enrich his followers' competence and self-sufficiency, and thereby to spare them a shared sense of victimization. By contrast, Milosevic's teaching not only reactivated the shared past trauma, but also spread fear of imminent (re)victimization. This fear of imminent oppression at the group level—even if it was mainly a fantasy—increased Serbs' sense of "we-ness" and encouraged a shared sense of being entitled to victimize the former Yugoslav Muslims. Serbian propaganda exaggerated (and distorted) Bosnian Muslims' aims and their leader Alija Izetbegovic's ideas about Islamic influence in Bosnia:

> By order of the Islamic fundamentalists from Sarajevo, healthy Serbian women aged 17 to 40 years are being separated out and subjected to special treatment. According to their sick plans going back many years, these women have to be impregnated by Orthodox Islamic seeds in order to raise a generation of Jannisaries[534] on the territories they surely consider to be theirs, the Islamic Republic. In other words, a fourfold crime is to be committed against the Serbian woman; to remove her from her own family, to impregnate her with undesirable seeds, to make her bear a stranger, and then to take him away from her.[535]

This piece of propaganda also clearly shows an attempt at "time collapse," as the propagandist digs up and reincarnates "Janissaries," a class of Ottoman soldiers out of use for centuries, to represent a supposed current threat and to evoke the continuity of distant past and present.[536]

It seems that the world community has not yet learned how to assess and respond to poisonous political teaching at early stages.[537] For example, when Slobodan Milosevic began to don the garb of nationalism, he did not publicly announce any plans to "restore" a Greater Serbia. However, behind the scenes, he supported certain academics in their research on the extent of the ancient Serbian empire, which would provide a legitimating "historical" basis for Serbian expansion into other parts of former Yugoslavia. Without intervention, societies in crisis can easily develop such *entitlement ideologies*;[538] assuming the availability of cash and weapons, "teaching" like Milosevic's can easily intensify until it prompts time collapse and malignant acts of "purification." But we can predict— and act to prevent—these eventualities in societies where identity modifications are visible. The international community must become more alert to political propaganda contaminated with a reactivated chosen trauma, and it must act to avert the corresponding blind trust and entitlement ideologies before they lead to sustained large-group regression and/or violence—even to genocide. Even after destructive leaders die or are removed from power, the societal effects of entrenched large-group regression can last for years—often decades—creating even more human misery before progression begins.

I observed this first-hand in Albania, a country that for four decades was a regressed state under a malignant leader. After the death of its leader, Albania experienced a choatic leaderless regression and only began to progress with tremendous difficulties. I am speaking of Enver Hoxha's Albania and post-Hoxha Albania. I will use Albania as a detailed case study to illustrate the psychology of large-group identity, rituals, and, as Albania's story demonstrates, the consequences of entrenched large-group regression and present attempts for progression.

/ part four: a case study

9 / albania: from regression to progression

Prison is impossible without dreaming ...
Yet I ...
I look and here my cigarette's burned out in my hand—
I never took a puff.

—Nazim Hikmet,"Amnesty"
  translated from Turkish by Randy Blasing and Mutlu Konuk

Fazile Godo (not her real name) was born in Tirana, Albania, at the end of 1943. Just three years later, Fazile's thirty-six-year-old father, an Italian-educated Albanian intellectual, was accused of opposing Albanian dictator Enver Hoxha and sentenced to a 101-year jail term. On a snowy winter day, two *Sigurimi* agents, members of Hoxha's secret police, forced Fazile, her twenty-five-year-old mother, and her two-year-old brother into a truck and drove them from their home in the Albanian capital of Tirana toward the mountain village of Deloirra, where they were to live in the internal exile customary for the families of prisoners. Going over the Tepelina Mountains, however, the truck broke down, and the two agents told Fazile's mother that they could not fix the truck. Since Fazile's mother and her children were "undesirables," the men left on foot to safety, abandoning the family to freeze to death on the snow-covered mountaintop.

More than 50 years later, Fazile's recollections of the episode are vivid. After the Sigurimi agents left, Fazile recalls, her mother managed to carry herself and her children to shelter: an abandoned ruin of a house without roof or doors. Then her mother collected some tree branches and started a fire. A pack of wolves with shining eyes came to attack them, Fazile reports, and kept their distance only because of the fire. But there were not enough tree branches to keep the fire going for long, and her mother believed that she and her children would soon be eaten alive. Suddenly they heard a noise: another truck was coming. Her mother decided to throw herself and her children under the approaching truck and be killed instantly rather than be torn apart by the wolves. Fortunately, the truck driver managed to stop in time and took the abandoned three to Deloirra to start their lives over as undesirable exiles.

Fazile and her mother and brother lived in Deloirra as "people's enemies" for two years. Other residents mostly avoided contact with the newcomers, and little Fazile began to sense that she was different from other people—that she was "bad." Two years later, Fazile's father was released from prison, and the whole family once more lived together in their own house in Tirana, though their furniture had been removed. Little Fazile could not recapture the sense of inner security that her home life had provided prior to her father's incarceration. Her father's release from jail did not end his family's undesirable status.

Her father had been badly tortured in prison, and he carried obvious physical evidence of his experience: his fingernails had been pulled out one by one, and his hands were further deformed and blackened because his jailers had bound his wrists together most of the time, cutting off circulation to his hands and fingers. In time, Fazile would learn the other details of her father's torture: hands tied behind his back, he would be hung upside down over a container full of water for hours at a time. Sometimes his tormentors would drop his head into the water and pull him up again before he drowned. At other times, the torturers would place boiled eggs in his armpits, burning his skin. In spite of "knowing" (if not the details, at least the terror of) what had happened to her father, little Fazile was subjected to absolute parental silence on the topic. If Fazile's parents had complained about Hoxha's regime, and if the children had talked about their parents' complaints in school, her father once more would be imprisoned, and the rest of the family would again be sent into internal exile. Fazile knew that she possessed the power to ruin her parents. When she experienced "normal" anger in the face of life's inevitable frustrations, she felt like a monster: if she expressed her anger against her parents and complained about them, she could literally destroy them.[539]

Of course, Fazile's recollections of what happened on the mountaintop and in the years immediately following the ordeal probably combine reality and fantasy: some accurate memories of real danger and elements of what her mother told her later mingled with a terrorized three-year-old child's perceptions of external threat. But the story is based on young Fazile's "psychic reality"—an inner conviction of truth about the event—and that psychic reality becomes the dominant organizing factor of an individual's internal world. Unfortunately, Fazile's story, while unusually dramatic in its outlines, reflects some general truths about many Albanians' experience under Hoxha. By establishing *de novo* a rigid social hierarchy of "good" and "bad"—and particularly by enlisting children in the project of enforcing that absolute binary—Hoxha, himself a paranoid individual, initiated and maintained a malignant group regression, creating what I will call a "paranoid society"[540] singularly unable to cope with the supreme leader's absence.

Albania is a small country (about the size of Massachusetts) situated on the eastern shore of the Adriatic Sea, separated from Italy by only 47 miles (76 kilometers) of water. Albania and its population of less than three and a half million people are unknown to most Americans. The formal relationship between the United States and communist Albania was broken off in 1946 and not re-established until March 1991. In fact, Albania was for a long time isolated from not just the United States but from nearly the whole of the world. From time to time, we heard stories about life in Albania that sounded as if they were written by George Orwell, but, unlike the Soviet Union, Albania under Hoxha posed no threat. Even if we did know of the sufferings of Albanians, we did not have reasons to identify with or have empathy for them. Only after NATO became involved in the Kosovo crisis in 1999 did Americans become more aware of Albanians as our television screens filled with the images of tens of thousands of ethnic Albanian Kosovars fleeing the region under Serbian pressure accelerated by NATO bombings. Then we watched the refugees return home, and we learned of atrocities, murders, and rapes as European and American forces set about trying the perhaps impossible task of creating a peaceful "co-existence" between Kosovo's Albanians and Serbs. Despite this new exposure, our awareness of Albanians living in Albania itself remained somewhat unclear.

My own first glimpse of Albania took place in 1974, when I drove with my family the length of the shore of the former Yugoslavia down to the Albanian border. I could see the mountains, which until 1913—"only yesterday," historically speaking—were part of the Ottoman Empire. Since I am of Turkish origin and thus belong to the heirs of the Ottoman Empire, I was very curious about Albania. A large number of people from Albania live in Turkey, and many of the heroes and villains of Albania were also the heroes and villains of the Ottoman Empire. So I felt a kind of kinship towards Albanians, but, in 1974, there was no way for my family and me, especially with our American passports, to cross the border from Yugoslavia into Albania.

Of course, Albanians have their own history, sentiments, and nationality, even though they were part of the Ottoman Empire for five centuries
and two-thirds of the Albanian population converted to Islam. From the
fourth to the fourteenth century, this part of the world belonged to the
Byzantine Empire, and before the Byzantines, from 146 B.C.E. to 395 C.E.,
Albania constituted part of the Roman province of Macedonia after
becoming a bridgehead of earlier Roman armies. Albanians feel, however,

that their original ancestors are the Illyrians, an Indo-European people who fought as well as intermingled with the ancient Greeks. All of these influences have left lasting marks on Albanian culture.

It was toward the end of the nineteenth century that modern Albanian nationalism was first roused.[541] In 1878, Albanian leaders gathered in the Kosovo town of Prizren and founded the League of Prizren to promote a unified and independent Albania.[542] After the first Balkan War (1912–1913),[543] Albanians declared their independence. In 1913, the European "Great Powers" (Great Britain, France, Germany, Russia, Austria, and Italy) recognized Albanian independence, but they were reluctant to create a Greater Albania—not least because it would be the only country on the continent of Europe dominated by Muslims (except some other European areas populated by Ottoman Muslims). Because of this reluctance, they left half of the ethnic Albanian population outside of independent Albania by keeping under Serbian control the two million Albanians in Kosovo, just less than half a million in Macedonia, and a smaller number in Montenegro.[544] The European powers imported a German prince, Wilhelm Zu Weid, to rule Albania only six months before World War I shook Europe, and during the war, other nations' armies controlled Albania.[545] After World War I, Britain, France, and Italy wanted to partition Albania among its neighbors, but U.S. President Woodrow Wilson intervened. In 1920, Albania became a member of the League of Nations.

After World War I, excepting a six-month effort at Western-style democracy, Albania was run by Ahmet Bey Zogu, who in 1928 crowned himself King Zog I. In 1939, Italy invaded Albania and Zog escaped to Greece. When independence came again in 1944, Albania found itself under the leadership of communist Enver Hoxha, who ruled the country until his death in April 1985, when he was replaced by Ramiz Alia. In a few years time, communist rule in Eastern Europe would collapse and its effects would be felt deeply in Albania, where intellectuals, the working class, and young people protested and demanded reforms. In December 1989, the Albanian Socialist Party—in reality a continuation of the Albanian Communist Labor Party—won Albania's first free elections since the mid-1920s. The communists that had ruled Albania since 1944 were still in power, but now under a different name. The name of the country changed from the People's Republic of Albania to the Republic of Albania; Alia was now called "Mr. President" instead of the "First Secretary;" and an economist named Fatos Nano became prime minister. But demonstrations continued, forcing new elections. In March 1992, the

Albanian Democratic Party, led by a young cardiologist-turned-politician, Sali Berisha, swept to a convincing electoral victory. Several former communist officials, including Alia and Nano, were arrested, tried for corruption of power, and given long jail sentences, though both Alia and Nano were released within a few years of their convictions.

Berisha, who was partially educated in France, assumed leadership with great energy. He initiated economic reforms and sought to tame the rampant public disorder of post-communist Albania. It soon became clear, however, that for Berisha, "democracy" meant militant anti-communism. He began using anti-democratic methods to turn his country into a "democratic" state. He was repressive towards his political opponents, interfered with the work of the Constitutional Court by removing its president, and restricted press freedoms. During the 1996 parliamentary elections in Albania, Berisha's methods caused some outrage in European circles. Meanwhile, Albania continued to be the poorest country in Europe. Paradoxically, a large number of Albanians felt that they were rolling in new wealth. Donkeys were displaced on the streets by Mercedes—85,000 of them registered by 1996, most of them stolen in Western Europe, according to officials. But, unfortunately, this new "wealth" was imaginary; in Tirana and other cities, cafes were filled all day "with a new class of espresso-sipping jobless."[546] Twenty pyramid schemes, which grew into murky empires, were the foundation of this imaginary wealth. Then, in March 1997, one of Albania's newest millionaires, Miksude Kademi, declared bankruptcy; she was the first pyramid operator to do so. Soon the others came tumbling down, swallowing an estimated $1.2 billion in savings (about half of Albania's gross domestic product) and "touch[ing] everything from Liberian shipping companies and German salami plants to New York bank accounts."[547] The pyramid schemes were so embedded in Albanian society that their collapse initiated a national uprising in which 1,500 people were killed. A multinational protection force led by an Italian commander eventually restored order and set up new elections that resulted in the defeat of President Sali Berisha and brought Fatos Nano back to power as the prime minister. Berisha's efforts to crystallize something like democracy in Albania were spoiled.

Auditors from PricewaterhouseCoopers and Deloitte & Touche, as well as other experts from the World Bank, Italy, Greece, and Turkey, arrived in Albania to unravel the pyramid finances. Their success was very limited because some powerful and influential Albanians, who were themselves connected with the missing money, stonewalled and interfered with the investigations. To the public, the unsuccessful auditors and experts became messengers carrying bad news, and popular opinion turned against them. In fact, some of them were threatened with machine guns. The failure of the pyramid system created a new wave of social disorganization that "piggybacked" on the chaos that had followed the collapse of communism in Albania.

As the new Nano government struggled to restart the economy, to achieve national reconciliation and democratization, and to prepare for macroeconomic stabilization and institutional reforms, the internal political climate remained volatile and confrontational. There existed no normal political dialogue between the government and Sali Berisha's Democratic Party, now the opposition party. In fact, the Democratic Party began to boycott Parliament and the Constitution Drafting Committee, and civil society remained very weak.

During Berisha's time in power, former U.S. president Jimmy Carter visited Albania, met the prime minister, and became interested in helping to develop democracy there. After Berisha fell from power and following the pyramid schemes disaster, the Atlanta-based Carter Center's interest in the country continued. In the second half of 1997, the Carter Center proposed to assist Albania in the development of a National Development Strategy (NDS) through a broad "participation" process.[548] In November 1997, during a visit to Albania by Carter Center staff, Prime Minister Nano officially requested that the Carter Center help organize and fund an Albanian NDS process.[549] The Carter Center's National Development Strategy process for Guyana a few years earlier had been a success story, and former diplomat Tom Forbord, who had worked on the Guyana project, went to Albania as the Center's representative. Armed with well-prepared plans, Forbord was to identify influential Albanians, choose participants for meetings to design economic strategies, and, once those strategies were developed, get feedback from the Albanian government and opposition, help to revise and improve the plans, pass them to authorities and influence the economic recovery in Albania. But Forbord immediately noticed that something was seriously wrong. He had many valuable and thoughtful conversations with Albanians one-on-one. Even with the prestige of a former U.S. president behind him and access to Albanian governmental officials at the highest levels, however, it was difficult for the diplomat to gather a group of influential Albanians to participate in serious discussions, compromises, or agreements about the future of the nation.

It became clear that a comprehensive analysis of Albania's developmental constraints and opportunities required a concurrent social, political, and psychological diagnosis of Albanian society, especially its rigid political divisions. The apartment that Tom Forbord wished to rent during his stay in Albania on the Carter Center project, for example, was owned by the mother-in-law of a student who had been shot and killed that spring and who had become a hero for the opposition Democratic Party. If the former diplomat rented this apartment, people might perceive that as taking Sali Berisha's "side" in the political fray. Even a simple living quarters arrangement could be politicized.

In late February 1998, Joyce Neu, then the assistant director of the Carter Center's Conflict Resolution Program,[550] Norman Itzkowitz of Princeton University, who is one of the world's leading scholars of Ottoman history, and myself, as a member of the Carter Center's International Negotiation Network (INN), arrived in Tirana from Zurich in a small Cross Airlines plane.[551] We were to stay in Albania for two weeks to make a "psychopolitical diagnosis" of the Albanian situation and to report back to the Carter Center. It would not take us long to realize that the large-group regression *without* a supreme leader in Albania in early 1998 was shaped and exacerbated by the malignant regression that the group had experienced *with* a totalitarian supreme leader. It was difficult to find thirty or so influential Albanians from different social backgrounds and different political views and keep them together for a series of collaborative meetings for any length of time because their individual senses of basic trust[552]—especially in the political arena—had been spoiled. They could not trust others, and so they could not cooperate even on these most-pressing shared problems. Hoxha's death had left the people to swim aimlessly in the "poison" that had flowed from the leader to the society during his decades of rule.

In early 1998, Tirana's small airport was obviously in need of a great deal of repair and organization. The American Embassy had arranged a van to pick us up, but, since the van had been stolen the night before (such things were common in Albania in the late 1990s), we took a dilapidated taxi to Tirana on a road full of potholes. As we approached the capital city, we saw hundreds and hundreds of concrete pillbox-shaped bunkers scattered across the landscape. In fact, there were an estimated 750,000 bunkers of various sizes built on Hoxha's orders in the years following his 1961 break with the Soviets. Though a communist, he was considered "bad" by

Moscow when he remained a Stalinist as the Soviet Union moved away from Stalin's legacy.[553] Furthermore, the Soviets, in 1968, invaded Czechoslovakia. There were realistic reasons for Hoxha to think of external enemies, but Hoxha's suspicions were extreme. He fantasized imminent invasion by outside enemies; his soldiers and followers would rush into these bunkers with their weapons and defend their land. When we visited Albania more than a decade after Hoxha's death, however, the bunkers, empty and run-down, remained: symbols of the dead leader's paranoia. Since they were durably constructed out of concrete poured over metal bars, they still stood even in areas where villages and towns had expanded since Hoxha's death. Apparently, no one had attempted to remove these concrete hulks before building new homes.

Seeing them for the first time was eerie, especially as none of the many books, papers, and reports on Albania I had read in preparation had mentioned the bunkers. Further, the contrast with the countryside we were driving through was extreme. Hoxha and his people, we were told, had learned to build terraced hillsides from the Chinese, and such terraces were everywhere, creating a soothing atmosphere. But these huge, ugly concrete mushrooms spoiled that beauty. Imagine the face of a person with smooth skin, and then imagine that person developing a dermatological problem that leaves the skin full of unsightly bumps. Having lived with these pillboxes for so long, Albanians did not seem to notice their existence. And, realistically speaking, post-Hoxha Albanian governments did not have funds to destroy them. Yet, perversely, these bunkers had actually become symbols of Albanians' large-group identity. In the handful of stores that sold souvenirs in Tirana in early 1998—when we were there we saw no foreign tourists; all foreigners were there for some kind of political or other business—we saw little bunkers, made of marble or wood, for sale alongside the Albanian flags that show a two-headed black eagle image superimposed on a dark red background. In fact, Albanians were still carriers of a "bunker mentality" in early 1998.[554]

Enver Hoxha, the man responsible for both the bunkers and the bunker mentality, was born in 1908 to a Muslim cloth merchant and his wife in Grijokastor, near the Greek border. He was somewhat exposed to French and American cultures while studying at the French Lycée at Korca and the American Technical School in Tirana, and in 1930 he went on a state scholarship to the University of Montpellier, France. From 1934 to 1936, he worked as a secretary at the Albanian Consulate General in Brussels, Belgium, where he also studied law. In western Europe, Hoxha watched as the new ideologies of socialism/communism and fascism/Nazism clashed. Germans, under the influence of Adolf Hitler, would choose Nazism, and Albanians, under the influence of Enver Hoxha, would choose communism.

Enver Hoxha returned to Albania in 1936 and became a teacher at his old school in Korca. Three years later, Fascist Italy, allied with Nazi Germany, invaded Albania. Hoxha refused to join the newly formed Albanian Fascist Party and instead opened a retail tobacco store in Tirana that also served as the headquarters for a communist cell. After the Nazis invaded Yugoslavia, the Yugoslav communists, who were fighting against the Nazis, helped Hoxha to start the Albanian Communist Party (later called the Party of Labor), and Hoxha became the political commissar of the Army of National Liberation. At this time, of course, his "bunker mentality" was based on the existing reality of his foreign political and military enemies.

When liberation finally came in 1944, Hoxha gained control of the government, married Nexhmiye Xhangolli, also a former active partisan, and remained as the supreme leader until his death in 1985. As dictator, he would break alliances with countries or friends, and make new alliances only to break away from them. For example, he broke relations with Josip Broz Tito of Yugoslavia in 1948 and became an admirer of Joseph Stalin.[555] After Stalin died, Hoxha broke relations with Nikita Khrushchev, and in 1961 became a close ally of the communist Chinese.[556] After the death of Mao Tse-tung, he broke relations with China, in 1978. He turned Albania into a country of almost complete isolation.[557]

At home, Hoxha transformed Albania from a semi-feudal remnant of the Ottoman Empire into an industrialized economy. During his reign, there was basic food for everyone; people could own or rent a house[558] and could walk in the streets in the middle of the night without fear. Epidemics of illiteracy and disease were stamped out under his regime. However, a closer look reveals that what the newly literate Albanians were permitted to read or study was limited and regulated, and the epidemics of physical illness were replaced with an epidemic of mental poisoning.[559] Indeed, Hoxha's techniques would have made Stalin proud—or even envious.

Most important, he created a fundamental split between what were called families with "good biography," who were perceived as loyal, and families with "bad biography," who were punished in various ways. It was on these pre-existing, but now enhanced, societal splits that Hoxha built this absolute division, on which all rewards and penalties were based. Ethnically, Albania has a relatively homogenous population, as ethnic Albanians account for about 90 percent of the people, but there are two major subgroups within the Albanian ethnicity: the Gegs (mostly in the north) and the Tosks (mostly in the south). The Gegs and the Tosks have their own distinct dialects, and there is a centuries-old historical split between the two. First, Hoxha helped to enhance this division by giving legal preference to persons of Tosk and Muslim origin; previously, the Gegs, slightly more than half of the Albanian population, had dominated Albanian politics. Then, Hoxha adopted a "standard literary Albanian language" based on the Tosk dialect.

The existing religious divisions in the society also helped Hoxha to maintain the societal splits initiated by him and his party. Seventy percent of Albanians living in Albania were Muslims, the remaining 30 percent Orthodox Christian or Catholic. By 1946, Hoxha had expelled all Roman Catholic priests, monks, and nuns from Albania, and Catholics were stigmatized as fascists even though only a minority of Albanian Catholics had collaborated during the Italian invasion. But, in fact, Enver Hoxha opposed all religious institutions, and officially subjugated them to the "laws of state" in 1949. Hoxha's anti-religious campaign peaked in the 1960s when he was inspired by China's Cultural Revolution; he seemed to be proud of creating the first truly atheist nation in the world. Religious names such as Pal (Paul) were discouraged (though if someone in the politburo had such a name, he could keep it). New, ideologically "correct" names appeared such as "Marenglen," which was a made-up combination of Marx, Engels, and Lenin; names such as Flamur (Flag) and Yll (Star) carried slightly less doctrinaire nationalistic or communist connotations. On the surface, then, Hoxha erased religious distinctions. But by opposing religions and their Gods—and by setting himself up as a kind of "god," as Adolf Hitler had done—he made people more aware, at a hidden level, of their pre-existing religious distinctions. One woman I interviewed in Tirana recalled how her mother-in-law hid the Koran between the covers of another book and how the young ones knew about it. They knew that this was a "courageous" gesture, and a gesture of great secrecy. In such a situation, the hidden symbol exerts power that is felt without being fully understood by the younger generation. As "forbidden fruit," former religious and cultural beliefs become both scary and desirable in hidden ways. As soon as Hoxha and the communist regime disappeared, people who on the surface did not have any investment in religion and its customs "returned" to their respective religions, even though many did not know the rituals of their religion or how to pray formally. One man I asked about his religion replied: "I am a Muslim," then added, "I think I am." Despite their lack of knowledge about religion, many people expressed a wish for their children to be raised as Muslims,

Orthodox, or Catholics. Mosques, churches, and religious schools have sprouted up everywhere since the arrival of "democracy."[560]

Hoxha also created a gap between Albanians and the customs, traditions, and heroes of the past. All but one of the nation's historic heroes were wiped from official memory,[561] essentially severing Albanians from their history and thereby destabilizing their shared identity. Into this gap, Hoxha inserted the image of himself as an omnipotent leader. This image and the made-up history and culture that subtended it were so well-internalized that those who had not been punished or tortured were quite slow to realize the rottenness of his regime. Afrim Dangellia, a psychiatrist at the Tirana University Medical Center, writes that it was not until the events of 1974–1975 that he began to wonder whether there might be something psychologically wrong with Hoxha. It was that year that Dangellia witnessed the elimination of certain members of the party, government, and military and realized that hundreds of families considered to be Hoxha's enemies had disappeared. He began to notice certain patterns in Hoxha's books and speeches: an inability to criticize himself, endless claims to be a superior being, constant references to "enemies," "evaders," and "saboteurs of socialism." Initially, Dangellia thought the "great leader" might be under stress as a result of his diabetes mellitus; only gradually did the psychiatrist realize that his leader had a paranoid personality. As Dangellia began to wonder whose turn it would be next to "disappear," he started to find his own individuality, not unlike Michael Sebek in the former Czechoslovakia.[562] Few were able to break Hoxha's spell as Dangellia did, so, when Hoxha died, many Albanians shed genuine tears. Nevertheless, when he was alive, the people's ambivalence towards his regime did sometimes manifest itself—for example, in the nicknames *Dulla*, "the ugly one," for Hoxha, and *Sorra*, "the crow," for his wife. Of course, one had to trust others absolutely when using such names. In the streets and the workplace, one was never sure who might be a spy for the regime.

On these foundations, then, Hoxha built his rigorous division of goodness and badness, loyalty and disloyalty. If someone was perceived to be against Enver Hoxha and his brand of communism, or expressed a wish to baptize a newborn relative, or even complained about not finding bread in the bakery on a certain day or was caught playing backgammon (a popular pastime during the Ottoman Empire period and so a link to past heritage and culture that Hoxha wanted broken), he or she would face a "black spot," or likely a prison term. Like backgammon, gambling and Italian television (which regime propaganda compared to pornography) were prohibited.[563] Interestingly, the qualities of goodness and badness were assigned to whole families, like a kind of contagion. Even the relatives of someone who wanted to marry a person from a family with a "black spot," would be punished. Often, one spouse would divorce a partner who developed a "black spot," as divorce would keep the spouse uncontaminated, and the children given to his or her custody would remain "good." If you were the child of a "bad" parent, however, even if you tried to remain "good," you very well might not be allowed to attend university when the time came.

At the same time, the system encouraged children to expose "badness" in their parents. As part of a constant propaganda barrage directed toward the young,[564] schoolchildren were required to recite: "I love Enver Hoxha, I love the Communist Party, I love Albania, I love my parents and family." Note the order of the "love objects" in this litany: parents and family were the fourth love objects and in practice, in order to maintain the love and loyalty to the first three, a child would or could—and according to the regime, should—give up the fourth object. Officials were sent to schools regularly to interview children about whether their parents spoke against Enver Hoxha in the privacy of their homes, and teachers were made to function as "spies" as well. One of our informants knew of two brothers, now adults, who as children had turned their father in to the system as an undesirable. The father was killed. I can only assume that the two brothers now live with guilt, whether they are conscious of it or not.

Parents had to whisper their true feelings about Enver Hoxha in the middle of the night in order for their children not to hear, for there were constant attacks on the link of basic trust between parents and their children. Through identification with their parents, children were unable to develop benign internal control systems (superegos) since they "knew" that parents had secrets, gave mixed messages, and were filled with fear and anxiety. The usual internal control systems that children develop were replaced by external controls. If one obeyed the external controls provided by Hoxha and his government, one could feel safe and avoid anxiety. To belong to the "good" family, one had to believe that Hoxha was a god-like, beloved, and feared father figure, and that the Communist Party, which took care of you and fed your needs, was like a mother figure. If one developed such beliefs, Albania and being Albanian gave one a shared idealized self-image. Still, the love for one's parents and family remained always a source of potential corruption. A person could try to remain "good," but anyone in the family who became "bad" could ruin you. Worse, an individual could internalize a sense of "badness" which would remain with him or her for life, as happened to Fazile Godo.

When Norman Itzkowitz and I interviewed Fazile in February 1998, she was working as a receptionist at a European organization in Tirana. She believed that, from an early age, she was different from other people she knew. There was, she felt, a "badness" in her, and, if she let it come out, she would destroy other human beings, even those whom she loved the most. While her internal "badness" made her "special," she knew that she was doomed to suffer because of it. The only other person she knew who possessed a similar internal "badness" was her mother, but they never spoke of their "secret," and Fazile never let her husband or children know about it. She said that she could tell us about it since we were strangers and were directly interested in her psyche, and she reported the story of her family in a matter-of-fact way, careful not to seek our sympathy.[565]

In fact, from work with children who have experienced drastic and horrible events, we know that Fazile's response to trauma is not at all atypical: because traumatized children cannot comprehend that parents or caretakers might be helpless or "bad" themselves, they often develop fantasies about being the cause of the tragedy. In my opinion, Fazile's original internal sense of "badness" (being the cause of the tragedy that befell her family as well as being the child of parents who were "enemies of the people," identifying with their "black spot") was intertwined with guilt over her power to hurt her parents. Indeed, I heard similar stories from many other Albanians we interviewed. In order to deal with the burden of guilt stemming from the possibility that a child can kill (or otherwise severely damage) his or her parents, these young people developed a division in their internal worlds, reflected in Fazile's image of herself as having "two identities" or "two faces." When wearing one face, she is a "good" girl protecting her saintly father and martyred mother. Her other face reflected the "badness" in her and could ruin her parents if she were not careful. Like other children, every school day, she had to recite that Hoxha was omnipotent and was to be most loved. The role of parents could not be held in high esteem, as constant propaganda attempted to replace traditional family ties with the idea that the people were all equal and would be taken care of as long as they adored the leader; it was not a family member whom one should trust but the leader and the party. As a child, Fazile was able to stabilize this internal division by developing many inhibitions and to manage her conflict by passivity and silence on any topic that might bring danger to loved ones. She could both honor her parents and remain "bad," but unique.

In adolescence, Fazile's continuing internal splitting helped her, to a great extent, to survive and live a "normal" life during the day, but at night she would plunge into a life of repeating terror. She had nightmares about wolves—the animals' eyes reflecting fire in her dreams—until the age of fifteen. As she came to understand more consciously the realities of the totalitarian regime, the frightening eyes of the wolves became more and more a part of her frightening external world. Once the whole world began to feel like wolves' eyes watching, her nightmares stopped; she was living the nightmare.

Eventually, Fazile fell in love with the son of a prominent physician, married, and had a son and a daughter. When her children were very young, her father, then sixty-five, was once more arrested and incarcerated. With this event, all of Fazile's childhood and teenage feelings were reactivated, and she felt she was "bad" once more: "My husband was suffering from my badness. I had to be more silent than ever so as not to share with him stories about my father and my inner horrors." When her children grew up, they were not permitted to go to university, since, as I mentioned earlier, the children of families with "black spots" were not allowed higher education. As education was revered in Fazile's family, she begged her husband to divorce her. If she were "kicked out" of the family, her husband and her children could denounce her and be a "clean" family. Then her children could have a university education. But her husband refused to divorce her, and she became increasingly inhibited about discussing her internal sense of "badness."

The death of Hoxha had pleased Fazile, but she was also aware that her feelings for him were very complicated. Fazile could not fully erase the part of her that had been subjected to propaganda about Hoxha's greatness. In the early post-communist period, a law passed which prohibited former *Sigurimi* agents and senior ex-communist officials—*Sigurimi* collaborators, those who had presented false evidence in political trials, committed crimes against humanity, or participated in the State Commission on Internment during the period of communist dictatorship—from working in senior posts in the state administration. But this law was not really put into practice. That torturers and tortured (and their heirs) were essentially asked to live together as if nothing remarkable had happened in the past especially disturbed Fazile. A personal experience made her even more miserable. Now that Fazile's children were free to gain higher education, her daughter went to a university and her son began to attend a technical school. When Fazile went to visit her son's school, she recognized the head administrator of the school as the son of a person who was involved in torturing her father. She was shocked and angry; paradoxically—but as we might expect, psychologically—her sense of inner "badness" overwhelmed her as she felt that her anger could actually result in harm to others. In early 1998, she still feared that her inner "badness" might hurt somehow her family.

Ramiz Alia, Albania's last communist leader, made sure that Hoxha had a magnificent tomb in the Martyr's Cemetery in Tirana. In 1992, however, after the final fall of communist power there, Hoxha's body was transferred to an ordinary public cemetery on the outskirts of Tirana, which we visited in 1998.[566] All the graves and tombstones looked alike. Hoxha's grave looked substantially like everyone else's: in death, one might say, he had finally become a true communist, "equal" to all others buried there. Still, we thought it remarkable to find Hoxha's grave decorated with colorful plastic flowers; it seems that there remained some Albanians whose hearts and minds were still touched with loyalty to the dictator. In fact, Fazile Godo's story shows us how even those who feel no such affection for the dead Hoxha nevertheless carry his regime with them internally long after it ceased to exist in external reality. The continuing effects of a strictly engineered malignant societal regression dovetailed all too neatly with the chaotic societal regression that followed the regime's demise.

As we have seen, Enver Hoxha had created a "paranoid society." When he was alive, his perceptions of real and imaginary enemies carried the force of law, and people knew how they were expected to respond to those identified as enemies. Without a supreme leader who, through manipulation and propaganda, directs the masses' behavior, controls the expressions of shared sentiments, and creates social order (even though it may be malignant), however, the societal paranoia thereby created leads to disorganization. Lacking the former rigid definitions of who the enemy is, members of the society become suspicious of everyone and every situation. They tend either to feel paralyzed in relating to others in an emotional, meaningful way or to strike out impulsively in desperation toward anyone regardless of his or her "innocence." The societal fragmentation and competition for leadership in large and small subgroups alike that tend to follow the fall of a dictatorship in turn create real new threats to individual safety and thus enhance paranoid thinking.

This is precisely what we saw in early 1998 post-communist Albania. Even though Nano's Socialist Party had gained a comfortable majority in the *Kuvend Popullove* (People's Assembly) in the 1997 elections, there was no one supreme leader (with accompanying absolute morality) for Albanians to rally around, as they had been used to doing for decades. The

result, from the highest levels of social organization to the most quotidian, was increased criminality. Despite the supposed arrival of democracy,
the country remained an armed camp, and the government had no control over some parts of the nation, as we observed firsthand.[567] The opposition, led by Berisha, refused to cooperate with the government in the
usual manner of established democracies. Instead, the relationship
between the opposition and the government was articulated through violent behavior, up to and including murder. At a restaurant outside of
Tirana, we saw literally hundreds of bullet casings on the ground around
the entrance; we were told that some people had celebrated an event the
night before by discharging their weapons. Another night, a young man
approached me near our hotel asking in English whether I wanted anyone
killed; the going rate, he said, was $500 per hit, but he would kill two of
my enemies for $600. At the same time, many young Albanian girls were
being kidnapped, sent to other European countries, and used as prostitutes. Parents in one village near Tirana told us that they would not allow
their teenage daughters to walk to the local school alone or in small
groups for fear that they would be kidnapped into prostitution. Two days
after our arrival in Tirana, a new, tougher anti-crime bill passed in the
Albanian's People's Assembly[568] allowed police to shoot without warning at
armed groups resisting police. It also permitted the Interior Ministry,
Defense Ministry, and intelligence services, as well as customs, municipal-
ity and tax police, to be supplied with weapons—merely exacerbating a
culture of violence in many Albanians' minds, since those who were given
guns under the new law did not seem trustworthy.

Besides the increase in "ordinary" criminal activity, the phenomenon
of *Hakmarrje-Akmaria*, or "revenge killings," enjoyed a resurgence in the
post-communist era. Albania's ancient rules and regulations about
revenge killings can be found in the arcane *Kanun of Lek Dukagjini*.[569] In
Turkish, *kanun* means legal code, and many kanuns existed in different
parts of the Ottoman Empire. But long before the Ottoman period in
Albania, the *Kanun of Lek Dukagjini*—or, as it is referred to in popular
speech, the "Law of Lek"—described how to deal with blood feuds, when
it was permissible to kill, and when the killing was prohibited, regulating
the anarchy in the rugged mountains of Northern Albania. Law of Lek
regulated revenge killings continued until the communists came to power
in 1944. During the Hoxha era, the practice was strictly forbidden. But by
the mid-1990s, about 2,000 blood feuds were in progress; in 1998, Dr.
Edmont Dragoti, then president of the Albanian Association of
Psychologists and head of the Department of Social Work and Applied

Psychology at the University of Tirana, informed me that, according to his statistics, there were an estimated 100 vendetta murders per year in post-communist Albania.[570] Now, as Dragoti observes, "unfortunately, blood-revenge is once again socially acceptable in Albania not only in the wilds but in Albanian cities as well."[571] A divorce, a car accident, even a drunken fight over a game of cards can escalate into a cycle of violence that leaves scores dead over the course of a decade or longer.[572]

But the revival of blood feuds is not somehow proof of an intrinsic Albanian violence resurfacing after years of suppression; there are material and psychological bases for this development. In 1994, pre-1944 landowners took their property back, evicting those who occupied them as a result of communist collectivization campaigns; land privatization (and other material impoverishment left in the wake of the Hoxha regime) was a significant factor in the return of the blood feuds. As one family displaced another on lands that had originally belonged to the first, those who were displaced tended to experience eviction as an affront to honor. Emin Spahia—general secretary of the All-Nation Reconciliation Mission, an organization dedicated to mediating peaceful conclusions to blood feuds in Albania—confirms not only that land disputes are at the root of many feuds but also that the phenomenon has now spread from the village to the city.[573] "The collapse of the state and the national economy has led many Albanians to once again openly embrace the traditional laws and loyalties of the village," investigative journalist Scott Anderson observes; "one's primary allegiance is to the clan and community, not to the state."[574] Dragoti thus accurately describes the practice's resurgence as a sort of "revival of the historical memory" in the absence of larger meaningful social structures and political authority.[575]

Still another factor—this an economic one—contributed to the post-communist destabilization of Albanian society. Within a few years of the 1991 introduction of freedom to travel, half a million Albanians—more than 12 percent of the population—left the country to find employment, creating another threat to the stability of the society. Most of those Albanians who emigrated went to northern Greece, working there illegally and creating a bad reputation for all Albanians among Greeks because Greeks perceive these migrant Albanians (both realistically and in fantasy) as "criminals." Meanwhile, with the collapse of the communist regime in the neighboring Yugoslavia, ethnic Albanians living in Kosovo began to speak about independence. The dilemma that Kosovar Albanians faced and their struggles with Serbs resonated with Albanians living in Albania.

But, because of the economic collapse and destruction of infrastructure in Albania, in 1998, many people felt that they had enough problems to worry about besides their fellow Albanians in Kosovo. In one village near Tirana, for example, sewer lines were broken and there was no money or organization to fix them. The sewers would rupture in the back-yards of peoples' homes, in the streets, or in the fields, creating stinking, bacteria-laden pools. In 1997, three small children in the village had fall-en into such pools and were drowned. These villagers therefore had no time to worry about Albanians living in the former Yugoslavia or even about Albanians living elsewhere in Albania. They felt bitter that no one from Tirana would come to help them and bitter about the general help-lessness of regional or national authorities. In turn, most people living in Tirana had little knowledge of what was happening in a village only twen-ty-five miles away, another indication of the extent to which the society was fragmented.

In Chapter 2, I described what had befallen the environment in Vladimir, Russia, during the Soviet period. There, in a regressed society focused on a central leader, the debasement of the milieu at least was done in an orderly fashion according to the ideology of communism and in the idealization of industry and the working class. As we have seen, under Enver Hoxha, the ruination of Albania's beautiful countryside was also performed in an orderly fashion according to the leader's "paranoid" expectations. In "leaderless" regressed Albania, as I observed it in early 1998, however, the ruination was being carried out haphazardly. People seemed to be competing to create a mess, pouring garbage not only into city streets, but also onto the lovely fields and forests of the countryside. There was something quite shocking and sad about the way that people seemed to attack anything beautiful. One night, for example, we went to hear a classical trio from Britain playing at the Albanian National Theatre at Skanderbeg Square in Tirana, but the audience seemed to be seeking ways to spoil the good music, talking and walking about during the per-formance. I could almost swear that the women had deliberately worn shoes with high heels in order to disrupt the beauty of the concert with ugly noise of their own.

Why should there be such a pattern in Albanian society at that time? I sensed a rage against mother earth—mother Albania. Some Albanian intel-lectuals spoke to me about a sense of shame that Albanians had allowed someone like Enver Hoxha to rule them; the garbage, I sensed, was an exter-nal representation of combined feelings of shame and rage turned inward. Like a helpless, angry child, the regressed society appeared to be bent on soiling its environment in symbolic rage with symbolic body waste.[576]

Nevertheless, not all the news was bad in the Albania of early 1998: some initial attempts were being made to deal with the poisons circulated by the totalitarian leader and in the subsequent leaderless regression. Artan Hoxha (no relation to the dictator) and Genc Ruli—foreign trade and finance ministers, respectively, in Sali Berisha's government—parted from Berisha and from what they called "the demonic temptation of power" to create a sort of think-tank, the Albanian Institute for Contemporary Studies. Unlike the Carter Center's efforts, they seemed to be successful at least in creating "an authority of thinkers" among some Albanians by conducting conferences on topics such as local governance. Listening to them, however, I noted that the discussions they sponsored still were intellectual in nature, and it was difficult for me to evaluate whether their think-tank could play a role in "healing" the deeper psychological and emotional splits in Albanian society. What was especially fascinating to me was that Artan Hoxha belonged to a persecuted family with a "black spot," whereas Ruli's family had been communists. Working together, as they were fully aware, pointed toward the possibility that Albania could become, as they said, a "normal country." Hoxha and Ruli were also aware of how Hoxha-era repression had been internalized across Albanian society; this internalization had been misunderstood as "forgiveness" when democracy came. There had been no "truth and reconciliation" efforts in Albania, they observed, like those in post-apartheid South Africa. For them, I sensed, the son of a family with a "bad biography" and the son of a family with a "good biography" working together was an opportunity to create a model for mending. Hoxha and Ruli were also aware that not only were the political parties re-enacting the former "demonization" policies, but they were also busy setting up (with or without justification) a demon in their former boss Berisha, just as they themselves had become part of a rigid split between those for and those against Berisha within the party.

At one point during our 1998 visit, we were introduced to Sali Berisha himself, and even this visit seemed to bode well for healing the societal regression in Albania. When Neu, Itzkowitz, and I met him at his party headquarters, I instantly liked him in spite of the fact that I would ordinarily strongly disapprove of some of his political activities. When I mentioned that I, like him, am a physician, Berisha responded that Albania was a "sick" society in need of physicians. I told him: "Mr. President, I am a visitor; I would not use such a term to describe your country. However, we can speak about a black-and-white division I have noted between Albania's politicians, between your party members and those who are now in power." He was easily able to understand the metaphor of "black and white." Feeling more comfortable, I asked him how he and his party could help those in power to use shades of gray. Apparently, he had never considered that he could cooperate with his antagonists; he himself had been involved deeply in the absolute division. My remarks intrigued him, and he said that he would think about what I had said. Soon he and the parliamentarians from his party began to attend the parliament sessions again and to participate in the political system. Unfortunately, however, this non-regressive behavior lasted only for a relatively short time.

Neu, Itzkowitz, and I were unable to return to Albania a year after our first visit, as we had planned, for the U.S. State Department warned us that such a visit would be too dangerous. Even the U.S Ambassador, Marisa Lino, left Albania for a time because of reports that Osama bin Laden was planning terrorist attacks there. Soon ethnic Albanians in Kosovo began to suffer Serbian attacks; the NATO bombing of Serbia followed, and, in the summer of 1999, some 450,000 Kosovar Albanians sought shelter in Albania. When these refugees flooded Albania's disused factories, sports stadiums, and city parks, it looked like the chaos there would reach its peak. But, as I followed the news from Albania, I began to notice that having an external enemy in the Serbs seemed to begin to "heal" splits within Albania and appeared to remove the malignant regression.

I finally returned to Albania in December 2000.[577] I could see the bunkers in the fields surrounding the airport as my plane descended to land at the Tirana airport on a sunny winter day: they still existed, but somehow did not appear to be as many in number. I wondered if the Albanians had begun to destroy them. The airport and the potholed road to the capital city, however, looked the same as they had two years before. I checked into the hotel next to the Albanian National Theatre, where in 1998, women wearing high-heeled shoes had competed with the members of a chamber orchestra, juxtaposing the ugly and the beautiful. One still could not climb up the steps to the theatre without stepping on trash.

There were, however, also noticeable changes in Tirana. In 1998, there had been virtually no shops; only small items such as cigarettes, lighters, chewing gum, and candy had been sold in booths in and around Skanderbeg Square. Now the booths, and their accompanying blaring music, were gone, and I could see different kinds of shops, from clothing to electronics stores. A neon sign had been installed just behind the statue of Skanderbeg, lighting up the back end of the horse atop which the hero sits. I was told that the Albanian mafia was investing in new hotels, some of which were under construction, and that the Catholic Church was busy creating a massive, handsome structure.

Anne Lindhardt—chair of the Department of Psychiatry at University Hospital in Copenhagen and, like myself, a temporary consultant to the World Health Organization (WHO)—and I took a UN jeep drive through Elbasan, where Hoxha had created a huge steel industry. Our driver described to us how Elbasan looked during Hoxha's days. His description brought to mind what I observed in the Soviet Union's Vladimir. Now Elbasan looked like a tornado had gone through it. A Turkish company was trying to re-start industry in the city, and entering and leaving the city we saw Turkish flags waving next to Albanian ones.

Surprisingly, taking in the Albanian refugees during the upheaval in Kosovo had improved the economy (officially, by 8 percent) as journalists and others poured in from abroad, stimulating government and private security industries. The threat of Osama bin Laden in Albania disappeared. After the war in Kosovo and after the refugees went back to their homes, Europeans and Americans began to pay more attention to Albania, appreciating what Albanians had done for the refugees. Meanwhile, a new leader, Ilir Meta, emerged and democracy tentatively began to crystallize. Roads in the countryside were much safer, and people could now travel to Tirana with relative confidence, even though traveling remained physically difficult due to the poor road conditions. Even the fact that I was in Albania for a meeting of 200 or so Albanian psychiatrists, psychologists, and other mental health professionals testified to broader changes in the society.

Swedish psychiatrist Birgitta Johansson, who was then attached to the WHO's Tirana office, had organized the meeting as part of her commitment to improving the mental health delivery system in Albania. Mental hospitals needed urgent attention; conditions were extremely poor, and in fact some patients were still handcuffed to their beds. Many mental health care workers at the meeting had stories to tell about the refugees as well as about how the suffering of Kosovar Albanians had emotionally affected Albanians in Albania proper. Fostering refugees had increased their nationalistic sentiments and self-esteem. The increased nationalistic sentiments, however, emotionally connected all Albanians, regardless of where they lived.

I met Majlinda Treska, director of the Joshua Trauma Center in Gjakova, near the Kosovo border. Treska and others from the Joshua Trauma Center were involved with helping the victims in Krusha e

Madhe, an agricultural village within the boundaries of Kosovo but only twenty minutes from Gjakova. During the war in Kosovo, Serbs had attacked this village of 740 families (5,200 people). Just over 200 people were massacred, leaving 138 widows and 400 orphans. Many more were left maimed and handicapped. There are incinerators in the village where most of the bodies of the massacre victims were burned, and to this day the widows and children wake up every morning to see the buildings in which the bodies of their murdered husbands, fathers, and other relatives were burned to ashes. But Treska's professional training did not include skills for dealing with such massive destruction. The strength that she finds to deal with this village comes not only from her personality, but also from her increased sense of Albanian nationalism. Treska had a nearly impossible task before her, but her resilience was immensely moving, and her stories and activities underlined how much the suffering in Kosovo had emotionally connected all Albanians.

I was also able to get back in touch with two people whom I had met during my previous visit. Edmont Dragoti came to see me at the WHO conference and confirmed that the Kosovo war was "welcomed" in a peculiar way by Albanian society: "Our closed society has become an open society," he added. Dragoti sees evidence that the chaos is disappearing and law and order are taking root. He did tell me, however, that the average Albanian income is only $100 per month and that prostitution is on the rise. Albanians feel that foreign investment and interest in their country are almost non-existent. "What Albanians did during the Kosovo war should make NATO and others want to help us more," Dragoti said, "It is pay time."

I had an emotional reunion with Fazile Godo, who was still working for the same international organization. She rushed to see me when she learned that I was in the city. We sat around a small table on the second floor dining room of the Miniri Hotel, next to the opera house, drinking sodas and watching school children in uniforms carrying backpacks or riding their bicycles on the street below. What moved me most were Fazile's remarks about how Itzkowitz's and my interview with her in 1998 had actually made a substantial difference in her internal world. Telling me about the "bad" core of her internal world and sharing her story had indeed been therapeutic for her, she said; her "bad" part was much tamed.[578] Fazile also told me about psychological changes in her father, now eighty-six years old, who had begun writing articles for the local newspaper about events during the Hoxha era. As most of that era's intellectuals had either been killed or had died from natural causes, he felt it was his duty to visit the past history and fill with "truth" the historical gap that Hoxha had created. Fazile said, "Everyone is visiting my father to hear his views on history."

While Fazile's father seemed to be a one-man missionary force trying to "heal" historical injuries, the "healing" that I noted in Albania in early 2000 has in fact not been the end result of a slow process of opening up the wounds gradually and appropriately—for the majority of Albanians, ventilating old helpless rage, shame, and guilt, and mourning over historic losses of people, dignity, and money. Circumstances in Albania are not ripe to have a "truth and reconciliation" activity as has happened in post-apartheid South Africa. Fazile's father could only be a rather lonely Desmond Tutu who could not have much impact on society in general. Thus, this "leaving behind" of regressed elements in Albania, I sensed, may simply be hiding them; only time will show whether these elements can truly disappear.

In addition to a no-more-than-partial development of democracy in the Albanian parliament,[579] there are other troubles brewing in this part of the world that may interfere with the slow disappearance of large-group regression, or may even initiate a different one. Even though it is not good politics to make such a statement in diplomatic circles, a kind of "Greater Albania" already exists. Albanians residing in Albania are now more connected through nationalistic feelings with ethnic Albanians in bordering Kosovo and Macedonia. For now, each group's particular economic and social difficulties tend to keep it preoccupied with its own affairs; still, one can hear and sense spoken and unspoken desires to unite the Albanians of Albania, Kosovo, and Macedonia under a single political umbrella. Europeans are aware of such possible developments, and they are also aware that such sentiments may become a new focal point for further troubles.

Ethnic Albanians populate the Western part of Macedonia. In fact, Albanians in Macedonia comprise 23 percent of the total population, while Slav-Macedonians make up 66 percent; the rest are Turks, Vlachs, Serbs, "Gypsies," and others. Unlike the Albanians in Albania proper, and without somebody like Enver Hoxha poisoning their lives, Albanians in Macedonia did not experience a gap in their history. Thus, they are not regressed in the same chaotic way that the Albanians of Albania are, though they may exhibit a regression of their own. While the two Albanian groups are different, political movements are likely to combine with nationalistic sentiments, propaganda, and manipulation to "unify" all Albanians, perhaps with drastic consequences.

Macedonia was "reborn" in 1992 after the collapse of the former communist Yugoslavia. In the newly independent Macedonia, the Macedonian-Slav majority, who are Eastern Orthodox Christians, naturally was involved in redefining the country's shared identity after such a drastic political change. Neighboring Greece initially opposed Macedonians' use of the name "Macedonia" and certain national symbols, such as the new Macedonian flag, because Greeks thought that the name of the new state and its symbols pointed to irredentism, as part of "old" Macedonia is in Greece. The Greeks' attitude in turn stimulated Macedonians to be more obsessive in defining their "new" identity, so Macedonian Christian and Slavic symbols can be seen everywhere. For example, one observes Orthodox religious and historic Slav characters and insignias on Macedonian money. There are few signs that represent Macedonia's mostly Muslim Albanians, who comprise one-third of the population, but their presence is clearly cause for concern among many Slav-Macedonians.

During my outing with Lindhardt, we changed UN cars at the border and entered Macedonia. Our new driver, a Slav-Macedonian, began telling us—both directly and indirectly—of Macedonian superiority over Albanians. It was true, as he noted, that there was a day-and-night difference in the physical road conditions between the two countries: driving on Albanian roads was like going on a boat in a stormy sea, but upon entering Macedonia, the ride smoothed dramatically. The driver's remarks, however, were not merely a physical comparison, but an emotional one concerning large-group identities and relations between the two ethnic groups. This concern is not limited to the working classes, however. The first night I was in Skopje, the capitol of Macedonia, I had dinner with some Slav-Macedonian scholars. I noted that they would very often return to discussing their shared identity, expressing anxiety about its security. For example, they spoke of Muslim/Albanians within their borders having more babies—and I do not know whether there is any factual basis to the claim—as a threat to their shared identity.

In early June 2001, after armed struggle broke out between Macedonian government forces and Albanian nationalist guerrillas, Georgi Efremov, chairman of the Academy of Sciences and Arts of Macedonia proposed that the best way to end the strife between majority Macedonian and minority Albanian communities was to divide Macedonia along ethnic lines. According to Efremov's plan, Macedonian-Albanians would be given the regions of Gostivar, Tetovo, and Debar, which later would be incorporated into Albania. In turn, Albania would hand over the town of Pogradec and the surrounding area near Prespa Lake to Macedonia. Emotions were already very high in Macedonia and were having a ripple effect on Albanians in Albania and Kosovo; Efremov's proposal evoked a furor among politicians and the majority of the public. He was probably thinking that such a division could be made quickly and peacefully and could prevent the possibility of bloody and destructive mayhem, which may end up dividing the country in one way or another anyhow. Of course, such a suggestion violated *realpolitik*: once a state is formed, it is usually quite difficult to partition it peacefully. Further, it was destined to go nowhere without the examination of alternative proposals and, more importantly, without serious preparatory work, including exploration of identity issues, unconscious fears, and examination of signs and symptoms of large-group regression and rituals, removing regression and turning group rituals into peaceful ones.

This is exactly what the Center for the Study of Mind and Human Interaction (CSMHI) had done in Estonia beginning in 1991: long-term preparatory work based on a psychoanalytic understanding of human relationships. After Estonia regained its independence in 1991 from the Soviet Union, the new state found itself with a one-third ethnic Russian population, rather like the one-third of the population of Macedonia who are Albanians. Estonians' emotions about the Russian minority were extremely intense, and there were serious questions about how to integrate them into Estonian society. Over five years of work there, we opened up dialogue, removed resistances against realistic discussion, created models of peaceful coexistence, and let decisions be made by the participants themselves: Estonians, Russian-speakers in Estonia, and representatives of Russia.[580]

In my opinion, a multi-year project such as the one that CSMHI carried out in Estonia was urgently needed in Macedonia. In the summer of 2001, it became clear that the Macedonian government could not overcome the crisis by itself. Its clumsy military campaign against Albanian guerrillas during the spring of 2001 had actually lent Albanian nationalists new legitimacy and strength. In June 2001, a six-day negotiation between Macedonian government and ethnic Albanian leaders ended without success, and Macedonian president Boris Trajkovski declared, "They [ethnic Albanian leaders] have dramatically changed their standpoint, practically asking for a two-nation state. They have no sincere intention of conducting a dialogue and finding effective and acceptable political solutions."[581] In early August, NATO Secretary General Javier Solana announced, smiling broadly, that Macedonia's rival factions had reached a breakthrough; only a day later, however, the fighting had resumed. With pressure from the international community, the deadlock was broken, and Albanian nationalists turned over their weapons to NATO peacekeeping troops. Meanwhile, European governments and the Bush administration began to exert pressure in favor of changes in the Macedonian constitution that would put the Albanian minority on an equal legal and political footing with Slavs, and this was done. Still, only time will tell whether such military and *realpolitik* interventions and changes in the constitution will result in long-lasting solutions. To my mind, ethnic Macedonian-Albanian coexistence within the state of Macedonia as well as peaceful relationships between Macedonians and Albanians outside Macedonia require a systematic "vaccination" against the eruption of violence, a process more satisfactory to all parties and more lasting if it involves psychologically-informed strategies.

/ coda

If we, as psychoanalysts, persist in restricting ourselves to an exclusively medical and clinical position, the research into collective behavior, for instance, research on the psychology of war, would proceed without our participation. Predictably, this would lead to a further plundering of analytic findings and theories without analysts having any effective share in the direction of the research, nor any means of protesting effectively.

—Alexander Mitscherlich, "Psychoanalysis and aggression of large groups"

Norman Itzkowitz, to whom this book is dedicated, has written a brief but moving paper about his own personal response to the September 11 tragedy. He tells us that despite the horror of watching the replay of the planes crashing into the Twin Towers day after day and despite experiencing grief and sadness at the loss of life, he could not mourn:

> Mourning for me is highly personal. I need to have known the deceased personally in order to engage in mourning. Although dictionaries give grieving and mourning as synonyms, for me they are not the same emotionally. To grieve and to experience the sorrow that accompanies it is a much more transitory matter than mourning. Mourning is a process, and you have to go through the entire process and emerge at the other end before you can let go of the deceased. As such, it takes time. Dictionaries neither grieve nor mourn, otherwise they would know the difference.[582]

Itzkowitz could not mourn because he did not know personally anyone who had died in the catastrophe. But when he received the November 7th issue of the *Princeton Alumni Weekly*, he saw, superimposed over images of an American flag and the university's seal, the names of thirteen alumni who had died in the tragedies of September 11th. The fifth name on the list was Robert J. Deraney, an alumnus of the class of 1980, whom Itzkowitz had known very well. Though, as Itzkowitz notes, Deraney was an Arab-American and he himself is a Jewish-American, he could now mourn.

Itzkowitz's story reflects a truth of human nature: when we do not know people personally, it is difficult to mourn their deaths.[583] South African Supreme Court Justice Richard Goldstone, who has examined human nature closely under terrible conditions, would agree. The work of the Goldstone Commission, which he led, uncovered the role of the police in fomenting and organizing violence between members of Inkatha Freedom Party and the African National Congress and formed the foundation of South Africa's Truth and Reconciliation Commission. Later, Goldstone served as the Chief Prosecutor for the United Nations international criminal tribunals of the former Yugoslavia and Rwanda and also investigated the atrocities committed in Kosovo. Two weeks after September 11, as the guest of the British Psychoanalytical Society in London, Justice Goldstone gave the 2001 Ernest Jones Lecture. There, echoing Itzkowitz, Justice Goldstone noted:

> It is a fact that as human beings we have regard and concern for those nearest and dearest and closest to us rather than people who are far away from us. Whether within our own micro-society, our own countries, our own continent and so forth, or whether it is religion, colour or language that keeps us together, we have a natural closeness, empathy and sensitivity for things that happen to those whom we hold close and near.[584]

For the 8,000 innocent Muslim boys who were slaughtered in cold blood outside Srebrenica by members of the Bosnian Serb army on the orders of General Mladic, Justice Goldstone reminded us, there had been "no great lines waiting to lay wreaths or to mourn in London or Washington or Paris."[585] As he observed, "there is this selectivity in relation to victims—depending on where they are, on what they look like and on how close they are to the major powers":[586]

> You can be absolutely certain that an international criminal tribunal would not have been set up for Rwanda, if Rwanda had happened before Yugoslavia. The precedent of the Yugoslavia Tribunal

enabled the Security Council to say—well, here is the precedent, Rwanda has requested an international tribunal, let's go along with it.[587]

With Justice Goldstone's words in mind, I try in this book to take us away from selectivity and bring us toward "universal" elements of human nature. Even after September 11 and the war in Iraq, we cannot simply divide the world into "us" and "them" and speak about how civilizations will clash. Instead, we can refer to man's need to identify some groups as allies and other groups as enemies.[588] This need evolves from individuals' attempts to protect their personal identities, which are intertwined with their experiences of ethnicity, nationality, religion, and other identifying circumstances. When large groups are threatened by conflict, members of the group cling evermore stubbornly to these circumstances in an effort to maintain and regulate their sense of self and their sense of belonging to a large group. At such times, large-group processes become dominant and large-group identity issues and rituals are more susceptible to political propaganda and manipulation.

Political, economic, legal, military, and historical factors usually figure prominently in any attempt to manage and solve large-group conflicts, but it is also necessary to consider the profound effect of human psychology, especially specific large-group processes that evolve under stress or after massive trauma and are manipulated by leaders. I try in this book to illustrate that psychoanalytic observations in the field and psychopolitical explanations should be given a genuine role in the study of large-group conflicts and in the development of strategies for a peaceful world.

/ acknowledgements

I acknowledge with deep gratitude the editorial help given to me by Danielle Pelfrey Duryea of the Department of English at the University of Virginia, who did more than edit this book; she gave me valuable leads to follow in my research. Simply put, writing this volume would not have been possible without our working alliance.

My special thanks also go to my son, Kurt Volkan, my agent, Theresa Park, my former editorial assistants, Cindalee Allan, Bruce Edwards, and Shelley Staples, at the University of Virginia School of Medicine's Center for the Study of Mind and Human Interaction (CSMHI), and to the former program director of CSMHI and managing editor of *Mind and Human Interaction*, Joy Boissevain.

/ notes

introduction

1.For a complete study of the concept of the need to have enemies and allies, see Vamık D. Volkan, *The Need to Have Enemies and Allies: From Clinical Practice to International Relationships.*

2.Erik H. Erikson developed the notion of basic trust in his seminal work *Childhood and Society.*

3.It may be useful to review briefly the distinctions between psychiatrists, psychologists, and psychoanalysts, three fields that are often mistaken for each other. Psychiatrists are physicians (M.D.s) who study and treat mental illness. Psychologists, who may hold Ph.D. or M.A. degrees, study the mind, emotions, and behavior, and how different external conditions affect them; not all psychologists are clinicians. In a process deriving from the work of Sigmund Freud, trained psychoanalysts—who may be M.D.s, Ph.D.s, M.A.s, social workers, or have other training altogether—work therapeutically with patients to discover the hidden sources of mental problems. Psychoanalysis involves three main areas: 1) a comprehensive theory of how the human mind evolves and functions; 2) using this understanding as an ameliorative tool for alleviating emotional suffering; and 3) using the theory to conduct research related to human understanding.

4.See Vamık Volkan, "Psychological concepts useful in the building of political foundations between nations (Track II diplomacy)"; *Bloodlines: From Ethnic Pride to Ethnic Terrorism.* See also Demetrios A. Julius, "The practice of Track Two diplomacy in the Arab-Israeli conferences."

5.Sigmund Freud, "Why war?" p. 207.

6.See Claudia Tate, "Freud and his 'Negro': Psychoanalysis as ally and enemy of African Americans."

7.See, for example, Sigmund Foulkes and E. James Anthony, *Group Psychotherapy*; Wilfred R. Bion, *Experiences in Groups*; D. Wilfred Abse, *Clinical Notes on Group-Analytic Psychotherapy*; and Malcolm Pines (Ed.), *The Evolution of Group Analysis.* See also: Vamık D. Volkan and David R. Hawkins, "The learning group."

8.See, for example, Manfred F. R. Kets de Vries, *The Irrational Executive*, for psychoanalytic exploration of organizations. Also see Howard F. Stein, *Euphemism, Spin, and the Crisis in Organizational Life.*

9.Vamık Volkan, "Psychoanalysis and Diplomacy: Potentials for and obstacles against collaboration."

10. Consider, for example, the important work of contemporary psychoanalytic theorists such as Didier Anzieu (*The Group and the Unconscious*), Janine Chasseguet-Smirgel (*The Ego Ideal*), and Otto F. Kernberg (*Internal World and External Reality*). They have observed that the large group represents an idealized, all-gratifying early mother (the "breast-mother") that repairs all narcissistic lesions. According to these theorists, leaders are chosen who promote such illusions of gratification, and mass aggression may occur in order to defend and preserve such fantasies if the group perceives that they are threatened.

11. There are others who are now contributing to this effort as well. For example, Peter Loewenberg, an historian as well as a practicing psychoanalyst in Los Angeles, has made psychoanalytic studies of a number of specific large-group events (Loewenberg, *Fantasy and Reality in History*). Norman Itzkowitz of Princeton University, another historian and psychoanalyst, has done similar work; Itzkowitz and I collaborated, for example, in examining a century of Turkish-Greek history through a psychoanalytic lens (see Vamık Volkan and Itzkowitz, *Turks and Greeks: Neighbors in Conflict*). John J. Hartman, a psychologist and psychoanalyst from the University of Florida and executive director of Remembrance and Reconciliation, Inc., has applied two psychoanalytic concepts—threats to identity and failure to mourn—to large-group dynamics (Hartman, "Polish-Jewish ethnic conflict: Threats to identity and the failure to mourn") as well.

Others have sought to bring psychoanalysts and the diplomatic establishment into closer relationship. Washington, D.C., psychoanalyst Afaf Mahfouz has worked for some time to promote communication between psychoanalysts and the United Nations. Stuart Twemlow, former director of the Erik Erikson Institute at Austen Riggs in Massachusetts, is applying psychoanalytic insights not only to international relations but also to school violence in the United States. Carroll Weinberg, a Philadelphia psychoanalyst, has been examining terrorism through a psychoanalytic lens (Weinberg, "Terrorists and terrorism: Have we reached a crossroad?"). In 1998 and again in 2001, South American psychoanalysts Moises Lemlij and Max Hernandez organized large and successful meetings in Lima, Peru, that brought psychoanalysts together with high-level diplomats and politicians. In India, psychoanalyst Sudhir Kakar has studied the December 1990 Hindu-Muslim riots in Hyderabad through a psychoanalytic lens (see Kakar, *The Colors of Violence*). In Israel, Rene Moses-Hrushovski and her late husband and fellow psychoanalyst Rafael Moses is and was a leader in applying psychoanalysis to diplomatic processes. Harold Saunders, former assistant secretary of state and present director of international affairs at the Kettering Foundation, and Joseph V. Montville, a former diplomat, are among those in the diplomatic arena incorporating psychoanalytic concepts into their work (see Saunders, *Public Peace Process;* Montville, "The arrow and the olive branch: A case for track two diplomacy"; "Psychoanalytic enlightenment and the greening of diplomacy"; and "Complicated mourning and mobilization for nationalism"). A number of other examples could be adduced, but collaboration between psychoanalysis and practical politics remains problematic.

After September 11, 2001, the International Psychoanalytic Association formed a Working Group on Terror and Terrorism under the chairmanship of Norwegian psychoanalyst Sverre Varvin. Members of the committee include Salman Akhtar (United States), Simon Brainsky (Columbia), Werner Bohleber (Germany), Abigail Golomb (Israel), Leopold Nosek (Brazil), Genevieve Welsh (France) and Vamık Volkan (United States). This Working Group has published a psychoanalytic study of terrorism [Sverre Varvin and Vamık D. Volkan (Eds.), *Violence or Dialogue? Psychoanalyitc Insights on Terror and Terrorism.*]

1

12. For a psychoanalytic description of individual identity, see Erik H. Erikson, "The problem of ego identity," and Salman Akhtar, *Broken Structures: Severe Personality Disorders and Their Treatment.* I have described in detail the psychodynamics of how an individual's core identity and his or her large-group identity become intertwined in *Bloodlines: From Ethnic Pride to Ethnic Terrorism, Das Versagen der Diplomatie,* and "Psychoanalysis and diplomacy, part 1: Individual and large-group identity."

13. On race, see the work of, among many others, Nancy Stepan, *The Idea of Race in Science: Great Britain 1800–1960,* and Noel Ignatieff, *How the Irish Became White*; on nationalism, see Benedict Anderson, *Invented Communities: Reflections on the Origin and Spread of Nationalism.*

14. Roger Scruton, *A Dictionary of Political Thought.*

15. George DeVos, "Ethnic pluralism."

16. Howard F. Stein, "International and group milieu of ethnicity."

17. Janine Chasseguet-Smirgel, "Blood and nation."

18. Scruton, ibid., p. 399.

19. Michael Barkun, "Religion, militias, and Oklahoma City: The mind of conspiratorialists" and "The Christian identity movement: Constructing millennialism on the racist Right."

20. W. Nathaniel Howell, "The evil that men do ... : Social effects of the Iraqi occupation of Kuwait."

21. Peter Loewenberg, *Fantasy and Reality in History.*

22. Loewenberg, "The psychological reality of nationalism"; Otto Bauer, *Die Nationalitatenfrage und Socialdemokratie.*

23. Rena Moses-Hrushovski, *Grief and Grievance: The Assassination of Yitzhak Rabin.*

24. Furthermore, those who belong to synthetic nations bring different perceptions, goals, and expectations to resolving the conflicts of others. I observed that whereas delegates from synthetic nations such as the United States tend to perceive that the best solution for ethnic conflict is to bring together the opposing parties in a kind of co-existence, delegates from ethnically homogeneous nations seem to understand more easily the conflicting parties' wishes to remain separate. That is, each delegate wishes to apply the model of their own nation to the situations of conflict that they are mediating. Of course, many political, economic, legal, and military considerations may complicate what delegates do as third-party facilitators.

The synthetic/nonsynthetic distinction I have drawn may be complicated by, for instance, the role of the nation in question in the history of imperialism. Delegates from nations that built empires—even if those empires have long since been dismantled—tend to evince a sort of pride as well as a certain comfort in the role of the powerful; further, they are likely to behave "generously" or "forgivingly"—a luxury, again, of the position of power. Those whose ancestors were ethnic minority subjects of empires often, on the other hand, move quickly to a sense of victimization; not forgetting and not forgiving tends to dominate their views of the conflict at hand. Even if a delegate's ethnic group itself held an empire before it was relegated to minority status within another empire, that delegate tends to remain aligned with the victim position. These effects of imperial history may, however, mitigate or shift as nations accrue collective postcolonial histories to bind them together. It may also be difficult to differentiate significantly between the form of nationalism—the aggregate of shared attachments that members of a group feel toward their own nation—shared by a group whose ancestors were colonized and that of a group whose ancestors were colonizers.

25. Rita R. Rogers, "Nationalism: A state of mind," p. 19.

26. William Petersen, "Concepts of ethnicity," p. 235. Petersen observes that the nationalism of any one individual may have its own nature and intensity and vary with time, place, and circumstance, and he adds the notion of the subnation, a unit smaller than a nation, which may be usefully applied to ethnic groups that are "seldom directly associated with the counterpart of a boundary-protecting state" (ibid., p. 235).

27. Hans Kohn, *Idea of Nationalism.*

28. George Orwell, "Notes on nationalism." Whatever Orwell's own ambivalent relationship with the imperial project of "forcing a particular way of life upon other people," (p. 362), his categorization of patriotism and nationalism remains opposite.

29. Orwell, ibid., p. 367.

30. See Dusan Kecmanovic, *The Mass Psychology of Ethnonationalism.* See also: Majid Tehranian, *Global Communication and World Politics*; Charles A. Kupchan (Ed.), *Nationalism and Nationalities in the New Europe.*

31. In reality, when Greece gained independence in 1821, only 40 percent of

the people were Greek Orthodox; 60 percent were Albanians, most of whom eventually left. There remains a tension even today between the official ethnic and religious homogeneity of the nation and the population's ethnic and religious (Catholic and Muslim—mostly Turkish) minorities, which are not fully integrated into the nation.

32. Joseph B. Gittler, "Toward defining an ethnic minority."

33. Norman Itzkowitz and Vamık Volkan, "The demonization of the other."

34. Itzkowitz and Volkan, ibid.

35. Vilho Harle, *The Enemy with a Thousand Faces: The Tradition of the Other in Western Political Thought and History*.

36. Itzkowitz and Volkan, ibid.

37. *Encyclopedia Britannica*, Macropedia, 1985, v. 15, pp. 360–366.

38. Commission on Human Rights Sub-Commission on Prevention of Discrimination and Protection of Minorities, United Nations, 1992.

39. Kemalism sought to unify the new Turkish state, led by Mustafa Kemal Ataturk, under the six principles of republicanism, nationalism, populism, etatism (interim state assistance to private enterprise), secularism, and revolutionism (ongoing reform). For details of the psychological dimensions of Kemalism, see Vamık Volkan and Norman Itzkowitz, *The Immortal Ataturk: A Psychobiography*.

40. Interestingly enough, some of Freud's only remarks on identity link individual psychology to large-group identity, if only in passing and without elaboration. In a speech read at a B'nai B'rith gathering, he pondered the fact that he himself felt bound to other Jews despite never having been instilled with the traditional Jewish ethnonational pride or religious faith. Although a nonbeliever, he noted, he felt a "safe privacy of a common mental construction," and "a clear consciousness of inner identity" as a Jew (Sigmund Freud, "Address to the Society of B'nai B'rith," p. 274). My work over the past twenty-five years has confirmed that Freud was quite right to link individual "mental construction" to large-group identity. We shall return to the mechanics of just how this bond develops in each individual later in the chapter.

41. Erik H. Erikson, "The problem of ego identity," p. 12. For other psychoanalytic writings on identity, see: Otto Fenichel, "Early stages of ego development"; Phyllis Greenacre, "Early physical determinants in the development of the sense of identity"; Edith Jacobson, *The Self and the Object World*; Otto F. Kernberg, *Object Relations Theory and Clinical Psychoanalysis*; and Margaret Mahler, *On Human Symbiosis and the Vicissitudes of Individuation*.

42. Emphasizing that each individual crystallizes his or her identity in adolescence, Erikson argued that, while identity-formation begins with earliest self-recognition, it is in actuality a lifelong process of development. For a discussion of personality, see Chapter 6.

43. Salman Akhtar, *Broken Structures: Severe Personality Disorders and Their Treatment*, p. 32

44. Sigmund Freud, "Inhibitions, symptoms, and anxiety."

45. James Glass, *Private Terror, Public Life*.

46. See L. Bryce Boyer, *Regression and Countertransference*; Ping-Nie Pao, *Schizophrenic Disorders*; and Vamık Volkan, *The Infantile Psychotic Self*.

47. Of course, as adults, we have no way of capturing or representing in language that experience of emotional, cognitive confusion.

48. See, for example, Robert Emde, "Development terminable and interminable I: Innate and motivational factors from infancy" and "Development terminable and interminable II: Recent psychoanalytic theory and therapeutic considerations"; Stanley Greenspan, *The Development of the Ego: Implications for Personality Theory, Psychopathology and the Psychotherapeutic Process*; and Daniel Stern, *The Interpersonal World of the Infant*.

49. The process that I have described here is known as the "object-relations" theory of development. See *Otto F. Kernberg, Object Relations Theory and Clinical Psychoanalysis* and *Aggression in Personality Disorders and Perversions*.

50. A child can identify with others even before he or she develops a clear "border" around the self, which is called "fusing" or "merging" identification. A "primitive" form of identification, it usually does not last very long, and is therefore of little relevance for our purposes here, though severely regressed adults can periodically experience fusion. A schizophrenic person may, for example, call "uncle" a person who wears a moustache like the one his uncle wears; in this situation, the schizophrenic "fuses" the images of two objects/persons.

51. Here I only mention adaptive, mental growth-inducing identifications. Though damaging, maladaptive identifications are of course also possible, they are not essential to our purposes in this chapter. I also omit discussion of certain other mental processes that, when combined with those mentioned here, make up the child's mind *in toto*.

52. For details, see Vamık Volkan, *The Need to Have Enemies and Allies*. Love relationships, marriage, parenthood, immigration, exile, or severe traumatic experiences in adulthood may unconsciously initiate internal work similar to that of the adolescent passage: elements of various identifications are re-examined and re-settled in modified forms within the individual's sense of self. In general, unconsciously examining childhood identifications in adulthood does not alter one's core identity unless the stress and trauma that instigate the re-examination are unusually severe.

53. Sigmund Freud, "Group psychology and the analysis of the ego."

54. See Vamık Volkan, *Das Versagen der Diplomatie*.

55. Edith Jacobson, *The Self and the Object World*; Margaret S. Mahler, *On Human Symbiosis and the Vicissitudes of Individuation*; Otto F. Kernberg, "A psychoanalytic classification of character pathology."

56. For example, a child develops the mental mechanism of repression to keep an unintegrated "bad" image contaminated with aggressive emotion—such as murderous rage toward his or her father as a response to experiencing the father

as a punitive figure—in his or her unconscious. This, obviously, is a vast topic beyond the scope of this book. For details see: Otto Kernberg, *Object Relations Theory and Clinical Psychoanalysis*, and H. G. Van der Waals, "Discussions of the mutual influences in the development of ego and id."

57. For details, see Jack Novick and Kerry Kelly, "Projection and externalization."

58. Erik H. Erikson, "Ontology of ritualization."

59. Vamık Volkan, *Bloodlines: From Ethnic Pride to Ethnic Terrorism.*

60. Finnish psychoanalysts Veikko Tahka, Kalle Achte, and Eero Rechardt ("Psychoanalyyttisia nakakohtie saunasta ja saunomista"), and other Finnish psychiatrists (O. Ihalainen, R. Hirvenoja, and M. Tuovinen, "Psychic factors in sauna bath habits") have written about Finns' shared conscious and unconscious fantasies surrounding sauna bathing.

61. The child's caretakers consciously and unconsciously direct the child to externalize his or her "good" unintegrated self-images and images of others onto certain items in their environment because these items are already accepted by the child's caretakers as amplifiers of their own cultural, ethnic, or national sentiments. Unintegrated "bad" images tend to be externalized onto other items, often those that belong to "others" or to enemy groups. (For further details, see Vamık Volkan, *Bloodlines* and *Das Versagen der Diplomatie.*)

62. Didier Anzieu (*The Group and the Unconscious*), Janine Chasseguet-Smirgel (ibid.), and Otto F. Kernberg ("Mass psychology through the analytic lens") have postulated that large groups represent for their members a "breast-mother" or "primitive maternal ego-ideal." Though Mother Russia, the Statue of Liberty, England's Boadicea, and many other examples of significant feminine symbols for large groups certainly support the idea that a nation represents certain maternal characteristics, I believe that there is more to large-group identity than this one aspect. In my work, I emphasize that the "good" mother-image that is attached to a large group is always condensed with the child's own unintegrated "good" self-images.

63. Robert Emde, "Positive emotions for psychoanalytic theory: Surprises from infancy research and new directions."

64. Peter Blos, *The Adolescent Passage.*

65. Sudhir Kakar, *The Color of Violence: Cultural Identities, Religion, and Conflict.*

66. Vamık Volkan, *Cyprus—War and Adaptation.*

67. Edith Jacobson, *The Self and the Object World*, p. 197.

68. Wayne C. Booth, "Pluralism in the classroom."

69. For a detailed report of the internal worlds of such analysands, see Vamık Volkan and Gabriele Ast, *Eine Borderline Therapie.*

70. When a child identifies with aspects of his or her parent, he or she also identifies with the parent's image of the child. Thus early identifications are shaped by absorbing not only what the parent is like, but also how the parent

regards the child both in reality and in his or her unconscious fantasies. See Hans Leowald, "On the therapeutic action of psychoanalysis."

71. Itzkowitz and Volkan, ibid.

72. John Lind, "The dream as a simple wish-fulfillment in the Negro." White psychiatrist Lind was very much a product of his time and place, conceiving of African Americans as "little children," psychologically speaking, and of their dreams as direct fulfillments of their wishes.

73. See H. J. Myers and Leon Yochelson, "Color denial in the Negro," and M. M. Vitols, H. G. Walters, and Martin H. Keeler, "Hallucinations and delusions in white and Negro schizophrenics."

74. S. W. Manning, "Cultural and value factors affecting the Negroes' use of agency services."

75. Charles Pinderhughes, "The origins of racism," and Charles Wilkerson, "Destructiveness of myths."

76. For a more-detailed exploration of this example, see Volkan, *Bloodlines*.

77. Itzkowitz and Volkan, ibid.

78. See MacGregor Burns, *Leadership*, for the concept of "transforming leaders." In Burns' explanation of the transforming leader, we may catch an echo of Max Weber's description of "charismatic" leaders. In *Wirtschaft und Gessellschaft*, Weber argues that charismatic leaders come to power at times of crisis within their groups; under these circumstances, the charismatic leader "is obeyed by virtue of personal trust in him and his revelation, his heroism, or his exemplary qualities so far as they fall within the scope of the individual's belief in his charisma" (p. 328). Abraham Zaleznik ("Charismatic and consensus leaders") adds that "charisma refers to any combination of unusual qualities in an individual which are attractive to others and result in special attachments, if not devotion, to his leadership" (p. 114). D. Wilfred Abse and Lucie Jessner ("The psychodynamic aspect of leadership"), Abse and Richard Ulman ("Charismatic political leadership and collective regression"), and Vamık Volkan and Norman Itzkowitz (*The Immortal Ataturk: A Psychobiography*) have suggested that the charismatic leader has both paternal and maternal characteristics; charismatic leaders provide a "total" parent image for their followers. Further, the charismatic leader inspires both love and awe and, at times, allows an occasional glimpse of brutality. "Certain it is," Abse and Ulman observe, "that the charismatic leader is both intimidating and encouraging, and he may alternate rapidly between these two ways of dealing with people" (p. 41).

79. Volkan and Itzkowitz, ibid.

80. See also Vamık Volkan, "On 'chosen trauma'"; *Bloodlines*; and "Psychoanalysis and diplomacy, part 1: Individual and large-group identity"; Vamık Volkan and Norman Itzkowitz, *Turks and Greeks: Neighbors in Conflict*.

81. See Judith Kestenberg and Ira Brenner, *The Last Witness*; Ilany Kogan, *The Cry of Mute Children: A Psychoanalytic Perspective of the Second Generation of the Holocaust*; and Vamık Volkan, Gabriele Ast, and William Greer, *The Third Reich*

in the Unconscious: Transgenerational Transmission and its Consequences, among many other contributions to this topic.

82. To understand the concept of depositing images, consider the following scenario: After a mother's first child dies, she becomes pregnant again and has a second child. In relating to her second child, the mother "deposits" her own mental representation of the deceased child into the developing identity of the second child, the "replacement child." Sometimes, the mother may be partly conscious of what she is doing; for example, she may name the second child after the first one. Replacement children with high adaptive capacity may not be injured by the deposited image of a dead relative if their activities and mental products match those that the parent(s) and/or other caregiver(s) expect from the now-idealized deposited image. For a less-adaptive replacement child, however, the deposited image may act like an irritating "foreign object" within his or her self-representation. For details, see A. C. Cain and B. S. Cain, "On replacing a child"; E. D. Poznanski, "The 'replacement child': A saga of unresolved parental grief"; and Vamık Volkan and Gabriele Ast, *Siblings in the Unconscious.*

I differentiate the concept of "deposited representation" from the more common "identification." The concept of identification refers to a subject's unconscious assimilation of another person's self-images, and the mental functions associated with them, through interactions with that other person. True identification is only possible after a child intrapsychically separates his or her self-representation from the representations of other people. Under these conditions, what comes from outside modifies, to some degree, the child's self-representation. In the identification process, the child is the more active partner in the interaction.

By contrast, the concept of deposited representation emphasizes the role of the parent or other significant person who unconsciously—and sometimes even consciously—forces aspects of him or herself, or aspects of his or her own internalized object-images, into the self-representation of the child. By depositing images and representations into the child's developing self-representation, the object influences the child's sense of identity and gives the child certain specific tasks to perform. In fact, the other person can pass his or her images, with associated affects, to the child even before the child achieves the separation between his or her own psychic boundaries and those of others. In the process of deposited representation, the more active partner is the significant other person, not the child whose self-representation functions as a reservoir. For additional details, see Vamık Volkan, *Six Steps in the Treatment of Borderline Personality Organization.*

83. Gerard J. Libaridian (Ed.), *Armenia at the Crossroads: Democracy and Nationhood in the Post-Soviet* Era.

84. Loewenberg, "The Uses of Anxiety," p. 515.

85. I have written extensively about this chosen trauma in *Bloodlines* and *Das Versagen der Diplomatie.* Norman Itzkowitz and I detailed a similarly distant chosen trauma for Greeks (the 1453 fall of Constantinople to the Ottoman Turks) in

Turks and Greeks: Neighbours in Conflict.

86. Peter Loewenberg, ibid., p. 515.

87. For additional details on this project, see Vamık Volkan, Bloodlines.

88. Sigmund Freud, *Interpretation of Dreams.*

89. Bernard E. Moore and Bernard D. Fine, *Psychoanalytic Terms and Concepts,* p. 192.

90. Hans Biederman, *Dictionary of Symbolism: Cultural Icons and Meaning Behind Them.*

91. Robert D. Kaplan, *Balkan Ghosts: A Journey Through History,* p. 39.

92. Barbara Ehrenreich, *Blood Rites: Origin and History of the Passions of War,* p. 212.

93. Robert G. L. Waite, *The Psychopathic God: Adolf Hitler,* p. 26.

94. See Heinz Werner and Bernard Kaplan, *Symbol Formation.*

95. A simple definition of political propaganda (from the Latin "to propagate" or "to sow") would encompass any communication and manipulation from a source of political authority that is directed toward its supporters and opposition at home and/or abroad as well as to those who might be described as "neutrals"; its aim, of course, is to further the propagandists' wishes and ideas. Emeritus professor of history at Princeton University Bernard Lewis suggests that *modern* political propaganda did not begin until the French Revolution (Bernard Lewis, "Propaganda in the Middle East"). Before the French Revolution, he argues, there was essentially no meaningful contact between the rulers and the ordinary people. The powerful had no need to communicate with or to manipulate the public—they simply ruled. After the seismic shift of the French Revolution, however, rulers began to need political propaganda in order to secure at least the appearance of consent from those they governed.

Of course, propaganda existed in earlier times, too. For example, Garth S. Jowett and Victoria O'Donnell (*Propaganda and Persuasion,* p. 2) describe how the concept of "propagating" ideas lost its neutrality: in 1622, *Sacra Conregatio de Propaganda Fide* (the "sacred congregation for propagating the faith" of the Roman Catholic Church) was established by the Vatican; the term "propaganda" became pejorative in Protestant Western Europe because it was associated with the project of spreading Catholicism in the New World at the expense of and in opposition to the "reformed" faiths.

Harold D. Lasswell, a pioneer in the study of psychosocial warfare, places modern propaganda's birth date even later, suggesting in 1938 that the "discovery of propaganda by both man in the street and the man in the study" took place during World War I (1914–1918) (Harold D. Lasswell, "Foreword," *Allied Propaganda and the Collapse of the German Empire in 1918,* G. G. Bruntz (Ed.) (p. v)). Elsewhere, in *Propaganda Technique in the World War,* Lasswell expressed his fear of propaganda's influence on the very nature of civil society:

A newer and subtler instrument must weld thousands and even millions of human beings into one amalgamated mass of hate and will and hope.

A new flame must burn out the canker of dissent and temper the steel of bellicose enthusiasm. The name of this new hammer and anvil of social solidarity is propaganda (pp. 220–221).

Lasswell's ideas were built on *learning theory*, based on a stimulus-response model.

When the "Great War" began, there was no public outcry about oppressed nationalities or religions and no interest in secret diplomacies; the war was fought by professional soldiers who required little knowledge of why they were fighting. As is depicted in World War I movies such as *Gallipoli*, soldiers shot and killed the enemy without hatred or even contempt. But as the war dragged on and began to affect peoples' lives more intimately, it became essential at once to stimulate the soldiers' will to fight and to explain the need for privation to the public at home. In order to justify the cost of operations it was necessary to inflate the fruits of victory with vague but lofty-sounding notions such as "self-determination" and "war to end all wars" (James A. C. Brown, *Techniques of Persuasion*, p. 91). Thus, Lasswell argues, political propaganda was "discovered"—more startling, he says, to the man in the street than to the man in the study: "The layman had previously lived in a world where there was no common name for the deliberate forming of attitudes by the manipulation of words (and word substitutes)" (Lasswell, "Foreword," p. v).

By World War I, communication technologies had drastically improved, enabling direct contact with the public on an unprecedented scale. In 1917, Woodrow Wilson's administration established the United States Committee on Public Information. The next year, an international committee of American, British, French, and Italian experts examined commercial advertising practices, which were already quite elaborately evolved, in order to refine techniques of political propaganda and manipulation to be directed at both the home front and enemy. Compared to the efforts of the victorious allies, it is now generally believed, German propaganda during World War I was weak and ineffectual (Leif Furhammer and Folke Isaksson, *Politics and Film*, p. 11). By the Second World War, of course, the German state was a master of propaganda. Adolf Hitler himself, as is well known, devoted two chapters of *Mein Kampf* to the proper design and execution of propaganda. Hitler asserted that propaganda should be aimed "only to a limited degree at the so-called intellect ... The art of propaganda lies in understanding the emotional ideas of great masses and finding through a psychologically correct form, the way to attention and thence to the heart of the broad masses" (Adolf Hitler, *Mein Kampf*, p. 180).

By the time Hitler was in power, psychoanalysis, which was developed by Sigmund Freud, was clearly established and Nazism and the war inspired psychoanalysts to write on large groups in conflict and the causes of massive destructions as well as how leaders manipulate the minds of thousands or millions of people. Besides Freud's papers on large-group psychology, psychoanalysts such as Ernst Kris ("The 'danger' of propaganda"; "Some problems of war propaganda: A note on propaganda new and old"; *Radio Propaganda: Report on Home Broadcasts*

During the War), Roger E. Money-Kyrle ("The psychology of propaganda"), and Edward Glover (*War, Sadism and Pacifism: Further Essays on Group Psychology and War*) examined the psychodynamics of how propaganda works. But after World War II, because psychoanalysis has sought to establish itself as a medical science (especially in the United States), the orientation of psychoanalysts has been restricted to the realm of clinical issues; few therefore even consider the possibilities of applying their skills beyond the therapeutic setting. Others have been discouraged by the pessimism of their predecessors. In a 1932 letter to Einstein, Freud saw little hope for an end to war and violence, or for the role of psychoanalysis in changing human behavior beyond the individual level, even though Freud himself had devoted considerable energy to understanding large groups (see Sigmund Freud, "Why war?").

Some psychoanalysts, such as Jacob Arlow ("Motivations for Peace"), have found some cautious optimism in some of Freud's writings on this subject. Freud's general pessimism was mirrored by many of his followers, and this fact, I believe, has played a key role in limiting the contributions made to diplomacy by psychoanalysts. Having seen what people are capable of doing to their fellow humans in many parts of the world over the last two decades, I cannot help but join Freud in his pessimism. Groups of human beings cannot completely refrain from committing acts of violence, mass destruction, and atrocity. So it is better for us, as psychoanalysts, to adopt a more practical, less idealistic attitude toward international relationships. I am optimistic about using psychoanalytic insights and concepts to deal with and modify certain limited international situations (see: Vamık Volkan, "The Tree Model").

Thus, psychoanalysts have written relatively little on the subjects of political decision-making, propaganda that aims to induce a sense of cohesiveness in a large group, or efforts to poison or heal the masses. In 1971, German psychoanalyst Alexander Mitscherlich stated that psychoanalysts need to collaborate with others, such as political and social scientists, in order to understand large-group dynamics (Alexander Mitscherlich, "Psychoanalysis and aggression of large groups"). Few, however, followed this route and ventured "beyond the couch" to apply their expertise in psychological processes to understanding collective human practices in politics, leader–follower relationships, political decision-making, and propaganda. I am one of these psychoanalysts who eventually came to follow this route.

2

96. "Survivor guilt" also entails a whole host of other psychological problems that I will not go into here. William Niederland's studies of Jewish survivors of the Holocaust are some of the first detailed descriptions of survivor guilt (Niederland, "Clinical observations on the 'survivor syndrome'").

97. Robert Lifton, for example, has studied the adaptive effects of artistic and

literary expression among survivors of the atomic bombing of Hiroshima. See Lifton, *Death in Life: Survivors of Hiroshima*.

98. Introjection simply means "taking in"; for example, a child takes in his or her parents', or society's, values and attitudes and identifies with them. Conversely, projection simply means "putting out" internal "devils": for instance, being harsh and blaming one's behavior on one's boss instead of taking responsibility for one's own rage. All of us use these mechanisms daily to one degree or another; but a regressed person uses them extensively and unconsciously *in place of* sorting out reality from fantasy. In a large-group setting, increased collective introjection results in very strictly incorporating new societal, political, or religious ideas or doctrines, as if the very identity of the regressed large group feeds on such ideas and doctrines to keep itself alive. Shared projection, on the other hand, magnifies the present dangers posed by "others." The magnified dangers become reservoirs for the envy, jealousy, and anger that are dangerous for members to own.

99. Sigmund Freud, "Group psychology and the analysis of the ego."

100. See, for example, Robert Waelder, "The principle of multiple function: Observation on over-determination."

101. Michael Sebek, "The fate of totalitarian objects." See also Nancy Hollander, *Love in Time of Hate: Liberation Psychology in Latin America* and "The legacy of state terror and the new social violence in Latin America"; the special issue of *Mind and Human Interaction* on "Defining Evil," vol. 11, no. 2.

102. Sayed Askar Mousavi, *The Hazaras of Afghanistan: An Historical, Cultural, Economic, and Political Study*.

103. Mousavi, ibid. The most numerous and powerful of these (now about 38 percent of the population) are known as the Pashtuns, speakers of the Pashto language. Tajiks now comprise 25 percent of the population, and Hazara 19 percent; the remainder of the population includes Uzbeks, Chahar, Aimak, Turkmen, Balochi, and others.

104. As the United States and its coalition partners considered a post-Taliban Afghanistan, they began to talk to the exiled King Zahir, who had not seen his country for three decades, and to consider the idea of his return to the country. Mohamed Zahir Shah, accompanied by interim leader Mohamed Karzai, returned from Italy to Afghanistan in April 2002.

105. Anthony Hyman, *Afghanistan Under Soviet Domination*; Peter Marsden, *The Taliban: War, Religion, and the New Order in Afghanistan*; Ahmad Rashid, *Taliban: Islam, Oil and the New Great Game in Central Asia*.

106. Patricia Pearson "In the balance: Afghan kids," *USA Today*, October 24, 2001, p. 15A.

107. Until 2000, the Taliban did earn money from opium and heroin production. Though the use of such drugs is prohibited by Islam, the Taliban claimed that selling it was not. In order to gain international recognition, the Taliban banned poppy cultivation in recent years, gaining multi-million dollar aid from

the United States as a result.

108. Rashid, ibid.

109. Rashid, ibid.

110. Robert Marquand, "The reclusive ruler who runs the Taliban," *The Christian Science Monitor*, October 10, 2001. Though this title makes universal claims, it is not accepted by Muslims outside Afghanistan.

111. Rashid, ibid. Mullah Omar belongs to a culture in which the veneration of holy places is typical. The Shrine of the Cloak is the most important holy place in Afghanistan, but there are many others that draw pilgrims seeking cures or happier fates.

112. Norimitsu Onishi, "A tale of the Mullah and Muhammad's amazing cloak," *The New York Times*, December 9, 2001, pp. B1 and B3. It is a Muslim custom in many parts of the world to have designated families as permanent keepers of holy places; Shawali inherited the responsibility from his father.

113. Onishi, ibid.

114. Qtd. in Onishi, ibid, p. B3.

115. Qtd. in Onishi, ibid.

116. Onishi, ibid.

117. Jeffrey Goldberg, "The education of a holy warrior," *The New York Times Magazine*, June 25, 2000.

118. Goldberg, ibid., pp. 32-27, 53, 63, 70.

119. Marta Cullberg-Weston, "When words lose their meaning: From societal crises to ethnic cleansing," p. 25.

120. See Robert S. Robins and Jerrold M. Post, *Political Paranoia: The Psychopolitics of Hatred*. Also see Joseph H. Berke, Stella Pierides, Andrea Sabbadini, and Stanley Schneider, *Even Paranoids Have Enemies*.

121. Marie Bonaparte, *Myths of War*.

122. Vamık Volkan, "Symptom formations and character changes due to upheavals of war: Examples from Cyprus."

123. Though this fear was to a degree based in reality, the extent of the change in cultural norms far exceeded the realistic threat.

124. Kurt Volkan, "Islam and identity in Central Asia." See also S. E. Wimbush, "The politics of identity change in Soviet Central Asia"; Alexandre Bennigsen and Marie Broxup, The *Islamic Threat to the Soviet Union*.

125. K. Volkan, ibid., p. 166.

126. K. Volkan, ibid., p. 167–168.

127. I suppose that, in psychoanalytic terms, this imagined weapon stood for a great phallus or an anal explosion.

128. A. de Swaan, "Widening circle of disidentification: On the psycho- and socio-genesis of the hatred of distant strangers; reflections on Rwanda."

129. Claudia Koonz, *Mothers in the Fatherland: Women, the Family and Nazi Politics*, p. 196.

130. Koonz, ibid., p. 196.

131. qtd. Koonz, ibid., p. 388.

132. Hitler, *Mein Kampf,* pp. 356-358.

133. Koonz, ibid., p. 388.

134. Jill Stephenson, "Propaganda, autarky, and the German housewife," pp. 121-122.

135. Betram Schaffner, *Fatherland: A Study of Authoritarianism in the German Family,* p. 35.

136. Stephenson, ibid., p. 136.

137. Stephenson, ibid., p. 137. In this, the Volkswirtschaft/Hauswirtschaft was not unlike "rural extension services" in the U.S. In the U.S., however, there was no comparable aim to intervene in every aspect of domestic life.

138. Sigrid Chamberlain's 1977 study of Haarer's books, "*Adolf Hitler, die deutsche Mutter und ihr erstes Kind*" ("Adolf Hitler, the German mother, and her first child"), noted that their practical admonitions in fact "were political propaganda" (p.8). Her plea to investigate the key role of interference in family dynamics in Nazi propaganda more generally has, however, gone largely unanswered in the scholarly investigations since. The present chapter attempts to amplify and to nuance her claim that "National socialist education was always an education that prevented bonding (child-parent) and the ability for relationships" (p.11). See also Johanna Haarer's other works, "*Mutterschaft und familienpflege imneuen Reich*" ("*Motherhood and family care in the new Reich*") and *Mutter, erzahl von Adolf Hitler* (*Mother, Tell About Adolf Hitler*).

139. *The German Mother and Her First Child* cast a surprisingly long and dark shadow over twentieth-century German child-rearing. Rather like the lingering, not-fully-conscious influence of Franz Anton Mesmer, the prescription for helpless children who would use excessive grandiosity to cope with misfortune continued in print until the late 1980s with slightly modified title—*The Mother and Her First-Born Child*—and content.

140. Koonz, ibid., p. 210.

141. Norman H. Baynes, ed., *The Speeches of Adolf Hitler,* Volume I (April 1922-August 1939), p.547.

142. Harry W. Flannery, *Assignment to Berlin,* p. 84.

143. Flannery, ibid.

144. Welch, *Propaganda and the German Cinema,* p. 66.

145. Qtd. in Wallace R. Deuel, *People Under Hitler,* p. 146 (SA refers to the Storm Troopers and SS stands for Elite Guards.)

146. Until adolescence, a child only has character *traits*; it is only in this phase that character (or personality) crystallization occurs (Peter Blos, *Adolescent Passage*). See also Vamık D. Volkan, *The Need to Have Enemies and Allies,* for how large-group (e.g., ethnic, religious, national) identity coalesces during adolescence.

147. In general, Nazi rules and regulations made mourning and feeling remorse difficult for all Germans. If someone died, he or she was no longer necessary for the survival of *Volksgemeinschaft*. The Party forbade families to make

"undue" displays of grief over loved ones. And, when civilians as well as soldiers died, the party asserted the right to determine the kind of clothes in which they might be laid out and the sorts of tombstones they might have over their graves (Deuel, ibid.). Soldiers were given quick burials, and there existed no national military cemetery. On May 18, 1937, the mayor of Pirmasens gave out a statement which read as follows: "It has been noted repeatedly that the dead have been laid out in expensive clothing and decorations. I call your attention to the fact that it is the duty of every citizen to see that the dead shall not be buried in expensive materials" (Deuel, ibid., p. 152). In January 1938, the Nazi Chamber of Arts, a section in the national Chamber of *Kultur* presided over by Joseph Goebbels, decided that every cemetery must have a certain basic landscaping and gravestones must be of approximately the same height and color.

Nazi military burial ceremonies at the Russian front were very brief: the unit commander would give a short speech and say, "He fell with honor for the Fuhrer, the people and the Fatherland." Images of dead heroes were included in the collective identity, but the Party interfered with the expression of individualized grief, which would have "piggybacked" on youngsters' developmental difficulties.

148. This is true only on certain levels; they were certainly trained to teach Nazi "racial theory."

149. Peter Loewenberg, *Decoding the Past: The Psychohistorical Approach*, pp. 240-283. We see such cases in our clinical practice when we treat children who had childhood physical/psychological hunger and who, as teenagers, have turned to grandiose religious cults or ideologies.

150. Welch, ibid., p. 65.

151. Welch, ibid., p. 77

152. For exceptions, see Edith Jacobson, *The Self and the Object World*, and Otto F. Kernberg, *Internal World and External Reality: Object Relations Theory Applied*.

153. Later, the adult male Nazi could use a Jewish woman prisoner in the camps as a sexual object, but she could not be a "proper" love object. Having sex with a Jew was forbidden but we know from anecdotal evidence that Nazi officers used Jewish women prisoners as sex objects.

154. Michael Sebek, "Anality in the totalitarian system and the psychology of post-totalitarian society," p. 54.

155. W. Ronald D. Fairbairn, a well-known psychoanalyst of his time, wrote in 1935 that communist ideology liquidated the family not as a social unit but as a psychological one. Michael Sebek has more recently described the destruction of the family under Soviet-style communism. See Fairbairn, "The sociological implications of communism considered in the light of psychoanalysis," and Sebek, ibid.

156. This team was assembled under the auspices of the University of Virginia Center for the Study of Mind and Human Interaction (CSMHI). Ambassador W. Nathaniel Howell (Ret.) is a resident diplomat of CSMHI. Team

members also included psychiatrists J. Anderson Thomson and Gregory Saathoff as well as psychiatric nurse and mediator Margie Howell.

157. Gregory Saathoff, "In the halls of mirrors: One Kuwaiti's captive memories" and "Kuwait's children: Identity in the shadow of the storm."

158. Anna Freud, "The ego and the mechanism of defense."

159. Peter Blos, *The Adolescent Passage.*

160. Based on our research, the CSMHI team suggested to Kuwaiti authorities a number of political and educational strategies to help the society to mourn its losses and changes and to speak openly about the helplessness and humiliation of the occupation in a way that would heal splits between generations as well as between subgroups within Kuwaiti society—for example, between those who fought against the Iraqis directly and those who escaped from Kuwait and returned after the invasion was over. When we tactfully presented our findings about children and adolescents to the authorities, however, Kuwaiti funding for the project stopped abruptly. It seems that, for political reasons, maintaining a shared denial was preferable to the systematic and therapeutic re-opening of Kuwaitis' psychological "wounds" so that they could heal in a more adaptive manner. Fortunately, we have not met with such strenuous resistance in most areas.

161. Janine Chasseguet-Smirgel, *Blood and Nation.*

162. Sebek, ibid., p. 54. Sebek, like Chasseguet-Smirgel (*Creativity and Perversion*), works from the Freudian theory of psychosexual development through oral, anal, and phallic phases, and sees life under a totalitarian regime as regressing to a developmentally primitive "anal world."

163. Of course, strictly speaking, it is not accurate to say that the group itself displays anal sadism; a society, after all, never has an infancy exactly as an individual does. What is actually happening is that individual members of a large group, not the group itself, regress to anal sadism. But we can say, by analogy, that a large group exhibits anal characteristics when members share anal regression.

3

164. Erik H. Erikson, *Toys and Reasons: Stages of Ritualization of Experience.*

165. Erikson, ibid., p. 82.

166. Erikson, ibid., p. 69.

167. Washington, D.C., psychoanalyst John Kafka (*Multiple Realities in Clinical Practice*) believes that ritual and ritualistic postures relate to a concern with boundaries, both spatial and psychological-temporal—including the boundaries between the individual and the group, between what is within and what is without, and between the concrete or concretized. I would add that ritualization also bears on the boundary separating two large groups, especially when the rituals are shared by members of both groups.

168. In *Bloodlines: From Ethnic Pride to Ethnic Terrorism*, I describe in detail my interviews with these Palestinian orphans. (See also As'ad Masri and Vamık

Volkan, "Children of Biet Atfal Al-Sommoud.")

169. See *Children in War*, a special issue of *Mind and Human Interaction*, Vol. 2, No. 2, October, 1990. During 1989–1990, Simon was Sigmund Freud Professor at the Hebrew University, Apfel a visiting professor at Hadassah Hospital.

170. The two Muslim families that kept the keys of the Church of the Holy Sepulchre in Jerusalem are the Nusseibehs and Djaudehs, old families of Muslim/Arab notables. One Nusseibeh family member was the mayor of Jerusalem during the early phase of the British League of Nations mandate in Palestine (1920–1948); another was Anwar Nusseibeh, a member of the Royal Jordanian cabinet under the late King Hussein.

171. This phenomenon is similar to one I observed among Cypriot Turks in the late 1960s. During the period in which they were forced to live under horrible conditions in enclaves surrounded by their enemies, Cypriot Turks created a symbol, a parakeet in a cage, to represent their imprisoned selves. As long as they could identify themselves with the fertile birds—thousands of them, in fact—who sang happily, Cypriot Turks maintained the hope that they would one day regain their freedom. For details, see Vamık Volkan, *Cyprus—War and Adaptation*.

172. The twenty-seventh of Nissan on the Hebrew calendar—May 2 on the 2000 Gregorian calendar—is observed as "Holocaust Day" in Israel.

173. George Pollock, *The Mourning-Liberation Process* (2 volumes), vol. 1, p. 231. (See also Vamık Volkan, *The Linking Objects and Linking Phenomena*, and Vamık Volkan and Elizabeth Zintl, *Life After Loss*.)

174. Pollock, ibid., vol. 1, p. 229.

175. For the classic psychoanalytic study, see Marie Bonaparte, "Time and the Unconscious."

176. I. L. Mintz, "The anniversary reaction: A response to the unconscious sense of time," p. 731.

177. E. Verissimo, *Mexico*.

178. Pollock, ibid., p.255.

179. For example, see Barbara Heimannsberg and Christoph Schmidt, *The Collective Silence: German Identity and the Legacy of Shame*; Vamık Volkan, Gabriele Ast and William Greer, *The Third Reich in the Unconscious*.

180. Gabriele Rothenthal, *Der Holocaust in Leben von drei Generationen* (Holocaust in the Life of Three Generations) and Annette Streeck-Fischer, "Naziskins in Germany: How traumatization deals with the past."

181. Vamık Volkan, *Bloodlines*.

182. Vamık Volkan, ibid. Also see Volkan, *The Need to Have Enemies and Allies*; *Das Versagen der Diplomatie*; and "Psychoanalysis and diplomacy, Part II."

183. Freud introduced and most thoroughly elaborated the psychology of minor differences in relation to individual psychology: "Each individual is separated from others by a 'taboo of personal isolation,' and ... it is precisely the minor differences in people who are otherwise alike that form the basis of

strangeness and hostility between them" ("Taboo of Virginity," p. 199). Later he mentioned briefly the role of minor differences between large groups, noting that Spaniards and Portuguese, English and Scots, and North and South Germans were preoccupied by constant comparisons and mutual ridicule ("Civilization and its Discontents"; see also "Group psychology and the analysis of the ego").

Of course, it is not a modern phenomenon: Anglo-Irish writer Jonathan Swift had sharply observed its fatal consequences as early as 1726. In *Gulliver's Travels*, Swift recounts a war between the fictional Lilliputians and Blefuscudians fought over the proper way to break an egg: in his satire, 11,000 suffer death rather than submit to breaking their eggs at the smaller end.

184. Israeli psychoanalyst Avner Falk has investigated the significance of these firmly fixed political borders for the individual: "Disputes over borders arise in different parts of the world and lead to armed conflict or even war. It is clear that the emotional meaning of one's country's borders, unconsciously, is fused with that of one's own boundaries" ("Border symbolism revisited," p. 218). Falk analyzes a young Israeli's dream of crossing the Israeli-Jordanian border, concluding that crossing an international border may carry the unconscious significance of crossing the incest barrier into the mother. Such crossings may, moreover, simultaneously symbolize internal barriers between impulses ("id impulses," in psychoanalytic parlance) and the mental functions (ego, superego) ranged against such impulses.

185. Donald W. Winnicott, "Berlin Walls," p. 224. While the physical border between the United States and Canada is flexible and permeable, there is a tendency in the United States, under certain conditions, to wish the border between the United States and Mexico were less so. Finnish historian Jouni Suistola ("Border and Identity: The Finnish army at the Russian border in 1941") has described Finnish–Russian border psychology and examined the Finnish relationship to space and boundaries.

186. Irene Misselwitz, "German reunification: A quasi-ethnic conflict," p. 81.

187. Falk, ibid.

188. See: Voila Bernard, Perry Ottenberg and Fritz Redlich, "Dehumanization: A composite psychological defense in relation to modern war," Rafael Moses, "On dehumanizing the enemy," and Salman Akhtar "Dehumanization: Origins, manifestations, and remedies."

189. Large-group purification rituals are part of a process of modification and resemble the adolescent passage in individual psychology. During adolescence, a teenager revisits his or her prior object relations and psychosexual conflicts and attempts to create new object relations and adaptations related to his or her "new" internal and external worlds. Peter Blos (*Adolescent Passage*) called this process the "second individuation," a term that also may be appropriate to large groups, especially when they become independent from colonial masters or centralized empires.

As in the individual, a large group does not truly eliminate its former identity through purification rituals, but reshuffles them in combination with modifications and additions. Rituals may enhance cohesion and a sense of sameness in the short term, but the core aspects and complexities of the large-group identity will persist.

190. Vamık Volkan, *Bloodlines*.

4

191. For an anthropological/psychoanalytic study of the Oklahoma City bombing see Howard Stein, *Beneath the Crust of Culture: Psychoanalytic Anthropology and the Cultural Unconscious in American Life*.

192. It is worth noting a certain tendency in the United States to identify the religious affiliation of large or subgroups when the population, or most of the population, is comprised of Muslims. For example, Croats living in Bosnia are referred to according to their ethnic identity and called "Bosnian Croats." However, when we refer to Muslims living in Bosnia, we typically call them "Bosnian Muslims" rather than "Bosniaks," despite the fact that some Bosniaks are religious, others secular. In 1998 and 1999, when I was involved in conducting workshops among Serb, Croat, and Bosniak mental health workers, I observed that the secular Bosniaks resented being called "Muslims" because they were then associated in the public's mind as "terrorists." The word "Christian" however, is not typically used to describe subgroups involved in violence; they are usually referred to according to ethnic or national affiliations.

193. Martin E. Marty and R. Scott Appleby, *Fundamentalism Comprehended*, p. 1.

194. The other members of this commission were: Professor Michael Barkun, a political scientist from Syracuse University; Joseph Krofcheck, a physician from Yarrow and Associates; Elizabeth W. Marvick, a lecturer at UCLA and a consultant on politics; Gregory Saathoff, a psychiatrist from the University of Virginia and also a member of the Center for the Study of Mind and Human Interaction; Stephen Sampson, director of psychology of Georgia Regional Hospital and a member of Georgia State University; Alan Sapp, professor of criminal justice, Central Missouri State University; and Robert Washington, professor of sociology at Bryn Mawr College.

195. The initial raid resulted in the deaths of four ATF agents and five Davidians. Twenty ATF agents and four Davidians, including Koresh, were wounded. The casualties brought FBI agents to the scene the next day, when the fifty-one day FBI siege of Mount Carmel began.

196. See: Gershon Gorenberg, *The End of Days: Fundamentalism and the Struggle for the Temple Mount*; Ernest R. Sandeen, *The Roots of Fundamentalism: British and American Millennarianism, 1800-1930*; and Charles B. Stozier, *Apocalypse: On the Psychology of Fundamentalism in America*.

There are exceptions to this general truth about fundamentalist sects and foundational texts. For example, the Order of the Solar Temple (an apocalyptic religious cult in Switzerland and Canada 53 members of which died in fires on the night of October 4, 1994) did not have a sacred text per se. However, one of its leaders, Luc Jouret, had written books and prepared tapes that the followers used much like sacred texts.

197. These figures were given by Michael Barkun to the members of the International Committee of the Group for the Advancement of Psychiatry (GAP), April 2000. See also, Michael Barkun, "Christian identity movement: constructing millenialism on the racist right"; "End-time paranoia: Conspiracy thinking at the millennium's close."

198. In the late 1920s, Lyman and Milton Stewart, two Union Oil tycoons in California, financed the publication of a series of pamphlets called *The Fundamentals* which enumerated five points essential for orthodoxy: biblical inerrancy, the virgin birth, Christ's atonement and resurrection, the authenticity of miracles, and dispensationalism. According to the Stewarts, then, "fundamentalists" were simply defenders of these five doctrines. See Randall Balmer, *Mine Eyes Have Seen the Glory: A Journey into the Evangelical Subculture in America.*

199. Qtd. in Edward J. Larson, *Summer for the Gods: The Scopes Trial and America's Continuing Debate over Science and Religion*, p. 50. The quote comes from the 1925 Tennessee House Bill 185.

200. Eventually, the Tennessee Supreme Court overturned the decision on a procedural technicality, but the constitutional issues were not actually addressed until 1968, when the U.S. Supreme Court finally overturned a similar law in Arkansas. Larson, ibid.

201. George Roche, *A World Without Heroes: A Modern Tragedy*, p.244.

202. Sigmund Freud, "The future of an illusion," pp. 43-44. Psychoanalysts who followed Freud suggest that the foundation of religious beliefs is established much earlier than the time a child deals with oedipal issues. See, for example, Donald W. Winnicott, "Transitional objects and transitional phenomena."

203. Roche, ibid., pp.171-172. Roche here misreads psychoanalysis and evolution as jointly reducing human beings to equivalent bio-psychological units, and thus seems to imply that it is consonant with the false equalization of communist ideology. In fact, psychoanalysis offers an explanation of how psychological evolution forms each individual distinctly, though all share the same basic derivatives of sexual and aggressive drives; actually existing communisms have never been sympathetic to psychoanalysis and have frequently prohibited its practice.

204. Barkun, ibid.

205. For a detailed and scholarly documentation of Christian millennialist movements see: Phillip Lamy, *Millennial Rage: Survivalists, White Supremacists, and the Doomsday Prophecy.* Lamy concludes that "millennialism tends to arise in periods of intense social change" (ibid., p.61). Richard Landes, professor of history and director of the Center for Millennial Studies at Boston University, interest-

ingly observes that historians have often ignored millennial beliefs in the thought of otherwise prominent people, such as Christopher Columbus and Isaac Newton, who have not become destructive leaders: "Accordingly, religious and secular historians alike have written a largely millennium-free history of the West, making millennialism a twice-untold tale, relegating it to the status of a recondite sideshow, largely ignored by serious scholars" (Landes, "The fruitful error: Reconsidering millennial enthusiasm," p. 89). As historian of millennialism Eugene Weber notes, however, millennial beliefs, not only among Christians but other religious groups as well, have proven so resilient that we cannot ignore them (Weber, *Apocalypses: Prophecies, Cults, and Millennial Beliefs Throughout the Ages*). We will turn to a non-Christian millennialism in the next chapter.

206. Most theologians agree that this view existed among the early church fathers until St. Augustine developed a doctrine known as "amillennialism." As years passed, amillennialism mostly faded away, and millennialism returned.

207. What happens to Muslims, Buddhists and others who are neither Christian nor Jewish when Christ comes back to earth? Since the Bible of course does not speak of them, there is not much concern about people of other faiths in the present literature on Christian millennialism. The focus is on the Jews surviving Armageddon who will accept Jesus as Lord and Savior. Only infrequent and general remarks appear about Muslims, Buddhists and so on; it appears to be assumed that they also will accept Jesus.

208. Some millennialists believe that the souls of those who are "saved," whether dead or alive, will not endure the harsh Tribulation; they will be "Raptured" up to join Jesus in heaven before the upheaval of Tribulation commences. It is generally also believed that only God can decide who is "saved" and that the number of individuals admitted to heaven is limited. Individuals who believe in this version of millennialism are known as "pretribulationists." Most fundamentalist churches in the United States are pretribulationists. There are also millennialists who believe that "saved" persons will be oppressed during the first half of Tribulation, but that the faithful will not endure the rule of the Antichrist. They will join Christ in the middle of Tribulation. In yet another variant, "postmillennialism," Jesus Christ returns after the perfect 1000 years.

209. See Stephen O'Leary, *Arguing the Apocalypse: A Theory of Millennial Rhetoric*.

210. The FBI ordered tanks to demolish the community's building and to spray CS gas through holes in the walls. Grenade launchers shot grenades containing the same gas into the compound. The deadly fire that apparently actually killed most of the Davidians started around noon on the same day, April 19, 1993, though how the fire started is still a subject of debate.

211. Olsson observes that the only diagnostic criterion of narcissistic personality disorder that does not seem to fit Koresh was that he could, at times, show powerful empathy; a person with NPD is not typically capable of doing so. Olsson argues, however, that Koresh's empathy was a kind of "self-absorbed empathy that

ultimately suits the exclusive narcissistic purpose of the leader. In fact, [Koresh] fit all the criteria for NPD" (Peter A. Olsson, "In search of their fathers-themselves: Jim Jones and David Koresh," p. 92).

212. See American Psychiatric Association's *Diagnostic and Statistical Manual of Mental Disorders*.

213. Salman Akhtar, *Broken Structures*; Vamık Volkan and Gabriele Ast, *Spekrum des Narzissmus*

214. Qtd. in Marc Breault and Martin King, *Inside the Cult: A Member's Chilling Account of Madness and Depravity in David Koresh's Compound*, p.24.

215. Breault and King, ibid., p. 28.

216. Catherine Wessinger, *How the Millennium Comes Violently: From Jonestown to Heaven's Gate*, p. 82.

217. Wessinger, ibid., p. 82.

218. Wessinger, ibid., p. 82.

219. The fights for leadership which ensued at the Mount Carmel Community, especially between George Roden and Vernon Howell are more complex than my scope here permits me to elaborate. See Wessinger, ibid.

220. See Dick J. Reavis, *The Ashes of Waco*; James D. Tabor and Eugene V. Gallagher, *Why Waco? Cults and the Battle for Religious Freedom in America* and Wessinger, ibid.

221. Wessinger, ibid., p. 84. See also Tabor and Gallagher, ibid.

222. Wessinger, ibid.

223. In clinical settings, we often see such mother/father-child role reversals in individuals with backgrounds similar to Koresh's.

224. Koresh himself was apparently unaware of the symbolic meanings of his actions. Only through outside examination can we interpret such symbolic actions.

225. Koresh was certainly not alone among fundamentalist leaders in developing this paternal image: Jim Jones, for example, the leader of the communal settlement of the Peoples Temple in Guyana, South America, where 918 people died in mass suicide on November 18, 1978, was actually called "Dad" or "Father" by his followers (Olsson, ibid.).

Olsson (ibid.) finds certain similarities in the personal backgrounds of Jones, Koresh, and Shoko Asahara (born Chizuo Matsumoto), who led the Japanese cult Aum Shinrikyo in the 1994 Tokyo subway gas attacks that killed twelve people and injured 5,000. All three had mental difficulties (lonely childhoods with intense parental rejection, separation, or neglect) and/or physical problems (Asahara was born sightless in one eye and partially blind in the other; Koresh was diagnosed with dyslexia) during childhood. Since they all experienced early rejections by their mothers, they exhibited adult behavior of controlling, seducing, or hurting women. They became strong father-figures as a result of their own weak or absent fathers; they functioned as "good father figures for others temporarily because they ... had to be premature parents for their own selves. At their unconscious core they are terrified of loneliness and insignificance" (Olsson, "Shoko Asahara: The malignant pied piper of Japan," p. 57).

226. There are, naturally, few psychoanalytic investigations of people who start or seek leadership of fundamentalist religious subgroups, simply because such leaders do not seek treatment on a psychoanalyst's couch. The rare psychoanalytic investigations of such individuals must therefore rely on data that is collected outside therapeutic offices, and the availability of psychologically significant data determines how much one can make a reasonable assessment of the mind of a person with whom the investigator never personally interacted. As I will describe at greater length in Part 3, primary and secondary sources of information about a leader permit us to see his or her personality and to make certain deductions about his or her internal world even without personal experience of that leader.

227. Wessinger, ibid., p. 96.

228. Marc Breault, who had become a Branch Davidian in 1986, was upset with Koresh's sexual activities, and he and his wife left Mount Carmel in 1989 for Australia. He persistently denounced Koresh as a "false prophet" and exposed Koresh's sexual conduct with young girls to a wide audience. He even claimed that Koresh was planning to commit child sacrifice and/or mass suicide. See Wessinger, ibid.

229. Wessinger, ibid.

230. Since I signed the Commission's report, I have had no more contact with the FBI; chairing the Commission was the only task I have carried out for the agency.

231. When necessary, the FBI consults with outside experts in dealing with critical events. The Commission, by suggesting to create a position of Resource Analyst, suggested that such consultations could be streamlined to be more effective.

232. Personal communication with Gregory Saathoff, 1996. For additional details on the Freemen standoff, see Wessinger, ibid.

233. Jaan Kaplinski, the famous Estonian poet and writer who was recently a candidate for the Nobel Prize, wrote to me in April 2002 to say that Estonians are now discovering "this interesting minority," the Russian Old Believers in Estonia. In the autumn of 2001, Kaplinski accepted an invitation to go to Varnja, not far away from Mustvee, where he saw "the church, a small museum, a school, and the restaurant where you can eat real, traditional Russian dishes." It was, he said "One of the most interesting meetings I ever had in Estonia." Kaplinski added, however, that there was "a lot of sadness in the air: the old way of life is vanishing, the younger people are not going to the church, they have no priest. But still, they are conscious of their identity, a revival is still possible."

234. Wessinger, ibid.

235. Derek Hopwood, "A movement in renewal in Islam," p. 109; Gregory Jaynes, "At Least 1,000 People Are Killed As Nigeria Crushes Islamic Sect," *The*

New York Times, January 12, 1981; Leon Dash, "Army Halts Muslim Feuding; Army Quells Orgy of Violence Among Nigeria's Feuding Muslims; Nigeria's Violent Spasm," *The Washington Post*, February 21, 1981.

236. Barkun, ibid.

237. See Olsson, ibid.

238. *Hamas*, which means "zeal" in Arabic, is a nickname for this group. The full name is *Harakatu l-Mujawamati l-islamiya* ("Islamic Resistance Movement"). To maintain the interest of its members, Hamas is also involved in healthcare and education issues and provides jobs for its members.

239. Hopwood, ibid., p. 109.

240. Wessinger, ibid., p. 56.

241. Reported in the *Boston Globe*, January 28, 1985.

242. Wessinger, ibid. It is sometimes difficult to clearly separate Wessinger's three categories, as a given group may move from one to another at different points in time. It is perhaps more useful to think of her divisions as states rather than as categories.

243. See Jean-Francois Mayer, "Apocalyptic millennialism in the West: The case of the Solar Temple."

244. See, for example, Sigmund Freud, "Totem and taboo"; "Moses and monotheism," and "The future of an illusion."

245. Sigmund Freud, "The psychopathology of everyday life," p. 19-20.

246. Phyllis Greenacre, "The transitional object and the fetish: With special reference to the role of illusion"; Arnold Modell, "Transitional objects and the creative art"; and Vamık Volkan, *Primitive Internalized Object Relations*.

247. If a toddler chooses an unusually hard and cold object, such as a stone or a jar, to control and keep around, clinicians should think of this as a clue to some disturbance in the early child-mother relationship and normal transitional activities.

248. Psychoanalysts call the temporal-developmental "space" in which this metaphorical lantern is located for each individual his or her "transitional space."

249. Winnicott also identified "transitional phenomena" such as bubbling sounds—and later certain songs—or touch sensations, that function similarly to tangible objects such as teddy bears.

250. I have often wondered whether advances in science create pressure on these "moments of rest." Certainly the expectation that, as scientific knowledge increased, "magical" beliefs would diminish has been disproven by historical events. Even in an age of science, human nature remains constant at its core; societies can still be overwhelmed by magical religious beliefs which may lead to massive sadistic or masochistic acts.

251. Winnicott, ibid., p. 16.

252. In a clinical setting, however, we see many adults whose childhood use of transitional objects was disturbed reactivate an adult version of transitional objects. Certain objects become magical to these adults, and they carry those

objects within themselves or use them as a buffer between themselves and others. For detailed clinical examples, see Vamık Volkan, ibid.

253. Marty and Appleby, ibid.

254. Rena Moses-Hrushovski, *Grief and Grievance: The Assassination of Yitzhak Rabin*, p. 133. The Ashkenazic Haredim is an orthodox religious subgroup in Israel dating from the late nineteenth century. They are not Zionist, nationalist, or democratic in ideology, but are preoccupied with studying holy scriptures as interpreted by Haredi rabbis. According to their beliefs, "since man cannot trust his own common sense, intelligence and integrity, he should not be able to think or decide for himself, to entertain thoughts and truths other than those deemed 'kosher' by the Haredi rabbis" (Moses-Hrushovski, ibid., p. 133).

255. Moses-Hrushovski, ibid.

256. Jeannie Mills, *Six Years with God: Life Inside Reverend Jim Jones's People Temple*, p. 13.

257. Olsson, ibid., p. 57

258. Emmanuel Sivan, discussion among Rabin Fellows, Yitzhak Rabin Center, Tel Aviv, February-May 2000. Sivan and I were colleagues during my fellowship at the Rabin Center in the spring of 2000. See also Gabriele A. Almond, Emmanuel Sivan, and R. Scott Appleby, "Fundamentalism: genus and species."

259. Qtd. in Wessinger, pp. 51-52.

260. Moses-Hrushovski, ibid. Between June 5 and 10, 1967, Israelis eliminated the Egyptian air force and took the Old City of Jerusalem, the Sinai, the Gaza Strip, the West Bank, and the Golan Heights in what is known as the Six-Day War.

261. Moses-Hrushovski (ibid.) argues that the various factions of Israel's ultra-religious community exaggerate the differences among them; in general they share the belief that the world must be transformed so that people obey religious law, the *Halaka*. The arrival of the Messiah is supposed to lead to a world governed by the *Halaka*.

262. Moses-Hrushovski, ibid., p. 94.

263. On the Jewish holy day of Yom Kippur, October 6, 1973, Egyptian and Syrian forces combined to attack Israel, with the Egyptians crossing the Suez Canal and the Syrians fighting on the Golan Heights. Israelis suffered heavy casualties, but were able to push their way into Syrian territory encircling the Egyptian Third Army by crossing the Suez Canal. A cease-fire was called on January 18, 1974, but it was not until March 26, 1979, that a full peace treaty (known as the Camp David Accords) ended the 30-year state of war between Israel and Egypt. Israel returned the entire Sinai peninsula to Egypt; in turn, Egypt recognized Israel's right to exist. The door was opened to establish normal diplomatic relations between the two countries.

264. The army did not use bullets, however, but white foam to drive the protesters back.

265. Gush Emunim differ significantly from the Haredi, whom I mentioned earlier in this chapter, insofar as they have actively sought to develop what they

see as Messianic intimations in the existing order. Among its members have been the heads of two terrorist organizations against Palestinians, the "Jewish Underground" and the "Temple Mount Plot." The Haredi, by contrast, believe that human beings should not attempt to influence or shape the Messianic process. Thus, the Haredi withdraws even from accepting the Jewish State. Nevertheless, they too have been involved in actions—legal and illegal—aimed at preventing other Jews from violating sacred laws. (See Menachem Friedman, "Jewish zealots: Conservative versus innovative.")

266. Moses-Hrushovski, ibid., p. 96.

267. As a counterexample, it is extremely important to tell the history of the Israeli return of Sharm El-Sheikh—called Ophira by the Israelis when they began to settle there in 1967—to its previous owners, Egypt. By the time the Sharm-El-Sheikh/Ophira settlers knew that they would have to move out, their population had risen to about 1,000. Unlike at Yamit, however, the Israeli withdrawal from Ophira was peaceful, in spite of the town's strategic importance: it controls access to the Aqaba (or Ellat) Gulf.

The story of the Israeli withdrawal from Ophira was told to me by the late Israeli psychoanalyst and good friend Rafael Moses and his wife, Rena Moses-Hrushowski, also a psychoanalyst and good friend, during our work together in the APA-sponsored Arab-Israeli dialogues. As it happens, the Moseses, psychologist Yona Rosenfeld, and Reuven Beumel, a social worker, were consulted by the head of the Ophira's Residents' Committee, who were concerned about what would happen to the settlers who were required to leave their homes. Viewing their task as crisis intervention, the team of four professionals traveled to Ophira, interviewing 120 people and taking part in Residents' Committee meetings. Initially, Ophira's settler residents were suspicious of Rafael Moses and his team, and they were reluctant to commit themselves to a new home, saying they did not know where they would settle.

Eventually, the team was able to learn that the idea of eviction induced among the settlers images and affects concerning past deportations. Perhaps unsurprisingly, the idea of evacuation was especially difficult for those residents who were also Holocaust survivors. Settlers exhibited various anxieties, such as fears about their children's futures and their own adjustments to new locations. Most of the time, their fears were somatized; they had sleep disorders, aches and pains. The team helped them to express their fears and to examine their feelings. During this process, the Moseses observed that the settlers' attitude concerning incoming Egyptians underwent changes:

About six weeks before the final evacuation, an advance group of 40 Egyptians, led by a General, arrived. One of the successful businessmen, a pillar of the community, had felt unsure of how he should deal with the Egyptians. He felt pulled into opposing directions—to represent his country, to serve the interests of the community, and to be himself, a person. Preferring at first to destroy some of his equipment rather than hand it over for nothing, he ended up inviting his opposite number to a sumptuous breakfast with Israeli delicacies sent daily from hundreds of miles away. On the day he did hand over the property—including those items which he had thought he might prefer to destroy—he was deeply touched when the Egyptian shyly told him how well he understood the intense pain of having to leave and give up what had been their homes. The Israeli wept for the first time in the arms of the Egyptian who shared his tears and his grief.

We came to understand that the leadership, as well as the populace, and the interrelations between the two played an important role in the successful adaptation to evacuating Ophira. The people, although inclined to be passive and private, were genuinely concerned about the welfare of all; the leaders were conscientious, able to accept criticism, and concerned about the common good. It was very impressive to see how harmonious and good, and truly democratic the relationship between the leaders and the led was.

We personally all valued this experience and feel that we ourselves changed in the course of it. We plan to report later on some generalizations derived from it, in the hope that they may be of some use to other groups required to abandon loved homes, in whatever part of the world.

It is clear that in Ophira, too, there were psychological impulses to be destructive, but they was avoided—with intentional, professional help. The peaceful withdrawal from Ophira could have provided a model for future withdrawals from Israeli settlements in the West Bank. History shows that this model has been wasted.

268. Gender ideologies are receiving new attention in the literature on comparative fundamentalisms; see, for example, John Stratton Hawley and Wayne Proudfoot, *Introduction to Fundamentalism and Gender*. Typically, fundamentalists exclude women from higher ranks (the case of Lois Roden presented earlier in this chapter, therefore, is an exception). Though many of the "New Religions" of Japan are led by women, Hawley and Proudfoot report,

[e]ven so, one of the hallmarks of these religions is their view that women ought to be subservient to men in ways that were institutionalized in the multigenerational, male-dominated household, which was forced aside when the Allied Forces recast the basis of Japanese law in 1947. On the whole, Japan's New Religions extol a return to this "golden age," when women entirely depended on men and habitually displayed the humility and self-sacrifice appropriate to their position. (Hawley and Proudfoot, ibid., p.7.)

269. Molly Moore, "Taliban: Most Statues Destroyed," *The Washington Post*, March 4, 2001, p. A22.

270. Pamela Constable, "Buddhas' Rubble Marks a Turn for Taliban," *The Washington Post*, March 20, 2001, p. A1.

271. Michael A. Sells, himself of Serbian American descent, describes both the ethnic and the cultural/historical cleansing in Bosnia-Herzegovina in detail (see Michael A. Sells, *Bridge Betrayed: Religion and Genocide in Bosnia*; see also, Vamık Volkan, *Bloodlines*).

272. Thomas Butler, "Yugoslavia mon amour."

273. David Freedberg, "The power of wood and stone: The Taliban is not the first to fear the mysterious lure of art," *The Washington Post*, March 25, 2001. Freedberg explains the event in ways that are very close to psychoanalytic understandings of such aggressive acts. See also David Freedberg, *The Power of Images*.

As Freedberg recalls, the Prophet Muhammad 's 9-year-old wife, Aisha, was allowed only to play with dolls that did not resemble people; in Islam, according to the hadith, artistic images are somewhat blasphemous. Since only God can give life, the artist's attempt to emulate him must be punished: "When ... the artist finally reaches heaven, God challenges him to breathe life into his creation. When the artist fails to do so, he is cast into hell to be tormented" ("The power of wood and stone: The Taliban is not the first to fear the mysterious lure of art," p. 82).

274. Freedberg, ibid.

5

275. J. Anderson Thomson, the assistant director of the Center for the Study of Mind and Human Interaction (CSMHI) at the University of Virginia, examines "male bonded coalitionary violence" ("Killer apes on American Airlines, or: How religion was the main hijacker on September 11," p. 74) which existed in the time before recorded history to understand the the terrorists who hijacked planes on September 11, 2001. He adds: "If we truly want to understand September 11 at its most fundamental level, we have to face the horror of our evolutionary history, the deadly legacy it has left in all men, and the violence that resides at the core of religion. The choice is ours." (p. 84)

276. Howell was U.S. ambassador to Kuwait during Iraq's 1990 invasion of that country.

277. W. Nathaniel Howell, "Islamic Revivalism: A cult phenomenon?" p. 100.

278. Howell, ibid.

279. Though Islam is a strictly monotheistic religion, the clash between "good" and "evil," exists in Islam. In Islam, as in Christianity and Judaism, the doer of "evil"—whether called Satan, the Devil, or Iblis—is one of God's creatures. In the clashes between God and this creature, however, we can find reflections of old dualistic religions such as Zoroastrianism, in which the devil is an independent power that struggles against God, the "superpower" of goodness. Bernard Lewis observes that at various stages Islam, especially in Iran, has been influenced by "the dualist ideal of cosmic clash of good and evil, light and darkness, order and chaos, truth and falsehood." See Lewis, "The roots of Muslim rage," p. 49.

280. Christopher Hitchens, "Why the suicide killers chose September 11," *The Guardian* (London), October 3, 2001, p.5

281. It is not that I find the durability of such a group trauma incredible: see Chapter 8 for my discussion of the reactivation of a 14th-century shared trauma in Serbia. An Arab such as bin Laden is unlikely to be so completely preoccupied with a significant 17th-century date in Turkish military history, since Arabs were in fact subject to the Ottoman Empire. Rather, bin Laden is apparently preoccupied with the more general Muslim loss of the Caliphate conjoined with the collapse of the Ottoman Empire in the early 20th century.

282. Turks arrived in Anatolia in the beginning of the 11th century and established the Seljuk Empire. The second Turkish empire, the Ottoman Empire, was established after the Mongols defeated the Seljuks in 1243. The Christian Crusades took place during the Seljuk Empire, not during the Ottoman period.

283. In truth, Islam was almost never as unified as Catholicism, experiencing major splits as soon as a century after the Prophet's death in 632 C.E. and riven by cult movements and regional power struggles throughout its history. Still, the Caliphate formed the titular head of at least Sunni Muslims (now 88-90 percent of Muslims) from the eighth century to the early 20th. From 1517, the Ottoman sultan combined the roles of emperor and religious leader, which is how Turkey's secularizing founder came to have the power to abolish it.

284. Political scientist Elie Kedourie's *The Chatham House Version and Other Middle-Eastern Studies* analyzes the British government's (and its agents') disastrous handling of the Middle East. According to Kedourie, the extremely widely-used *Chatham House Version of Middle-East History*, written by British historian Arnold Toynbee and his followers, was not truthful and was humiliating to the Arabs. To some extent European scholars even now follow *The Chatham House Version of Middle East History*.

See Elie Kedourie, *The Chatham House Version and Other Middle-Eastern Studies*, especially "Egypt and the Caliphate: 1915-52," chapter 7. See also: A. J. Toynbee, *The Study of History*, (12 volumes), and *Britain and The Arabs: The Need for a New Start*.

285. M. Hakan Yavuz, "The patterns of political Islamic identity: dynamics of national and transnational loyalties and identities," p. 356

286. Yavuz, ibid., p. 357

287. Yavuz, ibid., p. 357

288. Though Lewis was much in demand as a commentator in the weeks and months following September 11, 2001, his understanding of Islam is — as the late literary scholar and cultural critic Edward W. Said among others has observed— limited. In *Orientalism*, Said objected that Lewis sees Islam as a "cultural synthesis" that "could be studied apart from the economics, sociology, and politics of the Islamic people": "…with Bernard Lewis, you say that if Arab Palestinians oppose Israeli settlement and occupation of their lands, then that is merely 'the return of Islam,' or …Islamic opposition to non-Islamic peoples" (p. 105). Turkish politi-

cal scientist M. Hakan Yavuz concurs:

> Lewis's argument presupposes that Islam is the agent that determines the Muslim conduct. The diversity of the Muslim world from Malaysia to Albania does not support Lewis's claim but rather it illustrates that national, ethnic, territorial and linguistic identities have their own internal dynamics of loyalty. The second problem with Lewis's claim is that he posits agency with Islam as opposed to the individual Muslims. The Muslims are in fact the agents who construct and negotiate among different identities and loyalties. The third problem is that Lewis reduces Muslim conduct with the execution of Islamic norms. Muslims, for Lewis, are not active agents but rather behave according to fixed Islamic precepts. (ibid., pp. 346-47)

Lewis' understanding nevertheless retains validity for the extremist Islamic fundamentalists who are our concern here —those who share a feeling that they are under attack by Western intrusions.

289. Lewis, ibid., p. 59. Supplementing this understanding of the rise of Islamic fundamentalism as a response to suffering and humiliation, Saudi psychologist Hanan Al-Mutlaq has identified "non-spiritual rewards" to the fundamentalist Islamic Revival, elements which can attract people who are not deeply committed to fundamentalist religious ideas (Al-Mutlaq "Aspects of non-spiritual rewards of Islamic fundamentalism"). Beyond more usual non-spiritual rewards—such as the role of religion in assuring a sense of belonging and security, controlling individual aggression, satisfying wishes for fame, and scapegoating—the "Islamic Awakening" has, Al-Mutlaq observes, provided "rewards" specific to Arab culture, especially to Saudi culture. For instance, she suggests that, in the academic environment, "joining in" fundamentalist behavior exempts one from certain demanding scholarly tasks by denouncing them as unholy. She identifies an especially interesting "non-spiritual" reason for women to be fundamentalists. Statistically, she observes, mosque attendance by women has increased with the spread of Islamic fundamentalism:

> At first, this would seem logical, but if Islamic teaching is strictly followed, mosque attendance by women should decrease. Prophet Muhammad clearly stated that women are better off praying at home, but also stated that husbands cannot prevent women from attending prayer at the mosque if they so choose. (Al-Mutlaq, ibid., p. 95)

The "reward" for making this trip, then, seems primarily social rather than religious. The Islamic revival, paradoxically, is liberating these Saudi women from being homebound, as their culture demands. Such liberatory draws as Al-Mutlaq describes do not apply, however, under malignantly regressed extremist regimes that degrade women or demand other violent behavior.

290. Yavuz, ibid., p. 346

291. Though the *hadith*—"[e]ach ... attested to by a chain of authorities, in the form of 'I heard from...who heard from...who heard from... who heard the

Prophet say…'" — of course need to be treated with caution because they were collected and recorded over several generations during the lifetime and after the death of the Prophet, they remain a generally accepted source of information on the life of Muhammad (Subhash C. Inamdar, *Muhammad and the Rise of Islam: The Creation of Group Identity*, p. 101).

Other primary sources include Muhammad ibn Jarir Abu Jafar al-Tabari (839-923 C.E.), who lived during the time of the Abbasid Caliphs (Al-Tabari, *The History of al-Tabari*, 9 volumes), and Ibn Ishaq, who died in 761C.E. (Ibn Ishaq, *The Life of Muhammad: A Translation of Ishaq's Sirat Rasul Allah*, by A. Guillaume). Subhash C. Inamdar has presented a current and comprehensive review of Muhammad's life (Inamdar, ibid.).

There are even descriptions of his physical characteristics. He was of average height with a prominent forehead and hooked nose. He had a fair complexion, black eyes, and a pleasant smile. (See W. Montgomery Watt, *Muhammad: Prophet and Statesman*). When he was 63-years old he still had "the stature and grace of a much younger man" (Martin Lings, *Muhammad: His Life Based on the Earliest Sources*, p.).

292. Inamdar, ibid., p. 102.

293. Ibn Ishaq, ibid., p. 191.

294. In the context of his culture, Inamdar observes, this was not necessarily deviant behavior:

He grew up in a culture with few or no ascetic traditions and no tradition of strict monogamy. A culture that permits polygamous relationships allows for a freer attitude towards sexuality; celibacy would be almost incomprehensible. (Inamdar, ibid., p. 216)

Inamdar tells us, further, that in much of pre-Islamic Arabia (not including Mecca, however) the social system was matrilineal, and women were permitted to have more than one husband in matrilineal areas. Islam "now laid down a structure that defined marriage along patrilineal lines, but also retained some features of the matrilineal tradition by allowing a limited form of polygamy" (ibid., p. 216-217). The family came to surpass the clan and tribe in importance.

295. Believers understand such "contradictions" as a feature of the fact that various revelations were related to different historical events.

296. It is worth noting that jihad is not actually one of the traditional five "pillars," or essential tenets, of Islam. These five basic frameworks of the Muslim life are: faith (there is no god except God and Muhammad is the messenger of God), prayer, zakat (setting aside a portion of one's wealth for those in need – giving help to the poor is said to be like pruning plants to encourage new growth), fasting during the month of Ramadan, and pilgrimage (hajj) to Mecca. There are some Muslims, however, who consider jihad a sixth pillar.

297. Inamdar, ibid., p. 221. After the Prophet's death, other Muslim powers, Arabs and then Ottomans, used the same "propaganda" to form vast empires.

298. After Muhammad conquered Mecca, a myth developed that the

Quraysh were the keepers of the "secrets" of Islam. According to the myth, many Qurayshi "secret keepers" emigrated to Afghanistan, which may explain why Islamic mysticism (Sufism) is so widespread in that country. Sufis do not preach hatred of the "other," but intend to reflect the highest form of "inner understanding" beyond one's own faith. But the popularity of Sufism, with its mystical and magical aspects, paradoxically may also have helped make credible the claim of the Taliban's malignant fundamentalism to be a religion that would magically "cure" Afghanistan's war-related traumas (see Louis Palmer, *Adventures in Afghanistan*, pp. 5-6).

299. Sandra Mackey, *Passion and Politics: The Turbulent World of the Arabs*, p. 37.

300. Inamdar, ibid.

301. Norman Itzkowitz, *The Ottoman Empire and Islamic Tradition*, p.33.

302. Denis MacEoin, "The Shi'ite establishment in modern Iran."

303. Emmanuel Sivan, *Radical Islam: Medieval Theology and Modern Politics*, p. 2.

304. The Institute for the Propagation of Islam was founded at Qom, Iran, under the direction of Ayatollah Muhammad Kazim Shari'atamdari. In 1943, the Iranian *Anjuman-i Tablighat-i Islami* (Association for Islamic Propaganda) was founded by Ata Allah Shihabpur to disseminate conservative Shi'ite propaganda through wide-ranging publishing and preaching.

305. MacEoin, ibid., p. 99.

306. Richard Landes, "Apocalyptic Islam and bin Laden."

307. Sivan, ibid., p. 207

308. Conversely, there are, of course, voices that emphasize aspects of democracy in Islam. Abdulaziz Sachedina, professor of religious studies at the University of Virginia, for example, argues that it is necessary to re-examine traditional interpretations and replace outdated laws as Islam enters the 21st century (Sachedina, *The Islamic Roots of Democratic Pluralism*). See also Bernard Lewis, "Islam and liberal democracy: A historical overview."

309. Muslim terrorist organizations throughout history have used Prophet Muhammad 's Battle of Badr promise of immortality to play what one might call "the immortality card" with their students and inductees. In the late 11th and 12th centuries, a group of Shia Muslims called Nizaris, also known as "Assassins," opposed the dominant Sunni rulers. Hasan-i-Sabbah, the leader of the "Assassins," was born in Qom in present-day Iran in the mid-11th century. Hasan-i -Sabbah, also called the "Old Man of the Mountains," was a ruthless fanatic, who, according to legend, killed his own son for drinking wine. In order to impress his enemies, Hasan-i-Sabbah would order his followers to throw themselves from cliffs while wearing white clothes, under the supposition that seeing these acts would so frighten their opponents as to make them tremble. During and after the death of Hasan-i-Sabbah, the Assassins terrorized various enemies, including other Muslims and later Crusaders, for about 200 years, until

the 13th century Mongol invasion crushed them. Their stories, some fact and some legend, are still repeated in the Muslim world, providing models for future ruthless leaders who manipulate their followers with the promise of a better life after death.

310. Landes, ibid.

311. See for example, Vamık Volkan's study of Abdullah Ocalan, the leader of Kurdistan Workers Party (PKK) in *Bloodlines*.

312. Volkan, ibid., p. 162. It is obvious that not everyone with vulnerabilities in early identity formation seeks leadership or becomes preoccupied with this or that large-group identity. Psychoanalysts will need to acquire the necessary data to state with some certainty what makes a particular person seek a specific type of solution to his or her childhood separations, helplessness, shame, humiliation, and rage. In referring to fundamentalist or ethnic terrorist leaders, I am only referring to some observable general patterns.

313. The first was published in 1999—*Bin Laden: The Man who Declared War on America* by Yossef Bodansky, an Israeli who became a U.S. citizen and once headed the Congressional Task Force on Terrorism. The other, *A Warrior from Mecca: The Full Story of Osama bin Laden*, was published in Arabic in 2000 by Asad Khaled Khalil, a Saudi journalist and sympathizer with the Saudi royal house. See also Adam Robinson, *Bin Laden: Behind the Mask of the Terrorist*.

314. I am indebted to Avner Falk for this reference to the October 19, 2001, issue of *El Correro*, which includes a picture of the woman with some other youngsters, including bin Laden.

315. See also Avner Falk "Osama bin Laden and America: A psychobiographical sketch."

316. Robinson, ibid.; Falk, ibid.

317. Robinson, ibid., p. 39.

318. Robinson, ibid., p. 39.

319. Other sources list his age as 11 (for example, Jason Burke, "The making of the world's most wanted man," *The Observer*, October 28, 2001).

320. There is some disagreement about the vehicle of this event: Robinson, ibid., has it that the elder bin Laden died in a helicopter crash, though it is often reported that his father died while piloting his own airplane.

321. See, for example, Burke, ibid.

322. Azzam and his two sons were killed while on their way to a mosque in 1989 when three bombs exploded in their path. The killers were never found and rumors began to spread, including the particularly persistent report, especially among Palestinians, that the CIA had assassinated Azzam (Khaled Asad, *A Warrior from Mecca*), to which bin Laden may subscribe (Falk, ibid.) According to Khalil (ibid.), another of the rumors suggested that bin Laden himself may have played a role in the attack

323. Charles Socarides, "On vengeance: The desire to get even," p. 405.

324. Socarides, ibid.

325. Socarides, ibid., p. 425.

326. Landes, ibid. Landes usefully compares bin Laden's views to the fundamentalist revivalism familiar to students of American culture.

327. Landes, ibid.

328. Qtd. in "Religion: Bin Laden acknowledges support from Nigerian Muslims." *Africa News Service*, November 5, 2001. Bin Laden also frequently invokes the image of the medieval Christian Crusaders to characterize the enemy West.

329. Both Azzam and bin Laden were influenced by other Islamic thinkers such as Mohammed al-Quttub and Safar al Halawi.

330. See Uta Raschle, "Cologne 'Caliph' tied to terrorist links," *Frankfurter Allegmeine Zeitung* (English edition), October 6, 2000, p. 3. Turkish authorities wanted Kaplan returned to Turkey, but the German government refused. Kaplan was jailed in Germany in November 2001 for his role in the murder a rival religious leader in Berlin. The German Federal Office for the Protection of the Constitution now estimates that the number of Kaplan's followers is dwindling to less than 2,000. On December 12, 2001, German authorities raided cells of the ICCB around the country and banned the group's existence. At present, further discussions are taking place between Turks and Germans regarding Kaplan's return to Turkey.

331. Landes, ibid. Landes' analysis of bin Laden's apocalyptic views are partly based on his study of the website named in honor of the late Abdullah Azzam, bin Laden's former mentor and the co-founder (with bin Laden) of MAK, the forerunner of al Qaeda, and the writings of Saudi theologian Safar al Halawi. The website is located at www.azzam.com; see especially www.azzam.com/dayofwrath.

332. Landes, ibid. According to Landes, Islamic apocalyptic believers expect the Dajjal to lead a coalition of Christians and Jews to trample Al Haram al Sharif in Jerusalem, triggering the final cosmic battle. (Landes observes that Islamic apocalyptic discourse, as it has passed from Shi'ite to Sunni circles from Africa to Indonesia to America in the context of the last two decades of Arab-Israeli conflict, has incorporated many Western/biblical apocalyptic themes.) Thus, Landes concludes, the visit of Ariel Sharon to that site in the fall of 2000 was "desecrating" to those apocalyptic extremists among the Palestinians. According to Landes, some writers in the Middle East press

> ...exaggerated every one of [Sharon's] actions into those of the Dajjal. Aside from a tour of the mount with two hundred soldiers, it became an invasion of the Al Aqsa mosque with thousands of troops. This "reading" contributed its fuel to the attack of Muslim forces against the apocalyptic enemy of Israel. (Landes, ibid.)

333. Landes, ibid. This kind of apocalyptic violence is not a new phenomenon. Joseph Montville, formerly of the Center for Strategic and International Studies, writes: "All religions have at times in their history experienced periods of

hate-filled repression and violence led by "fundamentalist" authoritarian clerics. The Roman Catholic Church had such moments during the Crusades and the Inquisition aimed at Muslims and Jews in Spain. In British America, New England Christian Puritan leaders dealt harshly with dissenters. They hanged Quakers, burned rebellious servants to death, and maimed political deviants. Some political rabbis in Israel have used degrading and dehumanizing language against the Palestinian people, and even inspired the psychological environment that enabled the assassination of the peacemaking prime minister, Yitzhak Rabin, by a young, Jewish religious fanatic." (See Joseph Montville, "A disturbing presence: September 11 and the Islamic roots of democratic pluralism," p.2).

334. Palmer, ibid., p. 229.

335. Had they turned bin Laden over in 1997 (at the U.S. request), or even in 1999 (at the U.N. Security Council request), the Taliban might have obtained the international recognition it so craved, and Afghanistan might have been given seats in international organizations.

336. Ahmed Rashid, *Taliban: Islam, Oil, and the New Great Game in Central Asia*. Rashid estimates 25,000 unregistered madrassahs in 2000. A piece entitled "Medressahs and military" in the April 21, 2002, edition of the Pakistani newspaper *The Dawn* stated that there were only 138 madrassahs in Pakistan at the time of independence and that in spring 2002 there were 7000.

337. Estimates vary widely. Jeffrey Goldberg, "The education of a holy warrior," *The New York Times Magazine*, June 25, 2000, cites the one-million number.

338. Tariq Ali, "Former U.S. policies allowed the Taliban to thrive." *Turkish Daily News*, September 25, 2001, p. 16.

339. Rashid, ibid.

340. Rashid, ibid.

341. The term Wahhabism comes from the name of Mohammed Abdul Wahhab (1703-1792), who founded an ultra-traditional Islamic cult in Arabia in 1740, near where Riyadh stands now. Wahhabism demands extreme punishments, including execution, for sexual transgressions, drinking, and listening to music (with the exception of drums). From the 18th century on, Wahhabis are known to have murdered those who opposed the sect: for example, the Wahhabis killed about 2,000 ordinary citizens in the city of Qarbala in 1801 with the aim to wipe out any opposition. Wahhabism was infused with nationalism in the nineteenth century, and the British supported Wahhabi Arabs in their revolt against the Ottomans. Eventually, the founder of the Saudi kingdom, Ibn Saud, declared Wahhabism the official religion of the new state. Saudi Arabia has since supported the spread of Wahhabism into other Muslim areas. The Saudi-born bin Laden is himself Wahhabi. See: Albert Hourani, *A History of the Arab Peoples*; Mackey, ibid.

342. Rashid Ahmad Ganguhi (1829-1905) founded a madrassah in the 19th century in the Indian town of Deoband, following the ideology of another Indian Muslim, Mohammed Kasem Nanevtavi (1877-1933). The Deobandi movement

aimed to initiate an Islamic reform in the face of British rule. The first Deobandi school in Pakistan opened in 1947, and there were about 900 madrassahs following Deobandi ideology in Pakistan by the 1960s. See: Rashid, ibid.

343. Ali, ibid., p. 16.

344. Goldberg, ibid.

345. Rashid, ibid.

346. Goldberg, ibid., p. 34.

347. Goldberg, ibid., p. 36. Pakistan, it must be remembered, now has nuclear weapons. The anniversary of the day that Pakistan exploded a nuclear bomb, May 28, 1998 – now known as *Youm-e-Takbeer* ("the day of God's greatness")—is celebrated with great emotion in Tajikistan, Uzbekistan, and Chechnya, as well as in Pakistan. Unsurprisingly, then, Goldberg reports that "In Pentagon exercises, American war-gamers have mapped out a scenario in which Taliban-like extremists gain control of Pakistan's atomic arsenal during a violent break-up of the country" (ibid.).

348. Goldberg, ibid., p. 34.

349. Qtd. In "Bin Laden, Osama" Encyclopædia Britannica Online, http://www.britannica.com/eb/article?eu=135782&tocid=0&query=osama%20b in%20laden.

350. "Radiant," whose story was presented in Chapter 3, accompanied As'ad Masri, Nuha Abudabbeh, and myself to the orphanage.

351. Unfortunately, I do not know what has happened to any of these children, who would be in their early twenties now.

352. Vamık Volkan, *Bloodlines: From Ethnic Pride to Ethnic Terrorism*.

353. Naming the five Sabra and Shatila children "Arafat" (which also stood for victimized "Palestinian") further symbolized the superceding of their individual identities with their large-group identities.

354. See Chapter 2 for detailed discussion of how individual core identity is formed.

355. The contemporary phenomenon of suicide bombings in the Middle East was pioneered among Shi'ites during the Iraq-Iran war, then sprang to Beirut where it was adopted by Hezbollah, a Lebanese Shi'ite organization. Beginning in 1994, Hamas began to do the same.

356. David Van Biema, "Why the bombers keep coming" *Time*, December 17, 2001, p. 54.

357. Volkan, ibid. It should be recalled that students in their late teens were taught to become Kamikaze pilots and told that they would be happy forever if they died for their Emperor (God).

358. Lewis, ibid., p. 47. According to Lewis, "Muslim rage" is a general atmosphere that has strengthened all modern Islamic fundamentalist movements, not just those that have turned to overt violence.

359. Of course, no teenager's need for parental love and concern completely disappears.

360. Osama Bahar, for example, a Palestinian who blew himself up at the Ben Yehuda pedestrian mall in Jerusalem in 2001, had spent four years in an Israeli jail for his connection to Hamas. Apparently, before his death, he told a friend that, while he was in jail, Israeli interrogators "hung him by his arms from the ceiling, spat in his face, and mocked Islam (Israeli authorities had no comment)" (Van Biema, ibid., p. 54.).

361. Qtd in the unsigned editorial "Reaping the Whirlwind," *The Nation*, December 24, 2001, pp. 3-5.

362. Suicide bombers and attackers can also be found outside the situation at hand: the Japanese *Kamikaze* pilots of World War II, for example, and the Tamil Tigers of Sri Lanka, who have employed suicide bombings since they launched their first attack in 1987. The struggle between the Kurdistan Workers Party (PKK) and Turkish forces, especially between 1995 and 1999, produced some suicide bombings as well, and more recently Chechen rebels have become involved in a suicide bombing campaign. Though I have not studied the training of suicide attackers in any of the groups above, my hunch is that the basic psychological mechanisms of all suicide bombers (as well as of hunger-strikers such as those in Northern Ireland) are the same: an increased sense of large-group identity superceding a suppressed or fractured personal identity and submission to an absolute leader who is perceived to be an extension of or spokesperson for God and/or the shared group identity.

363. For this reason, perhaps the most effective aspect of the "war on terrorism" is the United States and its allies' interference in al Qaeda's financial stability.

364. According to French intelligence officials, it is believed that as many as 10,000 Islamic extremists from many continents have gone to camps in Afghanistan (reported in Peter Finn, "Hijackers depicted as elite group," *The Washington Post*, pp. 1, 10, November 5, 2001).

365. Since al Qaeda was founded in 1988, it has been held responsible for the World Trade Center bombing in 1993; the 1998 bombings of the American embassies in Kenya and Tanzania that killed 224 people, including 12 Americans, and injured over 5,000; the 2000 attack on the USS *Cole* in Aden Harbor, Yemen, which killed 17 American sailors; and, of course, the events of September 11, 2001.

366. These excerpts were released on September 28, 2001.

367. Toni Locy, "Ashcroft: Critics aid enemy," *The Washington Post*, December 7, 2001, p. 7A.

368. From President Bush's speech in Ontario, California, January 5, 2002.

369. See, for example, *The Dawn* (Karachi, Pakistan), December 30, 2001.

370. Fortunately, some senators reminded Ashcroft that diminishing civil liberties could hurt the U.S, both at home and abroad. Senator Russ Feingold of Wisconsin observed, "[The anti-terrorism bill that would broaden the Justice Department's powers sends] a terrible message to the rest of the world ... these

rules and procedures have to apply in times of war as well as in times of peace" (Qtd. in Locy, ibid.).

371. The United States has initiated a propaganda program designed to influence Americans as well as outsiders. The State Department named Charlotte Beers, former head of advertising agency Ogilvy & Mather, as undersecretary for Public Diplomacy and Public Affairs—her mission, to sell the official U.S. perspective on terrorism overseas (see Michael McCarthy, "Ad experts take fight to a new front," *USA Today*, p. B1, November 9, 2001).

6

372. I owe this anecdote to Tuvia Frilling, professor of history at Beer-Sheva University in Israel, who derives it from Hebrew-language sources: Erad Malkin and Zeev Ahahor, *Leaders and Leadership: Collected Essays*; Yehoshua Arieli, "National Consciousness, Judaism and Zionism in a violent world." Frilling, discussion among Inaugural Rabin Fellows, The Yitzhak Rabin Center for Israel Studies, Tel Aviv, March 2, 2000.

373. Frilling, ibid.

374. Douglas G. Hartle and Morton H. Halperin, "Rational and incremental decision-making," p. 126.

375. See Vamık Volkan, Salman Akhtar, Robert M. Dorn, John S. Kafka, Otto F. Kernberg, Peter A. Olsson, Rita R. Rogers, and Stephen B. Shanfield, "Leaders and decision-making."

376. Robert C. Tucker, *Stalin as a Revolutionary, 1879–1929: A Study in History and Personality*, p. xvi, emphasis in the original.

377. See: August L. von Rochau, *Grundsatze der Realpolitik*. "Official diplomacy" is the management of relations between states as well as relations between states and other organizations that have political power but do not have the legal recognition of statehood, such as the Palestinian Authority.

The rules and regulations that govern modern diplomacy date to the fifteenth century, when permanent missions between governments were first established. But we can easily imagine that conflicts between early human communities were not always settled by direct force, and that some precursor of diplomacy developed as humanity began to develop its earliest social groupings. The Greek root of the word diplomacy, *diplomata*, means "folded documents," suggesting that early "diplomats" may have been messengers offering official documents of negotiation.

Many of modern diplomacy's tenets were codified at the Congress of Vienna (1814–1815), which established the grades of diplomatic status as well as the concept of diplomatic immunity, based on three claims to privilege: *droit de chapelle*, the right to practice the religion of the homeland; *droit de quartier*, immunity from arrest by local police; and *droit de l'hotel*, the exemption of one's dwelling from local jurisdiction and taxation.

The tasks of modern official diplomacy can be broadly classified into six types

(Ronald Peter Barston, *Modern Diplomacy*):

1) Providing formal representation: The primary and most important task of a nation's embassy is to explain and defend its own policies and to interpret and negotiate the host nation's.

2) Serving as a listening post: An embassy identifies the key issues emerging from patterns of domestic or international events and relays this information to its own government.

3) Laying the groundwork for new diplomatic initiatives.

4) In case of conflict, reducing friction when advisable.

5) Managing change created by conflict.

6) Creating, drafting, and amending international norms and regulations that give structure to the international system.

In its efforts to resolve conflicts between states and other "actors" without recourse to armed force, official diplomacy operates according to established rituals and local customs. Indeed, there is a certain rigidity to the theory of formal diplomacy: derivatives of the work of such thinkers as Niccolo Machiavelli, Thomas Hobbes, John Locke, Karl Marx, Josef Engels, Mao Tse-tung, and Hubert Marcuse persist. Old theories color modern ones—for example, the notion of the balance of power, which dates to Thucydides, is clearly to be seen in Cold War theories of deterrence.

378. John A. Vasquez, "Morality and politics," p. 2–3.

379. A good summary of the considerations that comprise the rational-actor model is provided by Carol Barner-Barry and Robert Rosenwein (Psychological Perspectives on Politics), who propose a seven-stage "Rational-Comprehensive Model":

1. Identifying the problem to be solved.

2. Specifying and clarifying goals.

3. Ranking goals to show their relative priority.

4. Identifying alternative solutions.

5. Evaluating the costs and benefits of each alternative.

6. Making a comparative analysis of the alternative solutions.

7. Selecting the best alternative in light of the specified and ranked goals.

380. Christopher H. Achen and Duncan Snidal, "Rational deterrence theory and comparative case studies."

381. Charles Lindblom, "The science of muddling through." Barner-Barry and Rosenwein (ibid.) identify the five steps of the "incremental model":

1) Identify the problem, but allow modification to the problem formulation during the course of the decision-making process.

2) Specify goals, but give this step less attention than in the rational-comprehensive model.

3) Consider those alternative solutions which differ only incrementally from methods currently in use.

4) Evaluate alternatives not as final solutions but as a series of attacks on

the problem at hand.

5) Try various promising solutions, reprocessing and beginning again at Step 1 if necessary.

Critics of the incremental model asserted that it encouraged solutions that attack only symptoms and did not allow all possible solutions.

382. Amitai Etzioni, "Mixed scanning: A 'third' approach to decision-making."

383. Graham T. Allison, *The Essence of Decision: Explaining the Cuban Missile Crisis.*

384. Graham T. Allison and Morton H. Halperin, "Bureaucratic politics: A paradigm and some policy implications," p. 145.

385. During the Cold War, the term "deterrence theory" specifically referred to the nuclear arms race between the United States and the USSR.

386. Janice Stein and Raymond Tanter, *Rational Decision-Making: Israel's Security Choices.*

387. Harold D. Lasswell, *Psychopathology and Politics.*

388. Milton Rokeach defined a belief system as "the total universe of a person's beliefs about the physical world, the social world, and the self (Rokeach, "Belief system theory of stability and change," p. 123–124), whereas Alexander George limited his thinking to political belief systems (George, "The 'operational code': A neglected approach to the study of political leaders and decision-making").

389. A number of important new concepts in political science emerged from this confluence. What cognitive psychology refers to as "fundamental attribution errors" represent a human tendency to ascribe the worst possible motives to enemy groups and their leaders. During the Cold War, for example, the United States contended that the Soviet Union need not feel threatened by the U.S. nuclear arsenal by claiming that it would never launch the first warhead, but many in the United States worried that the same was not true of the Soviets, whose nuclear capabilities were close to, and in some cases beyond, American capacities. Cognitive theorists also speak of an "egocentric bias," which make one group see itself as the central point of reference when assessing the action of an opposing group; add the closely related "bias of overconfidence," and a group's judgment process is further complicated. For example, during the Vietnam War, American policy-makers finely differentiated the patterns of deployment of American forces in South Vietnam, confident that the other side was equally concerned. Leaders in Hanoi, however, were substantially unaware of American military leaders' preparations, and did not consider them in their own deployment activities (Janice Gross Stein, "Building politics into psychology: The misperception of threat"). "Proportionality bias," which leads decision-makers to expect their opponents to expend efforts proportionate to the ends they seek, (Robert Jervis, Richard Lebow, and Janice Gross Stein, *Psychology of Deterrence*) also inflates the perception of threat. When the Soviets invaded Afghanistan in 1979,

for instance, American decision-makers considered the political and military consequences of this invasion critical because of its high financial and personal cost to the USSR. Accordingly, they assumed that the invasion of Afghanistan would lead to the abrogation of SALT II and the disruption of détente, yet neither of these dire consequences actually ensued.

Cognitive models continued to assume that decision-makers that compare current situations to past events make those analogies consciously and rationally, but scholars such as Irving Janis and Leon Mann soon began to cast doubt on this presupposition. In 1977, Janis and Mann discussed "decisional conflict"—"simultaneously opposing tendencies within the individual to accept or reject a given course of action" (Irving L. Janis and Leon Mann, *Decision-making: A psychological analysis of conflict*, p. 46)—as a source of "emotional stress," with possible accompanying symptoms of "hesitation, vacillation, [and] feelings of uncertainty" (ibid., p. 45). According to Janis and Mann, an individual tends to continue in a given course of decision-making if the challenges or risks he or she encounters seem inconsequential. But a dilemma arises when the challenge or risk is serious, requiring the individual to ponder whether to continue with the original decision-making process or to modify it. If the solution is relatively simple, the decision-maker will show no symptoms of stress. But if the solution is complex and the risks of staying with or changing the decision-making process are both substantial, stress symptoms appear.

It is well established that people respond to the stress of making risky decisions with three main patterns of coping. *Vigilance* makes the decision-maker exceptionally alert and highly motivated to use sound decision-making procedures, such as searching for relevant information and carefully weighing consequences. Vigilance has positive value. *Hypervigilance*, (Robert Jervis, "Representativeness in foreign policy judgment") on the other hand, involves a frantic and inefficient search for the way out of a distressing dilemma. The hypervigilant decision-maker might even perceive a crisis where there is none or precipitate one through overreaction. The third coping pattern, also ineffective, is *defensive avoidance*, in which the decision-maker is engaged in wishful thinking and relies on illusions and rationalizations. In situations of defensive avoidance, three behaviors typically come into play: 1) procrastination—when there is no obvious penalty for postponing the decision, the decision-maker may avoid dealing with the problem; 2) responsibility-shifting—if procrastination involves risk or there is a tight deadline, the decision-maker may rationalize involving other people and may even blame others for failing to find a solution; and 3) bolstering tactics—the decision-maker may exaggerate favorable outcomes while minimizing unfavorable ones and may even deny the existence of or potential for unfavorable consequences.

390. Janis and Mann, ibid. One of the psychoanalytic cases Janis and Mann examined was Sigmund Freud's case of Dora (see Sigmund Freud "Fragment of an analysis of a case in hysteria"), an eighteen-year-old girl whose "decisional

conflict," to use Janis and Mann's terminology, concerned whether or not to have an illicit love affair with Mr. K., who was married and a friend of Dora's family. After deciding against the affair, Dora had much post-decisional regret and remained in "post-decisional conflict." Through their review of Freud's findings on the unconscious reasons why Dora could not "work through and resolve the post-decisional conflict in a normal fashion" (Janis and Mann, ibid., p. 100). (Of course, this is not the interpretation of Dora's situation that everyone sees in this case history; others have understood Dora's symptoms as deriving from trauma as a result of Mr. K.'s unwanted advances.)

391. In 1974, following the division of Cyprus into Turkish and Greek sectors, then Turkish Prime Minister Bulent Ecevit (Ecevit served again as prime minister in 1977, 1978–1979, and 1999–2002) noted the role of psychology in the long-standing conflict between these two neighboring nations. In response to this pertinent observation, I began to study the Cyprus problem, and later, with Princeton historian Norman Itzkowitz, researched 1,000 years of Turkish–Greek relations through a psychoanalytic lens (see Vamık Volkan, *Cyprus—War and Adaptation*; Vamık Volkan and Norman Itzkowitz, *Turks and Greeks: Neighbors in Conflict*).

392. The American Psychiatric Association (APA)'s Committee included psychiatrists Demetrios Julius and Rita Rogers as well as former diplomats Harold Saunders and Joseph Montville, who in 1987 joined me in establishing the Center for the Study of Mind and Human Interaction at the University of Virginia.

393. This is a difficult task indeed: it is often very difficult to examine fully the unconscious mind of a leader who never lies on a psychoanalyst's couch and to reconstruct his or her dominant unconscious fantasies from the patchwork resources available to any would-be biographer. It is not always possible to understand the mind of a political leader fully, even when the analyst is an expert in human psychology. There are, of course, many so-called "psychobiographies" written by people from various scholarly backgrounds giving reasons for the leader's various thought or action patterns. Some psychobiographies are sophisticated, some are not.

There is no single "correct" approach to writing psychobiography, however. As Avner Falk noted in "Aspects of political psychobiography," Sigmund Freud himself undertook biographical studies of Leonardo da Vinci and Moses in distinctly different ways ("Leonardo da Vinci and a memory of his childhood"; "Moses and monotheism"). Early psychoanalytic writings on the lives of famous artists and historical figures focused on interpreting the symbols they employed, but did not attempt to account for the directions of their creativity. Later, questions were raised about such symbol-based approaches, since, as Martin Bergmann has observed, "symbols are overdetermined and their meaning is less constant and less universal than Freud assumed" (Bergmann, "Limitations of method in psychoanalytic biography: An historical inquiry" p. 835). The evolution of child-development studies and ego psychology led to greater focus on the actual life history of the subject of a biography, especially on childhood traumas and later on adolescence as well. Critics continued to argue, however, that a psychoanalytic approach was reductionist, maintaining that unconscious instinctual forces cannot simply account for what is observable on the surface. Further research on child development illuminated the importance of dyadic child-mother experiences in the formation of a child's sense of self, ushering in object-relation theories and the examination of how a person establishes a cohesive sense of self (identity) and mental representations of others, enlarging our understanding of how personalities are formed—a great potential help to the biographer's attempt to understand his subject's inner world (Edith Jacobson, *The Self and the Object World*; Otto F. Kernberg, "Structural derivatives of object relations"). With Robert Waelder's principle of "multiple function," which established that a subject's decisions, actions, and productions have many conscious and unconscious meanings and sources, psychoanalytic writers began to consider more than one causal factor in examining an individual's artistic work, political ideology, and extreme or destructive actions (see Waelder, "Principle of multiple functions: Observations on over-determination"). Erik Erikson suggested that the biographer should focus on the adolescent years, during which a person expands his or her horizons beyond the family and neighbors to a wider social existence (Erikson, "Growth and crisis in the healthy personality"; *Young Man Luther*).

Combining what has been learned from ego psychology with what is useful from object relations theory, I believe it is possible to write a psychobiography based on a *developmental* approach. Norman Itzkowitz and I used such an approach in writing psychobiographies of Kemal Ataturk and Richard Nixon (Vamık Volkan and Norman Itzkowitz, *The Immortal Ataturk: A Psychobiography*; Vamık Volkan, Norman Itzkowitz, and Andrew Dod, *Richard Nixon: A Psychobiography*). I relied on the same approach when I presented the life of Abdullah Ocalan (also known as Apo), the leader of the Kurdistan Workers Party (PKK), in *Bloodlines: From Ethnic Pride to Ethnic Terrorism*.

This methodology examines information from the subject's infancy and early childhood, including the dyadic relationship between child and parent, construction of the subject's unconscious fantasies, and the parents' unconscious fantasies about their child which influence the subject's forming sense of self. From reports of the subject's childhood and adolescence, one can deduce the nature of the subject's Oedipal struggles, early traumas or growth-inducing experiences, developmental arrests, early symptom formations and adaptations to environment, and crystallization of personality organization during the adolescent passage. The researcher also examines, as deeply as primary resources permit, the subject's internal responses to external events, attempts to change the environment to fit internal demands, activities in the service of maintaining self-esteem, affective expressions or affect control, sexual adaptation, mate choices, and responses to parenthood. Finally, the psychobiographer considers transformations of identity, regressions and subsequent progressions in the reconsolidation of identity, midlife issues, and reactions to aging and the approach of death. The subject's entire life is thus looked at developmentally though a psychoanalytic lens. The researcher—so involved with the image of his or her subject—also must pay attention to his or her own "transference": the biographer's own fantasies and wishes projected onto the image of the subject.

The aim is a "total" history of the individual: the illumination of his or her psychic reality and its interaction with the external world in all its complexity. Obviously, the degree of success that can be achieved in writing a "total" psychobiography through this developmental approach depends on gaining access to information about the subject and on taming the writer's own transference distortions of his or her subject.

394. Of course, people in (and out) of the public eye may try to hide the neuroses that they feel are "alien." But it is generally not possible to hide personality permanently.

395. Tucker, ibid., p. xvi.

396. To review briefly: the first danger on Freud's list is the danger of losing an important person: the biological mother or other primary caretaker. The second involves the danger of losing the love provided by the mother or her substitute. The third, which occurs in children of approximately four to six years of age, concerns a fantasized dread of losing a highly invested body part. The fourth danger involves the loss of self-esteem that older children may experience when they believe that they are not living up to the real or imagined expectations of parents and important other people, such as teachers. As we can easily see, all of Freud's childhood dangerous situations relate to the concept of loss. The first one involves an actual loss—the death of a mother or the person who is performing the mothering role; the others are concerned with psychological losses. Children who are raised in nurturing environments tend to experience "losses" without a sense of utmost helplessness, extreme anxiety, and/or humiliation, and are able to gain something new from the experience of a loss, such as assuming certain useful functions of the lost object. These people will be less prone than people who were raised in a non-nurturing environment to react badly to the adult life situations that remind them (mostly unconsciously) of real or fantasized losses in childhood.

More recently, I have added another routine childhood danger situation to Freud's list, another threat of psychological loss. As I explained in Chapter 1, a child developing normally comes to know, by the third year of life, that he or she is really the same person both when frustrated and when pampered with love. The threat of loss occurs when the child fantasizes that he or she will lose his or her "good" self-images during the integration of "good" with "bad" into a realistic self-image. As the child learns how to "make gray" by putting the "black" and "white" parts of him or herself together, he or she may see the danger of ending up having an entirely "black" character, instead of a truly "gray" one. The following is a brief illustration, in the historical and political arena, of how this threatened loss may echo in adult lives: After the reunification of Germany in 1990, German psychoanalyst Gabriele Ast and I began to research Germans' reactions to reunification. Though our original plan to interview more than one hundred Germans had to be dropped for lack of funding, we were nevertheless able to conduct twenty-five in-depth interviews in which we noted that some Germans had perceived the reunification of East and West Germany as an internal danger signal. Through listening to their life stories, fantasies, daydreams, and dreams, we concluded that the external historical event—merging a formerly communist state with a democratic one—functioned as a reminder of childhood efforts to unite their opposing self-images and the accompanying danger of their "bad" aggressive sides dominating their "good" loving sides (Gabriele Ast, "Interview with Germans about reunification"; also see Vamık Volkan, Gabriele Ast, and William Greer, *The Third Reich in the Unconscious: Transgenerational Transmission and its Consequences*).

Now and then, without being fully aware of it, all adults relive the five major childhood dangers. For example, a woman may react to the news of the death of her best friend's mother with anxiety instead of sorrow. Looking closer at this response, we may learn that the death of her friend's mother reminded the woman of the childhood danger of losing her own mother (or her mother's love). In our ordinary conscious lives, however, we are often not aware that our experiences of events in the world may be linked to the seemingly unrelated psychological processes of our developmental years, substantially because people habitually mobilize certain psychological mechanisms in order to avoid anxiety. The more habitual those mechanisms are—such as trying to control our emotions and using intellectualization to explain away the causes of events in which we are intimately involved—the more they contribute to the complete picture of an individual's personality. One way to understand an individual's personality, then, is to identify what situations he or she perceives as dangerous, what psychological mechanisms he or she typically uses to cope with such situations, and what goals he or she consciously or unconsciously considers most important to achieve (Volkan, Akhtar, Dorn, Kafka, Kernberg, Olsson, Rogers, and Shanfield, ibid.). What a person tries desperately to avoid and what he or she is determined to achieve profoundly influence the kinds of decisions he or she makes in daily life.

397. For practical purposes, we can divide those who have personality disorders into two categories. The first is considered "higher-level" (meaning both more functional and less pathological) and is characterized by unconscious mental conflicts about authority, sexuality, competitiveness, control, and power. Like those who are considered to have "normal" personality traits, persons with this type of personality disorder possess an intact identity and retain a capacity for concern, empathy, ambivalence, and love. Under stress they exhibit anxiety and guilt. See Otto F. Kernberg, "A psychoanalytic classification of character pathology."

The second type of personality disorder exhibits "identity diffusion"; individuals with this type of personality disorder display pronounced contradictions in their self-concepts and in the way they relate to others. They have defective capacities for concern, empathy, ambivalence, love, and mourning. They oscillate between seeming to have high self-esteem and considering themselves inferior and unlovable. See Otto F. Kernberg, *Object Relations Theory and Clinical Psychoanalysis*, and Salman Akhtar, "The syndrome of identity diffusion."

398. Arthur S. Link, *Wilson: The Road to the White House*, p. 36–37.

399. Link, ibid., p. 90–91. Alexander L. George and Juliette L. George (*Presidential Personality and Performance*), who carried out a "personality study" on Wilson, offer extensive details on Wilson's childhood and his relationship with his father, Dr. Joseph Ruggles Wilson, a Presbyterian minister. According to their biographical sources, Dr. Wilson took total charge of Woodrow's early education, using very exacting teaching methods. He was a faultfinder—authoritarian, demanding and mocking—and Woodrow held him in high regard. Relatives commented on the father's caustic way of speaking, cruel teasing, and sharp tongue, noting how harshly he used them on his son. George and George note Woodrow Wilson's lifelong struggle with feelings of worthlessness and inadequacy and his subsequent striving, over and over again, to achieve self-esteem. With working hypotheses such as passive rebellion and repression of resentment, they suggest that Wilson strove in childhood to win his father's love and acknowledgement and continued to admire and to want to please his father. We might also speculate that Wilson's habitual successes, along with his decisions (conscious or unconscious) to spoil them, might relate to his identification with a father who wanted him to excel—an identification against which Wilson subsequently rebelled.

400. Volkan et al., ibid. Also see Robert C. Tucker, *Stalin as a Revolutionary, 1879-1929: A Study in History and Personality*; Robert S. Robins, "Paranoid ideation and charismatic leadership"; Robert S. Robins and Jerrold M. Post, *Political Paranoia: The Psychopolitics of Hatred*; and Salman Akhtar "Paranoid personality disorder: A synthesis of developmental, dynamic and descriptive features." For additional details on paranoid personality generally, also see David Shapiro, *Neurotic Styles*.

401. Tucker, ibid., p. 211. Stalin's psychoanalytically-informed biographers, such as Daniel Rancour-Laferriere (*The Mind of Stalin: A Psychoanalytic Study*) and Robert Tucker (ibid.) mention the savage beatings the young Stalin received from his father, who drank heavily, as significant elements in his personal development.

402. Nikita Sergeyevich Khrushchev, "The 'secret' speech delivered to the closed session of the Twentieth Congress of the Communist Party of the Soviet Union" (See Nikita Khruschev, *Khrushchev Remembers*.)

403. Parts of my two November 1990 interviews with Valentin Berezhkov appeared in Vamık D. Volkan, "An interview with Valentin Berezhkov: Stalin's interpreter."

404. It may be possible for such pathological personalities to ascend to lead-

ership when they are heirs to a throne, but this is not something that often happens in the modern world.

405. Matthew Holden, "Bargaining and command by heads of the U.S. government department."

406. In the United States, we might be able to compare the role of Franklin Delano Roosevelt—who was the closest the United States got to a long-term leader—to that of such long-term heads of state.

407. Shimon Shamir, personal communication, meetings sponsored by The Yitzhak Rabin Center for Israel Studies, Tel Aviv, May 2000. After serving as the Israeli ambassador to Egypt, Shamir became ambassador to Jordan. He presently teaches at the Tel Aviv University.

408. Shamir, ibid.

409. Peter Finn, "Settlement reported in Kohl scandal," *The Washington Post*, p. A22, February 9, 2001.

410. Psychoanalysts divide unconscious fantasies into various types. For example, Sigmund Freud stated that "unconscious phantasies have either been unconscious all along and have been formed in the unconscious, or—as is more often the case—they were once conscious phantasies, day-dreams, and have become unconscious through 'repression.'" See Freud, "Hysterical phantasies and their relation to bisexuality" (p. 161.).

411. See Susan Isaacs, "The nature and function of fantasy"; Jacob A. Arlow, "Unconscious fantasy and disturbances of conscious experience"; Lawrence B. Inderbitzin and Steven T. Levy, "Unconscious fantasy: A reconsideration of the concept"; and Vamık Volkan and Gabriele Ast, *Siblings in the Unconscious*.

412. U.S. Military Sales to Iran, qtd. in Marvin Zonis, *Majestic Failure: The Fall of the Shah*, p. 8

413. Zonis, ibid.

414. I will illustrate this in more detail in a discussion of Kemal Ataturk in Chapters 7 and 8.

7

415. Edith Wiegert, "Narcissism: Benign and malignant forms"; Vamık Volkan and Gabriele Ast, *Spektrum des Narcissmus*.

416. See Otto F. Kernberg, *Borderline Conditions and Pathological Narcissism*; Vamık Volkan, *Primitive Internalized Object Relations*; Vamık Volkan and Gabriele Ast, ibid.; Salman Akhtar, *Broken Structures*; Akhtar and J. Anderson Thomson, "Overview: Narcissistic personality disorder."

417. Typically, narcissistic individuals were somehow left emotionally hungry, ashamed, and helpless as children by their mothers or other primary caretakers. The caretaker may have been narcissistic him or herself and may have treated the child as a "beautiful toy" to exhibit to others while failing to express warmth toward the child. Alternately, the primary caretaker, grieving for signifi-

cant losses, may have been withdrawn and humiliated for his or her own psychological reasons and therefore unable to fulfill the child's psychological needs. Even though the child experiences the caretaker as cold and uncaring, the caretaker sees the child as someone "special," perhaps as his or her future savior, someone who will repair grief or humiliation, or restore the family name. For example, one grieving mother saw her son as a link to a dead sibling, whom she imagined as already immortal and omnipotent. Although the mother's grief made her distant and ungiving from the second child's point of view, she nevertheless engaged in an intense relationship with him, pushing him to match the idealized image of the dead sibling. Though the second child became narcissistic in order to inhabit the "number one" position in his mother's eyes, he would now and then do "stupid" things in order to defeat the image of the "perfect" dead sibling he had internalized from his mother. In another situation, a Catholic mother fantasized that her son would grow up to become the Pope (i.e., an idealized father to replace the bad father she herself had experienced as a child), while her routine mothering functions left the child deprived of ordinary affection and approval for just being an average child. This perception of her child as unique was conveyed into the developing self of the small child and became the foundation for the child's future sense of his own grandiosity. Around such an element of imagined "specialness," the child collects his or her own idealized images of others, creating what we have envisaged as the large, good piece of the pie. The child then pushes away—in technical terms, "splits"—the "hungry" and frustrated self-image, along with the devalued image he or she has of the "cold" primary caretaker (and others), creating the smaller, spoiled part of the pie.

418. Narcissistic individuals often do not wish to come to treatment since they (overtly) feel omnipotent and have no need for help from others, including a psychoanalyst. It is usually after experiencing some frustration, shame, or even brief depression that such an individual seeks help. For example, a narcissistic individual may seek help if he considers himself to be the most intelligent person to ever attend college, but fails to make a passing grade. Once the crisis is over, however, the person often reverts to using the unspoiled section of the pie. If the patient is already in analysis, and the analyst is experienced with treating such individuals, the patient will voluntarily remain in treatment, even developing illusions (transference) that the analyst is "stupid"; the patient then feels "great" compared to the analyst. Or the patient may experience the analyst as "wonderful," but simply an extension of the patient's glorious existence. Such transferences are worked through during the patient's analysis.

419. Vamık Volkan, "The glass bubble of a narcissistic patient"; Volkan and Ast, ibid. See also Arnold Modell, "The holding environment and the therapeutic action of psychoanalysis," who refers to such fantasies as cocoon fantasies. Although I have no objection to this notion, I suggest that the analogy of a glass bubble is more useful because it describes a transparent enclosure that permits its occupant to assess the outside world without being encroached upon, enhancing

the sense of omnipotence and self-sufficiency.

420. "Glass bubble" fantasies usually come to the narcissistic person's mind before he goes to sleep. In a sense, such people need to protect their good part, reestablishing their sense of omnipotence before surrendering themselves to sleep in a lonely kingdom under a protective umbrella.

421. See Chapter 1 for more discussion of externalization and the related process of projection.

422. However well it may be hidden, I see the feeling of envy as chronic to the narcissistic personality, and it can become acute when exacerbated. But narcissistic people frequently dismiss any strong feeling of envy by the ready device of concluding that, although the object of envy did accomplish something noteworthy, they themselves continue to be superior in more important ways, making no room for humiliation. In this regard, thoughts, decisions, and actions often come quickly to narcissistic people. For example, one narcissistic woman went to a country club several times a week to display herself for admiring men, though she felt no concern or affection for them as human beings and felt rather empty despite the flattery. She was consumed with envy when a woman entered the club in a dress similar to hers, but handled the situation by deciding that the "rival" had "thick ankles," a criterion on which she could resume her typical position of superiority. Protecting this sense of omnipotence and grandiosity is the narcissist's essential task.

423. Volkan and Ast, ibid. It can easily be imagined that practically no one with severe malignant narcissism comes to lie on the analyst's couch. On very unusual occasions, however, an analyst may treat a person with a mild form of malignant narcissism who is not involved in mutilating or murdering others. Gabriele Ast and I have described the full analysis and recovery of an individual with malignant narcissism who achieved his "aggressive triumphs" by machine-gunning animals whenever he felt threatened by his "bad" piece. He was a hunter, but not a sportsman.

424. Michael H. Stone, "Murder."

425. Volkan and Ast, ibid., pp. 9–10.

426. Lloyd Etheridge ("Hardball politics: A model") states that narcissistically oriented people develop intense attachments to certain institutions or offices that are denied. They believe their grandiose part will be attacked if they are not a leader in such an institution or if they fail to attain an office.

427. Max Weber, *Wirtschaft und Gesellschaft*. See also D. Wilfred Abse and Lucie Jessner, "The psychodynamic aspect of leadership"; D. Wilfred Abse and Richard Ulman, "Charismatic political leadership and collective leadership"; Robert C. Tucker, "The theory of charismatic leadership."

428. Turks did not have surnames until 1934, so it was often difficult to differentiate one Mehmet or Mustafa from another. It was Mustafa Kemal who decided that surnames should be adopted, and he modeled the new practice by legally adopting the surname of Ataturk.

429. Particularly since September 11, 2001, there has been a great deal of debate about the intertwining of religion and politics in Islam. In this context, Ataturk's Turkey gains new importance: here is a model of separating religion from state power in an Islamic country.

430. The new Turkey adopted a civil code modeled on that of the Swiss, a penal code adopted from Italy, and a code of business law drawn from Germany.

431. Kemal Ataturk, *Ataturk'un Soylev ve Demecleri* [Speeches and Statements by Ataturk] Vol. 2, p. 183.

432. Further, as Dankwart A. Rustow, distinguished university professor of political science at the City University of New York Graduate School, observes:

Readers of a generation inured to the mass murders of a Hitler and a Stalin ... should at once be reminded that in an average day those regimes killed off more victims than the Kemalist regime did in all its two decades. ... Although the exact arithmetic is hard to establish, it is clear that those who lost their lives for political reasons in Turkey in the twenties and thir-ties numbered several dozen, at most a few hundred." (Rustow, "Ataturk as founder of a state," p. 221)

For additional details on this topic, see Volkan and Itzkowitz, ibid.

433. Qtd. in Sevket Sureyya Aydemir, *Tek Adam (The Singular Man)*, Vol. 3, p. 484.

434. Aydemir, ibid., p. 482.

435. Aydemir, ibid.

436. After the failure of his brief marriage (1923–1925) to Latife Usakligil, Ataturk adopted many daughters. Gokcen was a twelve-year-old orphan at the time of her adoption. She became one of the most famous aviators of her time and died in 2001.

437. Ataturk's first memory appears in the January 10, 1922, edition of *Vakit*, a Turkish daily, in an interview with Ahmet Emin Yalman.

438. Attendance records were kept for these events.

439. Ataturk's drinking had a long history, although he replaced alcohol with coffee when on the battlefield or when preparing certain civil activities. He never appeared drunk in public.

440. Ataturk, ibid., p. 183.

441. Volkan, Itzkowitz, and Dod, *Richard Nixon*. For the Ehrlichman refer-ence see: p. 94.

442. Volkan, Itzkowitz, and Dod, ibid.

443. Theodore H. White, *The Making of the President,1968*, p. 53.

444. Blema Steinberg, *Shame and Humiliation: Presidential Decision-making on Vietnam: A Psychoanalytic Interpretation*.

445. Volkan, Itzkowitz, and Dod, ibid. We spent more than three years trying to understand Nixon's personality and internal world.

446. Steinberg, ibid., p. 170.

447. Steinberg, ibid., p. 172.

448. Ted Szulc, *The Illusion of Peace*, p. 62.

449. Seymour M. Hersh, *The Price of Power: Kissinger in the Nixon White House*.

450. Richard Nixon, *RN: The Memoirs of Richard Nixon*, p. 380.

451. Steinberg, ibid.

452. Henry Kissinger, *The White House Years*, p. 242.

453. Kissinger, ibid.

454. Qtd. Stephen E. Ambrose, *Nixon: the Triumph of a Politician, 1962–1972*, p. 258.

455. Kissinger, ibid., p. 247.

456. Steinberg, ibid., p. 177.

457. Steinberg, ibid.; Volkan, Itzkowitz, and Dod, ibid.; Bruce Mazlish, *In Search of Richard Nixon: A Psychohistorical Inquiry*; Ambrose, ibid.

458. James D. Barber, *The Presidential Character: Predicting Performance in the White House*, p. 429.

459. Ambrose, ibid., p. 185.

460. Qtd. in Ambrose, ibid., p. 345.

461. Qtd. in Steinberg, ibid., p. 191.

462. Kissinger, ibid., pp. 492–493. Though we learn a great deal about Nixon's psychology from Kissinger, Steinberg reminds us that Kissinger's own behavior during the same time period provides a typical example of the role of a follower in a narcissistic leader's need to be victorious over, in Nixon's case, real and fantasized enemies. Kissinger "submitted" himself to a narcissistic leader's wish to remain unchallenged, and his observations must be treated accordingly.

463. Kissinger, ibid., p. 498. Lewis Beale wrote that Nixon screened *Patton* twice during the week that he began the secret bombing of Cambodia in 1970 (*Los Angeles Times*, August 4, 2003, p. E5)

464. Steinberg, ibid., p. 206.

465. Steinberg, ibid., p. 205.

466. H. Robert Haldeman, *The Haldeman Diaries: Inside the Nixon White House*.

467. In order to understand Nixon's reactions to various threats of shame and humiliation, it is necessary to carefully explore his background, which reveals a childhood that was far from ideal. His early experiences with loss, adversity, and bereavement suggest that his behavior as president echoed a personality organization formed early in life—one in which shame and humiliation were intolerable. The interested reader may look at our in-depth study of how Nixon's personality evolved (see Volkan, Itzkowitz, and Dod, ibid.).

468. Abse and Ulman, "Charismatic leaderships and collective regression."

469. These various possible psychological influences cover a large range: the effect on his mother's mental condition of the deaths of three older siblings in infancy before Hitler's birth, the fact that Hitler's father was illegitimate and prone to violent outbursts at home (he may also have been alcoholic), the births

of younger siblings, the death of Hitler's younger brother when Hitler was 11, the death of his father three years later, his mother's cancer and treatment by a Jewish physician, and her death when Hitler was 18 (see, for example, T. G. Waite, *The Psychopathic God: Adolf Hitler*; Norbert Bromberg and Verna V. Small, *Hitler's Psychopathology*; Helm Steirlin, *Adolf Hitler:A Family Perspective*). There also have been those who thought not psychological developmental elements but outside factors determined Hitler's destructive mind. For example, Leonard L. Heston and Renate Heston argued that Hitler's use of amphetamines, which were prescribed by his doctor, Theodore Morrell, induced an addiction that resulted in paranoid psychosis; thus, the Hestons implied, Hitler's anti-Semitism and legislation of mass murder were iatrogenically created (Leonard L. Heston and Renate Heston, *The Medical Casebook of Adolf Hitler: His Illness, Doctors, and Drugs*).

Actually, the first psychobiographical study of Hitler, commissioned by the head of the U.S. Office of Strategic Services during World War II and written by Cambridge, Massachusetts, psychiatrist Walter C. Langer (Walter C. Langer, *The Mind of Adolf Hitler: The Secret Wartime Report*), is perhaps the most incisive among the many books on Hitler's psychology, in spite of certain shortcomings. Originally a secret report, it was not published for public view until after the war, and Langer did not have some data about Hitler that became available to later investigators such as Fritz Redlich, former chair of the Department of Psychiatry at Yale University, whose meticulously researched 1998 volume is the most recent of the major books on Hitler's life. Whereas Langer's work tried to understand the Hitler phenomenon from a psychological point of view, Redlich's study did not intend "to demonstrate that psychological factors are the most important factors in an appraisal of Hitler" (Fritz Redlich, *Hitler: Diagnosis of a Destructive Prophet*, p. xv). But Redlich has provided some valuable new data about Hitler's life, as well as highlighting and enlarging knowledge from the previously available data. His systematic study of Hitler's physical and mental health concludes that what Morrell prescribed may have intensified, but did not cause, the Fuhrer's pre-existing mental and physical problems. Further, an examination of Hitler's physical health led Redlich to conclude that Hitler was born with two congenital defects: spina bifida occulta and hypospadius (a deformity of the penis). Such medical conditions may have exacerbated other key factors in the development of Hitler's mind.

In any event, it remains clear that there is little solid data concerning the development of Hitler's internal world and his transformation into a dictator. As Ira Brenner, a leading expert on the psychological impact of the Holocaust on subsequent generations, has observed, what Redlich sees as psychoanalysis's limited ability to "explain" Hitler "reflects a general difficulty in comprehensively formulating people with extraordinary abilities or people under extraordinary circumstances rather than a devaluation of analytic theory itself" (Ira Brenner, "Review of *Hitler: Diagnosis of a Destructive Prophet*, by Fritz Redlich"). Brenner continues, in what I believe to be the best brief summary of what psychoanalytic biographies could say about Hitler's mind and its development:

> As he [Hitler] and his baby sister, Clara, were the only survivors of his parents' six children, he may have had an unconscious fantasy that his father, who was a bastard both literally and figuratively, was the dangerous source of [syphilis] (Hitler considered syphilis a 'Jewish' disease and lived in mortal dread of it). He may have also ascribed his congenital defects as well as his mother's cancer to his father. Whatever sense of inner badness he may have felt would have been externalized and blamed on others through displacement from the father and projected onto the 'degenerate and inferior' groups like Jews, Gypsies, homosexuals, the mentally ill, and the physically handicapped. In so doing, all of his doubts about his ancestry, his sexuality, his physical and mental well being would have been disowned and ascribed to others. It is also conjectured that a reason he had no children was because of a deep fear of transmitting his genetic defects (Brenner, ibid., pp. 103–104).

470. Ernst K. Bramsted, *Goebbels and National Socialist Propaganda 1925–1945*. Goebbels's ministry was, incidentally, extraordinarily well-funded: in 1934, its budget totaled two million pounds sterling, a staggering amount at the time for a single government agency. In later years, that annual budget would be doubled.

471. Victor Reimann, *Goebbels: The Man Who Created Hitler*, p. 2.

472. ibid., p. 6.

473. At the same time, of course, Mein Kampf was ubiquitous, distributed at official ceremonies and to soldiers.

474. ibid., p. 4. It is fascinating to note that the greeting "Heil Hitler" can be translated as "heal Hitler," "treat Hitler," or "make him restore."

475. Langer, ibid., p. 64.

476. Hermann Rauschning, *Revolution of Nihilism*, reported in Langer, ibid., p. 64.

477. William Teeling, *Know Thy Enemy*, p. 2.

478. Langer, ibid., p. 64.

479. This statement comes from Judith Stern, an Israeli psychologist who studied extensively the psychology of the German people under the Third Reich (personal communication, March 2001, Tel Aviv).

Hitler's thought and action contained a paradox: Hitler himself certainly did not embody the Aryan superman.

480. Stern, ibid.

481. Reported in Reimann, ibid., p. 40.

482. ibid., p. 44.

483. Arno Gruen, *Der Frende In Uns (The Stranger Within Us)*. Also see Gruen, "Surrendering identity: Herman Goering and Rudolf Hess."

484. Qtd. in Joachim C. Fest, *The Face of the Third Reich*, p. 190. See also Gruen, ibid.

485. Qtd. in Fest, ibid., p. 189.

486. Peter Loewenberg, "The uses of anxiety," p. 521. In spite of the propaganda machinery used to present Hitler as above any malicious feelings, the Fuhrer at times needed to illustrate his ruthlessness.

487. Judith Stern, ibid. See also Judith Stern, "Deviance in Nazi Society."

488. Vamık Volkan, "An interview with Valentin Berezhkov: Stalin's interpreter."

489. Zarubina has described her memories of that career in the book *Inside Russia: The Life and Times of Zoya Zarubina*, by Inez Cope Jeffrey.

490. This led the other *Politburo* members to fear that Beria could seal up the Kremlin at any time.

491. Volkan, ibid., p. 78.

492. See Daniel Rancour-Laferriere, *The Mind of Stalin: A Psychoanalytic Study*, which lists 22 nicknames bestowed on Stalin by the Soviet media during the dictator's lifetime.

8

493. Indonesia's troubles continued under his successor, President Addurrahim Wahid. Wahid was forced out of power in 2001 and replaced by Megawati Sukarnoputri, daughter of the "founding father" of postcolonial Indonesia, President Sukarno.

494. *The Wall Street Journal*, August 6, 1998, p. 6.

495. K. B. Richburg, "Indonesians debate truth of rape reports." *The Washington Post*, September 24, 1998, p. A32. The actual number of assaults has continued to be hard to pin down.

496. These old Turkish and Tanzanian words come from a common Arabic root. In Turkey, in a later linguistic purification, the Arabic-rooted word "muallim" was replaced by the word "ogretmen."

497. Vamık Volkan and Norman Itzkowitz, *The Immortal Ataturk: A Psychobiography.*

498. "Ghazi" is a title given to veterans of wars.

499. The Arabic writing system can represent three vowel sounds and their elongation. The Turkish system has eight vowels. This meant, in effect, that one written word had more than one pronunciation and meaning.

500. In Turkey, Islam's prohibition against alcohol functioned mainly as a prohibition against the *public* consumption of alcohol.

501. Kemal Ataturk, *Ataturk' un Soylev ve Demecleri (Speeches and Statements of Ataturk)*, p. 256.

502. Volkan and Itzkowitz, ibid., pp. 285–286. See the previous chapter for Ataturk's childhood and "repair" fantasies.

503. The former colonies of Tanganyika and Zanzibar united in April 1964 to form one sovereign state: the United Republic of Tanzania. More than 35 million

people now live in Tanzania, best known abroad for the national symbol Mount Kilimanjaro (thanks in no small part to Ernest Hemingway's book, *The Snows of Kilimanjaro*). The majority of Tanzanians belongs to the Bantu tribe, but the population comprises more than 130 other tribes and a small minority of other ethnic groups. Most Tanzanians are Christian (45 percent) or Muslim (35 percent).

504. Though I have psychobiographical knowledge of Ataturk, I do not have any such information about Nyerere's internal world, unconscious motivations, or personality development. Thus I can report here only Nyerere's activities as a political leader who acted as a teacher in the public arena.

505. See Willard Wolfe, *From Radicalism to Socialism: Men and Ideas in the Formation of Fabian Socialist Doctrine, 1881–1889*.

506. Yusef Kassam, *The Adult Education Revolution in Tanzania*. See also H. Hinzen and V. H. Hundsdorfer, *The Tanzanian Experience: Education for Liberation and Development*.

507. Budd L. Hall and J. Roby Kidd (eds). *Adult Education for Action*.

508. Nyerere was diagnosed with leukemia in 1998, and died while undergoing treatment in a London hospital on October 14, 1999.

509. Economic development remained particularly elusive: at the time of Nyerere's resignation, Tanzania was still one of the world's poorest countries.

510. A few notable developments in psychoanalytically-influenced studies of teaching and learning processes: A zoology teacher named M. L. J. Abercrombie became disappointed in the effects that studying science seemed to have on her students' habits of thinking. She noted that when she asked her students to describe what they saw while dissecting an animal or looking through a microscope, her students often did not distinguish sharply between what was actually there and what they were told "ought" to be there (Abercrombie, *The Anatomy of Judgment*). Aware of research on visual perception concerning the part played by past experience and present attitude in determining what we see, Abercrombie developed a specialized teaching project influenced by the work of psychoanalysts Sigmund Heinrich Foulkes and James Anthony with small therapy groups (Foulkes and Anthony, *Group Psychotherapy*). Medical students in groups of twelve attended eight sessions, each lasting one and a half hours. Intellectual discussions of heuristic concepts such as seeing, language, classification, evaluation of evidence, and causation accompanied small group activities using free associations according to techniques evolved by Foulkes and Anthony. As Abercrombie had hypothesized, this approach enhanced students' ability to reach valid judgments.

For five years, from 1968 to 1973, I taught clinical psychiatry and psychodynamic concepts to psychiatric residents using a method I developed based on Abercrombie's work, called the Field Work Method (See Vamık Volkan and David R. Hawkins, "The 'Field Work Method' of teaching and learning clinical psychiatry" and "The learning group"). Seven to ten first-year residents met with the same teacher twice a week throughout the academic year while observing behind a one-way mirror one resident's treatment of an inpatient. A group discussion as well as an intellectual examination of what had been observed followed each treatment hour.

Each group of residents in the Field Work program met with the teacher for about 225 hours throughout the academic year, much longer than Abercrombie's groups, which met for only a total of 12 hours. The Field Work groups thus developed more-intense small-group psychodynamics which, with my help, could be used to help reorganize the residents' stores of experience so that they could make more valid clinical judgments in the future.

The Field Work Method combined the students' actual observations and internal experiences with intellectual explanation. It was based on a "show and tell" sort of interaction between teacher and students and engaged resistances to learning and concepts, struggles against identification with the teacher, and acquisition of intellectual and emotional autonomy.

Two relatively recent books also deal with one-to-one and small-group teaching–learning processes. The first of these books is written by psychoanalyst Robert Gardner (*On Trying to Teach: The Mind in Correspondence*), who uses personal anecdotes from everyday life concerning teaching and learning from a psychoanalytic perspective. The second book is by a psychoanalytically-informed professor of English, Jeffrey Berman (*Diaries to an English Professor: Pain and Growth in the Classroom*), who describes a methodology he developed while teaching a course entitled "Psychoanalysis and English."

Both Gardner and Berman emphasize the roles that emotional subtlety and mutuality in human relationships play in classroom teaching. When I read their work, I also noted an echo of a concept used as the basis of teaching at the Hanna Perkins School in the 1960s. Anne Katan, who directed this therapeutic nursery school, observed that verbalization leads to a mastery of the ego over affects and drives (Katan, "Some thoughts on the role of verbalization in early childhood,"): teaching young children the names of the emotions that they discharged psychosomatically had a therapeutic impact on the children.

Classroom teaching is unsuccessful when a teacher disregards the students' readiness, interests, and emotional states and believes that only the teacher has the answers. Teaching is more successful when it integrates intellectualization with emotions. For example, Berman promoted interaction with his college students by having them write diaries. With the students' permission, Berman read anonymous diary entries to the class for twenty minutes once a week. Students wrote mostly about problems of being children of divorced parents and having eating disorders or depression. Discussions opened avenues of empathy among the members of the class, which, in turn, allowed the students to develop themselves intellectually, since the teacher also provided intellectual feedback on what they were writing in their diaries. Berman's methodology and Gardner's emphasis on playfulness and unconscious communication resonated with Abercrombie's efforts and the Field Work method.

511. Margaret S. Mahler, *On Human Symbiosis and the Vicissitudes of Individuation*.

512. Berman, ibid., p. 227.

513. In psychoanalysis, these expectations and distortions are technically called "transferences."

514. Unless, of course, a gradual, systematic effort is made to change or influence the minds of group members, such as was made by the Nazi propaganda system.

515. James MacGregor Burns, *Leadership*.

516. "Kemalism" refers to certain ideological principles published in a manifesto on April 20, 1931. They were later enshrined in the constitution. It concerns eliminating the Ottoman dynasty and giving sovereignty to the nation, extending equal rights to all citizens, granting state assistance to private enterprise in order to develop Turkey's economic future, and, most importantly, establishing secularism.

517. Some aspects of Kemalism were eventually modified under the presidency of Turgut Ozal (1989–1993). In 2002, a new political party, the Justice and Development party, which has Islamic roots, came to power in Turkey. The ruling party continues to support the secular laws and immediately became involved in Turkey's efforts to join the European Union.

518. Though I have read Mandela's autobiography and other fine books written about him (Nelson Mandela, *Long Walk to Freedom: The Autobiography of Nelson Mandela*; James Gregory, *Goodbye Bafana: Nelson Mandela, My Prisoner, My Friend* ...; Brian Frost, *Struggling to Forgive: Nelson Mandela and South Africa's Search for Reconciliation*; Martin Meredith, *Nelson Mandela: A Biography*; Anthony Sampson, *Mandela: The Authorized Biography*), I am not prepared to offer psychoanalytic explorations of why he has been able to accomplish all that he has, not least because I have not sufficiently studied the culture in which Mandela was raised to understand the interactions between his family history and his cultural and historical context.

519. Mandela, ibid., p. 495.

520. Qtd. Frost, ibid., p. 6.

521. Frost, ibid.

522. This story of this episode comes from John Carlin, "Master of his Fate," *New York Times Book Review*, p. 9, September 19, 1999. Carlin covered South Africa for the British newspaper *The Independent* from 1989 to 1995.

523. Qtd. Carlin, ibid., p. 10

524. Qtd. Carlin, ibid

525. Qtd. Carlin, ibid.

526. E. M. Swift, "Bok to the Future," *Sports Illustrated*, p. 32, july 3, 1995

527. Swift, ibid.

528. Qtd. Swift, ibid.

529. Swift, ibid.

530. Though I have never met Nelson Mandela, I came to know Desmond Tutu in the mid-1990s on a few occasions at the Carter Center in Atlanta while we were both members of the International Negotiation Network, chaired by former President Jimmy Carter.

531. E. Vulliamy, *Season in Hell: Understanding Bosnia's War*, p. 157.

532. For more detailed consideration of these events, see Vamık Volkan, *Bloodlines*. Other targets included Croats and Slovenes.

533. Norman Mailer, "Milosevic and Clinton." *The Washington Post*, May 24, 1999, p. A25.

534. The Ottoman army.

535. Roy Gutman, *Witness to Genocide*, p. x.

536. Here we catch echoes of Nazi propaganda as well as the ideology of Osama bin Laden. Another ideology similar to Milosevic's teachings is the *Megali Idea* (Great Idea), which is also connected to the reactivation of chosen trauma (see Michael Herzfeld, *Ours Once More: Folklore,Ideology, and the Making of the Modern Greece*; Kenneth Young, *The Greek Passion: A Study in People and Politics*). The chosen trauma associated with the Greek Megali Idea is the fall of Constantinople (Istanbul) to the Ottomans in 1453. The Megali Idea, which calls for the reunification of the Byzantine Empire under a greater Greece, was not expressed as a political ideology until the mid-nineteenth century, but existed beneath the surface. Kyriakos Markides, a Cypriot-born Greek sociologist, describes the role of the Megali Idea as reflected in the Cyprus conflict. Cypriot Greek leaders, such as the late Archbishop Makarios, who fought for the island's union with Greece, were busy reactivating or strengthening the Megali Idea. Markides writes: "One could agree that the "Great Idea" had an internal logic, pressing for the realization [of the idea] in every part of the Greek world which continued to be under foreign rule. Because the Greeks of Cyprus have considered themselves historically and culturally to be Greeks, the "Great Idea" has had an intense appeal. Thus, when the church fathers called upon the Cypriots [Greeks] to fight for union with Greece, it did not require much effort to heat up emotions." (Kyriakos Markides, *The Rise and Fall of the Cyprus Republic*, pp. 10–11.)

Megali Idea is no longer a "politically correct" term among most Greek scholars. Greek membership in the European Union and the recent rapprochement with Turkey have helped to diminish this concept and the ideals associated with it.

537. We have evolved one strategy at the Center for the Study of Mind and Human Interaction that requires psychoanalysts' collaboration with other disciplines (See Volkan, "Tree Model"). Briefly, this method, nicknamed the "tree model" to reflect that the slow growth and branching of a tree are analogous to the way our process unfolds, has three basic components or phases:

1) Psychopolitical diagnosis of the situation
2) Psychopolitical dialogues between members of opposing groups

3) Collaborative actions and institutions that grow out of the dialogue process

During the first phase, which includes in-depth interviews with a wide range of members of the groups involved, the interdisciplinary team of clinicians, historians, political scientists, and others begins to understand the main aspects of the relationship between the two groups and the surrounding situation to be addressed. During the psychopolitical dialogues—which consist of a series of multi-day meetings over several years—resistances are brought to the surface, articulated, and interpreted so that more realistic communication can take place. In order for the insights gained to have an impact on social and political policy as well as on the populace at large, the final phase requires the collaborative development of concrete actions, programs, and institutions. This methodology allows several disciplines to work together to articulate and work through underlying psychological and historical aspects of the tensions and then operationalize what is learned so that more peaceful coexistence can be achieved.

538. A process similar to the development of an entitlement ideology is revanchism. "Revanchists are those with a grievance which they seek to rectify at all costs, the world being out of joint for them until retribution is exacted" (Roger Scruton, *A Dictionary of Political Thought*, p. 405). Examples of revanchism among modern political movements include the Israeli-Palestinian conflict and the conflict in Northern Ireland. The groups involved reactivate feelings of victimhood and feel an enhanced sense of entitlement for revenge. In this context, with two groups in conflict, and each feeling entitled to the same land, creating lasting agreements on crucial issues is almost impossible.

9

539. Gabriele Ast has written about a German man she analyzed whose experience was similar to Fazile's. When this man was four years old, his parents planned to escape from East Berlin to West Berlin. They could not speak openly in front of their child about their plans for fear that the child would tell others. Though German, they had originally lived in Hungary and also spoke Hungarian, so when making their plans they spoke only in Hungarian. But the little boy nevertheless knew what was happening. Furthermore, he knew that if he screamed or called the police as the escape was taking place, he could in essence kill his parents. The family escaped to West Berlin successfully, but the boy internalized and kept his power to destroy. When this man, as an adult, came to see Dr. Ast, he still felt guilt for possessing the power to damage or kill his parents. He had developed a rigid, obsessive personality organization in order to keep his "power" under control. See Gabriele Ast, "A crocodile in a pouch."

540. Robert S. Robins, a professor of political science at Tulane University, and Jerrold M. Post, a professor of psychiatry at George Washington University, have studied the malign power of paranoia in a variety of contexts and suggest

that the paranoid dynamic has been a factor in every social disaster of this century. They illustrate how a leader's innate suspiciousness and wish to protect his or her followers from dangerous "others" can sometimes overshoot benevolent objectives with disastrous results (see Robert S. Robins and Jerrold M. Post, *Political Paranoia: The Psychopolitics of Hatred*).

541. The underground writings of Naim and Sami Frasheri, two brothers, were instrumental in creating a sense of patriotism among Albanians in this period.

542. The Serbs consider Kosovo as a location of their group "soul." Since Prizren is also in Kosovo, Albanians also feel that this province is sacred for them. The situation to some extent is similar to Israeli and Palestinian arguments about Jerusalem, which is "sacred" for both parties.

543. In 1913, Serb, Greek, and Bulgarian armies defeated their former rulers, the Ottomans, who still controlled Albania. The war broke out because Serbia, Greece, and Bulgaria wanted to expand into Ottoman territory they considered rightfully theirs.

544. Some Albanians also fled to Turkey at this time. Today, in addition to Albanians living in Kosovo, about 23 percent of ethnic Albanians live in Macedonia; Montenegro has far fewer.

545. During World War I, Austrian, French, Italian, Greek, Montenegrin and Serb armies were on Albanian soil.

546. Robert Frank: "Jungle accounting: Auditors in Albania pick through rubble of pyramid schemes," *The Wall Street Journal Europe*, August 6, 1998, pp. 1, 7.

547. Frank, ibid., p. 1.

548. The Carter Center was following the World Bank's definition of the term "participation": "Participation is a process through which stakeholders influence and share control over development initiatives and the decisions and resources which affect them" (*The World Bank Participation Sourcebook*, Washington: IBRD/The World Bank, p.xi. This book outlines methods for "stakeholders'" consultation and various outreach techniques to garner the public input.). Implicit in this definition is the identification of "stakeholders" as the people affected by the development initiatives—in this case, the Albanians.

549. There were private individuals and organizations in Albania who also were giving serious thought to Albanian economic development. Among them was Vebi Velija, a prominent industrialist originally from Macedonia (see Vebi Velija, *Quo Vadis Albania?*). He had a vision for economic development strategy, but when I met him in 1998 at his plush office, he expressed frustration with those in power who, he said, would interfere with his attempts for their own personal and political reasons.

550. In 2000, Joyce Neu became the director of the Joan B. Kroc Institute for Peace and Justice at the University of San Diego in California.

551. Joyce Neu, Norman Itzkowitz and I already had many years experience

of working together. Dr. Neu and I had accompanied former president Jimmy Carter, Rosalynn Carter, and other International Negotiation Network (INN) members on a 1995 trip to Senegal for discussions and evaluations of the political conditions in various African states. The three of us were among the veterans of the Center for the Study of Mind and Human Interaction and the Carter Center's joint project in Estonia, where we brought together Estonian parliamentarians and influential citizens to have a series of "unofficial" psychopolitical dialogues with the Russian ambassador to Estonia, Russian parliamentarians, and scholars and leaders of the Russian community living in Estonia (Vamık D. Volkan, *Bloodlines*; Joyce Neu and Vamık D. Volkan, "Developing a methodology for conflict prevention: The case of Estonia").

552. See Chapter 2 for a discussion of the psychological concept of basic trust.

553. See Nikita Khrushchev, *Khrushchev Remembers*.

554. I am indebted to Joyce Neu for coining this term.

555. Nicolas C. Pano, "Albania."

556. William E. Griffith, *Albania and the Sino-Soviet Rift*; see also, Elez Biberaj, *Albania and China: A Study of an Unequal Alliance*.

557. This ruthlessness—or perhaps capriciousness—may have extended to Hoxha's personal life as well. When Mehmet Shehu—Hoxha's closest friend, commander of the Partisan resistance during the National Liberation War, and second-in-command in Enver Hoxha's administration—died in 1981, many Albanians believed that Shehu committed suicide. But others believed that Shehu had been shot by his "friend," Enver Hoxha, because Shehu had recently opposed the regime's isolationist policies and had been accused of being a Yugoslav spy.

Albanian psychologist Edmont Dragoti told me in 1998 that he had read a letter that Shehu wrote to Hoxha not long before he died, which is apparently in the possession of an Albanian physician who was close to Hoxha and now lives in Denmark. According to Dragoti, Shehu writes that he knows that the dictator no longer accepts him and complains that Hoxha is treating him as he treated Nacho Spiro (another member of the communist elite who had committed suicide). In the letter, Shehu also begs Hoxha not to punish his (Shehu's) children. It is this statement that convinces Dragoti that Shehu did in fact commit suicide, for suicides were "punished after death" under the Hoxha regime by being declared enemies of the state, thereby afflicting their families with a "black spot."

Dragoti has told me that one of the reasons that Hoxha turned against his right-hand man involved an indirect association with another family bearing a "black spot." Shehu's eldest son became engaged to a young woman who, it became known, had relatives living in the United States who opposed Hoxha. Some weeks after Shehu died, this son, twenty-three years old, killed himself. Shehu's widow was imprisoned, and his remaining son and daughter sent into internal exile.

As a youth, Dragoti was a friend of Skender Shehu, the second son. After his friend's exile to a mountainous location, Dragoti and another student were sent to do some work in the village where the young man was living. One afternoon, the two youth came across Skender on the village road; young Dragoti wanted to rush to greet his friend, whatever enemy his father may have been to the state. As Dragoti tried to approach, Skender cried out, tears in his eyes, "Do not come near me—it will be dangerous for you!" A few months later, Dragoti learned that Skender too had committed suicide. As an adult, Dragoti named his only son after his lost friend.

558. I have been told that, under the Hoxha regime, rent for an apartment could be as cheap as ten cents per month.

559. See: Amnesty International's 1984 report: *Albania: Political Imprisonment and the Law*; Anton Logoreci, *The Albanians: Europe's Forgotten Survivors*; Arshi Pipa, "Party ideology and purges in Albania"; Gjon Sinishta, *The Fulfilled Promise: A Documentary Account of Religious Persecution in Albania*; and Bernhard Tonnes, "Religious Persecution in Albania."

560. Many village mosques are being built with funds coming mostly from rich Arab countries. The imams make sure that children are attracted to the mosques. In early 1998 Tirana, Hafiz Sabri Koci was the head of the Muslim community, and he tried to re-establish Muslim customs as they had existed during the Ottoman period. Enver Hoxha had imprisoned him for twenty-five years. He seemed to me resolved to erase the "godlessness" of the Hoxha regime with a silent and stubborn determination. The Albanian Catholic leader, Rvok Mirdita, had lived in the United States until after the communist period and was able to raise sufficient funds to repair and modernize the Catholic Cathedral in Tirana. In fact, in 1998 the Cathedral stood out as the only manicured area in the middle of dilapidated buildings in the city. The orthodox patriarch in Istanbul selected an outsider, a Greek archbishop, to reconstruct the Albanian Autocephalous Orthodox Church. In 1998, this appointment continued to be a source of controversy within the Albanian orthodox community.

561. The only hero from Albania's past whose representation was allowed during the Hoxha regime was Skanderbeg. Born George Castriotes in 1405, Skanderbeg converted to Islam, but, in 1443, after the Ottomans lost to the Serbs at Nish, Skanderbeg collected about 12,000 men, massacred the Turks in Albania, and reconverted to Christianity. Pope Nicholas V declared him a champion of Christendom. He died in 1467, and by 1502, all Albania was under Ottoman control. My visit to the Skanderbeg museum in Krujes, not far from Tirana, gave the impression that Hoxha may have seen himself as a kind of extension of this past national hero; though his religious associations were ignored, Skanderbeg did function as a symbol for Hoxha's own revolt against existing authority.

562. Afrim Dangellia, personal communication, June 2001. For discussion of Sebek, see Chapter 2.

563. For some reason, drinking alcoholic beverages was not prohibited. Some Albanians with whom I spoke in 1998 mentioned that they found this odd, since

all other "pleasures" were outlawed.

564. In the schools, teachers constantly preached the idea that Hoxha was a god-like figure with magnificent powers of clairvoyance, an echo of the Nazi propaganda I discussed in the last chapter. School-distributed propaganda also equated Hoxha with the nation, isolating his image from the dangerous and envious rest of the world, making him unique among all humanity in his goodness, power, and knowledge. Again, as in Nazi schools, Hoxha-era Albanian schools were one of the regime's instruments for undermining children's sense of basic trust.

565. When communism collapsed in Albania, Fazile was aware that many people who had suffered under Enver Hoxha much less severely than she asked for compensation for their sufferings. She could not bring herself to seek financial help for herself, however; as we understand it, filing for compensation would have ruined her unique sense of inner "badness."

566. Westerners may remember the remarkable images of similar symbolic "demotion" that occurred across the former communist countries. When Hoxha was alive, his colossal gilded statue dominated the main square of Tirana, the Skanderbeg Square. When my colleagues and I were in Tirana in early 1998, all public signs of Hoxha had been erased, so I never saw this statue, which was demolished in 1991. After seeing photographs of it, however, I have since realized that I have seen its "twin" in Gori, the Republic of Georgia, where Joseph Stalin was born. The statue of Stalin in Gori still stands.

567. On our first day in Albania, we learned of unrest in Shkodra, a city of the north. The next day, the U.S. ambassador, Marisa Lino, advised us not to travel more than 25–30 miles out of Tirana. At night, we heard gunshots. Our observations were therefore limited to Tirana, villages outside of Tirana, and towns such as Kruje, Durres, and Kavaje.

568. Berisha and parliamentarians from his party were not present when the vote was taken.

569. The name refers to the powerful tribal chiefs in Northern Albania, the Dukagjini, mentioned in Vatican documents as early as 1216. When the Ottomans came, Dukagjini chiefs became Muslims and ancient Albanian beliefs and customs were merged with Islamic laws. The village elders interpreted the Law of Lek and decided when blood should be shed to the honor of the injured and so on.

570. In 1994, a "Blood Feud Reconciliation" agency was established in the northern Albanian city of Shkodra to deal with the situation, but most efforts were unsuccessful.

571. Edmont Dragoti, personal communication.

572. See Scott Anderson, "The curse of blood and vengeance," *The New York Times Magazine*, pp. 28–35. 44. 54–57, December 26, 1999

573. Anderson, ibid., pp. 55–56. Interestingly, Spahia's organization cements each successful mediation with a formal ceremony including all members of both

families; "'Otherwise, someone can decide they are not bound by the peace, and the blood [feud] will start again'" (qtd. Anderson, ibid., p. 55).

574. Anderson, ibid., p. 31.

575. Dragoti, "Blood revenge: Ancient crimes return to haunt Albania."

576. My observations of Albania in early 1998 strongly echoed Nancy Caro Hollander's writings on the legacy of state terror in Latin America *(Love in Time of Hate: Liberation Psychology in Latin America*; "The legacy of state terror and the new social violence in Latin America"; "The secret behind the uniform: An evil partnership"). Hollander, based at the Psychoanalytic Center of California, has studied in great depth the cruel domination of terrorist states in Latin America from the 1960s through the 1980s. Wherever terrorist or Stalinist regimes ruled in Latin America, the governments implemented policies of "disappearing," torturing, and murdering citizens in order to impose a passive consensus within the population. Individual behavior in terrorist states was therefore characterized by silence, inexpressiveness, inhibition and self-censorship, use of "primitive" defense mechanisms (such as projection, splitting, magical thinking, an inability to distinguish between internal anxiety and external fear), and difficulty in mourning or inability to mourn. The terrorist state splits society into victimizers, victims, and bystanders who, as Hollander notes, live under constant threat and anticipatory anxiety of suddenly being thrust into the victim position. When the terrorist state comes to an end, such sentiments do not altogether disappear since they are internalized over time. If political leadership following state terror is not sufficiently strong, confusion ensues and problems of basic trust complicate relationships,leading to further societal regression.

577. My Finnish psychiatrist friend Henrik Wahlberg had been working for the World Health Organization (WHO) in neighboring Macedonia. He was instrumental in my receiving a temporary consultant position at the WHO and my visits to both Albania and Macedonia in late 2000.

578. Ordinarily, people do not experience such drastic changes after only a few "therapeutic" interviews with a psychoanalyst. During my travels to traumatized societies, however, I have observed on several occasions that in certain circumstances—such as Fazile's decades-long silence and her sense of safety with Itzkowitz and me—traumatized individuals can experience dramatic internal changes following brief interventions.

579. One night during my 2000 visit, Sali Berisha's party members held a rally at the Skanderbeg Square, shouting slogans against the existing Albanian government, whom they consider to be an extension of old communists. I was told that Berisha himself would speak, so I began walking through the crowd toward the podium in the hopes of meeting him again. But he was not present after all, and being in the middle of so many people directed by the same emotion—and not sharing that emotion—suddenly frightened me, and I quickly left the Square.

580. See also Joyce Neu and Vamık Volkan, "Developing a methodology for

conflict prevention: The case of Estonia" and Vamık Volkan, *Bloodlines*.

581. See William Drozdiak, "NATO Set to Send Troops to Macedonia," *The Washington Post*, June 21, 2001, p. A19.

coda

582. Norman Itzkowitz, "Unity out of diversity," pp. 173–174.

583. Obviously some people whom we do not know symbolically represent people who are close to us, such as a leader who functions as a father figure for an individual. In such a case, mourning for a person whom we do not know is possible.

584. Richard Goldstone, "Crimes against humanity—forgetting the victims," The 2001 Ernest Jones Lecture, The British Psychoanalytical Society, September 25, 2001.

585. Goldstone, ibid.

586. Goldstone, ibid.

587. Goldstone, ibid.

588. Vamık Volkan, *The Need to Have Enemies and Allies*.

/ bibliography

Abercrombie, M.L.J. (1960). *The Anatomy of Judgment*. London: Hutchinson.

Abse, D. Wilfred (1974). *Clinical Notes on Group-Analytic Psychotherapy*. Charlottesville, VA: University Press of Virginia.

Abse, D. Wilfred and Lucie Jessner (1961). The psychodynamic aspect of leadership. *Daedalus*, 90: 693–710.

Abse, D. Wilfred and Richard Ulman (1977). Charismatic political leadership and collective regression. In Robert S. Robins (Ed.), *Psychopathology and Political Leadership* (pp. 35–52). New Orleans: Tulane University Press.

Achen, Christopher H. and Duncan Jane Snidal (1989). Rational deterrence theory and comparative case studies. *World Politics*, 41: 143–169.

Akhtar, Salman (1984). The syndrome of identity diffusion. *American Journal of Psychiatry*, 141: 1381–1385.

——— (1990). Paranoid personality disorder: A synthesis of developmental, dynamic, and descriptive features. *American Journal of Psychiatry*, 44: 5–25.

——— (1992). *Broken Structures: Severe Personality Disorders and Their Treatment*. Northvale, NJ: Jason Aronson.

——— (2003). Dehumanization: Origins, manifestations, and remedies. In Sverre Varvin and Vamık D. Volkan (Eds.) *Violence or Dialogue? Psychoanalytic Insights on Terror and Terrorism* (pp. 131–145). London: International Psychoanalysis Library.

Akhtar, Salman and J. Anderson Thomson (1982). Overview: Narcissistic personality disorder. *American Journal of Psychiatry*, 139: 12–20.

Allison, Graham T. (1971). *The Essence of Decision: Explaining the Cuban Missile Crisis*. Boston: Little Brown.

Allison, Graham T. and Morton H. Halpern (1972). Bureaucratic politics: A paradigm and some policy implications. *World Politics*, 24: 40–79.

Almond, Gabriel A., Sivan, Emmanuel, and Appleby, R. Scott (1995). Fundamentalism: genus and species. In Martin E. Marty and R. Scott Appleby (Ed.), *Fundamentalism Comprehended* (pp. 339-424). Chicago: The University of Chicago Press.

Ambrose, Stephen E. (1989). *Nixon: The Triumph of a Politician*, 1962–1972. New York: Simon and Schuster.

Anderson, Benedict (1990). *Imagined Communities: Reflections on the Origin and Spread of Nationalism*. Philadelphia: Routledge.

Anzieu, Didier (1984). *The Group and the Unconscious*. London: Routledge & Kegan Paul.

Arieli, Yehoshua (1977). National consciousness, Judaism, and Zionism in a violent world. *Mifne*, 16: 4–11.

Arlow, Jacob (1969). Unconscious fantasy and disturbances of conscious experience. *Psychoanalytic Quarterly*, 38: 1–27.

——— (1973). Motivations for peace. In H. Z. Winnik, Rafael Moses, and M. Ostow (Eds.), *Psychological Basis of War* (pp. 193–204). Jerusalem: Jerusalem Academic Press.

Asad, Khaled K. (2000). *A Warrior from Mecca: The Full Story of Osama bin Laden*. (in Arabic). London: PD.

Ast, Gabriele (1991). Interview with Germans about reunification, *Mind and Human Interaction*, 2:100–104

——— (1997). A crocodile in a pouch. In Vamık D. Volkan and Salman Akhtar (Eds.), *The Seed of Madness: Constitution, Environment, and Fantasy in the Organization of the Psychotic Core* (pp. 133-154). Madison, CT: International Universities Press.

Ataturk, Kemal (1952). *Ataturk'un Soylev ve Demecleri (Speeches and Statements of Ataturk)* (Vols 1–2). Istanbul: Turk Inkilap Tarihi Enstitusu.

Aydemir, Sevket Sureyya (1969). *Tek Adam (The Singular Man)* (Vols. 1–3). Istanbul: Remzi Kitabevi.

Balmer, Randall (1989). *Mine Eyes Have Seen the Glory: A Journey into the Evangelical Subculture in America*. New York: Oxford University Press.

Barber, James D. (1977). *The Presidential Character: Predicting Performance in the White House*. Englewood Cliffs, NJ: Prentice-Hall.

Bauer, Otto (1907). *Die Nationalitatenfrage und die Sozialdemokratie*, Reprint, Vienna: Europaverlag, 1975.

Barkun, Michael (1996). Religion, militias, and Oklahoma City: The mind of conspiratorialists. *Terrorism and Political Violence*, 8: 50–64.

——— (1997). The Christian identity movement: Constructing millennialism on the racist right. In Thomas Robbins and Susan Palmer (Eds.), *Millennium, Messiahs and Mayhem* (pp. 247–260). Philadelphia: Routledge.

——— (1999). End-time paranoia: Conspiracy thinking at the millennium's close. In Christopher Kleinhenz and Fanny LeMoine (Eds.), *Fearful Hope: Approaching the New Millennium* (pp. 170-181). Wisconsin: University of Wisconsin Press.

Barner-Barry, Carol and Robert Rosenwein (1985). *Psychological Perspectives on Politics*. Englewood Cliffs, NJ: Prentice-Hall.

Barston, Ronald P. (1988). *Modern Diplomacy*. New York: Longman.

Baynes, Norman H. (1942). *The Speeches of Adolf Hitler*, April 1922–August 1939 (two volumes). New York: Oxford University Press.

Bennigsen, Alexandre and Marie Broxup (1983). *The Islamic threat to the Soviet Union*. Beckenham: Croom Helm.

Bergmann, Martin S. (1973). Limitations of method in psychoanalytic biography: A historical inquiry. *Journal of the American Psychoanalytic Association*, 21: 833–850.

Berke, Joseph H, Stella Pierides, Andrea Sabbadini, and Stanley Schneider (1998). *Even Paranoids Have Enemies*. London: Routledge.

Berman, Jeffrey (1994). *Diaries to an English Professor: Pain and Growth in the Classroom*. Amherst: University of Massachusetts Press.

Bernard, Viola W., Perry Ottenberg, and Fritz Redlich (1973). Dehumanization: A composite psychological defense in relation to modern war. In N. Sanford and C. Comstock (Eds.), *Sanctions of Evil: Sources of Social Destructiveness* (pp. 102–124). San Francisco: Jossey-Bass.

Biberaj, Elez (1986). *Albania and China: A Study of Unequal Alliance*. Boulder, CO: Westview Press.

Biedermann, Hans (1992). *Dictionary of Symbolism: Cultural Icons and the Meaning Behind Them* (J. Hulbert, Trans.). New York: Facts on File.

Bion, Wilfred R. (1961). *Experiences in Groups*. London: Tavistock Publications.

Blos, Peter (1979). *The Adolescent Passage: Developmental Issues*. New York: International Universities Press.

Bodansky, Yossef (1999). *Bin Laden: The Man Who Declared War on America*. New York: Random House.

Bonaparte, Marie (1940). Time and the unconscious. *International Journal of Psycho-Analysis*, 21: 427–468.

———— (1947). *Myths of War*. London: Imago.

Booth, Wayne C. (1986). Pluralism in the classroom. *Critical Inquiry*, 12: 468–479.

Boyer, L. Bryce (1998). *Regression and Countertransference*. Northvale, NJ: Jason Aronson.

Bramsted, Ernest K. (1965). *Goebbels and National Socialist Propaganda*. East Lansing, MI: Michigan State University Press.

Breault, Marc and King, Martin (1993). *Inside the Cult: A Member's Chilling Account of Madness and Depravity* in David Koresh's Compound. New York: Signet Books.

Brenner, Ira (2002). Book review and commentary: *Hitler: Diagnosis of a Destructive Prophet*, by Fritz Redlich. *Journal of Applied Psychoanalytic Studies*, 4: 99–105.

Broomberg, Norbert and Verna V. Small (1983). *Hitler's Psychopathology*. New York: International Universities Press.

Brown, James A. C. (1963). *Techniques of Persuasion: From Propaganda to Brainwashing*. Middlesex, England: Penguin Books.

Burns, James M. (1978). *Leadership*. New York: Harper Torchbooks.

Butler, Thomas (1993). Yugoslavia mon amour. *Mind and Human Interaction*, 4:120-128.

Cain, A. C. and B. S. Cain (1964). On replacing a child. *Journal of American Academy of Child Psychiatry*, 3: 443–456.

Chamberlain, Sigrid (1997). *Adolf Hitler, die deutsche Mutter und ihr erstes Kind Uber zwei NS-Erziehungsbucher* (Adolf Hitler, the German Mother, and her First Child: About two National Socialist Education Books). Giessen: Psychosozial Verlag.

Chasseguet-Smirgel, Janine (1984). *The Ego Ideal*. New York: W. W. Norton.

——— (1990). Creativity and Perversion. New York: W. W. Norton.

——— (1996). Blood and nation. *Mind and Human Interaction*, 7:31–36.

Cullberg-Weston, Marta (1997). When words lose their meaning: From societal crisis to ethnic cleansing. *Mind and Human Interaction*, 8:20–32.

de Swaan, Abram (1996). Widening circle of disidentification: On the psycho-socio-genesis of the hatred of distant strangers; Reflections on Rwanda. Paper presented at the conference "Civilization and its Enduring Discontents," Bellagio, Italy, September.

Deuel, Wallace (1942). *People Under Hitler*. New York: Harcourt, Brace, and Company.

DeVos, George (1975). Ethnic pluralism: Conflict and accommodation. In George De Vos and L. Komanucci-Ross (Eds.), *Ethnic Identity: Cultural Continuities and Change* (pp. 5–41). Palo Alto, CA: Mayfield.

Dragoti, Edmond (1996). Blood revenge: Ancient crimes return to haunt Albania. *Psychology International*, 7:4:1-3. Washington: American Psychological Association Office of International Affairs.

Ehrenreich, Barbara (1997). *Blood Rites: Origins and History of the Passions of War*. New York: Metropolitan Books.

Emde, Robert N. (1988a). Development terminable and interminable I: Innate and motivational factors from infancy. *International Journal of Psycho-Analysis*, 69: 23–41.

——— (1988b). Development terminable and interminable II: Recent psychoanalytic theory and therapeutic considerations. *International Journal of Psycho-Analysis*, 69: 283–296.

——— (1991). Positive emotions for psychoanalytic theory: Surprises from infancy research and new directions. *Journal of American Psychoanalytic Association* (Supplement), 39: 5–44.

Erikson, Erik H. (1950). Growth and crisis in the healthy personality. *In Identity and the Life Cycle*. New York: International Universities Press.

——— (1956). The problem of ego identity. *Journal of the American Psychoanalytic Association*, 4: 56–121.

——— (1958). *Young Man Luther*. New York: Norton.

——— (1966). Ontogeny of ritualization. In Rudolph Loewenstein (Ed.), *Psychoanalysis: A General Psychology* (pp. 601–621). New York: International Universities Press.

——— (1977). *Toys and Reasons: Stages in the Ritualization of Experience*. New

York: W.W. Norton.

——— (1985). *Childhood and Society*. New York: W. W. Norton.

Etheredge, Lloyd (1979). Hardball politics: A model. *Political Psychology*, 1: 3–26.

Etzioni, Amitai (1967). Mixed scanning: A "third" approach to decision-making. *Public Administration Review*, 27: 385–392.

Fairbairn, W. Ronald (1935). The sociological significance of communism considered in the light of psychoanalysis. In Ronald Fairbairn (Ed.), *Psychoanalytic Studies of the Personality* (pp. 233–246). New York: Routledge, 1986.

Falk, Avner (1974). Border symbolism. *Psychoanalytic Quarterly*, 43: 650–660.

——— (1983). Border symbolism revisited. *International Review of Psycho-Analysis*, 10: 215–220.

——— (1985). Aspects of political psychobiography. *Political Psychology*, 6: 605–619.

——— (2001). Osama bin Laden and America: A psychobiographical study. *Mind and Human Interaction*, 12: 161–172.

Fenichel, Otto (1937). Early stages of ego development. In *The Collected Papers of Otto Fenichel*, Vol 2 (pp. 25–48). New York: Norton.

Fest, Joachim C. (1970). *The Face of the Third Reich*. New York: Pantheon.

Flannery, Harry W. (1942). *Assignment to Berlin*. New York: A. A. Knopf.

Foulkes, Sigmund H. and E. James Anthony (1957). *Group Psychotherapy*. London: Penguin Books.

Freud, Anna (1936). The ego and the mechanisms of defense. In *The Writings of Anna Freud* (Vol. 2). New York: International Universities Press.

Freud, Sigmund (1900). The interpretation of dreams. *The Standard Edition of the Complete Psychological Works of Sigmund Freud* (James Strachey, Trans.), 4-5: ix–xxxii, 1–267. London: Hogarth Press, 1953.

——— (1901). Fragments of an analysis of a case of hysteria. *The Standard Edition of the Complete Psychological Works of Sigmund Freud* (James Strachey, Trans.), 7: 3–122. London: Hogarth Press, 1955.

——— (1901). The psychopathology of everyday life. *The Standard Edition of the Complete Psychological Works of Sigmund Freud* (James Strachey, Trans.), 6: London: Hogarth Press, 1955.

——— (1908). Hysterical phantasies and their relations to bisexuality. *The Standard Edition of the Complete Psychological Works of Sigmund Freud* (James Strachey, Trans.), 9: 155–166. London: Hogarth Press, 1959.

——— (1910). Leonardo da Vinci and a memory of his childhood. *Standard Edition* (James Strachey, Trans.), 7: 3–122. London: Hogarth Press, 1955

——— (1913). Totem and taboo. *The Standard Edition of the Complete Psychological Works of Sigmund Freud* (James Strachey, Trans.), 13: 1-162. London: Hogarth Press, 1955.

——— (1917). Taboo of virginity. *The Standard Edition of the Complete Psychological Works of Sigmund Freud* (James Strachey, Trans.), 11: 191–208. London: Hogarth Press, 1961.

———— (1921). Group psychology and the analysis of the ego. *The Standard Edition of the Complete Psychological Works of Sigmund Freud* (James Strachey, Trans.),18: 63–143. London: Hogarth Press, 1955.

———— (1926). Inhibitions, symptoms and anxiety. *The Standard Edition of the Complete Psychological Works of Sigmund Freud* (James Strachey, Trans.), 20: 77–175. London: Hogarth Press, 1959.

———— (1927). The future of an illusion. *The Standard Edition of the Complete Psychological Works of Sigmund Freud* (James Strachey, Trans.), 21: 5-56. London: Hogarth Press, 1961.

———— (1930). Civilization and its discontents. *The Standard Edition of the Complete Psychological Works of Sigmund Freud* (James Strachey, Trans.), 21: 59–145. London: Hogarth Press, 1961.

———— (1932). Why war? *The Standard Edition of the Complete Psychological Works of Sigmund Freud* (James Strachey, Trans.), 22: 194–215. London: Hogarth Press, 1964.

———— (1939). Moses and monotheism, *The Standard Edition of the Complete Psychological Works of Sigmund Freud* (James Strachey, Trans.), 23: TK. London: Hogarth Press, 1964.

———— (1941). Address to the Society of B'nai B'rith. *The Standard Edition of the Complete Psychological Works of Sigmund Freud* (James Strachey, Trans.), 20: 271–274. London: Hogarth Press, 1961.

Friedman, Menachem (1990). Jewish zealots: Conservative versus innovative. In Emmanuel Sivan and Menachem Friedman (Eds.) *Religious Radicalism and Politics in the Middle East* (pp. 120-152). Albany, NY: SUNY Press.

Frost, Brian (1998). *Struggling to Forgive: Nelson Mandela and South Africa's Search for Reconciliation*. London: Harper Collins.

Furhammer, Leif and Folke Isaksson (1971). *Politics and Film*. New York: Praeger.

Gardner, M. Robert (1994). *On Trying to Teach: The Mind in Correspondence*. Hillsdale, NJ: The Analytic Press, Inc.

Gedo, John E. (1972). The methodology of psychoanalytic biography. *Journal of the American Psychoanalytic Association*, 20: 638–649.

George, Alexander L. (1969). The "operational code": A neglected approach to the study of political leaders and decision-making. *International Studies Quarterly*, 23: 190–222.

George, Alexander L. and Juliette L. George (Eds.) (1998). *Presidential Personality and Performance*. Boulder, CO: Westview.

Gittler, Joseph B. (1977). Toward defining an ethnic minority. *International Journal of Group Tensions*, 7: 4–19.

Glass, James (1989). *Private Terror/Public Life: Psychosis and Politics of Community*. Ithaca, NY: Cornell University Press.

Glover, Edward (1947). *War, Sadism, and Pacifism: Further Essays on Group Psychology and War*. London: Allen and Unwin.

Gorenberg, Gershom (2000). *The End of Days: Fundamentalism and the Struggle for the Temple Mount*. New York: Free Press.

Greenacre, Phyllis (1958). Early physical determinants in the development of the sense of identity. *Journal of the American Psychoanalytic Association*, 6: 612–627.

——— (1970). The transitional object and the fetish: With special reference to the role of illusion. *International Journal of Psycho-Analysis*, 51: 447-456.

Greenspan, Stanley (1989). *The Development of the Ego: Implications for Personality Theory, Psychopathology and the Psychotherapeutic Process*. Madison, CT: International Universities Press.

Gregory, James (1995). *Goodbye Bafana: Nelson Mandela, My Prisoner, My Friend*. London: Headline Book Publishing.

Griffith, William E. (1963). *Albania and the Sino-Soviet Rift*. Cambridge, MA: MIT Press.

Gruen, Arno (2000) *Der Fremde in uns (Stranger Within Us)*. Frankfurt: Klett-Corta.

——— (2001). Surrendering identity: Herman Goring and Rudolf Hess. *Mind and Human Interaction*, 12: 35–51.

Guttman, Roy (1993). *A Witness to Genocide*. New York: MacMillan.

Haarer, Johanna (1937). Mutterschaft und Familienpflege imneuen Reich" (Motherhood and Family Care in the New Reich) in *Beitrage zur Volkslehr und Gemeinschaftspflege (Essays on Ethnology and Community Care)*. Munich: Herausgegeben von der Volksbildungs Kanzlei.

——— (1942). *Die Deutche Mutter und ihr erstes Kind. (The German Mother and Her First Child.)* Munich: J.F. Lehmann.

——— (1943). *Mutter, erzahl von Adolf Hitler (Mother, Tell about Adolf Hitler)*. Munich: J. F. Lehmanns Verlag.

Haldeman, H. Robert (1994). *Haldeman Diaries: Inside the Nixon White House*. New York: G.P. Putnam and Sons.

Hall, Budd L. and J. Robby Kidd (Eds.) (1978). *Adult Education: A Design for Action*. Oxford: Pergamon.

Harle, Vilho (2000). *The Enemy with a Thousand Faces: The Tradition of the Other in Western Political Thought and History*. Westport, CT: Praeger.

Hartle, T. W. and M. J. Halperin (1980). Rational and incremental decision-making: An exposition and critique with illustrations. In M.J. White (Ed.), *Managing Public Systems: Analytic Techniques for Public Administration*. North Scituate, MA: Duxbury Press.

Hartman, John J. (2000). Polish-Jewish ethnic conflict: Threats to identity and the failure to mourn. *Mind and Human Interaction*, 11: 27–41.

Hawley, John S. and Proudfoot, Wayne (1994). Introduction. In John S. Hawley (Ed.) *Fundamentalism and Gender* (pp. 5-44). New York: Oxford Universities Press.

Heimannsberg, Barbara and Christoph J. Schmidt (1993). *The Collective Silence: German Identity and the Legacy of Shame*. Hillsdale, NJ: The Analytic Press, Inc.

Hemingway, Ernest (1938). *The Fifth Column and the First Forty-Nine Stories.* New York: Charles Scribner's Sons.

Hersh, Seymour M. (1983). *The Price of Power: Kissinger in the Nixon White House.* New York: Summit Books.

Herzfeld, Michael (1986). *Ours Once More: Folklore, Ideology, and the Making of Modern Greece.* New York: Pella.

Heston, Leonard and Renate Heston (1980). *The Medical Casebook of Adolf Hitler: His Illnesses, Doctors, and Drugs.* New York: Stein and Day Publishing.

Hinzen, H. and V.H. Hundsdorfer (1979). *The Tanzanian Experience: Education for Liberation and Development.* Hamburg: UNESCO Institute for Education.

Hitler, Adolf (1925, 1927). *Mein Kampf (My Struggle).* Boston: Houghton Mifflin Company, 1962.

Holden, Matthew (1988). Bargaining and command by heads of U.S. government departments. *The Social Science Journal,* 25: 255–276.

Hollander, Nancy (1997) *Love in Time of Hate: Liberation Psychology in Latin America.* New Jersey: Rutgers University Press.

———— (1999). The legacy of state terror and the new social violence in Latin America. Paper presented at the International Conference "At the Threshold of the Millennium," Lima, Peru, April 14–21.

———— (2000). The secret behind the uniform: An evil partnership. *Mind and Human Interaction,* 11: 108-118.

Hopwood, Derek (1983). A movement in renewal in Islam. In Denis MacEoin and Ahmed Al-Shahi (Eds.) *Islam in the Modern World* (pp. 109-118). New York: St. Martin Press.

Hourani, Albert (1991). *A History of the Arab Peoples.* Cambridge, MA: Belknap Press.

Howell, W. Nathaniel (1995). "The evil that men do…": Societal effects of the Iraqi occupation of Kuwait. *Mind and Human Interaction,* 6: 150–169.

———— (1997). Islamic revivalism: A cult phenomenon? *Mind and Human Interaction,* 5: 97-103.

Hyman, Anthony (1984). *Afghanistan Under Soviet Domination.* London: McMillan Books.

Ignatiev, Noel (1995). *How the Irish Became White.* London: Routledge.

Ihalainen, O., R. Hirvenoja, and M. Tuovinen (1972). Psychic factors in sauna bath habits. *Psychiatria Fennica,* 3: 207–212.

Inamdar, Subhash C. (2001). *Muhammad and the Rise of Islam: The Creation of Group Identity.* Madison, CT: Psychosocial Press.

Ishaq, Ibn (1955). *The Life of Muhammad: A Translation of Ishaq's Sirat Rasul Allah* (A. Guillaume, Trans., with introduction and notes). London: Oxford University Press.

Inderbitzin, Lawrence B. and T. Levy Steven (1990). Unconscious fantasy: A reconsideration of the concept. *Journal of the American Psychoanalytic Association,* 38: 113–130.

Isaacs, Susan (1948). The nature and function of fantasy. In Melanie Klein, Paula Heimann, Susan Isaacs and Joann Riviere (Eds.), *Development of Psychoanalysis* (pp. 67–121). London: Hogarth Press, 1973.

Itzkowitz, Norman (1972). *The Ottoman Empire and Islamic Tradition*. New York: Alfred A. Knopf.

———— (2001). Unity out of diversity. *Mind and Human Interaction*, 12: 173–175

Itzkowitz, Norman and Vamık D. Volkan, The demonization of the other. Unpublished paper.

Jacobson, Edith (1964). *The Self and the Object World*. New York: International Universities Press.

Janis, Irving L. and Leon Mann (1977). *Decision Making: A Psychological Analysis of Conflict, Choice, and Commitment*. New York: Free Press.

Jeffery, Inez Cope (1999) *Inside Russia: The Life and Times of Zoya Zarubina*. Austin: Eakin Press.

Jervis, Robert N. (1986). Representativeness in foreign policy judgment. *Political Psychology* 7:483–505.

Jervis, Robert N., Richard N. Lebow and Janice G. Stein. (1985). *Psychology of Deterrence*. Baltimore: The John Hopkins University Press.

Jowett, Garth S. and Victoria O'Donnell (1992). *Propaganda and Persuasion*. New York: Sage Publications.

Julius, Demetrios (1991). The practice of Track Two Diplomacy in the Arab-Israeli Conferences. In Vamık Volkan, Joseph Montville, and Demetrios Julius (Eds.), Unofficial Diplomacy At Work, vol. 2 of *The Psychodynamics of International Relationships* (pp. 193–205). Lexington, MA: Lexington Books.

Kafka, John (1989). *Multiple Realities in Clinical Practice*. New Haven: Yale University Press.

Kakar, Sudhir (1996). *The Colors of Violence: Cultural Identities, Religion and Conflict*. Chicago: The University of Chicago Press.

Kaplan, Robert D. (1993). *Balkan Ghosts: A Journey through History*. New York: Vintage Books.

Kassam, Yusef (1978). *The Adult Education Revolution in Tanzania*. Nairobi: Shungwaya Publishers Ltd.

Katan, Annie (1961). Some thoughts about the role of verbalization in early childhood. *The Psychoanalytic Study of the Child*, 16: 184–188. New York: International Universities Press.

Kecmanovic, Dusan (1996). *The Mass Psychology of Ethnonationalism*. New York: Plenum.

Kedourie, Elie (1970). *The Chatham House Version and Other Middle Eastern Studies*. London: Weidenfeld & Nicholson.

Kernberg, Otto F. (1966). Structural derivatives of object-relationships. *International Journal of Psychoanalysis*, 47: 236–253.

————. (1970). A psychoanalytic classification of character pathology. *Journal of*

340 / vamık volkan

the American Psychoanalytic Association, 18: 800–822.

———— (1975). *Borderline Conditions and Pathological Narcissism*. New York: Jason Aronson.

———— (1976). *Object Relations Theory and Clinical Psychoanalysis*. New York: Jason Aronson.

———— (1980). *Internal World and External Reality: Object Relations Theory Applied*. New York: Jason Aronson.

———— (1989). Mass psychology through the analytic lens. Paper presented at the meeting "Through the Looking Glass: Freud's Impact on Contemporary Culture," Philadelphia September 23.

———— (1992). *Aggression in Personality Disorders and Perversion*. New Haven: Yale University Press.

Kestenberg, Judith and Brenner, Ira (1996). *The Last Witness*. Washington, DC: American Psychiatric Press.

Kets de Vries, Manfred (Ed.) (1984) *The Irrational Executive: Psychoanalytic Explorations in Management*. New York: International Universities Press.

Khalil, Asad K. (2000). *A Warrior from Mecca: The Full Story of Osama bin Laden*. (in Arabic). London: PD.

Kissinger, Henry A. (1979). *The White House Years*. Boston: Little, Brown.

Kogan, Ilany (1995). *The Cry of Mute Children: A Psychoanalytic Perspective of the Second Generation of the Holocaust*. London: Free Association Books.

Kohn, Hans (1944). *Idea of Nationalism*. New York: Macmillan.

Koonz, Claudia (1987). *Mothers in the Fatherland: Women, the Family and Nazi Politics*. New York: St. Martin's Press.

Kris, Ernst (1941). The "danger" of propaganda. In *Selected Papers of Ernst Kris*, pp. 409–432. New Haven: Yale University Press (1975).

———— (1943). Some problems of war propaganda: A note on propaganda new and old. *Psychoanalytic Quarterly*, 12: 381–399.

———— (1944). *Radio Propaganda: Report on Home Broadcasts During the War*. New York: Oxford University Press.

Khrushchev, Nikita (1970). *Khrushchev Remembers*. Boston: Little, Brown.

Kupchan, Charles A. (ed.) (1995). *Nationalism and Nationalities in the New Europe*. Ithaca, NY: Cornell University Press.

Lamy, Phillip (1996). *Millennial Rage: Survivalists, White Supremacists, and the Doomsday Prophesy*. New York: Plenum.

Landes, Richard (2001). Apocalyptic Islam and bin Laden. Paper presented at the Committee of International Relations, Group for the Advancement of Psychiatry (GAP) conference. November 8–10, 2001. White Plains, NY.

———— (2001). The fruitful error: Reconsidering millennial enthusiasm. *Journal of Interdisciplinary History*, 22: 89-98.

Larson, Edward J. (1997). *Summer for the Gods: the Scopes Trial and America's Continuing Debate over Science and Religion*. New York: Basic Books.

Langer, Walter C. (1972). *The Mind of Adolph Hitler*. New York: Basic Books.

Lasswell, Harold D. (1927). *Propaganda Technique in the World War*. New York: Knopf.

——— (1930). *Psychopathology and Politics*. Chicago: University of Chicago Press.

——— (1935). *Propaganda and Promotional Activities*. Minneapolis: University of Minnesota Press.

——— (1935). *World Politics and Personal Insecurity*. New York: McGraw-Hill Book Co.

——— (1938). Foreword. In G. G. Bruntz (Ed.), *Allied Propaganda and the Collapse of the German Empire in 1918* (pp. v–viii). Stanford: Stanford University Press.

Lewis, Bernard (1990). The roots of Muslim rage. *The Atlantic Monthly*, September 20, pp. 47-60.

——— (1996). Islam and liberal democracy: A historical overview. *Journal of Democracy*, 7: 52-63.

——— (2000). Propaganda in the Middle East. Paper presented at the International Conference in Commemoration of the 78th Birthday of Yitzhak Rabin: Patterns of Political Discourse: Propaganda, Incitement, and Freedom of Speech. Sponsored by The Yitzhak Rabin Center for Israel Studies, Tel Aviv, February 28–March 1.

Libaridian, Gerard Jinair (Ed.) (1991). *Armenia at the Crossroads: Democracy and Nationhood in the Post-Soviet Era*. Watertown, MA: Blue Crane Books.

Lifton, Robert (1968). *Death in Life: Survivors of Hiroshima*. New York: Random House.

Lind, John E. (1914). The dream as a simple wish-fulfillment in the Negro. *Psychoanalytic Review*, 1: 295–300.

Lindblom, Charles (1959). The science of muddling through. *Public Administration Review*, 19: 79–88.

Lings, Martin (1983). *Muhammad: His Life Based on the Earliest Sources*. Rochester, VT: Inner Traditions.

Link, Arthur S. (1974). *Wilson: The Road to the White House*. Princeton: Princeton University Press.

Loewald, Hans (1960). On the therapeutic action of psychoanalysis. *International Journal of Psycho-Analysis*, 41: 16–33.

Loewenberg, Peter (1991). Uses of anxiety. *Partisan Review*, 3: 514–525.

——— (1994). The psychological reality of nationalism: Between community and fantasy. *Mind and Human Interaction*, 5: 6–18.

——— (1995). Fantasy and Reality in History. New York: Oxford University Press.

——— (1996). *Decoding the Past: The Psychopolitical Approach*. New Brunswick: Transaction Publishers.

Logoreci, Anton (1977). *The Albanians: Europe's Forgotten Survivors*. Boulder, CO: Westview Press.

MacEoin, Denis (1983). The Shi'i establishment in modern Iran. In Denis

MacEoin and Ahmad Al-Shahi (Eds.) *Islam in the Modern World* (pp. 88-108). New York: St. Martin Press.

Mackey, Sandra (1992). *Passion and Politics: The Turbulent World of the Arabs.* New York: Dutton Press.

Mahler, Margaret S. (1968). *On Human Symbiosis and the Vicissitudes of Individuation.* New York: International Universities Press.

Malkin, Erad and Zeev Zhahor (1992). *Leaders and Leadership: Collected Essays* (in Hebrew). Jerusalem: Zlaman Shezar Center and Israeli Historical Society.

Mandela, Nelson (1994). *Long Walk to Freedom: The Autobiography of Nelson Mandela.* New York: Little, Brown and Company.

Manning, S.W. (1960). Cultural and value factors affecting the Negroes' use of agency services. *Journal of Social Work,* 5: 3–13.

Markides, Kyriakos (1977). *The Rise and Fall of the Cyprus Republic.* New Haven, CT: Yale University Press.

Marsden, Peter (1998). *The Taliban: War, Religion, and the New Order in Afghanistan.* London: Zed Books.

Marty, Martin E. and Appleby, R. Scott, eds. (1995). *Fundamentalism Comprehended.* Chicago: University of Chicago Press.

Masri, As'ad and Vamık D. Volkan (1990). The children of Biet Atfal Al-Sommoud. *Mind and Human Interaction,* 2: 51–53.

Mayer, Jean-Francois (1998). Apocalyptic millennialism in the West: The case of the Solar Temple. Paper read at the University of Virginia, The Critical Incident Analysis Group, November 13.

Mazlish, Bruce (1972). *In Search of Richard Nixon: A Psychohistorical Inquiry.* New York: Basic Books.

Meredith, Martin (1998). *Nelson Mandela: A Biography.* New York: St. Martin's Press.

Mills, Jeannie (1979). *Six Years with God: Life Inside Reverend. Jim Jones's People Temple.* New York: A & W Publishers.

Mintz, I. L. (1971). The anniversary reaction: A response to the unconscious sense of time. *Journal of the American Psychoanalytic Association,* 19: 720–735.

Misselwitz, Irene (2003). German reunification: A quasi-ethnic conflict." *Mind and Human Interaction,* 13: 77–86.

Mitscherlich, Alexander (1971). Psychoanalysis and aggression of large groups. *International Journal of Psycho-Analysis,* 52: 161–167.

Money-Kyrle, Roger E. (1941). The psychology of propaganda. *British Journal of Medical Psychology,* 19: 82–94.

Modell, Arnold H. (1970). The transitional objects and the creative art. *Psychoanalytic Quarterly,* 39: 240-250.

——— . (1976). The holding environment and the therapeutic action of psychoanalysis. *Journal of the American Psychoanalytic Association,* 24: 255–307.

Montville, Joseph V. (1987). The arrow and the olive branch: A case for Track Two Diplomacy. In John McDonald and D. B. Bendahmane (Eds.), *Conflict*

Resolution: Track Two Diplomacy (pp. 5–20). Washington, DC: U.S. Government Printing Office.

———— (1989). Psychoanalytic enlightenment and the greening of diplomacy, *Journal of the American Psychoanalytic Association*, 37: 297–318.

———— (1995). Complicated mourning and mobilization for nationalism. In Jerome Braun (Ed.), *Social Pathology in Comparative Perspective: The Nature and Psychology of Civil Society* (pp. 159–174). New York: Praeger.

———— (2001). A disturbing presence: September 11 and the Islamic roots of democratic pluralism. *Preventive Diplomacy News*, p. 2. Washington: Center for Strategic and International Studies.

Moore, Burness E. and Bernard D. Fine (1990). *Psychoanalytic Terms and Concepts*. New Haven: American Psychoanalytic Association and Yale University Press.

Morgenthau, Hans J. (1948). *Politics Among Nations: The Struggle for Power and Peace*. New York: Alfred A. Knopf.

Moses, Rafael (1990). On dehumanizing the enemy. In Vamık D. Volkan, Demetrios A. Julius and Joseph V. Montville (Eds.), *The Psychodynamics of International Relationships* (Vol. 1) (pp. 111–118). Lexington, MA: Lexington Books.

Moses-Hrushovski, Rena (2000). *Grief and Grievance: The Assassination of Yitzhak Rabin*. London: Minerva Press.

Mousavi, Sayed Askar (1998). *The Hazaras of Afghanistan: An Historical, Cultural, Economic, and Political Study*. London: Curzon.

Al-Mutlaq, Hanan (1996) Aspects of non-spiritual rewards of Islamic fundamentalism. *Mind and Human Interaction*, 7: 91–96

Myers, H.J. and Leon Yochelson (1948). Color denial in the Negro. *Psychiatry*, 11: 39–46.

Neu, Joyce and Volkan, Vamık (1999). *Developing a Methodology for Conflict Prevention: The Case of Estonia*. Atlanta, GA: The Carter Center Special Report Series. Winter.

Niederland, William (1968). Clinical observation on the "survivor syndrome." *International Journal of Psycho-analysis*, 49: 313–315.

Nixon, Richard M. (1978). RN: *The Memoirs of Richard Nixon*. New York: Grosset and Dunlap.

Novick, Jack and Kerry Kelly (1970). Projection and externalization. *Psychoanalytic Study of the Child*, 25: 69–95.

O'Leary, Stephen (1994). *Arguing the Apocalypse: A Theory of Millennial Rhetoric*. Cambridge, MA: Harvard University Press.

Olsson, Peter A. (1994). In search of their fathers-themselves: Jim Jones and David Koresh, *Mind and Human Interaction*, 5: 85-96.

———— (1996). Shoko Asahara: The malignant pied piper of Japan, *Mind and Human Interaction*, 7: 54-57.

Orwell, George (1945). Notes on nationalism. In S. Orwell and L. Angus (Eds.)

The Collected Essays, Journalism, and Letters of George Orwell (Vol. 3) (pp. 361–380). New York: Harcourt Brace Jovanovich, 1971.

Palmer, Louis (1990). *Adventures in Afghanistan*. London: Octagon Press.

Pano, Nicholas C. (1982). Albania. In Milorad M. Drachkovitch (Ed.) *The Last Bastion of Stalinism in East Central Europe: Yesterday, Today, Tomorrow*, 187-218. Stanford: California Hoover Institution Press.

Pao, Ping-Nie (1979). *Schizophrenic disorders: Theory and Treatment from a Psychodynamimc Point of View*. New York: International Universities Press.

Petersen, William (1980). Concepts of ethnicity. In S. Thermstorm (Ed.), *Harvard Encyclopedia of Ethnic Groups* (pp. 234–242). Cambridge, MA: Harvard University Press.

Pinderhughes, Charles A. (1969). The origins of racism. *International Journal of Psychiatry*, 8: 934–941.

Pines, Malcolm (Ed.) (1983). *The Evolution of Group Analysis*. London: Routledge & Kegan Paul.

Pipa, Arshi (1984). Party ideology and purges in Albania. *Telos*, 59: 69-100.

Pollock, George H. (1989). *The Mourning-Liberation Process* (Vols. 1-2). Madison, CT: International Universities Press.

Poznanski, E. O. (1972). The "replacement child:" A saga of unresolved parental grief. *Behavioral Pediatrics*, 81: 1190–1193.

Rancour-Laferriere, Daniel (1988). *The Mind of Stalin: A Psychoanalytic Study*. Ann Arbor, MI: Ardis.

Rashid, Ahmad (2000). *Taliban: Islam, Oil, and the New Great Game in Central Asia*. London: I. B. Tauris.

Rauschning, Hermann (1939). *The Revolution of Nihilism*. New York: Alliance Book Corporation.

Reavis, Dick J. (1995). *The Ashes of Waco: An Investigation*. New York: Simon and Schuster.

Redlich, Fritz (1998). *Hitler: Diagnosis of a Destructive Prophet*. New York: Oxford University Press.

Reimann, Victor (1976). *Goebbels: The Man Who Created Hitler*. (Stephen Wendt, Trans.). New York: Doubleday.

Robins, Robert S. (1986). Paranoid ideation and charismatic leadership. *Psychohistory Review*, 5: 15–55.

Robins, Robert S. and Jerrold M. Post (1997). *Political Paranoia: The Psychopolitics of Hatred*. New Haven: Yale University Press.

Robinson, Adam (2002). *Bin Laden: Behind the Mask of the Terrorist*. New York: Arcade Publishing Inc.

Roche, George (1987). *A World without Heroes: The Modern Tragedy*. Hillsdale, Michigan: The Hillsdale College Press.

Rogers, Rita R. (1994). Nationalism: A state of mind. *Mind and Human Interaction*, 5: 19–21.

Rokeach, Milton (1984). Belief system theory of stability and change. In S. J. Ball-

Rokeach, M. Rokeach, and J. W. Grube (Eds.), *The Great American Values Test: Influencing Behavior and Belief through Television* (pp. 17–38). New York: Free Press.

Rosenthal, Gabriele (Ed.) (1998). *The Holocaust in Three Generations: Families of Victims and Perpetrators of the Nazi Regime*. London: Cassell Academic.

Rustow, Dankwart A. (1970). Ataturk as founder of a state. In Dankwart A. Rustow (Ed.), *Philosophers and Kings: Studies in Leadership* (pp. 208–247). New York: George Braziller.

Saathoff, Gregory B. (1995). In the halls of mirrors: One Kuwaiti's captive memories. *Mind and Human Interaction*, 6: 170–178.

——— (1996). Kuwait's children: Identity in the shadow of the storm. *Mind and Human Interaction*, 7: 181–191.

Sachedina, Abdulaziz (2001). *The Islamic Roots of Democratic Pluralism*. Washington, DC: CSIS Press.

Said, Edward (1979). *Orientalism*. New York: Vintage Books.

Sampson, Anthony (1999). *Mandela: The Authorized Biography*. New York: Alfred A. Knopf.

Sandeen, Ernest R. (1970). *The Roots of Fundamentalism: British and American Millenarianism, 1800-1930*. Chicago: University of Chicago Press.

Saunders, Harold H. (1999). *Public Peace Process: Sustained Dialogue to Transform Racial and Ethnic Conflicts*. New York: St. Martin's Press.

Schaffner, Bertram (1948). *Father Land: A Study of Authoritarianism in the German Family*. New York: Columbia University Press.

Scruton, Roger (1982). *A Dictionary of Political Thought*. New York: Harper and Row.

Sebek, Michael (1992). Anality in the totalitarian system and the psychology of post-totalitarian society. *Mind and Human Interaction*, 4: 52–59.

——— (1996). The fate of the totalitarian object. *International Forum of Psychoanalysis*, 5: 289–294.

Sells, Michael A. (1996). *Bridge Betrayed: Religion and Genocide in Bosnia*. Berkeley, CA: University of California Press.

Shapiro, David (1972). *Neurotic Styles*. New York: Basic Books.

Sinishta, Gjon (1976). *The Promise: A Documentary Account of Religious Persecution in Albania*. Santa Clara, CA: H and F Composing Service Printing.

Sivan, Emmanuel (1985). *Radical Islam: Medieval Theology and Modern Politics*. New Haven, CT: Yale University Press.

Socarides, Charles (1977). On vengeance: The desire to "get even." In Charles Socarides (Ed.) *The World of Emotions: Clinical Studies of Affects and Their Expressions* (pp. 403-425). New York: International Universities Press, 1966.

Stein, Howard F. (1990). International and group milieu of ethnicity: Identifying generic group dynamic issues. *Canadian Review of Studies in Nationalism*, 17: 107–130.

——— (1998). *Euphemism, Spin, and the Crisis in Organizational Life*. Westport, CT: Greenwood Publishing Group.

——— (2004). *Beneath the Crust of Culture: Psychoanalytic Anthropology and the Cultural Unconscious in American Life*. Amsterdam, Holland: Rodopi.

Stein, Janice (1988). Building politics into psychology: The misperception of threat. *Political Psychology*, 9: 245–271.

Stein, Janice and Raymond Tanter (1980). *Rational Decision-Making: Israel's Security Choices*, 1967. Columbus, OH: Ohio State University Press.

Steinberg, Blema (1996). *Shame and Humiliation: Presidential Decision-Making on Vietnam*. Montreal: McGill-Queen's University Press.

Stepan, Nancy (1982). *The Idea of Race in Science: Great Britain 1800–1960*. Hamden, CT: Archon Books.

Stephenson, Jill (1983). Propaganda, autarky and the German housewife. In D. Welch (Ed.) *Nazi Propaganda: The Power and the Limitations* (pp. 117-142). London: Croom Helm.

Stern, Daniel N. (1985). *The Interpersonal World of the Infant*. New York: Basic Books.

Stern, Judith (2001). Deviance in the Nazi Society. *Mind and Human Interaction*, 12: 218–237.

Stierlin, Helm (1976). *Adolf Hitler: A Family Perspective*. New York: Psycho-history Press.

Stone, Michael H. (1989). Murder. In Otto F. Kernberg (Ed.), *Narcissistic Personality Disorder, The Psychiatric Clinics of North America*, 12: 643–651. Philadelphia: W. B. Saunders.

Streeck-Fischer, Annette (1999). Naziskins in Germany: Traumatization in the past and present. *Mind and Human Interaction*, 10: 84–97.

Strozier, Charles B. (1994). *Apocalypse: On the Psychology of Fundamentalism in America*. Boston: Beacon Press.

Suistola, Jouni (2001) Border and identity: The Finnish Army at the Russian border in 1941. *Mind and Human Interaction*. 12: 133–141.

Swift, Jonathan (1726). *Gulliver's Travels*. Paul Turner (Ed.). London: Oxford University Press (1998).

Szulc, Ted (1978). *The Illusion of Peace*. New York: Viking Press.

al-Tabari (1988). *The History of al-Tabari*, (9 volumes). Albany, NY: State University of New York Press.

Tabor, James D. and Gallagher, Eugene V. (1995). *Why Waco? Cults and the Battle for Religious Freedom in America*. Berkeley: University of California Press.

Tahka, Veikko, Erro Rechart, and Kalle A. Achte (1971). Psychoanalytic aspects of the Finnish sauna bath. *Psychiatrica Fennica*, 2: 63–72.

Tate, Claudia (1996). Freud and his "Negro:" Psychoanalysis as ally and enemy of African-Americans. *Journal for the Psychoanalysis of Culture and Society*, 1: 53–62.

Teeling, William (1939). *Know Thy Enemy*. London: Nicholson.

Tehranian, Majid (1999). *Global Communication and World Politics: Domi-*

nation, Development, and Discourse. New York: Lynne Rienner.

Thomson, J. Anderson (2003). Killer apes on American Airlines, or: How religion was the main hijacker on September 11. In Sverre Varvin and Vamık D. Volkan (Eds.) *Violence or Dialogue? Psychoanalytic insights on Terror and Terrorism* (pp. 73–84). London: International Psychoanalysis Library.

Tonnes, B. (1982). Religious persecution in Albania. *Religion in Communist Lands*, 10: 242-55.

Toynbee, Arnold J. (1933–1948). *A Study of History* (10 vols.) London: Oxford University Press.

Tucker, Robert C. (1970). The theory of charismatic leadership. In Dankwart A. Rustow (Ed.), *Philosophers and Kings: Studies in Leadership* (pp. 69–94). New York: George Braziller.

———— (1973). *Stalin as a Revolutionary, 1879–1929: A Study in History and Personality*. New York: Norton.

Van der Waals, H. G. (1952). Discussions of the mutual influences in the development of the ego and id. *Psychoanalytic Study of the Child*, 7: 18–19.

Varvin, Sverre and Volkan, Vamık D. (Eds.) (2003). *Violence or Dialogue: Psychoanalytic Insights on Terror and Terrorism*. London: International Psychoanalysis Library.

Vasquez, John A. (1986). Morality and politics. In John A. Vasquez (Ed.), *Classics of International Relations* (pp. 1–8). Englewood Cliffs, NJ: Prentice-Hall.

Velija, Vebi (1996). *Quo Vadis Albania? A Version of the Economic Recovery Program of Albania*. Tirana: Onufri.

Verissimo, E. (1962). *Mexico*. Garden City, NY: Dolphin Books.

Vitols, M.M., H.G. Walters, and Martin H. Keeler (1963). Hallucinations and delusions in white and Negro schizophrenics. *American Journal of Psychiatry*, 120: 472–476.

Volkan, Kurt (1992). Islam and identity in Central Asia. *Mind and Human Interaction*, 4: 165–168.

Volkan, Vamık D. (1976). *Primitive Internalized Object Relations*. New York: International Universities Press.

———— (1979a). *Cyprus—War and Adaptation: A Psychoanalytic History of Two Ethnic Groups in Conflict*. Charlottesville, VA: University Press of Virginia.

———— (1979b). Symptom formations and character changes associated with the upheavals of war: Examples from Cyprus. *American Journal of Psychotherapy*, 33: 239–262.

———— (1979c). The glass bubble of a narcissistic patient. In Joseph Le Boit and Attilio Capponi (Ed.), *Advances in Psychotherapy of the Borderline Patient* (pp. 405–431). New York: Jason Aronson.

———— (1981) *Linking Objects and Linking Phenomena: A Study of the Forms, Symptoms, Metapsychology and Therapy of Complicated Mourning*. New York: International Universities Press.

———— (1987a). Psychological concepts useful in building the political foundations between nations (Track II diplomacy). *Journal of the American Psychoanalytic Association*, 35: 903–935.

———— (1987b). *Six Steps in the Treatment of Borderline Personality Organization*. Northvale, NJ: Jason Aronson.

———— (1988). *The Need to Have Enemies and Allies: From Clinical Practice to International Relationships*. Northvale, NJ: Jason Aronson.

———— (1991a). An interview with Valentin Berezhkov, Stalin's interpreter. *Mind and Human Interaction*, 2: 77–80.

———— (1991b). On "chosen trauma." *Mind and Human Interaction*, 3:13.

———— (1995). *The Infantile Psychotic Self: Understanding and Treating Schizoprenics and Other Difficult Patients*. Northvale, NJ: Jason Aronson.

———— (1997). *Bloodlines: From Ethnic Pride to Ethnic Terrorism*. New York: Farrar, Straus, and Giroux.

———— (1999a). *Das Versagen der Diplomatie: zur Psychoanalyse nationaler, etnischer und religiöser Konflikte (The Failure of Diplomacy: The Psychoanalysis of National, Ethnic and Religious Conflicts)*. Giessen: Psychosozial-Verlag.

————. (1999b). Nostalgia as a linking phenomenon. *Journal of Applied Psychoanalysis*, 1:169–179.

———— (1999c). Psychoanalysis and diplomacy: Part I. Individual and large group identity. *Journal of Applied Psychoanalytic Studies*, 1: 29–55.

———— (1999d). Psychoanalysis and diplomacy: Part II: Large-group rituals. *Journal of Applied Psychoanalytic Studies*, 1: 223–247.

———— (1999e). Psychoanalysis and diplomacy: Part III: Potentials for and obstacles against collaboration. *Journal of Applied Psychoanalytic Studies*, 1: 305–318.

———— (1999f). The Tree Model: A Comprehensive psychopolitical approach to unofficial diplomacy and the reduction of ethnic tension. *Mind and Human Interaction*, 10: 142–210.

Volkan, Vamık D, Salman Akhtar, Robert M. Dorn, John S. Kafka, Otto F. Kernberg, Peter A. Olsson, Rita R. Rogers, and Stephen B. Shanfield (1998). The psychodynamics of leaders and decision-makers. *Mind and Human Interaction*, 9: 130–181.

Volkan, Vamık D. and Gabriele Ast (1992). *Eine Borderline Therapie*. Gottingen: Vandenhoeck & Ruprecht.

———— (1994). *Spektrum des Narzissmus (Spectrum of Narcissism)*. Gottingen: Vandenhoeck & Ruprecht

———— (1997). *Siblings in the Unconscious*. Madison, CT: International Universities Press.

Volkan, Vamık D, Gabriele Ast, and William Greer (2002). *The Third Reich in the Unconscious: Transgenerational Transmission and its Consequences*. New York: Brunner-Routledge.

Volkan, Vamık D. and David R. Hawkins (1971). The "Fieldwork" method of teaching and learning clinical psychiatry. *Comprehensive Psychiatry*, 12: 103–115.

———— (1972). The learning group. *American Journal of Psychiatry*, 128: 1121–1126.

Volkan, Vamık D. and Norman Itzkowitz (1984). *The Immortal Ataturk: A Psychobiography*. Chicago: Chicago University Press.

———— (1994). *Turks and Greeks: Neighbours in Conflict*. Cambridgeshire, England: Eothen Press.

Volkan, Vamık D., Norman Itzkowitz, and Andrew Dod (1997). *Richard Nixon: A Psychobiography*. New York: Columbia University Press.

Volkan, Vamık D. and Elizabeth Zintl (1993). *Life After Loss: The Lessons of Grief*. New York: Charles Scribner's & Sons.

von Rochau, August L. (1853). *Grundsätze der Realpolitik*. Frankfurt, Germany: Ullstein (1972).

Vulliamy, Ed (1994). *Season in Hell: Understanding Bosnia's War*. New York: St. Martin's Press.

Waelder, Robert (1930). The principle of multiple function: Observations on over-determination. *Psychoanalytic Quarterly*, 5: 45–62, (1936).

Waite, Robert G.L. (1977). *The Psychopathic God: Adolf Hitler*. New York: Basic Books.

Watt, W. Montgomery (1961). *Muhammad: Prophet and Statesman*. New York: Oxford University Press.

Weber, Eugene (1999). *Apocalypses: Prophesies, Cults, and Millennial Beliefs Through the Ages*. Cambridge, MA: Harvard University Press.

Weber, Max (1925). *Wirtshaft und Gessellshaft (Economy and Society)* (Vols. 1–2). Tubingen: J. C. B. Mohr.

Weigert, Edith (1967). Narcissism: Benign and malignant forms. In Robert W. Gibson (Ed.), *Crosscurrents in Psychiatry and Psychoanalysis* (pp. 222–238). Philadelphia: Lippincott.

Weinberg, Carroll (1992) Terrorists and terrorism: Have we reached a crossroad? *Mind and Human Interaction*, 3:77–82.

Welch, David (1983). *Propaganda and German Cinema, 1933-1945*. New York: Oxford University Press.

Werner, Heinz and Bernard Kaplan (1963). *Symbol Formation*. New York: Wiley.

Wessinger, Catherine (1997). Millennialism with and without mayhem. In Thomse Robbins and Susan Palmer (Ed.) *Millennium, Messiahs, and Mayhem* (pp. 47-60). New York: Routledge.

———— (1999). *How the Millennium Comes Violently: From Jonestown to Heaven's Gate*. New York: Seven Bridges Press.

White, Theodore H. (1969). *The Making of the President, 1968*. New York: Pocket Books.

Wilkerson, Charles B. (1970). Destructiveness of myths. *American Journal of Psychiatry*, 126: 1087–1092.

Wimbush, S. Enders (1984) The politics of identity change in Soviet Central Asia. *Central Asian Survey*, 3: 69–79.

Winnicott, Donald W. (1953). Transitional objects and transitional phenomena. *International Journal of Psycho-Analysis*, 34: 89-97.

————. (1969). Berlin Walls. In C. Winnicott, R. Shepherd and M. Davis (Eds.), *D. W. Winnicott: Home Is Where We Start From* (pp. 221–227). New York: W.W. Norton, 1986.

Wolfe, Willard (1975). *From Radicalism to Socialism: Men and Ideas in the Formation of Fabian Socialist Doctrine, 1881–1889*. New Haven: Yale University Press.

Yavuz, M. Hakan (1995). The patterns of political Islamic identity: dynamics of national and transnational loyalties and identities. *Central Asian Survey*, 14: 342–372.

Young, Kenneth (1969). *The Greek Passion: A Study in People and Politics*. London: J. M. Dent and Sons.

Zaleznik, Abraham (1984). Charismatic and consensus leaders: A psychological comparison. In M. F. R. Kets de Vries (Ed.), *The Irrational Executive* (pp. 112 –132). New York: International University Press.

Zonis, Marvin (1991). *Majestic Failure: The Fall of the Shah*. Chicago: University of Chicago Press.

/ index

Abercrombie, M.L.J., 320
Abraham, 142, 146
Abse, D. Wilfred, 265, 272, 314, 316
Abu Bakr, 147
Abu Talib, 143
Abudabbeh, Nuha, 92, 301
Achen, Christopher H., 304
Achte, Kalle, 271
adaptive behaviors, 228
Afghanistan, 11, 24, 160, 278, 297; bin
    Laden and, 25, 137, 154, 156–157;
    Buddha statues and, 137–138; children in,
    64, 156, 164; ethnicity of population, 277;
    history of, 63–64; Islamic fundamental-
    ism in, 154–156; map of, 65; propaganda
    in, 66; purification rituals and, 137–138;
    al Qaeda and, 25, 66, 137, 154, 163, 302;
    Soviet invasion of, 64, 153, 155–156,
    305–306; Sufism in, 297; Taliban and, 25,
    63–66, 137–138, 155, 165, 277, 300, 306;
    United States and, 64, 155, 164–166, 277;
    war orphans in, 64
aggression, 70, 90, 101, 266, 270, 276, 285,
    293, 295, 310, 314; identity protection
    and, 69; Nazi Germany and, 68, 76;
    regression and, 67–68, 86; rituals and, 107
aggressive triumphs, 192, 211
Agnew, Spiro, 206
Ahahor, Zeev, 303
Aimak, 277
Aisha, 147, 293
Akhtar, Salman, 267, 269, 283, 287, 303,
    310–312
Al Haram al Sharif, 134, 299
Alawiyah, Tuty, 216
Albania, 329; Albanians living outside of,
    27, 235, 237, 250–251, 253, 256–259;
    All–Nation Reconciliation Mission, 250;

Army of National Liberation, 242; "bad
    biography" in, 242, 252; basic trust and,
    245; bin Laden and, 253–254; "black
    spot" and, 67, 244–247, 252, 326; "bunker
    mentality" in, 241–242; Carter Center
    and, 239–240, 252; Catholicism and,
    243–244, 254, 327; Communist Party,
    237, 242, 245; Consulate General of, 241;
    Enver Hoxha and, 67–68, 72, 74, 233–235,
    237, 240–252, 254–256, 326–328; Fazile
    Godo and, 233–234, 245–248, 255–256,
    324, 328–329; "Greater Albania," 256; his-
    tory of, 72, 235–238, 241–244; identity
    and, 241, 244, 257–258; Islam and, 237,
    241, 243–244, 257, 327–328; Kosovo and,
    235, 237, 250–251, 253–256, 258, 325;
    large-group regression in, 67, 230, 233,
    235, 240, 248, 252–253, 256; Law of Lek,
    249, 328; Macedonia and, 236–237,
    256–259; mafia in, 254; map of, 236;
    National Theatre of, 251, 253; non-
    regressive behavior, 253; Ottoman Empire
    and, 235–236, 242, 244, 327; as "paranoid
    society," 68, 235, 241, 244, 248, 251; Party
    of Labor in, 242; People's Assembly in
    248; political parties in, 237–240; propa-
    ganda, 244–248, 256; pyramid scheme in,
    238–239; Sigurimi agents, 233, 247; size
    of, 235, "truth and reconciliation" in, 252,
    256
Alfred P. Murrah Federal Building, 113
Algeria, 149
Ali, Tariq, 155, 300–301
Alia, Ramiz, 237–238, 248
Allison, Graham T., 174–175, 305
Almond, Gabriele, 290
Amamullah, King, 63
ambivalence, 35
Ambrose, Stephen, 316
"American Model," 173
American Psychiatric Association, 15, 176,
    287, 291, 307
American Psycho (2000), 192
amillennialism, 286
Aminah, 142–143
Amir, Yigal, 28, 135
Amnesty International, 327
Anderson, Scott, 328–329, 250
Andres, Walter G., 139
anniversary reactions, 97–100
Anthony, James, 265, 320

351

/ about the author

Vamık D. Volkan, M.D., is an emeritus professor of psychiatry and the founder of the Center for the Study of Mind and Human Interaction (CSMHI) at the University of Virginia School of Medicine. CSMHI studies large groups in conflict and counts psychoanalysts, psychiatrists, psychologists, historians, former diplomats, and political scientists among its multidisciplinary faculty. He is an emeritus training and supervising analyst at the Washington Psychoanalytic Institute as well as a past president of both the International Society of Political Psychology (ISPP) and the Virginia Psychoanalytic Society.

In the 1990s, he served as a member of the Carter Center's International Negotiation Network, headed by former president Jimmy Carter. In 1995, he chaired a Select Advisory Commission to the Federal Bureau of Investigation's (FBI's) Critical Incident Response Group. In 1999, he gave the twenty-seventh Annual Sigmund Freud Lecture in Vienna, Austria. In 2000, he served as an Inaugural Rabin Fellow at The Yitzhak Rabin Center for Israel Studies in Tel Aviv. In February 2001, he was a visiting professor of Law at Harvard University. In 2003 he was a visiting professor of psychiatry at Ege University, Izmir, Turkey, was selected to be a member of the Board of the Freud Society in Vienna, Austria, and received the Sigmund Freud Award given by the city of Vienna in collaboration with the World Council of Psychotherapy. In 2003–2004 he was an Erik Erikson scholar at The Austen Riggs Center, Stockbridge, Massachusetts.

Dr. Volkan is also the founder and emeritus editor of the quarterly journal *Mind and Human Interaction*, which opens meaningful dialogues between the disciplines of history, culture, politics, and psychoanalysis. He is the author or coauthor of thirty books and the editor or coeditor of ten more. His work has been translated into Dutch, German, Greek, Hebrew, Italian, Japanese, Romanian, Russian, Serbian, Spanish, and Turkish.